Queer Approaches to Tolkien

ALSO OF INTEREST
AND FROM MCFARLAND

Tolkien in the New Century: Essays in Honor of Tom Shippey (edited by John Wm. Houghton, Janet Brennan Croft, Nancy Martsch, John D. Rateliff and Robin Anne Reid, 2014)

The Body in Tolkien's Legendarium: Essays on Middle-earth Corporeality (edited by Christopher Vaccaro, 2013)

Queer Approaches to Tolkien
Essays on the Many Paths to Middle-earth

Edited by ROBIN ANNE REID,
CHRISTOPHER VACCARO *and*
STEPHEN YANDELL

STUDIES IN TOLKIEN

Series Editor Robin Anne Reid

McFarland & Company, Inc., Publishers
Jefferson, North Carolina

This book has undergone peer review.

Studies in Tolkien Advisory Board

Maria K. Alberto	Bradford Lee Eden
Amy M. Amendt-Raduege	Craig Franson
Aurélie Brémont	Perry Neil Harrison
Sara Brown	Kristine M. Larsen
Gerry Canavan	Mariana Rios Maldonado
Sonali Arvind Chunodkar	Robert T. Tally, Jr.
Cait Coker	Helen Young
Janet Brennan Croft	

LIBRARY OF CONGRESS CATALOGING-IN-PUBLICATION DATA

Names: Reid, Robin Anne, 1955– editor | Vaccaro, Christopher editor | Yandell, Stephen editor
Title: Queer approaches to Tolkien : essays on the many paths to Middle-earth / edited by Robin Anne Reid, Christopher Vaccaro and Stephen Yandell.
Description: Jefferson, North Carolina : McFarland & Company, Inc., Publishers, 2026. | Series: Studies in Tolkien | Includes bibliographical references and index.
Identifiers: LCCN 2025031028 | ISBN 9781476694627 paperback ∞
   ISBN 9798368600024 ebook
Subjects: LCSH: Tolkien, J. R. R. (John Ronald Reuel), 1892–1973—Criticism and interpretation | Queer theory | LCGFT: Literary criticism | Essays
Classification: LCC PR6039.O32 Z7956 2025 | DDC 823/.912—dc23/eng/20250725
LC record available at https://lccn.loc.gov/2025031028

ISBN (print) 978-1-4766-9462-7
ISBN (ebook) 979-8-3686-0002-4

© 2026 Robin Anne Reid, Christopher Vaccaro and Stephen Yandell. All rights reserved

No part of this book may be reproduced or transmitted in any form or by any means, electronic or mechanical, including photocopying or recording, or by any information storage and retrieval system, without permission in writing from the publisher.

Front cover image by Denis Belitsky (Shutterstock)

Printed in the United States of America

McFarland & Company, Inc., Publishers
  Box 611, Jefferson, North Carolina 28640
     www.mcfarlandpub.com

Table of Contents

Acknowledgments — vii

Abbreviations — ix

Preface
  Robin Anne Reid, Christopher Vaccaro *and*
  Stephen Yandell — 1

Introduction
  Robin Anne Reid, Christopher Vaccaro *and*
  Stephen Yandell — 11

Part I. Queer Moralities

The Problematic Perimeters of Elrond Half-elven and
  Ronald English-Catholic
  Kristine Larsen — 27

I Dream of Gandalf: or, How I Was Raised by Wizards
  Jes Battis — 43

The End Is Queer: *Cleanness* and Tolkien's Apocalyptic
  Landscape
  Stephen Yandell — 56

Part II. Queer Intersections

Mother or Other: Tolkien's Shelob and the "Monstrous-
  Feminine"
  Sara Brown — 77

Éowyn and/or Dernhelm: Reading Éowyn's (Trans)Masculine
  Disguise
  Gavin Foster — 92

"Something Mighty Queer": Destabilizing Gender, Intimacy
and Family in Tolkien's Legendarium
   DANNA PETERSEN-DEEPROSE   107

Part III. Intra-Male Queerness

"For he would take no wife": Surface Reading, Eärnur and
the Queering of the Unmarried Male in *The Lord of the Rings*
   NICHOLAS BIRNS   125

"Bending over with naked blade": The Erotics of Suffering and
Male-Male Penetration in Tolkien's Legendarium
   ZACHARY CLIFTON ENGLEDOW   140

Frodo, Sam and the Ring of Power: A Queer Erotic Triangle
   CHRISTOPHER CAMERON   153

"Saruman [?Pardoned]": The Queerness of Sex in Tolkien's
The Lord of the Rings
   CHRISTOPHER VACCARO   168

Part IV. Queer Transformations

"and stooping he raised Beleg and kissed his mouth":
Queering Canon with Tolkien Fanfiction
   MARIA K. ALBERTO   189

"What care I for the hands of a king?": Tolkien Fanfiction
and Narratives of the Transgender Self
   CORDELIAH G. LOGSDON   201

Tolkien and Alterity: A Bibliography
   JORDAN AUDAS   215

About the Contributors   229

Index   233

Acknowledgments

The three editors would like to jointly thank the following, starting with our contributors who have walked with us along many paths and have taught us so much along the way. We appreciate the faith Layla Milholen and McFarland had that this volume would contribute to the field of Tolkien Studies, and we would like to thank our anonymous peer reviewers for their feedback, which improved the final work.

Some of the most important support for all scholars comes from the archivists and librarians who provide ongoing support in the face of budget cuts and ongoing attacks. We are especially grateful to:

Catherine Coker, associate professor at University of Illinois Urbana–Champaign
Janet Brennan Croft, associate university librarian, University of Northern Iowa
William M. Fliss, Tolkien archivist, Raynor Library, Marquette University

In addition, all of us benefited from the growing number of conferences that gave us opportunities to share our work with others, both online and face-to-face. We are grateful to these organizers and communities and would like to thank the following:

The International Medieval Congress, University of Leeds (imc.leeds.ac.uk/)
The Mythopoeic Society Online MidWinter Seminar 2024: "Something Mighty Queer" (mythsoc.org/oms/oms-2024.htm).
Tolkien at Kalamazoo, International Congress on Medieval Studies, Western Michigan University (wmich.edu/medievalcongress)
The Tolkien Society Seminar Summer 2021 on "Tolkien and Diversity" (Tolkiensociety.org/events/Tolkien-society-summer-seminar/)
Tolkien Studies Area, PCA/ACA: Popular Culture Association (pcaaca.org/)

Tolkien at the University of Vermont (Tolkienvt.org)

We would also like to acknowledge those whose support and insights over the years made a difference: Annie Brust, Olivia K. Burgham, Gideon Cooper, Nathan Fredrickson, Virginia Elizabeth King, Yvette Kisor, Hannah Mendro, Brooke Petersen, Melissa Sloat, Christiane Steinwascher, and Eva Wijman.

Robin Anne Reid—I would like to thank Judy Ann Ford. I also want to acknowledge the queer students, faculty, and staff who became my friends during my twenty-seven years in Texas and how much they taught me during those years about joy and survival. Additional thanks go to Chris and Steve who read my rather incoherent email about a possible "Queer Tolkien" project and agreed to become editors.

Christopher Vaccaro—I would like to thank the thousands of queer activists at local, regional, national, and global levels who continue to fight in the streets and in their writing for LGBTQ+ rights. I would also like to thank the lovers and loved ones who have supported me in numerous ways in my work. Thanks also go to the library services team at Howe Library, University of Vermont.

Stephen Yandell—I would like to thank my spouse, Joel Chanvisanuruk, for his endless support. I appreciate the ongoing encouragement from my colleagues in the Arts and Sciences Dean's office, and for every sanity-preserving lunch with Amy Whipple. I am also indebted to my two co-editors; one of the real joys of this project was sharing our passion while learning from their expertise.

Abbreviations

Each essay has its own Works Cited section, but the editors asked everyone to follow a few guidelines for consistent citation across the essays, abbreviating titles the same way and identifying direct quotations from *The Lord of the Rings* by volume title, book number, chapter number, and pagination. The abbreviations below follow those generated for earlier journals and publications on Tolkien.

However, new publications have been issued since our contributors began writing; in this case, we had to add an abbreviation for the revised and expanded edition of *The Letters of J.R.R. Tolkien*, which was published in 2023, fairly late in the process of the anthology. Some of our authors used the original edition (*Letters 1*) and others the revised and expanded one (*Letters 2*). All provide the letter number (using the #) and page number. The new edition does not change the first edition's numbering of the original letters; instead, the new letters are inserted chronologically in between the original ones and given the same number as the preceding original plus a small letter (a, b, c, etc.).

The Legendarium

Children: *The Children of Húrin*, edited by Christopher Tolkien, Houghton Mifflin Company, 2007.
FGH: *Farmer Giles of Ham*. Various editions cited by authors.
FR: *The Fellowship of the Ring*. Various editions cited by authors
H: *The Hobbit*. Various editions cited by authors.
Lays: *The Lays of Beleriand*, edited by Christopher Tolkien, Houghton Mifflin, 1985. Vol. 3: *The History of Middle-earth*.
Letters 1: *The Letters of J.R.R. Tolkien*, edited by Humphrey Carpenter, assisted by Christopher Tolkien, Houghton Mifflin, 1981.
Letters 2: *The Letters of J.R.R. Tolkien*, edited by Humphrey Carpenter,

assisted by Christopher Tolkien, Revised and Expanded ed., Harper Collins, 2023.

Lost Road: *The Lost Road and Other Writings*, edited by Christopher Tolkien, Houghton Mifflin, 1987. Vol. 5: *The History of Middle-earth*.

LotR: *The Lord of the Rings*. Various editions cited by authors.

LT I: *The Book of Lost Tales Part I*, edited by Christopher Tolkien, Houghton Mifflin, 1984.

LT II: *The Book of Lost Tales Part II*, edited by Christopher Tolkien, Houghton Mifflin, 1984.

Morgoth: *Morgoth's Ring: The Later Silmarillion Part One*, edited by Christopher Tolkien, Houghton Mifflin, 1993. Vol. 10: *The History of Middle-earth*.

Nature: *The Nature of Middle-earth*, edited by Carl F. Hostetter, Houghton Mifflin, 2021.

OED: *Oxford English Dictionary*.

OFS: *On Fairy Stories*. Various editions cited by authors

Peoples: *The Peoples of Middle-earth*, edited by Christopher Tolkien, Houghton Mifflin, 1984. Vol. 12: *The History of Middle-earth*.

RK: *The Return of the King*. Various editions cited by authors

S: *The Silmarillion*, edited by Christopher Tolkien, Houghton Mifflin, 2001.

Sauron: *Sauron Defeated including The History of* The Lord of the Rings *Part Four*, edited by Christopher Tolkien, Houghton Mifflin, 1988. Vol. 9: *The History of Middle-earth*.

SGGK: *Sir Gawain and the Green Knight, Pearl, and Sir Orfeo*. Translated by J.R.R. Tolkien, Allen & Unwin, 1975.

Shadow: *The Return of the Shadow: The History of* The Lord of the Rings *Part One*, edited by Christopher Tolkien, Houghton Mifflin, 1988. Vol. 6: *The History of Middle-earth*.

Shaping: *The Shaping of Middle-earth: The Quenta. The Ambarkanta and The Annals*, edited by Christopher Tolkien, Houghton Mifflin, 1986. Vol. 4: *The History of Middle-earth*.

T&L: *Tree and Leaf*. HarperCollins, 2001.

Treason: *The Treason of Isengard: The History of* The Lord of the Rings *Part Two*, edited by Christopher Tolkien, Houghton Mifflin, 1989. Vol. 7: *The History of Middle-earth*.

TT: *The Two Towers*. Various editions cited by authors

UT: *Unfinished Tales of Numenor and Middle-earth*, edited by Christopher Tolkien, Houghton Mifflin, 1980.

WJ: *The War of the Jewels: The Later Silmarillion Part Two*, edited by Christopher Tolkien, Houghton Mifflin, 1994. Vol. 11: *The History of Middle-earth*.

WR: *The War of the Ring: The History of* The Lord of the Rings *Part Three*, edited by Christopher Tolkien, Houghton Mifflin, 1988. Vol. 8: *The History of Middle-earth*.

Journals

JTR: *Journal of Tolkien Research*
ML: *Mythlore*
Mal: *Mallorn*
TS: *Tolkien Studies*

Reference Works

Artist: Hammond and Scull's *J.R.R. Tolkien: Artist and Illustrator*
Bio: Carpenter's *J.R.R. Tolkien: A Biography*
C&G: Hammond and Scull's *The J.R.R. Tolkien Companion and Guide*
RC: Hammond and Scull's The Lord of the Rings: *A Reader's Companion*

Preface

ROBIN ANNE REID,
CHRISTOPHER VACCARO *and*
STEPHEN YANDELL

As we write this Preface in late 2024, we must note that any current consideration of queerness in J.R.R. Tolkien's writings ought also to consider, even tangentially, the connections between its intersections with religious readings and the growing attacks on any attempts to discuss issues relating to "diversity" in his body of work. Explorations of Christian themes in Tolkien's writings began the moment *The Lord of the Rings* was published, and more formal studies gained momentum during his lifetime.[1] In the decades after his death, these studies expanded into research on religious imagery and broader moral implications in his works, employing both Christian[2] and non–Christian lenses.[3] The field has only broadened in successive decades, but the most popular (as opposed to academic) offerings have grown increasingly Christian in nature, popular in style, and devotional in form.[4]

However, Christianity's relationship to Tolkien's writings has always been conflicted, just as its relationship has been to fantasy literature generally. Stories have invoked magic and secondary worlds for centuries, of course, and Christian responses have typically been anxious over any possible invocations of magic; some Christians have inevitably equated the supernatural with the occult. It is not surprising, then, that a portion of the reading public also watched nervously as *The Lord of the Rings*' popularity rose in the late twentieth century. A number of major works have pointed to Tolkien's Catholic identity as a primary (for some, the sole) lens by which one should appreciate *The Lord of the Rings*' ethical, moral, and social themes. In *The Magical World of the Inklings*, Gareth Knight outlines numerous ways in which good and evil structure Tolkien's novel. Although these themes exist in myth, Knight reminds readers that Tolkien's stories

1

are Christian rather than pagan: "there is nothing that is at variance with Tolkien's Christian orthodoxy" (131). Similarly, in challenging critics who "find no religious element at all in Tolkien's Middle-earth" (115), Richard Purtill argues that Tolkien's moral messages are foundational to understanding his works, and that "[his] morality is essentially Christian morality" (95). However, Purtill contrasts Tolkien's style of writing with that of other Inklings: "Tolkien, practically a cradle Catholic, was less inclined to talk about religion than [C.S.] Lewis, the convert to Christianity" (121). Although slightly more critical of the degree to which Tolkien "presents a cogent interpretation of...'motions of grace'" in *The Lord of the Rings* (4), Gunnar Urang argues in *Shadows of Heaven* that Tolkien's writings articulate Christian tenets as effectively as some of Christianity's foundational theological texts: "what we have found unbelievable is not the other world of ... Middle-earth ... but what has now become for us the other world of the *Consolation of Philosophy* or the *Summa*" (170).

Tolkien's self-professed Catholic identity made little difference for some readers, but for American evangelicals, especially those for whom Catholicism represented a pagan-riddled Christianity (Chick 1985), that identification was damning. Christianity's earliest efforts to separate itself from pagan cultures meant denouncing all non–Christian practices, but various branches of Christianity have embraced that charge with varying levels of fervency over the centuries. For example, leaders of evangelical Christianity in the 1970s, around the same time Tolkien's writings were becoming well known in the United States, became particularly obsessed with denouncing any perceived invocation of the supernatural.[5]

It is within this context that Jack Chick, American conservative, cartoonist, born-again Christian, and founder of Chick Publications in 1970, began creating comic books and tracts as a method of evangelization. While Chick's writings addressed a broad swath of topics cast as an infernal plot to destroy humanity — not simply Satanism and witchcraft but also Muslims, Catholics, gay rights, and evolution — one tract proves particularly useful in documenting Christianity's conflicted relationship with Tolkien.

Chick's "Dark Dungeons" tract, first published in 1984, warns of the threat of role-playing games such as *Dungeons and Dragons*, set in secondary worlds and employing magic. One panel of the cartoon invokes Acts 19:19 as a call for Christians to burn all materials that in any way suggest the occult, and one footnote makes explicit that this directive "include[es] C.S. Lewis and Tolkien, both of which can be found in occult bookstores" (19). In subsequent publications, however, the tract was revised and the reference to Lewis and Tolkien was removed. In its place was a series of related Biblical verses. Scholar P.D. Magnus requested clarification of this edit from a representative of chick.com ("Secrets"). The organization explained that details of occult connections to Lewis and Tolkien could not be verified, and therefore "the information was dropped." In *Harry Potter, Narnia, and* The Lord of the Rings, Richard Abanes offers a tentative answer to the longstanding conflict between Christianity and fantasy literature: "Why does *The Lord of the Rings* continue to be interpreted by some as a kind of promotion of occultism? Though it may be due in some part to unfamiliarity with the work, a more notable cause may be society's obsession with occultism in general..." (102). Reception of Tolkien has grown more positive amongst Christians in recent decades, but a publishing industry still remains in place to guide anxious Christians through various literary uses of magic.[6]

While the editors are aware of this culture of Christian anxiety, we also know that from the moment Tolkien's writings appeared, careful, passionate counter-cultural readers eagerly offered a stream of creative scholarship drawing on a wide variety of theoretical lenses, reflecting a range of ideological, philosophical, and religious approaches. These scholars, both academic and independent, professional and amateur, drew on new approaches for accessing, processing, and challenging Tolkien's works. Of particular value have been the increasingly robust number of studies successful at shining light on overlooked corners of the legendarium. Researchers have explored class-coded dialects in Tolkien, have highlighted female characters, and have begun to interrogate presentations of race.[7] During the past twenty years, scholars have only begun exploring queerness in Tolkien's writings. Seven essays stand out as groundbreaking in the first twenty years of Queer Tolkien studies (Battis; Chance; Craig; Reid, "Thrusts in the Dark"; Rohy; Vaccaro; and Yandell) and establish the context in which, alongside that of Christian anxiety, we offer the following collection of essays that celebrate the counter-cultural work of Tolkien that marks both the author and his texts as queer. Our aim in this volume is to continue challenging previous assumptions while celebrating the growing field of Queer Tolkien studies by publishing some of the most recent, creative queer scholarship, and by championing a new, long-overdue, era of Queer Tolkien scholarship.

We are not surprised at the time it has taken for readers to turn their attention to queer topics. Their reluctance is understandable on multiple fronts. A study of this nature must acknowledge the risk that far-right extremists (FRE) will target any attempt to explore questions of diversity including, but not limited to, queer readings. Members of the far right have been quick to denounce a "cancel culture" amongst anyone to the left of them. However, they themselves have been responsible for reactionary calls to ban books (including *The Lord of the Rings*), ideas, and individuals they have deemed dangerous or blasphemous ("Banned"). This danger is often tied an imagined public or national identity the FRE feel they have a divine calling to defend. Some of the same readers have also felt emboldened (indeed, divinely ordained) by centuries of dehumanizing, anti-queer rhetoric. The result has been a culture that has discouraged publications in queer theory while simultaneously enabling personal attacks on scholars.

On June 9, 2021, the Tolkien Society posted the program for its virtual "Tolkien and Diversity" seminar which included the group's Call for Proposals (CFP) and the scheduled presenters' names and presentation titles. Six of the sixteen presenters spoke on early versions of their essays which had been accepted for our anthology. Comments attacking the theme and the speakers immediately appeared on the Tolkien Society's Facebook group only to be deleted by the moderators. Between June 10 and July 8, 2021, nineteen articles were published in a variety of alt-right periodicals, blogs, and forums, most of which offered angry responses, and many of which allowed public comments. The majority of attacks singled out the presenters whose paper titles included the word "queer" (Reid, "J.R.R. Tolkien, Culture Warrior")

Tolkien's own enigmatic identities and contradictory statements play a significant role in this conflict. Tolkien had a queer relationship with audiences for as long as he has been writing.[8] As Verlyn Flieger points out in her recent work, Tolkien's work contains multiple contradictory statements that resist easy labelling or categorization. Tolkien's work has proven challenging even within the (admittedly diverse) audience of Christian readers.[9] For example, Tolkien founds his legendarium on the creative work of a single God, but he also offers readers a pantheon of lesser divine beings responsible for interacting with humanity. Some Christian readers are uncomfortable processing such a proposition (Baldassarro). Similarly, the mere inclusion of magic in Middle-earth marks Tolkien's writing for other readers as a dangerous invitation to the occult and the Satanic. The distinct categories of divinity and non-divinity, magic and ordinary, mortal and immortal are all challenged throughout the legendarium.

Other Christian scholars have also been quick to note a related phenomenon; they concede the warmth with which a majority of Christians have embraced the writings by J.R.R. Tolkien (and other Inkling writers such as C.S. Lewis) because of their self-identified Christian beliefs, while distinguishing Tolkien and Lewis from the overwhelming rejection given to works of other fantasy authors such as J.K. Rowling. As Richard Abanes notes in *Harry Potter and the Bible: The Menace Behind the Magick*, "the ongoing positive portrayals of occultism in society have a profound effect on people…. An extremely important distinction must be made between [the works of J.R.R. Tolkien and C.S. Lewis] and J.K. Rowling's Harry Potter books" (222–3). In *Harry Potter, Narnia, and The Lord of the Rings*, Abanes similarly warns about the need for a clear division between works of fantasy: *The Lord of the Rings* has value for Christians because it "presents magic as a seductive and dangerous force that does not rightly belong to humans.... In Rowling's world, however, wizards are humans, and their powers are tapped and increased via practices that have real-world occult parallels" (171).

Abanes works hard to ignore an inherently queer slipperiness in Tolkien's writings. However, other authors have more accurately acknowledged the rigidity brought by other readers of Tolkien. In an online piece for *Illuminati News*, Wes Penre describes binary thinking amongst some Christian readers; texts are placed either in a secular or spiritual category, and once there remain either shunned or embraced:

> Christians are divided into two camps with regards to Tolkien's books. One camp says there are allegorical links between his myth and Biblical truth, while the other camp points out the occult links, and emphasizes that "Lord of the Rings" was written to deceive and mislead people, and steer them away from God and into the occult.

For some, the mere invocation of a fantastic world places a work of literature in an unclear category, and thus warrants shunning: what can the binary-thinking reader do with a Middle-earth that cannot be easily defined as a world "saved by Jesus Christ," for example?

Our volume embraces Verlyn Flieger's 2014 reminder that readers misunderstand J.R.R. Tolkien's work if they place weight on any single position he articulated as opposed to acknowledging the contradictions throughout his work ("But What Did He Really Mean?"). Multiple "Tolkiens" exist, she argues, offering textual evidence about perspectives that changed according to his audience and to his changing positions over a lifetime (1892–1973) that, as Dimitra Fimi has shown, encompassed the breakup of the British Empire, two world wars, various movements for social justice and civil rights, and revolutions in science and technology (*Tolkien, Race, and Cultural History: From Fairies to Hobbits*).

In contrast to the majority of the earlier scholarship on queer Tolkien, our contributors reject the limited meaning of "queer" as "homosexual" as well as the exclusive focus on the outdated question of whether Tolkien intended any of his characters to be homosexual, or gay, queer, or straight.[10] Without downplaying innovative research focusing on "queer" as limited to meaning a broad range of differences such as ethnicity, race, class, sex, or gender but excluding sexuality/sexual identities, we have chosen to showcase the diversity of queer theories in the multi-disciplinary and multiple period specialties in Tolkien scholarship represented by our contributors. We have also chosen to move beyond focusing only on Tolkien's legendarium to explore queer transformative works by fans, including two essays on queer Tolkien fanfiction (see Maria K. Alberto's and Cordeliah G. Logsdon's essays in the "Queer Transformations" section).[11]

The editors of this volume see the collection as bridging long-standing gaps in Tolkien scholarship and in Queer scholarship on literature. For readers who know Tolkien primarily as a lifelong Catholic and are familiar with interpretations that highlight Catholic themes, processing queerness in the texts may seem unimaginable. At the same time, some queer theorists who have done phenomenal work with interrogating queerness in all sorts of texts have simply overlooked the work of an author like Tolkien who has declared himself so publicly a Christian. Tolkien's skills as a literary author are complicated for other readers trying to situate him as an early twentieth-century medievalist, linguist, and author with phenomenal impact on popular culture. The contributors to this volume thus offer invaluable service in helping to bridge multiple gaps that remain not only in Queer scholarship, but also in Tolkien scholarship as a field.

NOTES

1. Clyde S. Kilby, Professor of English at Wheaton College and friend of J.R.R. Tolkien, had the opportunity to read unpublished drafts of *The Silmarillion*, and offered one of the earliest such works. He describes in *Tolkien & The Silmarillion* Christian themes he identified while helping Tolkien organize the manuscript in the summer of 1966.

2. See, for example, Devin Brown's *The Christian World of* The Hobbit, Philip Ryken's *The Messiah Comes to Middle-earth: Images of Christ's Threefold Office in* The Lord of the Rings, Mark Eddy Smith's *Tolkien's Ordinary Virtues: Exploring the Spiritual Themes of* The Lord of the Rings, and Ralph C. Wood's *The Gospel According to Tolkien: Visions of the Kingdom in Middle-earth*. Tom Emanuel's recent essay, "'It is "about" nothing but itself': Tolkienian Theology Beyond the Domination of the Author," critiques the earlier tendency to evangelize from Tolkien's fiction and presents a counter-argument drawing on "progressive Christian and Jewish hermeneutics and Tolkien's own writings on intent and the freedom of the reader, [to] propose a theological framework for reading Tolkien that honors his Catholic foundations, the sub-creative integrity of his secondary world, and the religious diversity of the readers who find it so enchanting" (32).

3. Examples include Anna Milon's collection *Tolkien the Pagan? Reading Middle-earth Through a Spiritual Lens*, David Loy and Linda Goodhew's *The Dharma of Dragons and Daemons: Buddhist Themes in Modern Fantasy*, and Claudio Testi's *Pagan Saints in Middle-earth*.

4. Short, applicable chapters for personal reflection with a specifically Christian lens of applicability define this growing genre, including Sarah Arthur's *Walking with Frodo: A Devotional Journey Through* The Lord of the Rings, Devin Brown's *Hobbit Lessons: A Map for Life's Unexpected Journeys*, and Ed Strauss's *A Hobbit Devotional: Bilbo Baggins and the Bible*.

5. These responses were led in large part by authors such as Mike Warnke (claiming the status of ex-satanist high priest in his 1972 *The Satan Seller*), Lowell Hart (*Satan's Music Exposed*), and Bob Larson (*Rock: Practical Help for Those Who Listen to the Words and Don't Like What They Hear*).

6. Richard Abanes's *Harry Potter and the Bible: The Menace behind the Magick* warns of the dangers of J.K. Rowling's pagan-based books, explicitly distinguishing them from those by Christian writers like J.R.R. Tolkien. Abanes's 2005 *Harry Potter, Narnia, and The Lord of the Rings: What You Need to Know About Fantasy Books and Movies* offers a more nuanced position, helping nervous parents identify moral messages in fantasy literature generally while recognizing that Christian uses of the supernatural in some books affect young readers very differently from pagan presentations of magic.

7. See in this volume, "Tolkien and Alterity: A Bibliography," by Jordan Audas, which covers scholarship published from 1970 to 2023 that focuses on "alterity" which "can be narrowly defined as a state of Otherness relating to aspects of difference; it is broadly defined in this work as aspects of humanity that can be/are marginalized, stigmatized, or discriminated against, such as race, gender, sexuality, etc." (215).

8. Jane Chance explores Tolkien's own self-identification of being a "queer creature" in her 2016 monograph, *Tolkien, Self and Other: "This Queer Creature."*

9. The Tolkien Society's 2023 event, "Tolkien and Religion in the Twenty-first Century," shows the multidisciplinary, thematic, and potentially "contradictory" breadth of the theme of "religion and Tolkien" ("Tolkien Society Online Seminar").

10. Alexander Doty, in *Flaming Classics*, identifies six different definitions of "queer" that he sees functioning in queer theory and scholarship. The definitions range from the straightforward "synonym for either gay, or lesbian, or bisexual" to the more "radical understanding of queer ... [as] something apart from established gender and sexuality categories" (6-7). The work done by our contributors draws on a number of the different definitions of "queer" that Doty describes.

11. Tolkien fandom originated in the 1950s and has been growing ever since (Coker). However, relatively little attention was paid to fandom as culture or to transformative works by fans until recently. See: Abrahamson; Alberto; Booker; Brayton; Coker; Felagund; Gwynne; McCormack; Piatti-Farnell; Reid ("Making or Creating Orcs"; "Thrusts in the Dark") Sturgis; Viars and Coker; and Walls-Thumma.

Works Cited

Abrahamson, Megan. "J.R.R. Tolkien, Fanfiction, and 'The Freedom of the Reader.'" *Mythlore* vol. 32, no. 1, 2013, pp. 55-74, dc.swosu.edu/mythlore/vol32/iss1/5.

Abanes, Richard. *Harry Potter and the Bible: The Menace Behind the Magick*. Horizon Books, 2001.

———. *Harry Potter, Narnia, and The Lord of the Rings: What You Need to Know About Fantasy Books and Movies*. Harvest House Publishers, 2005.

Alberto, Maria. "'The Effort to Translate': Fan Film Culture and the Works of J.R.R. Tolkien." *Journal of Tolkien Research*, vol. 3, iss. 3, article 2, 2016, scholar.valpo.edu/journaloftolkienresearch/vol3/iss3/2.

Arthur, Sarah. *Walking with Frodo: A Devotional Journey Through The Lord of the Rings*. Tyndale House Publishers, 2003.

"Banned and Challenged Classics." *Banned and Challenged Books*. The ALA Office for Intellectual Freedom, ala.org/advocacy/bbooks/frequentlychallengedbooks/classics. Accessed 10 Sept. 2024.

Baldassarro, M. Wolf. "Banned Books Awareness: 'Lord of the Rings' by J.R.R Tolkien." *Banned Book Awareness*, Deep Forest Productions, 13 Mar. 2011, bbark.deepforestproductions.com/column/2011/03/13/banned-book-awareness-lord-rings-jrr-tolkien.

Battis, Jes. "Gazing Upon Sauron: Hobbits, Elves, and the Queering of the Postcolonial Optic." *MFS Modern Fiction Studies*, guest editor Shaun F.D. Hughes, vol. 50, no. 4, 2004, pp. 908-26, doi.org/10.1353/mfs.2005.0001.

Booker, Susan. "Tales Around the Internet Campfire: Fan Fiction in Tolkien's Universe." *Tolkien on Film: Essays on Peter Jackson's The Lord of the Rings*, edited by Janet Brennan Croft, Mythopoeic P, 2004, pp. 259-282.

Brayton, Jennifer. "Fic Frodo Slash Frodo: Fandoms and *The Lord of the Rings*." From

Hobbits to Hollywood: Essays on Peter Jackson's Lord of the Rings, edited by Ernest Mathijs and Murray Pomerance, Rodopi, 2006, pp. 137–153.

Brown, Devin. *The Christian World of* The Hobbit. Abingdon P, Illustrated ed., 2012.

Chance, Jane. "'In the Company of Orcs': Peter Jackson's Queer Tolkien." *Queer Movie Medievalisms*, edited by Kathleen Coyne Kelly and Tison Pugh, Ashgate Publishing, Routledge, 2009, pp. 79–96.

Chick, Jack. "Are Roman Catholics Christians?" Chick Publications, 1985.

———. "Dark Dungeons." Chick Publications, 1984.

Coker, Cait. "Fandom." *A Companion to J.R.R. Tolkien*, 2nd ed., edited by Stuart D. Lee, Wiley 2022.

Craig, David M. "'Queer Lodgings': Gender and Sexuality in *The Lord of the Rings*." *Mallorn*, vol. 38, Jan. 2001, pp. 11–18, journals.tolkiensociety.org/mallorn/article/view/145/139. Rpt. "Queer Lodgings: Gender and Sexuality in *The Lord of the Rings*—Reprinted with a New Introduction by the Author, *Mallorn*, Vol. 61, 2020, pp. 20–29.

Doty, Alexander. *Flaming Classics: Queering the Film Canon*. Routledge, 2000.

Emanuel, Tom. "'It Is "about" Nothing but Itself': Tolkienian Theology Beyond the Domination of the Author." *Mythlore*, vol. 42, no. 1, article 3, 2024, pp. 29–53, dc.swosu.edu/mythlore/vol42/iss1/3.

Felagund, Dawn. "Data on Tolkien Fanfiction Culture and Practices (1st Edition)." *Fiction and Research of Dawn Walls-Thumma*. 15 Apr. 2019, dawnfelagund.com/data-on-tolkien-fanfiction-culture-and-practices.

Fimi, Dimitra. *Tolkien, Race and Cultural History*. Palgrave Macmillan, 2010.

Flieger, Verlyn. "The Arch and the Keystone," *Mythlore*, vol. 38, no. 1, article 3, 2019, pp. 7–19, dc.swosu.edu/mythlore/vol38/iss1/3.

———. "But What Did He Really Mean?" *Tolkien Studies*, vol. 11, 2014, pp. 149–166.

Gwynne, Owain. "Fan-Made Time: *The Lord of the Rings* and *The Hobbit*." *Fan CULTure: Essays on Participatory Fandom in the 21st Century*," edited by Kristin M. Barton and Jonathan Malcolm Lampley, McFarland, 2014, pp. 76–91.

Hart, Lowell. *Satan's Music Exposed*. Amg Publishers, 1981.

Kilby, Clyde S. *Tolkien & The Silmarillion*. Harold Shaw P, 1976.

Knight, Gareth. *The Magical World of the Inklings*. Element Books, 1990.

Larson, Bob. *Rock: Practical Help for Those Who Listen to the Words and Don't Like What They Hear*. Tyndale House Publishers, 1980.

Loy, David, and Linda Goodhew. *The Dharma of Dragons and Daemons: Buddhist Themes in Modern Fantasy*. Wisdom Publications, 2000.

Magnus, P.D. "Secrets of Dark Dungeons." fecundity.com/pmagnus/darkdung.html. Accessed 10 Oct. 2024.

McCormack, Una. "Finding Ourselves in the (Un)Mapped Lands: Women's Reparative Readings of the Lord of the Rings." *Perilous and Fair: Women in the Works and Life of J.R.R. Tolkien*, edited by Janet Brennan Croft and Leslie A. Donovan, Mythopoeic P, 2025, pp. 309–326.

Milon, Anna. *Tolkien the Pagan? Reading Middle-earth Through a Spiritual Lens*. Luna P Publishing, 2019. Peter Roe Series XIX.

Penre, Wes. "J.R.R. Tolkien and C. S. Lewis: The Occult Overtones in Their Writings." *Illuminati News*. 1 Jan. 2005. illuminati-news.com/tolkien-occult.htm.

Piatti-Farnell, Lorna, editor. *Fan Phenomena: The Lord of the Rings*. Intellect, 2016.

Purtill, Richard. *Lord of the Elves and Eldils: Fantasy and Philosophy in C. S. Lewis and J.R.R. Tolkien*. Zondervan Books, 1974.

Reid, Robin Anne, "J.R.R. Tolkien, Culture Warrior: The Alt-Right's Crusade Against the Tolkien Society's 2021 Summer Seminar on 'Tolkien and Diversity.'" *Journal of Tolkien Research*, vol. 16, iss. 2, article 4, 2023, scholar.valpo.edu/journaloftolkienresearch/vol16/iss2/4.

———. "Making or Creating Orcs: How Thorinsmut's Free Orcs AU Writes Back to Tolkien." *Journal of Tolkien Research*, vol. 11, iss. 2, article 3, 2020, scholar.valpo.edu/journaloftolkienresearch/vol11/iss2/3.

_____. "Thrusts in the Dark: Slashers' Queer Practices." *Extrapolation*, vol. 50, no. 3, Jan. 2009, pp. 463–83, doi.org/10.3828/extr.2009.50.3.6.

Rohy, Valerie. "On Fairy Stories." *MFS: Modern Fiction Studies*, J.R.R. Tolkien Special Issue, guest editor Shaun F.D. Hughes, vol. 50, no. 4, 2004, pp. 927–48.

Ryken, Philip. *The Messiah Comes to Middle-Earth: Images of Christ's Threefold Office in The Lord of the Rings*, Hansen Lectureship Series, IVP Academic, 2017.

Smith, Mark Eddy. *Tolkien's Ordinary Virtues: Exploring the Spiritual Themes of* The Lord of the Rings. CreateSpace Independent Publishing Platform, 2001.

Strauss, Ed. *A Hobbit Devotional: Bilbo Baggins and the Bible*. Barbour Books, 2012.

Sturgis, Amy H. "Reimagining Rose: Portrayals of Tolkien's Rosie Cotton in Twenty-First Century Fan Fiction," *Mythlore*, vol. 24, no. 3, article 10, 2006, pp. 165–187. dc.swosu.edu/mythlore/vol24/iss3/10.

Testi, Claudio. *Pagan Saints in Middle-earth*. Walking Tree Publishers, 2018. Cormarë Series No. 37.

"Tolkien Society Online Seminar 2023: Tolkien and Religion in the Twenty-first Century." *Tolkien Society*. 26 Nov. 2023, tolkiensociety.org/events/tolkien-society-online-seminar-2023-tolkien-and-religion-in-the-twenty-first-century/.

Urang, Gunnar. *Shadows of Heaven: Religion and Fantasy in the Writing of C.S. Lewis, Charles Williams, and J.R.R. Tolkien*. United Church P, 1971.

Vaccaro, Christopher. "Saruman's Sodomitic Resonances: Alain de Lille's *De Planctu Naturae* and J.R.R. Tolkien's *The Lord of the Rings*." *Tolkien and Alterity*, edited by Christopher Vaccaro and Yvette Kisor, Palgrave Macmillan, 2017, pp. 123–47.

Viars, Karen, and Cait Coker. "Constructing Lothíriel: Rewriting and Rescuing the Women of Middle-Earth [sic] from the Margins," *Mythlore*, vol. 33, no. 2, article 6, 2015, pp. 15-48, dc.swosu.edu/mythlore/vol33/iss2/6/.

Walls-Thumma, Dawn M. "Affirmational and Transformational Values and Practices in the Tolkien Fanfiction Community," *Journal of Tolkien Research*, vol. 8, iss. 1, article 6, 2019, scholar.valpo.edu/journaloftolkienresearch/vol8/iss1/6.

Warnke, Mike. *The Satan Seller*. Logos International, 1972.

Wood, Ralph C. *The Gospel According to Tolkien: Visions of the Kingdom in Middle-earth*. Westminster John Knox P, 2003.

Yandell, Stephen. "Cruising Faery: Queer Desire in Giles, Niggle, and Smith." *Tolkien and Alterity*, edited by Christopher Vaccaro and Yvette Kisor, Palgrave Macmillan, 2017, pp. 149–79.

Introduction

ROBIN ANNE REID,
CHRISTOPHER VACCARO *and*
STEPHEN YANDELL

The three editors—two medievalists and one postmodernist—saw the need for an anthology that explored the "many paths" of queer approaches to J.R.R. Tolkien, his legendarium, adaptations and transformative works, more than a decade ago.[1] We began imagining a shape for it in 2017, well before Covid-19 changed everything. We created a Call for Proposals (CFP) inviting submissions for paper sessions in the Tolkien Studies Area for the 2018 annual Popular Culture and American Culture conference. We received enough proposals to schedule two paper sessions that explored a number of queer approaches to Tolkien's legendarium, and then we began the process of soliciting more proposals for an anthology. The impact of the pandemic and the resulting lockdowns was felt by all the editors and the contributors, but that hiatus also gave us the opportunity to carefully and consciously develop this collection over seven years to make sure we are representing the best work being currently done, are paying attention to the scholarly shifts currently taking place in Tolkien scholarship, and are making sure we adequately respond to the changing context in this critical period of time. Some of the original presenters at the conference and the first round of submissions chose not to pursue publication with us; others had to withdraw (primarily due to the impact of Covid on their lives and jobs), and we added essays by other authors along the way.

As we revise this introduction in spring 2025, we are all aware of the contemporary socio-political and historical context in which our collection exists (2017–2025), a context in which far-right extremist (FRE) movements in the United States have not only accelerated legislation against LGBTQ+ rights, reproductive rights, civil rights, immigrant rights, and voting rights but have also accelerated hate crimes, violent protests, and insurrection ("FBI Releases"). These efforts in the public and political spheres are reflected in and supported by online campaigns against popular media as Alexandra Minna Stern documents in *Proud Boys and the White Ethnostate: How the Alt-right Is Warping the American Imagination* (2019).[2] As we began to prepare the manuscript to submit to McFarland for peer review, we watched the growth of fascist and authoritarian movements in the United States and around the world; as we came to the end of the process (October 2024), we saw the unprecedented spectacle of President Joseph Biden, the incumbent candidate for the 2024 presidential election, withdrawing from the race on July 21, 2024, and, half an hour later, endorsing Vice President Kamala Harris to replace him. Two weeks later, Vice President Harris named the governor of Minnesota, Tim Walz, as her vice-presidential nominee. In 1999, Walz, then a high school geography teacher and assistant coach in Minnesota, agreed to serve as the "first-ever gay–straight alliance advisor at Mankato West High School after being approached by one of his students" (Maskell).

Despite our growing optimism in the wake of this political shift, we knew that even if Harris and Walz won the election, a great deal of work would remain to address inequalities caused by metastasizing homophobia, misogyny, nativism, racism, and xenophobia which all have deep historical roots in the United States. As it turned out, Donald Trump won the election by a narrow margin and in the last few months has accelerated the attempted destruction of the United States as a democracy. This collection was created as legislatures in gerrymandered red states enabled unprecedented growth in the number of challenged and banned books in school and public libraries while passing laws that established criminal penalties for librarians breaking them (American Library Association, Bailey, Meehan, et al.). Many of the banned books focus on LGBTQ+ themes, a clear backlash against recent progressive changes, while others engage with the histories and realities of Black, Indigenous, and People of Color (BIPOC). All of our lives and work have been shaped in different ways by the decades-long conflict between the far-right and progressive movements in this country.

Stephen Yandell: This conflicted shifting between the categories of spiritual and secular certainly defines my own earliest experiences with Tolkien. I read *The Hobbit* for the first time while attending a Christian, Protestant, evangelical junior-high school, and was surprised that while some instructors held up Tolkien as a positive Christian influence, others were quick to label him a Catholic, and thus, by some evangelical standards, not a true Christian. One family at the same school typified for me the most extreme form of binary thinking. I remember distinctly the afternoon I learned one set of parents had pulled their son from the school after learning he was being asked to read C.S. Lewis's *The Lion, the Witch, and the Wardrobe*. The fantastic had no place in this Christian family's life. As I was told, any book that "depicted Jesus as an animal" should be shunned as both secular and dangerous.

Robin Anne Reid: As a queer feminist autist, intersectional queer theory is important to me. I was, as a child, a lukewarm Presbyterian at best until my family stopped attending the church because of conflict over a donation to Angela Davis's Legal Defense Fund (Tangeman). My animism was enhanced, if not caused, by my falling in love with *The Fellowship of the Ring*, *The Two Towers*, and *The Return of the King* (the authorized Ballantine editions, of course, which we found in a local drugstore's rack of paperbacks) in 1965 when I was ten. I did not realize I was an atheist until my fifties. That realization was what raised my consciousness of the conflicts around "Tolkien" and "religion" that had not been particularly relevant to me before. Two specific incidents are key: first, the vitriolic attacks against the "Tolkien and Diversity" 2023 Summer Seminar (see the "Preface" in this volume; Reid, "J.R.R. Tolkien, Culture Warrior"; Emanuel 2023), and, second, a published response to a conference presentation by Donald Williams in *Mythlore* in which he argues that Verlyn Flieger's essay on the contradictions in Tolkien's work was the result of her ignorance of "the Christian philosophy of history, the biblical eschatology, that underlies Tolkien's work" (198) (Reid, "A Queer Atheist Feminist Autist Responds"). Those two events are a microcosm of the larger "culture wars," primarily related to two of the seven mountains (of the Seven Mountain Mandate) in this country: media and arts/entertainment (Poythress). However, during my quarter-century plus as a college teacher in rural Texas where I taught contemporary critical theories and marginalized literatures, I also watched as more and more of the books I taught were challenged and/or banned.

Christopher Vaccaro: I'm a "querd"—a queer nerd. I came to Tolkien's Middle-earth through my role-playing group—a religiously, ethnically, and sexually diverse bunch of boys—who used the Advanced Dungeons and Dragons system to help narrate our own stories rooted on the eastern shores of the *Middle-earth Role-playing* (MERP) map (Maliszewski). At the same time as my wizard was establishing himself as the bane of Balrogs, I was reading that being "homosexual" was sinful in the *Catholic Encyclopedia*. Like me, my characters got queerer and queerer. After being chased down alleys and protesting the lack of HIV/AIDS research with ACT UP and Queer Nation, my readings and interpretations have got queerer and queerer too. You could say I have an agenda! Part of that agenda for this collection is to showcase the need for more queer fantasies/interpretations of Tolkien, given the past dominance of the straight fantasies in criticism (Reid; Vaccaro; Yandell, "Queer Lodgings Interview").

Queer Tolkien scholarship is a relatively new field which we argue originated in David Craig's 2001 essay "'Queer Lodgings': Gender and Sexuality in *The Lord of the Rings*," a groundbreaking exploration of how homosocial, homoerotic, homoamorous, and possibly homosexual elements of the novel reflect the historical context of friendships between men during World War I that Tolkien experienced during his service. In 2016, the first monograph on the topic, Jane Chance's *Tolkien, Self and Other: "This Queer Creature,"* takes a different approach, placing Tolkien's fiction alongside his scholarship to argue that Tolkien's own life as a Catholic in England, a medievalist at Oxford, an Englishman born in South Africa, and a "queer creature" who created languages, and their worlds, illustrates how his non-normative identities, knowledges, and activities fall under the generic definition of "alterity." Chance draws on Tison Pugh's work to analyze Tolkien's queer medieval aesthetics.

The first, and so far only, as of the writing of this introduction, bibliographic essay on queer readings of Tolkien is by Yvette Kisor in her 2017 "Queer Tolkien: A Bibliographic Essay on Tolkien and Alterity" (Vaccaro and Kisor). Her essay covers queer scholarship on Tolkien from 2001 to Jane Chance's monograph, published in 2016. The publications by Craig and Chance exemplify the two different types of queer approaches that Kisor identifies in her essay. The first type are those works focusing on questions relating to "queer sexuality and identity," about characters in *The Lord of the Rings*, while the second draws on the broadest meaning of "queer" as "alterity," or, simply, difference, which includes any identity or all identities that are non-normative in any way (18). Kisor identifies five essays (2001–2005), which, although disagreeing on whether or not Frodo and Sam's relationship in the novel is homosexual, fall into the first category (Craig; Rohy; Smol; Saxey; and Timmons). She identifies ten essays, and a monograph, that focus on the broader concept of "alterity," with scholars addressing a larger range of characters than Frodo and Sam, including Orcs, and analyzing how systems of ethnicity or race, class, and gender function in Tolkien's work (Battis; Chance [four essays; the monograph]; Dawson; Komornicka; Opreanu; Saxton; and Tadie).

Kisor argues that future scholarship should move beyond the "singular focus on the question of the homosexuality of characters in *The Lord of the Rings*" to consider other characters in Tolkien's legendarium as well as adaptations of his works, such as film and fan creations. She also encourages scholars to use "a broader concept of the queer than just the sexual, as the division of essays in this overview proposes," including questions of genre (drawing on Pugh) (Kisor 25–6). She concludes her bibliographic essay by listing three "queer abiding concerns for future scholarship: the relation with the Other, the response to difference, and the negotiation with the queer" (27). She employs this broader concept in "'We Could Do with a Bit More Queerness in These Parts': An Analysis of the Queer against the Peculiar, the Odd, and the Strange in *The Lord of the Rings*." In her 2023 essay she closely examines the distribution of vocabulary related to the various speakers and context in which the word "queer" is used, concluding that Tolkien crafted "in *The Lord of the Rings* an association with Hobbits and a very specific set of resonances for the term that embed it in provincial mistrust, a sense of real outside threat, and places within the ancient natural world that appear foundationally opposed to the ordinary realm of civilization" (21).

This collection picks up Kisor's charge on all three fronts; and, as people who are queer, or "Othered," in ways that Tolkien never was, we would add to Kisor's three final concerns three additional questions which shaped this collection and which we argue require further exploration: What do "the Other[s]" and "the Queer[s]" have to say about Tolkien's legendarium, the adaptations and transformative works, and the global phenomenon of the readership that has flourished during the past seven decades? Given the dominance of the heterosexist interpretations in scholarship, when will "the Straight" (or "the Normative") scholars acknowledge the limitations of their subject positions when interpreting texts rather than assuming their (personal sense of) universality is, well, universal? Finally, how can Tolkien scholars change the academic spaces we inhabit to become more diverse and intersectional in the future? We see our anthology as offering one small step, indeed a collection of several small steps, in that direction.

Clearly, there is still more work to be done, many more paths to explore in the future, with a growing and more diverse group of readers and scholars who can begin to fill the gaps that still exist. The most significant gap is the default Whiteness of queer (and gender, and feminist) approaches to Tolkien. As far as we can discover, there are few intersectional analyses of race, ethnicity, sexuality, and gender, although Jane Chance's (2008) and Jes Battis's 2004 essays have made a start. Given the lengthy time we ended up spending in the early stages of the anthology, we had the opportunity to make multiple attempts through both targeted open calls and personal emails to scholars to encourage intersectional submissions. We failed. Another gap is the absence of queer feminist (and feminist queer) approaches to female characters in Tolkien.[3] A third gap we consider significant is the question of queer theological approaches to Tolkien.[4]

Our purpose in this collection has always been to foreground a diverse group of voices from multiple disciplinary perspectives and periods, some of which have been minimal or absent in previous scholarship applying queer theories to Tolkien's legendarium. Our contributors' work shows the diversity of queer theories and the range of scholarly periodizations as well as multiple generations of scholars. In terms of queer approaches to Tolkien, there is the medieval queer (exemplified by the work of Tison Pugh in medieval studies, though his own work does not touch on Tolkien), which employs contemporary queer theories to analyze Tolkien's work in the context of the medieval works which were his professional and personal passion. When Jane Chance created the Tolkien at Kalamazoo sponsoring group for the International Congress on Medieval Studies in 2000 and proceeded to edit a number of anthologies from sessions she organized for the conference, the long-standing connection between Tolkien studies and medieval studies was established.

But there is also a growing postmodern queer body of work by scholars specializing in post-medieval historical/literary periods and applying queer theories from multiple theorists to analyze Tolkien's work in the context of the twentieth and twenty-first centuries. This expansion of periodization seems to correlate with the release of the live-action films directed by Peter Jackson (2001–2003) which transformed what was already a multi-disciplinary field to include people trained in contemporary and inter-disciplinary fields such as cultural studies, film studies, gender studies, and reception studies.[5] A major periodical marking this change in Tolkien scholarship is the 2004 Tolkien issue of *MFS: Modern Fiction Studies*, J.R.R. Tolkien Special Issue, guest edited by Shaun F.D. Hughes. *MFS* is an academic journal published by Johns Hopkins University Press which has the goal of publishing essays "that analyze the important aesthetic, cultural, political, and environmental developments currently shaping today's academic and public conversations" (*MFS*). The 2004 issue features two essays on "*The Lord of the Rings* and Race" (Rearick; Kim) and three on "Queering *The Lord of the Rings*" (Battis; Rohy; Smol) and has been, until this anthology appears, the single largest collection of queer approaches (and of critical race approaches) in Tolkien studies.

The editors are pleased, therefore, that our anthology is the first to feature a more comprehensive focus on queer approaches to Tolkien's legendarium that is grounded in the existence of our queer bodies and pleasures rather than on either generic "differences" or "homosexuality." All three editors have long and queer personal engagements with Tolkien's work that influenced their academic training, their choices of queer theorists in their scholarship, and, frankly, their own queer identities. We also embody the range of literary periods, from medieval to postmodern, that exists in twenty-first-century Tolkien scholarship as do the authors of the other essays. The pre-modern queer, exemplified by the work of medievalist Tison Pugh, is joined by postmodern queer works by scholars trained in post-medieval periods. The scholarship in this collection foregrounds the multiple queer theories that exist, including but not limited to the works of Sara Ahmed, Alexander Doty, Sigmund Freud, Gérard Genette, René Girard, Jack Halberstam, Annemarie Jagose, Julia Kristeva, Jay Prosser, Tison Pugh, Eve Kosofsky Sedgwick, Susan Stryker, and Richard Zeikowitz.

Queer Approaches to Tolkien: Essays on the Many Paths to Middle-earth is organized into four sections following the Preface and Introduction, ending with a bibliography on "Tolkien and Alterity." The first section has three essays that focus on alternative ethical frameworks. The second has three essays that explore the interactions of intersectional interpretive strategies that address gaps in previous Tolkien scholarship. The third section has four essays on queer relations between male characters including, but not limited to, Frodo and Sam, and the final section has two essays on transformative Tolkien fanfiction. The final contribution, "Tolkien and Alterity: A Bibliography" is included because we acknowledge the need to highlight the importance of multiple axes of difference to work toward an intersectional queer scholarship in future.

Overview of Essays

Part I, "Queer Moralities," has three essays focusing on alternative types of ethical frameworks.

In "The Problematic Perimeters of Elrond Half-elven and Ronald English-Catholic," Kristine Larsen argues that Tolkien presents himself significantly in the figure of Elrond. The shared minority positions of author and creation help champion the deep impact of homosocial bonds, revealing self-identification to be of vital importance for individuals residing in liminal spaces.

In "I Dream of Gandalf: or, How I Was Raised by Wizards," through discussions of queerness, wizardly willfulness, and neurodiversity, Jes Battis examines Gandalf as a figure of power and hope. Gandalf's queerness is part of this discussion, but so is the wizard's refusal of categories. Battis likewise explores the wizardly mind (Gandalf's and Merlin's) as something delightfully queer, in line with contemporary work on neurodiversity by M. Remi Yergeau and Julia Rodas.

In "The End Is Queer: *Cleanness* and Tolkien's Apocalyptic Landscape," Stephen Yandell argues that Tolkien borrowed heavily from the fourteenth-century poem *Cleanness* (also titled "Purity"). Tolkien's best challenge to *Cleanness's* homophobia is in his championing of an alternative moral code, one grounded in the original Sodom story: the call to offer hospitality to the outsider. This queer ethic proves central in determining one's character in the legendarium, and in challenging fixed boundaries between insider and outsider. Yandell argues that Tolkien queers not only his medieval source text *Cleanness*, but also the medieval apocalyptic genre.

Part II, "Queer Intersections," highlights through its three essays an important attribute of the collection overall, the complicated interactions of intersectional interpretive strategies that address gaps in previous scholarship.

In "Mother or Other: Tolkien's Shelob and the 'Monstrous-Feminine,'" Sara Brown draws on postmodern queer theory and third-wave feminist scholarship by Jack Halberstam and Judith Butler to develop an intersectional argument analyzing Shelob as an example of gender performativity, in which her actions demonstrate a modern femininity that draws on traditionally masculine power structures. In conversation with Julia Kristeva's concept of abjection and Barbara Creed's description of the "monstrous-feminine," Brown shows how Shelob's queerness as a mother subverts the norm entirely. By placing Shelob next to Grendel's mother, Brown illustrates how transgressive female characters are punished via the medium of language.

In "Éowyn and/or Dernhelm: Reading Éowyn's (Trans)Masculine Disguise," Gavin Foster analyzes Tolkien's representation of gender performativity in his construction of Dernhelm. While not intending to suggest that Éowyn is necessarily trans-coded, Foster argues that her disguise substantively blurs the boundaries between masculinity and femininity, and that said blurring may be usefully read through the perspectives of transgender theorists such as Jay Prosser, Jack Halberstam, and Susan Stryker. Ultimately, the goal is to demonstrate how an introduction of these new lenses might provide further insight into the ways gender and gender performance function in Tolkien's works.

In "'Something Mighty Queer': Destabilizing Gender, Intimacy and Family in Tolkien's Legendarium," Danna Petersen-Deeprose argues that, while Tolkien's texts reinforce gender norms at a surface level, they simultaneously, and more significantly, destabilize them. Drawing on work by Audre Lorde and Lewis Seifert, Petersen-Deeprose analyzes how the races of Dwarves, Elves, and Ainur reveal this gender non-conformity and how the breadth of non-heterosexual partnerships and non-normative families complicate essentialist ideas of gender and destabilize contemporary cis-hetero amatonormative structures.

Part III, "Intra-Male Queerness," offers four essays centered around queer relations between male characters from *The Silmarillion* and *The Lord of the Rings*.

In "'For he would take no wife': Surface Reading, Eärnur and the Queering of the Unmarried Male in *The Lord of the Rings*," Nicholas Birns argues that Eärnur, the last king of Gondor, is a model of queer defiance. His childlessness, refusal to settle down, and love-hate relationship with the Witch-king of Angmar align Eärnur with other bachelor figures in the legendarium. The same traits contribute to Tolkien's depiction of male sexuality, and ultimately demand a new consideration of Aragorn, whose reproductivity proves contingent on Eärnur's queer unattachment.

In "'Bending over with naked blade': The Erotics of Suffering and Male-Male Penetration in Tolkien's Legendarium," Zachary Clifton Engledow argues that the relationship of Beleg and Túrin is born of intense, perverse desire, drawing on work by Tison Pugh and Richard Zeikowitz. The characters' romance is predicated on the pleasures of holding to a damaged identity where trauma and shame bind bodies through time and beyond narrative frameworks. Pleasure is shown to reside in the partial, the failure, and the lack.

In "Frodo, Sam and the Ring of Power: A Queer Erotic Triangle," Christopher Cameron questions how evidence that Tolkien and the Shirefolk frequently refer to Frodo and Bilbo (both lifelong bachelors) as "queer" is often understood by readers to mean "odd" and is read as male intimacy without sexual connotations. Cameron makes a case for a queer reading of Tolkien's characters through the application of queer and psychoanalytical theory by René Girard and Sigmund Freud. Exploring Frodo and Sam's erotic feelings for each other and building on Carol Bernard's analysis of Frodo and Sam's relationship as an erotic triangle with Gollum, Cameron argues that the Ring, as a fetishized object of libidinal desire, should be positioned within that triangle.

In "'Saruman [?Pardoned]': The Queerness of Sex in Tolkien's *The Lord of the Rings*," Christopher Vaccaro analyzes early drafts and sketches of *The Lord of the Rings* held at Marquette University using theories by Annemarie Jagose, Julia Kristeva, and Eve Kosofsky Sedgwick to argue that the changes in Saruman's fall and potential future offer rich insights into Tolkien's rhetorical shifts and opinions toward the queer figure, sexuality, and primal carnality. Saruman's vices not only reinforce a medieval template of the "sodomitic," they point to Tolkien's changing attitudes towards a suitable punishment for the wizard and reveal a shifting discomfort with all that he signifies.

Lastly, Part IV, "Queer Transformations," offers two essays that analyze the transformative worlds of Tolkien fanfiction.

In "'and stooping he raised Beleg and kissed his mouth': Queering

Canon with Tolkien Fanfiction," Maria K. Alberto demonstrates that fans who create transformative fictions based on J.R.R. Tolkien's legendarium exemplify how canon(s) can be queered. Building from, but also expanding on, queer reading practices such as those described by Alexander Doty, Alberto argues that these fans treat the construct of an authoritative textual category as itself something to be engaged. Alberto focuses on Beleg and Túrin's "canon kiss" (kisses which occur between the heroes in multiple versions of Túrin's story) to show how fans rewrite structural elements, genre norms, and linguistic signifiers.

In "'What care I for the hands of a king?' Tolkien Fanfiction and Narratives of the Transgender Self," Cordeliah G. Logsdon builds on previous scholarship about transformative fiction by fans that centers female characters from the edges of Tolkien's texts by expanding the transformational scope to include transgender stories and realities. Drawing on personal reflection and an examination of Anglachel's *Hands of the King*, their analysis blends the interpretation of fan story with the personal experiences of one of its transgender readers. Logsdon's work creates a model for exploring source texts and transformative fiction in a way that values queerness, challenges the presumptive supremacy of cisgender readings, and creates spaces for transgender thought, themes, and characters.

Finally, in "Tolkien and Alterity: A Bibliography," Jordan Audas presents an extensive bibliography compiled using searches which matched "Tolkien" and "Alterity." "Tolkien" as a search term includes anything related to J.R.R. Tolkien (biographical information, personal or attributed views, the process of creating and writing his academic and literary outputs, etc.) as well as related to the literary world he created (criticisms and close-text readings of his novels, character interactions and motives, adaptations and transformative works, etc.). The matching search term, "Alterity," for the purpose of this project, is broadly defined in this work as aspects of humanity that can be/are marginalized, stigmatized, or discriminated against, such as race, gender, sexuality, etc., rather than all states of difference.

The three editors of this volume hope that the essays herein speak to the interests, fantasies, and curiosities of its readers and provide new and exciting paths into Middle-earth.

Notes

1. The reference to "many paths" in *Queer Approaches to Tolkien: Essays on the Many Paths to Middle-earth*, comes from a song by Bilbo that the four hobbits are singing on the first night of their journey just before they meet the Elves in the Shire (*The Fellowship of the Ring* [*FR*], I, iii, 114–15).

2. The backlash against Amazon (whose preliminary marketing for the Amazon *Rings*

of Power adaptation was attacked for months before the first episode of the first season of the series aired) is a typical example of this phenomenon (Barraclough).

    3. See Reid, "Thrusts in the Dark: Slashers' Queer Practices," for an example of this approach.

    4. Fantasy scholarship, like Tolkien scholarship, has only recently begun to engage with queer theory and approaches, a recent example being Taylor Driggers's 2022 monograph, *Queering Faith in Fantasy Literature: Fantastic Incarnations and the Deconstruction of Theology*, Bloomsbury.

    5. The three founding and arguably best-known scholars in Tolkien scholarship in terms of their monograph and essay publication are two medievalists (Jane Chance, in literature, and Tom Shippey, philology) and comparative mythology (Verlyn Flieger). Medieval texts are texts produced during the historical period defined as the Middle Ages, roughly 500–1500 CE; medievalist, or neomedieval, texts (labeled as medievalism) are those works produced after that period that draw on what is known about the "medieval" at a later time. In the past, medievalist content tended to be found mostly in historical fiction and films. Since Tolkien, genre fantasy, fiction, film, and games increasingly draw on what is popularly known about the "medieval." Medievalists have argued whether or not these recent appropriations should perhaps be considered "neomedieval" to distinguish contemporary or postmodern views of "the medieval" from work published in previous centuries. *Studies in Medievalism*, the International Society for the Study of Medievalism's (ISSM) scholarly journal, has dealt with the debate in a number of its issues which focus on "the interdisciplinary study of the popular and scholarly reception of the Middle Ages in postmedieval times. Medievalism is the continuing invention, reinvention, construction, and reconstruction of the global medieval past, broadly" ("About"). The growing scholarly consensus seems to be that there are multiple manifestations of medievalism and neomedievalism, and always have been, based on different constructions of "the medieval" in scholarship and popular culture (Fugelso, *Studies in Medievalism XIX*). A review of scholarly backgrounds of contributors to *Tolkien and Alterity* is representative of the contemporary field's range of different periods and specializations: the anthology includes work by medievalists (Vaccaro; Kisor; Holmes; Yandell) as well as academics specializing English or British literature (Amendt-Raduege, Arul); eighteenth-century literature (Dawson); comparative mythology (Flieger); astronomy (Larsen); queer theory (Rohy), and critical race theory (Reid).

Works Cited

Amendt-Raguege, Amy. "Revising Lobelia," Vaccaro and Kisor, pp. 77–93.

American Library Association. "Censorship by the Numbers." *Banned and Challenged Books*. American Library Association, ala.org/bbooks/censorship-numbers#. Accessed 10 Oct. 2024.

Arul, Melissa Ruth. "Silmarils and Obsession: The Undoing of Fëanor," Vaccaro and Kisor, pp. 225–39.

Bailey, Charles W. "Red States Threaten Librarians with Prison—As Blue States Work to Protect Them." *Digital Koans*, 18 Apr. 2024, digital-scholarship.org/digitalkoans/2024/04/18/red-states-threaten-librarians-with-prison-as-blue-states-work-to-protect-them. Accessed 10 Oct. 2024.

Barraclough, Leo. "'Rings of Power' Cast Slams Racist Backlash at Monte-Carlo Television Festival, Teases 'Action-Packed' Season 2." *Variety*. 18 June 2023, variety.com/2023/scene/global/rings-of-power-lord-of-the-rings-monte-carlo-television-festival-1235648051.

Battis, Jes. "Gazing Upon Sauron: Hobbits, Elves, and the Queering of the Postcolonial Optic." Hughes, pp. 908–26.

Chance, Jane. "'In the Company of Orcs': Peter Jackson's Queer Tolkien." *Queer Movie Medievalisms*, edited by Kathleen Coyne Kelly and Tison Pugh, Routledge, 2009, pp. 79–96.

———. "'Queer'" Hobbits: The Problem of Difference in the Shire." *The Lord of the Rings: The Mythology of Power*, Rev. ed., UP of Kentucky, 2001.

———. "Subversive Fantasist: Tolkien on Class Difference." *Proceedings of the Conference on The Lord of the Rings, 1954–2004: Scholarship in Honor of Richard E. Blackwelder*, edited by Wayne G. Hammond and Christina Scull, Marquette UP, 2006, pp. 153–68.

———. "Tolkien and the Other: Race and Gender in the Middle Earth." *Tolkien's Modern Middle Ages*, edited by Jane Chance and Alfred K. Siewers, Palgrave, 2008, pp. 171–86.

———. *Tolkien, Self and Other: This Queer Creature*. Palgrave, 2016.

Craig, David M. "'Queer Lodgings': Gender and Sexuality in *The Lord of the Rings*." *Mallorn*, vol. 38, Jan. 2001, pp. 11–18, journals.tolkiensociety.org/mallorn/article/view/145/139. Rpt. "Queer Lodgings: Gender and Sexuality in *The Lord of the Rings*—Reprinted with a New Introduction by the Author." *Mallorn*, Vol. 61, 2020, pp. 20–29.

Dawson, Deidre. "Language and Alterity in Tolkien and Lévinas," Vaccaro and Kisor, pp. 183–203.

Driggers, Taylor. *Queering Faith in Fantasy Literature: Fantastic Incarnations and the Deconstruction of Theology*, Bloomsbury, 2022.

Eaglestone, Robert, editor. *Reading* The Lord of the Rings: *New Writings on Tolkien's Trilogy*, Continuum, 2006

Emanuel, Tom. "Recovering Race in Middle-earth." *Queer and Back Again*. 20 May 2023, queerandback.substack.com/p/recovering-race-in-middle-earth.

"FBI Releases 2023 Hate Crime Statistics." *Facts and Statistics*, U.S. Department of Justice. 23 September 2024, justice.gov/hatecrimes/hate-crime-statistics.

Flieger, Verlyn. "The Orcs and the Others: Familiarity as Estrangement in *The Lord of the Rings*," Vaccaro and Kisor, pp. 205–22.

Fugelso, Karl. *Studies in Medievalism XIX: Defining NeoMedievalisms*. Boydell & Brewer, D.S. Brewer, 2010, Studies in Medievalism.

Holmes, John. "The Oher as *Kolbítr*: Tolkien's Faramir and Éowyn as Alfred and Æthelflæd," Vaccaro and Kisor, pp. 241–61.

Hughes, Shaun F.D., guest editor. *J.R.R. Tolkien Special Issue*. *MFS: Modern Fiction Studies*, J.R.R. Tolkien Special Issue, vol. 50, iss. 4, Winter 2004.

International Society for the Study of Medievalism (ISSM). "Overview." *About*. medievalisms.org. Accessed 10 Oct. 2024.

Kim, Sue. "Beyond Black and White: Race and Postmodernism in *The Lord of the Rings* Films." *MFS: Modern Fiction Studies*, J.R.R. Tolkien Special Issue, guest editor Shaun F.D. Hughes, vol. 50, no. 4, 2004, pp. 875–907, doi.org/10. 1353/mfs.2005.0005.

Kisor, Yvette. "'We Could Do with a Bit More Queerness in These Parts': An Analysis of the Queer Against the Peculiar, the Odd, and the Strange in *The Lord of the Rings*." *Journal of Tolkien Research*, vol. 16, iss.1, article 4, 2023, scholar.valpo.edu/journaloftolkienresearch/vol16/iss1/4.

———. "Queer Tolkien: A Bibliographical Essay on Tolkien and Alterity." Vaccaro and Kisor, pp. 17–32.

Komornicka, Jolanta N. "The Ugly Elf: Orc Bodies, Perversion and Redemption in *The Silmarillion* and *The Lord of the Rings*." *The Body in Tolkien's Legendarium: Essays on Middle-earth Corporeality*, edited by Christopher Vaccaro, McFarland, 2013, pp. 83–96.

Lewis, C.S. *The Lion, the Witch, and the Wardrobe*. Collier Books, 1973.

Maliszewski, James. "Retrospective: Middle-earth Role Playing." *Grognardia*, 23 Dec. 2020, grognardia.blogspot.com/2020/12/retrospective-middle-earth-role-playing.html.

Maskell, Emily. "Tim Walz Praised for His Work as Gay-straight Alliance Advisor in the 1990s: 'He Has a Great Heart.'" *Pink News*. 7 Aug. 2024, thepinknews.com/2024/08/07/tim-walz-praised-for-his-work-as-gay-straight-alliance-advisor.

Meehan, Kasey, Jonathan Friedman, Sabrina Baêta, and Tasslyn Magnusson. "Banned in the USA: The Mounting Pressure to Censor." 1 Sept. 2023, *Pen America*, pen.org/report/book-bans-pressure-to-censor.

MFS: Modern Fiction Studies. Johns Hopkins University Press. press.jhu.edu/journals/mfs-modern-fiction-studies. Accessed 10 Oct. 2024.

Opreanu, Lucia. "The Inescapable Other—Identity Transitions and Mutations in the

Constructions of Tolkien's Gollum/Sméagol." *University of Bucharest Review*, vol. 1, no. 1, 2011, pp. 151–59.

Poythress, Justin N. "How Evangelicals Lose Will Make All the Difference: A Critique of the Seven Mountain Mandate." "Bible and Theology," *The Gospel Coalition*, July 10, 2023, thegospelcoalition.org/article/seven-mountain-mandate.

Rearick, Anderson. "Why Is the Only Good Orc a Dead Orc? The Dark Face of Racism Examined in Tolkien's World." *MFS: Modern Fiction Studies*, J.R.R. Tolkien Special Issue, guest editor Shaun F.D. Hughes, vol. 50, no. 4, 2004, pp. 861–74, doi.org/10.1353/mfs.2005.0008.

Reid, Robin Anne. "J.R.R. Tolkien, Culture Warrior: The Alt-Right's Crusade Against the Tolkien Society's 2021 Summer Seminar on 'Tolkien and Diversity.'" *Journal of Tolkien Research*, vol. 16, iss. 2, article 4, 2023, scholar.valpo.edu/journaloftolkienresearch/vol16/iss2/4.

———. "A Queer Atheist Feminist Autist Responds to Donald Williams's 'Keystone or Cornerstone? A Rejoinder to Verlyn Flieger on the Alleged "Conflicting Sides" of Tolkien's Singular Self.'" *Mythlore*, vol. 40, no. 2, article 14, 2022, pp. 196–220, Dc.swosu.edu/mythlore/vol40/iss2/14.

———. "Race in Tolkien Studies: A Bibliographic Essay." Vaccaro and Kisor, pp. 33–74.

———. "Thrusts in the Dark: Slashers' Queer Practices." *Extrapolation*, vol. 50, no. 3, 2009, pp. 463–483.

Reid, Robin, Chrisopher Vaccaro, and Stephen Yandell. "Queer Tolkien Anthology Interview with Robin Reid, Chris Vaccaro, and Steve Yandell." *Queer Lodgings: A Tolkien Podcast*, Ep. 16, Alicia, Grace, and Leah. 28 Sept. 2023, queerlodgings.com/episodes/queer-anthology-interview.

Rohy, Valerie. "Cinema, Sexuality, Mechanical Reproduction." Vaccaro and Kisor, pp. 111–122.

Saxey, Esther. "Homoeroticism." Eaglestone, pp. 124–137.

Saxton, Benjamin. "Tolkien and Bakhtin on Authorship, Literary Freedom, and Alterity." *Tolkien Studies*, vol 10, 2013, pp. 167–83.

Smol, Anna. "'Oh ... oh ... Frodo!': Readings of Male Intimacy in *The Lord of the Rings*." Hughes, pp. 949–79.

Stern, Alexandra Minna. *Proud Boys and the White Ethnostate: How the Alt-Right Is Warping the American Imagination*. Beacon P, 2019.

Stuart, Robert. *Tolkien, Race, and Racism in Middle-earth*. Palgrave, 2022.

Studies in Medievalism. International Society for the Study of Medievalisms (ISSM), medievalisms.org/studies-in-medievalism. Accessed 10 Oct. 2024.

Tadie, Joseph. "'That the World Not Be Usurped': Emanuel Levinas and J.R.R. Tolkien on Serving the Other as Release from Bondage." *Tolkien Among the Moderns*, edited by Ralph C. Wood, U of Notre Dame P, 2015, pp. 219–45.

Tangeman, Fred. "LIVE: The Angela Davis Legal Defense Fund 50 Years Later." Presbyterian History, Presbyterian Church, 21 Sept. 2021, pcusa.org/news/2021/9/21/phs-live-angela-davis-legal-defense-fund-50-years.

Timmons, Daniel. "Hobbit Sex and Sensuality in *The Lord of the Rings*." *Mythlore*, vol. 23, no. 3, article 7, 2001, pp. 70–29, dc.swosu.edu/mythlore/vol23/iss3/7.

Tolkien, J.R.R. *The Fellowship of the Ring*. Ballantine Books, 1965.

———. *The Hobbit*. Rev. ed. Ballantine Books, 1975.

———. *The Return of the King*. Ballantine Books, 1965.

———. *The Two Towers*. Ballantine Books, 1965.

Vaccaro, Christopher. "Saruman's Sodomitic Resonances." Vaccaro and Kisor, pp. 123–47.

Vaccaro, Christopher, and Yvette Kisor, editors. *Tolkien and Alterity*. Palgrave, 2017.

Williams, Donald T. "Keystone or Cornerstone? A Rejoinder to Verlyn Flieger on the Alleged 'Conflicting Sides' of Tolkien's Singular Self." *Mythlore*, vol. 40, no. 1, article 13, 2021, pp. 210–26, dc.swosu.edu/mythlore/vol40/iss1/13.

Yandell, Stephen. "Cruising Faery: Queer Desire in Giles, Niggle, and Smith." Vaccaro and Kisor, pp. 149–79.

PART I
Queer Moralities

The Problematic Perimeters of Elrond Half-elven and Ronald English-Catholic

Kristine Larsen

Introduction

In a 1956 draft letter, J.R.R. Tolkien mused, "As far as any character is 'like me' it is Faramir" (*The Letters of J.R.R. Tolkien* [*Letters 2*] #180, 336). This statement begs the question of what it means to be "like" Tolkien? Jane Chance opines that the philologist and author "resists classification," for example, in "his creation of a queer-non-normative-mythology based on a privilege of the marginal" (*Tolkien, Self and Other* 5). Elsewhere Chance further explains that one of the strengths of Tolkien's tales is his propensity to "make his heroes marginal beings, ordinary and even antiheroic. Frodo is a Baggins, but half Brandybuck, that is, a family that hales from Buckland, where, as Old Noakes says, 'folks are so queer'" ("Tolkien and the Other" 179). It is therefore striking that Tolkien proclaimed in a 1958 letter that he was not, in fact, most like Faramir, but rather a Hobbit, due to his enjoyment of "gardens, trees and unmechanized farmlands" as well as pipes and "plain food" (*Letters 2* #213, 411–12).

Like Hobbits, Tolkien eschewed travel in his later years, although his earliest decades of life were marked by a harrowing personal journey. From Bloemfontein, South Africa, to the Shire-like English countryside, the industrial landscape of Birmingham to foster homes and school halls, and finally to the battlefield of the Somme, Tolkien endured many personal battles, before finding a semblance of peace as a married academic and father. But even in this "victory" his was a queered position on the margins, both as a devout Roman Catholic in a majority Anglican nation, and a medieval philologist in academia. It is therefore no wonder that

"Tolkien sides with 'the little guy,' the ignominious exile," as Jane Chance notes ("Tolkien and the Other" 177).

Indeed, the exiled and expatriated play central roles in the great tales of Middle-earth, tales filled with personal and intergenerational trauma (King 170). Tolkien's tales of the Noldorin Elves are filled with sorrow (including being barred from returning to the Blessed Realm), as are those of the Sindarins who never arrived there in the first place. Palpable is the pain of the refugees from the destruction of the Elvish kingdoms of Gondolin and Doriath, and the survivors of the Great Battle between the forces of Morgoth and the Valar at the end of the First Age. Victory against Sauron at the end of the Second Age was achieved only through the blood of the brothers-in-arms of the Last Alliance of Men and Elves. But one character stands above the rest in this august group, representing through his complex bloodlines and personal sacrifices the price that must be paid for the attainment of peace and the greater good—Elrond Half-elven.

One of Tolkien's earlier characters (dating back to the "Sketch of the Mythology" c.1920s, published in *The Shaping of Middle-earth* [*Shaping*]), Elrond resists binary categorization to a greater degree than any other of Tolkien's characters. In *The Hobbit* he is described as being "as noble and as fair in face as an elf-lord, as strong as a warrior, as wise as a wizard, as venerable as a king of dwarves," evoking at least four sentient species (*H* 49). In *The Fellowship of the Ring* (*FR*), his face is described as "neither old nor young, though in it was written the memory of many things both glad and sorrowful.... He was the Lord of Rivendell and mighty among both Elves and Men" (*FR*, II, i, 239).

A closer scrutiny of Elrond's background reveals significant parallels with the author himself. Orphaned, fostered with a brother so close in age that they were nearly twins, Tolkien's life, like Elrond's, was greatly impacted by the choice of his mother to identify with a particular group. Known more widely for their fellowship with male compatriots than their marriages, and veterans of traumatic wars that killed their closest male companions, both Tolkien and Elrond afterwards settled into decidedly domestic roles focused on home and scholarly pursuits. While they were undoubtedly impacted by the trauma they suffered, they never let their trauma define them, and turned their experiences to the service of others, as teachers, mentors, and loremasters (King 171). Indeed, in their gendered relationships and familial ties, deliberate choices of self-identification (their exertion of free will), and singular roles as masters of lore, both Tolkien and Elrond honor the choices of their mothers. In addition, both fluidly crossed the sometimes-problematic perimeters between two seemingly exclusory domains (Human and Elf in the case of Elrond, the modern and the medieval for Tolkien). Even the name *Elrond* rolls off the tongue in much the same way as Tolkien's preferred name, *Ronald*, and is nearly an anagram. Tolkien's life experiences are reflected in the details of the most tragic life event endured by Elrond's sons, the loss of their mother Celebrían. I therefore argue that while Tolkien may have consciously self-identified with Faramir or the Hobbits, it is actually Elrond Half-elven who not only best reflects his creator but also encapsulates much of what was queer (in the sense of transcending culturally normative categories [Doty 11–12]) about Tolkien.

Gendered Relationships and Familial Ties

It is widely noted that Tolkien's works are dominated by male characters and male-male relationships, although he certainly created notable and powerful women characters (Croft and Donovan 2). This androcentric focus is not surprising, given the seminal roles played in Tolkien's life by male-dominated groups, especially the TCBS (Tea Club, Barrovian Society) while a student at King Edward's School and, much later, the Inklings. Esther Saxey notes of *The Lord of the Rings* that male-male relationships are particularly important, often reflecting a deep personal devotion. Furthermore, "Passionate allegiance is often named 'love'; Faramir is referred to in relation to Beregond as the captain whom he loved" (Saxey 132). Another interesting case of significant homosocial bonding occurs in the early *Silmarillion* texts in *The Lost Road*, where Tulkas, the warrior of the Valar, has "great love" for Manwë's son, Fionwë. Afterwards it is noted that Tulkas' wife is the Vala Nessa (*Lost Road* 206). The order of the two statements is interesting, if taken in a hierarchical sense, as it clearly highlights the centrality (to the story, if not the individuals involved) of the homosocial relationship.

Christopher Vaccaro argues that, due to changing definitions of terms such as homosexuality and love, over place and time, "homoamory" might be the preferred terminology for such intense male-male relationships. Vaccaro notes that "it implies something different ... 'homoamory' gives space for a reader to supply the dimensions of this love" (2). There is certainly historical precedence for this; as David Craig points out, the "boundaries between male friendship and homosexuality were somewhat fluid" at the time of Tolkien's service in the Great War (World War I) (15).

There are many such "Great Wars" in the history of Middle-earth, with one in particular paralleling (at least in a superficial way) Tolkien's experience in World War I: the Last Alliance "of Men and Elves, or 'Allies,'"[1] against the "Central Powers" of Sauron and his Orcs (and others). As Elrond recounts at his famed Council, he had experienced "many defeats, and many fruitless victories" as he had been the "herald of Gil-galad and marched with his host" (*FR*, II, ii, 256). As is often true of Elrond, this description downplays his centrality to the tale and pushes him towards the margins. At the end of *The Silmarillion* (*S*) proper we read that Gil-galad was the king of Elves who remained in Middle-earth at the end of the First Age "and with him was Elrond Half-elven, son of Eärendil the Mariner and brother of Elros first king of Númenor" (*S* 286). Elrond was not just "with" Gil-galad, but apparently a trusted councilor of mighty ancestry mentioned in the same breath as the High-king he served. For example, Sauron avoided Lindon because both Gil-galad and Elrond saw through his "fair-seeming" and jointly denied him admission to their realm (*S* 287). According to "The Tale of Years" (*The Return of the King* [*RK*], "Appendix B," 364), 1695 years passed between the end of the First Age and the invasion of Eriador by Sauron's forces, when Gil-galad sent Elrond with a force to meet Sauron in battle. It is insinuated that until this time, the two were inseparable (*Unfinished Tales* [*UT*] 237–8).

Two years later Elrond was forced to retreat, and founded a valley refuge, Imladris, which famously ultimately became the "Last Homely House" (*H* 44) after successfully being defended against the onslaught of Sauron's forces until reinforcements arrived from Númenor (*UT* 238–9). This was the first of many times that Elrond was able to offer safety and protection to others through a defensive rather than offensive stance. Therefore, Elrond's founding of a military base was also the first step towards the important and life-changing experiences of Aragorn, Bilbo, and Frodo (among others) in the House of Elrond in Rivendell. Afterwards, Elrond's wisdom in this regard was rewarded, the White Council declaring Imladris the main Elvish stronghold in the region; Gil-galad thereafter entrusted the Elvish ring of power Vilya to Elrond as his vice-regent (*UT* 239). Seventeen centuries of relative peace followed until Sauron attacked Gondor, and the Last Alliance between Men and Elves was formed.

Tolkien suffered the loss of two of his three closest friends, Robert Gilson and Geoffrey Bache Smith, as a result of the Battle of the Somme, and while Christopher Wiseman survived, the brotherhood of the TCBS was irrevocably broken. Likewise, Elendil and Gil-galad, brothers-in-arms as the leaders of the Last Alliance, died in the assault on Mordor while Isildur and Elrond (their respective seconds-in-command) survived. The loss of Gil-galad after a nearly 3500-year relationship unequivocally affected Elrond in deep and significant ways (no matter how one views their affiliation on the homoamory scale), as the loss of Gilson and Smith did to Tolkien. As Tolkien reflected, "One has indeed personally to come under the shadow of war to feel fully its oppression.... By 1918 all but one of my close friends were dead" (*FR*, "Foreword," 7). Similar words would have not sounded out of place coming from Elrond's mouth. Perhaps more poetically, in a letter to Smith after Gilson's death Tolkien famously wrote "something has gone crack.... I feel a mere individual at present—with intense feelings more than ideas but very powerless" (*Letters 2* #5, 6). After the Great War, Tolkien made a hard shift from the homosocial atmosphere of the battlefield, significant male-male relationship of officer and batman, and hypermasculine role as soldier, to the domestic sphere, becoming a husband, father, and academic. Similarly, after the death of Gil-galad, Elrond returned to Imladris and settled into a domestic role as the head of one of the few remaining Elvish enclaves in Middle-earth and a great loremaster. While Tolkien had married before being sent to the front, and became a father not long after, Elrond's transition from long-time bachelor Elf to the more traditional roles of husband and father are Entish in their lack of haste, especially in light of Tolkien's statement that the Eldar normally married in their youth, around age fifty, and "marriage, save for rare ill chances or strange fates, was the natural course of life for all the Eldar" (*Morgoth's Ring* [*Morgoth*] 210). It is therefore instructional to explore the evolution of Elrond's marriage in Tolkien's various revisions.

Esther Saxey notes of *The Lord of the Rings* that the "appendices heterosexualize many of the characters, giving wives and children to Merry and Pippin, and heirs to Aragorn" (128). The same is true of Elrond, as this is the source of most of our scarce information about his marriage to Celebrían, in the form of largely repetitive information in Appendix A and the timeline in Appendix B, "The Tale of Years." In the latter Tolkien explains that Elrond married Celebrían, daughter of Galadriel and Celeborn, in TA 109, and their twin sons Elladan and Elrohir were born in TA 130. Arwen's birth followed in TA 241 (*RK*, "Appendix B," 366). In TA 2509 Celebrían's travel party was attacked by Orcs and she received a "poisoned wound," resulting in her leaving for the West the following year (*RK*, "Appendix B," 368). In Appendix A we only glean the additional information that she had been rescued by her sons, not her husband, and although Elrond was able to heal the physical wound, her trauma was apparently too much to bear, which necessitated her travel into the West seeking peace (*RK*, "Appendix A," III, 323).

The torturous history of Elrond's road to fatherhood highlights the fact that the royal house of the Noldor is a relative failure in passing along their genes. Gil-galad, like most of the High Kings before him, died childless. Turgon, King of Gondolin, had produced a child, a daughter Idril, grandmother of Elrond; the lack of a male heir shifted the kingship to Turgon's cousins, and ultimately to Gil-galad. While the office of the High-king died with Gil-galad, it was vital to the future of Middle-earth that the lines of the first king of the Noldor, Finwë, and of Lúthien, did not end; otherwise, there would have been little hope for the world of Men when the last of the High Elves went oversea. Fortunately, both lines are united in Elros (the forefather of Aragorn) and Elrond. It was therefore vital that Elrond procreate, and necessarily (in the eyes of the strict Roman Catholic Tolkien) first marry. However, the sole direct reference to Celebrían in the main text of *The Lord of the Rings* is Galadriel's gifting to Aragorn of the Elfstone, which she had passed to "Celebrían my daughter, and she to hers" (*FR*, II, iv, 366).

In *The Peoples of Middle-earth*, Christopher Tolkien points out that during his father's revisions of the appendices of *The Lord of the Rings* there was a "general reduction, compression ... omission of allusive passages, notably the story of Celebrían" (*Peoples* 265). The timeline of Elrond's marriage is also shifted; in the initial versions of Appendix B, their marriage does not occur until TA 2500, with Celebrían killed in the Orc attack a mere 100 years later (*Peoples* 226; 249). She survives in the fourth draft, but she is traumatized by the experience and soon departs over sea, leaving her husband alone after a mere 209 years of marriage (*Peoples* 236). In all these versions Elrond does not wed Celebrían until over two millennia after the death of Gil-galad, cohabitating in Middle-earth for only a century or two.

The significant shift of Elrond's marriage to early in the Third Age is more aligned with statements in "Of the Laws and Customs Among the Eldar" in *Morgoth's Ring* concerning the natural status of Elves as wedding in their youth. The same essay also explains that because the conception and bearing of children requires so much strength and effort, they also reproduced while young (*Morgoth* 212). In these various drafts and the published version of Appendix B, Elrond was either over 3500 or 5500 years old (in solar years) when he became a father; the later date (from the drafts) would have further queered his assumption of the traditional masculine roles of husband and father. Tolkien revisited the timing of Elrond's marriage in his circa 1959 essay "Time-scales and Rates of Growth" and other related essays published in *The Nature of Middle-earth* [*Nature*]. Here, Tolkien revisits the rate of aging of the Elves, and using detailed calculations demonstrates that physically Elrond and Celebrían were still in their prime when married (*Nature* 65–6). Tolkien further blames the delay in their marriage on war in Middle-earth (*Nature* 65). Throughout several related essays, Tolkien continues to tweak his calculations, always drawing upon Elrond and Celebrían as his central test case to demonstrate internal consistency. The mathematical gymnastics needed to align the timing of Elrond's marriage with Elvish heteronormative standards is a testament to how queer Tolkien's original plans for Elrond and Celebrían—to have them wait until two millennia into the Third Age to marry—had been.

Interestingly, another possible interpretation of Gil-galad and Elrond's relationship is as between two asexual individuals, which would also lend credence to the delay in Elrond's marriage. Rory Queripel has convincingly proposed an alternative reading of Aldarion and Erendis's problematic marriage as between an asexual man and heteronormative woman "situating his choices within an oppressive set of social norms that are, in fact, anathema to him" (1). The asexuality of certain characters can be interpreted as highlighting their queer aspects. For example, in, "'For He Would Take No Wife': Surface Reading, Eärnur and the Queering of the Unmarried Male in *The Lord of the Rings*" (this volume), Nicholas Birns notes that Boromir's description as being similar to King Eärnur, who had never married, is "ostentatiously associating him with the queer," as Boromir, like Eärnur before him are eschewing their responsibilities to the throne to produce a (presumably male) heir (130). As Birns points out, "Dynastic marriage is one of the few cases where reproduction is more of a motive than sexual desire," further pointing out that "the way royal marriage unharnesses reproductivity from erotic pleasure also lends royal marriage an inherently queer aspect" (131). Seen in this light, Elrond's uncharacteristically significant delay in marrying Celebrían and producing heirs not only makes more sense (without chronological gymnastics) but further queers him.

Celebrían's limited role in the story is similar to that of the wife of the titular character of *Farmer Giles of Ham*, who, as Stephen Yandell argues, "helps maintain a public display of heteronormativity. Nevertheless, her presence does not make him any less queer a figure" (159). The same could be said of Elrond and Celebrían, whose union follows a trend noted by Valerie Rohy (927) of the marriages of Sam, Aragorn, and Faramir: "romances seem oddly incomplete ... because they are never started; the culmination of each relationship feels arbitrary because so little story has preceded it."[2] However, the decision to send Celebrían over sea, away from her husband and three children, is surprising when seen through the lens of Tolkien's 1904 sketch entitled "Home." Dating to the period when Mabel Tolkien's diabetes was becoming fatal, the artwork shows Tolkien and his aunt Jane's fiancé, Edwin Neave, "seated before the fire, darning socks and mending pants, with a caption reading 'What is Home Without a Mother (or a Wife)'" (Chance, *Tolkien, Self and Other* 20). In the case of Imladris, all indications are that it was a comfortable (and comforting) picturesque home indeed, with Elrond playing the multiply gendered roles of father/mother/ruler.

Like Tolkien, a number of important characters in the legendarium suffer the tragic loss of one or more parents and are fostered, signifying them as liminal (compared to the heteronormative family structure).

Most familiar to readers is Aragorn, who was brought to Imladris after his father's death and fostered by Elrond (*RK*, "Appendix A," I, v, 338). Unless the reader is familiar with *The Silmarillion*, they are unaware that Elrond himself was fostered, along with his twin brother, Elros, by the sons of Fëanor (in the earlier versions Maedhros, and later Maglor).[3] Previously, Dior, son of Beren and Lúthien, had been killed by the sons of Fëanor over his family's Silmaril, and Dior's young sons were abandoned to die in the woods (*S* 237). Dior's daughter, Elwing, escaped with their family heirloom Silmaril and fled with other refugees from Doriath to the mouths of the River Sirion. There she met and married the other half-elven, Eärendil, a refugee from the fall of Gondolin. In some versions of the legendarium her sons were born while her husband was on one of his many sea voyages and therefore never met their father, further "queering" Elrond's family status (*The Lost Road* [*Lost Road*] 143).

Both Elrond and Tolkien had few (if any) memories of their fathers, and also lost their mothers under tragic circumstances, being orphaned at a young age. The sons of Fëanor attacked during Eärendil's absence; Elwing jumped into the sea with the heirloom Silmaril and was reunited with Eärendil. The duo then sailed West seeking the aid of the Valar against Melkor, believing that their twin sons, Elrond and Elros, only a few years old, had been slain. Instead, Maglor lovingly fostered the twins, and they were thus raised by their family's sworn enemies (*S* 247). Tolkien was separated from his father when he was only three years old, moving with his mother and brother from South Africa to England, with his father dying a year later. After the death of his mother, Tolkien and his brother, Hilary, were fostered by a surrogate father figure, Father Francis Morgan.

Tolkien's decision to make Elrond and Elros twins is interesting, further queering Elrond by disturbing the normative and highlighting his liminal status because twins are rare among Tolkien's Elves (*Peoples* 353). There are ten instances of twins in Tolkien's works; three of these are among Elrond's family tree (Larsen, "Seeing Double" 140). Twins have historically been considered with both awe and suspicion; for example, in medieval Catholicism the birth of twins was considered "an evil omen, indicative of an adulterous union" (Ward 3; Rowland and Jennings 108). Therefore twins (and their mothers) were considered liminal beings, the result of a "queer" conception.

Ronald and Hilary Tolkien were technically not twins but were born only 25 months apart. The Tolkien boys had much in common with not only the sons of Elwing, but also with her brothers; for example, Elwing and her brothers were exiled, losing their parents and their home at tender ages. In "The Genealogies" in *The Lost Road* it is said that Elboron was born in FA 192 and Elbereth in 195, and the "Earliest Annals of Beleriand" gives their deaths in FA 206 (*Lost Road* 403; *Shaping* 307). They were therefore fourteen and eleven when they were orphaned, suspiciously similar to Ronald and Hilary, who were twelve and ten, respectively, when their mother died.

This parallel suggests a resolution to the question of why Tolkien ultimately decided to spare Celebrían's life and send her into the West. There was certainly precedence for widowing an elf lord and depriving an elf maid of her mother—for example, Elrond's paternal great-grandparents Turgon, King of Gondolin, and his wife Elenwë, who was tragically lost at the harrowing crossing of the icy wastes of Helcaraxë in the First Age (*S* 90). It has been argued elsewhere (Larsen, "Half-Elven and Half-Orphans") that Tolkien's personal identification with Elrond (either consciously or unconsciously), or an identification of himself and Hilary with Elrond's twin sons, Elladan and Elrohir, shifted Celebrían's fate. In leaving the fate of Elrond's sons ambiguous, Tolkien leaves open the possibility that they might eventually sail West and be reunited with their parents (*Letters 2* #153, 288). Such a resolution would have been a comfort to the young orphan inside Tolkien's psyche who had been traumatized by the loss of his own parents. In addition, by painting Elrond's familial relationships as non-normative, Tolkien effectively queers himself, highlighting his own liminality.

Throughout his youth Elrond lived among exiles, first the refugees of Gondolin and Doriath, and later with the sons of Fëanor (*Shaping* 308–9). Similarly, Tolkien's early family life was punctuated by impermanence and uncertainty as he moved from South Africa to rural England, then industrial Birmingham. After his mother's death he was shuttled between relatives until finally finding relative stability in his fosterage under Father Francis Morgan. Elrond's first real sense of permanence was in the Second Age, first with Gil-galad in Eregion, and later in Imladris. Here we see a seminal example of what Chance (*Tolkien, Self and Other* 20) terms the "importance of 'home' and its lack" a central theme in Tolkien's works, as well as his life.

Tolkien said of his non-traditional father figure, Father Morgan "was more than a father to me. I first learned charity and forgiveness from him," echoing the Icelandic tradition that "a fourth of a foster-child's strength comes from the foster-father" (Coren 434; Rose 398). Perhaps both Tolkien and Elrond are excellent examples of this.[4] In their self-identification as foster fathers, Elrond and Maglor each make a conscious decision to exercise their free will and redefine the bonds of family for a vulnerable orphan, setting into motion a great chain of events that reverberate down through the history of Middle-earth. Similarly, a significant act of self-identification and free will on the part of Tolkien's mother forever changed the lives of her sons and set them on an irrevocable path to Father Morgan's fosterage and beyond.

Self-Identification and Free Will

Patronymic designations highlight the importance of heredity and heraldry in the legendarium. Tolkien was also quite cognizant of the importance of heredity in some segments of the Primary World. In a draft letter to a German publisher, Tolkien noted that he unfortunately had no Jewish ancestors, but nevertheless regarded his "German name with pride" (*Letters 2* #30, 48). Tolkien's deep connection to the name inherited from his father's family is seen in the nickname by which his friend C.S. Lewis affectionately referred to him, Tollers (e.g., *Letters 2*, #294, 531). A similarly strong connection with family names is seen in a variety of Tolkien's characters, for example Tuor son of Huor. Elrond's most common appellation—Elrond Half-elven—appears to deviate from this trend, until one remembers that he shared this epithet with his father, Eärendil. This nomenclature simultaneously accentuates and greatly simplifies Elrond's mixed heritage as a descendent of all three great houses of the Edain as well as the kings of the Noldorin and Sindarin Elves (and the sister of the king of the Vanyar Elves [*Morgoth* 207]). Elrond also claims descent from the Maia Melian through his famed foremother, Lúthien.

In an often-cited 1954 letter to Peter Hastings, Tolkien recognized that there were "scientific" difficulties in the separate fates for humanity and elvenkind (*Letters 2* #153, 283). Indeed, he realized that Humans and Elves had to be in "biological terms one race" or they would not have been able to produce fertile children (*Letters 2* #153, 283). As Tolkien further reflected, in Elrond and Elros (and later Arwen and Aragorn) "the problem of the Half-elven" had been combined into a single lineage (*Letters 2* #153, 283). This designation of the Half-elven as a "problem" highlights their queer status in disturbing the accepted order of things. The existence of Half-elven also problematizes "elf" and "human" as distinct, well-defined categories: it queers their individual definitions.

In her detailed analysis of the thorny issues of race in Tolkien's works, Dimitra Fimi draws particular attention to Tolkien's use of "race" in Letter #181 which she argues is "a word that carries ideological and political baggage" (132). Fimi argues that this reflects Tolkien's awareness of racist views of "'human hybridisation' ... which distinguished between fertile offspring produced by 'eugenesic' or closely allied races and infertile offspring resulting from the intermarriage of 'non-eugenesic' or remotely allied races" (152–3).[5] One can also interpret Tolkien's usage more simplistically, reflecting the common misuse of the word *race* when meaning *species* (for example when referring to *Homo sapiens sapiens* as the human *race* instead of the human *species*). Scientifically Tolkien is here describing Humans and Elves as one species, because they can procreate and produce fertile offspring. There are numerous examples in his writings of "race" as a synonym for "species." For instance, Frodo describes the cry of seabirds "whose race had perished from the earth" (*FR*, II, vi, 366). Therefore, we should acknowledge the difference between scientific and popular uses of these terms.

Regardless of whether we are to think of Humans and Elves as different *species* or *races*, the term "Half-elven" initially smacks of hierarchy to the modern ear, as the term "half-breed" has generally been used in a pejorative sense in our Primary World, for example in referring to children born of a European and a member of an indigenous people (e.g., Parsons 144). For example, in a 1972 letter, Tolkien identifies Arwen as not an Elf but a "half-elven who abandoned her elvish rights" (*Letters 2* #345, 593). Putting aside the point that Arwen was genetically closer to three-quarters Elvish, I would argue that this highlights not only her liminal status, but more importantly the fact that as one of this special class of beings, she is given a *choice* to decide both her "kind" and her ultimate fate. I would therefore argue that the nomenclature Elrond *Half-elven* celebrates rather than disparages his mixed lineage, while simultaneously highlighting his queer position within Arda. This positivity is certainly very different from the lived experience of many mixed-race individuals in our Primary World.

Fimi notes that the Half-elven play a crucial role in Arda: they "provide an enrichment of the 'racial' structure of Tolkien's invented world: they 'ennoble' the Men of Middle-earth and prove 'race mixture' to be beneficial" (154). I would also argue that we can read this in reverse, that the introduction of human genetics tempers the problematic pride of the Noldor, and perhaps even the siren's call of the sea for the Sindar.[6] Of course, other interpretations are also possible. Chance notes that we also see such beneficial blending of the various Hobbit lineages in Bilbo and Frodo (*Tolkien, Self and Other* 244; 165). While she argues that the existence of such "a hybrid hero who mingles tribal differences ontologically" provides a "solution to the problem of alterity in class, place of origin, or race" (*Tolkien, Self and Other* 165), in the Half-elven Tolkien creates a new type of alterity—the alterity that derives from perhaps the ultimate exercise of individual free will in Arda—defining one's relationship with mortality.[7]

The exercise of free will by women in particular is not only central to Tolkien's fiction, but his life. Not only did Edith break off an engagement to marry Tolkien, but perhaps the most important choice by a woman in his life was his mother Mabel's conversion to Catholicism, which set into motion a domino effect that ultimately led to his meeting Edith. One cannot stress too deeply the life-changing nature of this choice. As Tolkien wrote to his son Michael in 1963, as a child he could only partially comprehend the "heroic sufferings" of his mother as a result of her conversion (*Letters 2* #250, 477). Daniel Timmons notes that throughout the legendarium we read of individuals great and small who are "presented with momentous choices.... In every case, these individuals shape their destinies, affect the lives of others, and influence, sometimes catastrophically, the history and even the geography of the world" (221). Important examples range from Melkor and his desire to change the music of creation, and continue through Míriel and her son Fëanor, Túrin, Lúthien, and her descendent Arwen. All of these non-normative—in other words, queer—choices involve the conscious exercise of free will, and change their lives in irreversible ways.

Seen in this context, the choices of Elrond and Ronald to be of the same kind as their mother meant that they would forever occupy a queer position within society, forever associated with a qualifier (Half-elven, English-Catholic[8]). There would also always be life-altering complications associated with such a choice. In addition, the similar making of an irrevocable choice as to the "kind" with which one is identified (and all the responsibilities, triumphs, and tragedies pursuant thereto) is a repeated refrain in the legendarium; as Chance points out, it begins with the Valar (*Tolkien, Self and Other* 72), who accepted the offer to go into the world and to have their lives tied to its history (*S* 20). Fimi notes that the first division of the Elves into the Eldar and the Avari is based on the latter's "irrevocable choice" to not embark on the journey from their birthplace in Cuiviénen to the Blessed Realm (143). The Eldar were afterwards further subdivided when some of the Teleri chose to remain in Middle-earth with their king Elwë and his queen, the Maia Melian, and became known as the Sindar. Melian also made the choice to love one of the First Born Children of Ilúvatar, and her daughter, Lúthien, one of the Second Born Children, an irrevocable choice that reverberates through the Second and Third Ages down to Arwen.[9]

Lore-Masters and Masterful Lore

We have demonstrated that multiple parallels exist between the experiences and life choices of Tolkien and his fictional creation Elrond Half-elven, many of which highlight their liminal, non-normative, queer status in their respective societies. These include their identity as orphans, twins, foster sons, and their life-altering decision to honor the choice of their mothers as to which kind they would be. But there is one last important choice that Elrond may or may not have had a chance to make, one that

Tolkien is remarkably silent about. In the early versions of the legendarium, before Tolkien conceived of Númenor, Elros, or Gil-galad, it is said that although most of the Elves left Middle-earth for the Blessed Realm at the defeat of Melkor, Elrond remained and "ruled in the West of the World" (*Lost Road* 144). *The Lord of the Rings* and later writings instead established Gil-galad as the last High King of the Elves in Middle-earth, and, importantly, the "last male descendent of Finwë except Elrond the Half-elven" (*Peoples* 347).[10]

In light of his heredity, one wonders why Elrond didn't become High-king after the death of Gil-galad. Clearly he was the obvious choice, having been vice-regent and entrusted with one of the Rings of Power. Was it because of Elrond's half-elvish blood, or simply the fact that he was a descendent of Finwë through his grandmother, Idril, daughter of Turgon, and not a male relative? Perhaps Tolkien intended to highlight the fading of the Elves and elevate the role of Aragorn as the King of Men. Did Elrond reject the crown out of respect for Gil-galad, whom he had once been very close to, or because he realized that the seat was seemingly cursed? Or, was Elrond, like Tolkien, simply more at home in the role of homebody, scholar, and lore-master than soldier or administrator? Any of these motivations would have highlighted some aspect of Elrond's liminal relationship with Middle-earth, whether it be his bloodline, his personal experiences, or his personal preferences. If I had to hazard a guess, I would personally connect it to a combination of the passing of Middle-earth from Elves to Men and Elrond's innate similarities to Tolkien himself.

Regardless of the ultimate reason, *The Silmarillion* reports that in Imladris Elrond preserved "the memory of all that had been fair; and the house of Elrond was a refuge for the weary and the oppressed, and a treasury of good counsel and wise lore"[11] (*S* 297–8). Note the stressing of *memory*, *wisdom*, and *counsel* as the true treasures, rather than jewels, gold, or land (the spoils of war), an emphasis on caretaking (a stereotypically feminine role), and a respect for the liminal, specifically those shoved to the edges of society. These are some of the very same values that were stressed in Tolkien's classroom, home office,[12] and the Inklings' famed literary meetings at *The Eagle and Child* pub, where Tolkien distinguished himself as scholar, teacher, mentor, and myth-maker (in other words, a lore-master par excellence). We also see a little of Tolkien as the "Elf-friend," the revealer or discoverer of the legendarium rather than its author, pushing his role towards the margins (Flieger 185).

Yandell points out that in *Leaf by Niggle* "Niggle and Parish's male-only household in the afterlife proves more generative than anything either had experienced while alive. In fact, the art they jointly create becomes an artistic legacy, clearly suggesting to readers an alternative form of progeny" (163). Similarly, Elrond not only sired the Evenstar of his people but also gave birth to and fiercely protected a domestic sphere tucked away in the valley of the Bruinen that provided a much-needed sanctuary to all the peoples of Middle-earth. Ronald was not only father to his four children and professor to his students, but also father, mother, and foster parent to an entire Secondary World, in the process teaching invaluable lessons to those of us otherwise trapped in our Primary one. Vaccaro and Kisor remind us that in Middle-earth "[w]ise and benevolent characters see through the veils of culturally-constructed binaries and are the better for their expansive, even cosmopolitan awareness of their world's diversity" (5). It was through their positions as liminal beings, as "queer" compared to the majority positions of their respective societies, that Elrond and John Ronald Reuel Tolkien ultimately transformed their personal pain and suffering into very public hope. Their shared legacy is the inspiration they continue to provide to multiple generations of lore-masters and lore-lovers far beyond their time on this *middel-erde*.

Notes

1. The Alliance also included the Dwarves of Khazad-dûm.
2. Tolkien did play with an aborted back story to the courtship of Elrond and Celebrían in the post-*LOTR* work "Concerning Galadriel and Celeborn" in which Galadriel and her daughter travel to Imladris circa 1800 SA, and it is here that "Elrond first saw Celebrían, and loved her, though he said nothing of it" (*UT* 240).
3. For a detailed analysis of the fostering relationships of Elrond in light of Northern European tradition, see Larsen, "Medieval Fostering in the First and Third Ages of Middle-earth: Elrond as Fóstri and Fóstr-son."
4. A fostering relationship could not exist between Gil-galad and Elrond, who differed in age by only a few decades, an insignificant gap in Elvish terms.
5. We should not refer to the offspring of Elf-Human relationships as "hybrids"; in biological terms, the most successful hybrids between closely related species, such as donkeys and horses, are sterile.
6. The concept of *hybrid vigor* (or more scientifically *heterosis*) in which cross-breeding diverse strains of plants or animals result in healthier, more robust individuals has been discussed in the scientific literature since at least the early 1900s (Shull 439).
7. Technically the Elves were not immortal since their existence was tied to the existence of Arda, the world, which itself was not eternal (*Letters 2*, #153, 283).
8. The term "Anglo-Catholic" has a very specific meaning in common use, and does not refer to an English Roman Catholic, but rather a movement within the Anglican Church.
9. One can also argue that in marrying Tolkien, Edith Bratt also made an irrevocable choice as to which kind she would be, as she first had to convert to Catholicism, and therefore shared in his "fate," as in the case of Eärendil and Elwing (although Elwing chose first).
10. As described in *The Peoples of Middle-earth* (349–51), Tolkien went through several iterations concerning Gil-galad's parentage. In all cases, he was clearly the final male descendent of Finwë through a strictly male line of inheritance.
11. For further analysis of the importance of Elrond as lore-master, see Larsen, "A Journey Down the Rabbit Hole of the OED in Search of the Meaning of 'Master' Elrond."
12. Tolkien was known to meet with his students, including women, in the domestic space of his home. See, for example, Carpenter (121–2).

Works Cited

Carpenter, Humphrey. *J.R.R. Tolkien: A Biography*. Houghton Mifflin, 2000.
Chance, Jane. "Tolkien and the Other: Race and Gender in Middle-earth." *Tolkien's Modern Middle Ages*, edited by Jane Chance and Alfred K. Siewers, Palgrave Macmillan, 2005, pp. 171–6. The New Middle Ages.
Chance, Jane. *Tolkien, Self and Other: "This Queer Creature."* Palgrave Macmillan, 2016.
Coren, Michael. "Morgan, Father Francis." *J.R.R. Tolkien Encyclopedia: Scholarship and Critical Assessment*, edited by Michael D.C. Drout, Routledge, 2007, pp. 434–5.
Craig, David M. "'Queer Lodgings': Gender and Sexuality in *The Lord of the Rings*." *Mallorn*, vol. 38, Jan. 2001, pp. 11–18, journals.tolkiensociety.org/mallorn/article/view/145/139. Rpt. "Queer Lodgings: Gender and Sexuality in *The Lord of the Rings*—Reprinted with a New Introduction by the Author." *Mallorn*, vol. 61, 2020, pp. 20–29.
Croft, Janet Brennan, and Leslie A. Donovan. "Introduction." *Perilous and Fair: Women in the Works and Life of J.R.R. Tolkien*, edited by Janet Brennan Croft and Leslie A. Donovan, Mythopoeic P, 2015, pp. 1–7.
Doty, Alexander. *Flaming Classics: Queering the Film Canon*. Routledge, 2000.
Fimi, Dimitra. *Tolkien, Race and Cultural History*. Palgrave Macmillan, 2010.
Flieger, Verlyn. "The Footsteps of Ælfwine." *Tolkien's* Legendarium: *Essays on* The History of Middle-earth, edited by Verlyn Flieger and Carl F. Hostetter, Greenwood Press, 2000, pp. 183–98.
King, V. Elizabeth. "'The Burnt Hand Teaches Most About Fire': Applying Trauma Exposure and Ecological Frameworks to Narratives of Displacement and Resettlement Across Elven Cultures in Tolkien's Middle-earth." *Tolkien and Diversity*, edited by Will Sherwood, Luna P Publishing, 2023, pp. 167–90.
Larsen, Kristine. "Half-Elven and Half-Orphans: The Choices and Consequences of 'Crossing Over.'" *Journal of Tolkien Research*, vol. 15, iss. 1, 2002, article 6, scholar.valpo.edu/journaloftolkienresearch/vol15/iss1/6.
⸻. "A Journey Down the Rabbit Hole of the OED in Search of the Meaning of 'Master' Elrond." *Journal of Tolkien Research* vol. 7, iss. 1, 2019, article 9, scholar.valpo.edu/journaloftolkienresearch/vol7/iss1/9.
⸻. "Medieval Fostering in the First and Third Ages of Middle-earth: Elrond as Fóstri and Fóstr-son." Part One, *Amon Hen*, iss. 264, March 2017, pp. 11–14; Part Two, *Amon Hen*, iss. 265, May 2017, pp. 11–13.
⸻. "Seeing Double: Tolkien and the Indo-European Divine Twins." *Mythlore*, vol. 40, no. 2, 2022, pp. 139–69, dc.swosu.edu/mythlore/vol40/iss2/10.
Parsons, Elsie Clews. "Half-breed." *The Scientific Monthly*, vol. 18, 1924, pp. 144–8.
Queripel, Rory. "The Mariner (and His Wife): Queering Aldarion's (A)sexuality." *Journal of Tolkien Research*, vol. 18, iss. 2, 2023, article 12, scholar.valpo.edu/journaloftolkienresearch/vol18/iss2/12.
Rohy, Valerie. "On Fairy Stories." *MFS: Modern Fiction Studies*, J.R.R. Tolkien Special Issue, guest editor Shaun F.D. Hughes, vol. 50, no. 4, 2004, pp. 927–948.
Rose, H.A. "Fosterage in Brittany and Iceland." *Folklore*, vol. 37 no. 4, 1926, pp. 398–9.
Rowland, Beryl, and Margaret Jennings. "Unheavenly Twins." *Neuphilologische Mitteilungen*, vol. 85, no. 1, 1984, pp. 108–14.
Saxey, Esther. "Homoeroticism." *Reading* The Lord of the Rings, edited by Robert Eaglestone, Continuum, 2006, pp. 124–37.
Shull, George H. "What Is 'Heterosis'?" *Genetics*, vol. 33, 1948, pp. 439–46.
Timmons, Daniel. "Free Will." *J.R.R. Tolkien Encyclopedia: Scholarship and Critical Assessment*, edited by Michael D.C. Drout, Routledge, 2007, pp. 221–2.
Tolkien, J.R.R. *The Fellowship of the Ring*. Houghton Mifflin, 1993.
⸻. *The Hobbit*. Houghton Mifflin, 2007.
⸻. *The Letters of J.R.R. Tolkien*, edited by Humphrey Carpenter, assisted by Christopher Tolkien, Revised and Expanded ed., HarperCollins, 2023.
⸻. *The Lost Road and Other Writings*, edited by Christopher Tolkien, Houghton Mifflin, 1987. The History of Middle-earth, vol. 5.

_____. *Morgoth's Ring: The Later Silmarillion, Part One*, edited by Christopher Tolkien, Houghton Mifflin, 1993. The History of Middle-earth, vol. 10.
_____. *The Nature of Middle-earth*, edited by Carl F. Hostetter, Houghton Mifflin, 2021.
_____. *The Peoples of Middle-earth*, edited by Christopher Tolkien, Houghton Mifflin, 1996. The History of Middle-earth, vol. 12.
_____. *The Return of the King.* Houghton Mifflin, 1993.
_____. *The Shaping of Middle-earth*, edited by Christopher Tolkien, Houghton Mifflin, 1986. The History of Middle-earth, vol. 4.
_____. *The Silmarillion,* edited by Christopher Tolkien, Houghton Mifflin, 2001. The History of Middle-earth, vol. 4.
_____. *Unfinished Tales: Of Númenor and Middle-earth,* edited by Christopher Tolkien, Houghton Mifflin, 1980.
Vaccaro, Christopher. "'Dyrne Langad': Secret Longing and Homo-amory in *Beowulf* and J.R.R. Tolkien's *The Lord of the Rings.*" *Journal of Tolkien Research*, vol. 6, iss. 1, 2018, article 6, scholar.valpo.edu/journaloftolkienresearch/vol6/iss1/6.
Vaccaro, Christopher, and Yvette Kisor, "Introduction." *Tolkien and Alterity*, edited by Christopher Vaccaro and Yvette Kisor, Palgrave Macmillan, 2017, pp. 1–13.
Ward, Donald. *The Divine Twins.* University of California Press, 1968.
Yandell, Stephen. "Cruising Faery: Queer Desire in Giles, Niggle, and Smith." *Tolkien and Alterity*, edited by Christopher Vaccaro and Yvette Kisor, Palgrave Macmillan, 2017, pp. 149–79.

I Dream of Gandalf: or, How I Was Raised by Wizards

Jes Battis

This essay will focus on Gandalf the Grey, Tolkien's famous wizard, as an unexpectedly queer character in Middle-earth. Through discussions of queerness, wizardly willfulness, and neurodiversity, I want to talk about Gandalf as a figure of power and hope for many readers. I'm also interested by the in-between spaces that Tolkien's wizards occupy, and, in particular, Gandalf's many transformations (between Maiar/Istar, human/divine, grey/white). Gandalf's queerness is part of this discussion, but so, in general, is the wizard's refusal of categories. I want to discuss, as well, the wizardly mind as something delightfully queer, in line with contemporary work on neurodiversity by M. Remi Yergeau and Julia Miele Rodas. Since reading about wizards affected me so profoundly as a queer and neurodivergent kid, I also have to bring myself into this discussion. We all should. Wizards belong to everyone.

Gandalf as a character seems cloaked in queerness, even if they seem to evade definition. Ian McKellen, the actor who plays Gandalf in Peter Jackson's film franchise, has joked slyly about Gandalf's sexuality across multiple interviews. In his 2021 essay on masculinity and desire in Tolkien's work, Derek Pacheco links Gandalf with "the form of gossip that circulates upon Bilbo's return" (277) and notes how Gandalf's many tales are a "queer fulfillment" of Bilbo's journey. Jane Chance's *Tolkien, Self and Other* describes Tolkien himself as a "queer creature" who also "queered the medieval by remaking it his own imaginary" (12). But in spite of the gauzy queerness that clings to many of Tolkien's characters, Gandalf is rarely remarked upon as a queer figure. This essay proposes reading Gandalf along a spectrum of queerness and transness, as a spirit, a changeling, a wizard with impeccable comedic timing, and a figure who defies categories. My Gandalf has always been queer and trans, and I want to weave in some personal details alongside a more traditional analysis. We're talking about wizards, after all, who are slippery by nature.

What I remember, growing up, was the green, leather-bound volume of *The Hobbit* with gold runes that framed the cover, like a mirror into another world. That edition had its own box, where the book fit snugly. We mostly had cheap paperbacks when I was growing up, aside from the almost mythical *Encyclopædia Britannica* set that my father had paid for in precarious installments. *The Hobbit* was the only other book that had that kind of weight to it—an emerald reliquary from another earth. I read it alongside other self-conscious fantasy texts: *Watership Down*, *The Last Unicorn*, *A Wind in the Door*. My father cried when Progonoskes, the many-eyed Seraphim, died in L'Engle's novel. I've taught all of those books now, years later, but *The Hobbit* (H) (and *The Lord of the Rings* [LotR]) was special because it had wizards.

Gandalf, Saruman, Radagast—they fascinated me with their otherworldly minds, and their magic that so often failed. Tolkien's epic story was never really about the wizards, but I always wanted to know what they were up to. What's Radagast doing in the forest? How does Saruman pass time in Orthanc? Staring wistfully into the Palantír, searching for something beyond recovery? What does Gandalf think about when the hobbits aren't on their mind?

I will be using they/them pronouns for Gandalf throughout this discussion. Tolkien's wizards are essentially angelic beings, which makes them non-binary, and all the more important for young readers. In his "Essay on the Istari," Tolkien notes that these beings are "clad in bodies as of Men, real and not feigned" (*Unfinished Tales of Númenor and Middle-earth* [UT] 389). This makes them subject to a variety of pains, temptations, and desires. At the same time, the Istari are "forbidden to reveal themselves in forms of majesty" (*UT* 389), which reminds us that they are, in fact, non-binary by nature. Perhaps, when reading Tolkien's phrase "bodies … [as] of Men," we might think instead of the Old English noun "mann," which is gender neutral. The Istar become people, not simply men, even if the few active wizards in Middle-earth do resemble cis men. Tolkien's wizards might serve as unique role models—particularly for non-binary and neurodivergent readers who connect with the wizard as a shifting figure. Why do these medievalist demi-gods still resonate for LGBTQ+ readers? What can old wizards teach us about how to survive our current world?

The wizards of Middle-earth borrow from a number of medieval traditions, including Arthurian literature, Norse epic poetry, and Middle English alliterative verse. Tolkien was a medievalist, after all, and in Gandalf we can see echoes of Odin, Loki, Merlin, and Morgan le Fay. As a medievalist text, *The Lord of the Rings* would go on to influence decades of contemporary fantasy literature, and its wizards remained for many years the gold standard for *Dungeons & Dragons* and other gaming tie-ins. They cast a long shadow. I think what first drew me to Gandalf was how they were always changing. Even their name changed: Olórin, Mithrandir, Gandalf, Grey, White. The idea of having a secret name—one you fear to reveal, or one you can't reveal—might connect with all kinds of transitions, processes of self-naming, and experiences of passing in a world that doesn't quite see you. Tolkien's wizards aren't particularly masculine (beards aren't necessarily male), and instead appear at a remove from social interaction, wearing robes that make them appear soft and indistinct. Throughout *The Hobbit* and *The Lord of the Rings*, Gandalf also has a slyness, a wit, that separates them from more binary characters. We will call it a neuroqueer way of thinking.

Gandalf's queerness is similar to what we might call neuroqueerness. Nick Walker defines this in a number of ways, including "being neurodivergent and approaching one's neurodivergence as a form of queerness" and "engaging in practices intended to 'undo' one's cultural conditioning toward conformity and compliance with dominant norms" (Walker, *Neurocosmopolitanism* n.p.). You can queer your brain; your brain can be queer; and your way of thinking can be an act of queerness, just as powerful as any erotic or relational act. In *Authoring Autism*, M. Remi Yergeau defines neuroqueerness as a type of nontraditional rhetoric often shared by people on the spectrum. In their passionate manifesto for the rights of autistic people, they state: "I want a rhetoric that tics, a rhetoric that stims, [...] [a] rhetoric that averts eye contact" (Yergeau 31). Their central argument is that autistic people are not seen as possessing rhetoric, which means that we aren't seen as possessing humanity. Neuroqueerness insists upon alternative mental rhetorics, brain runes, like the rune scratched on Bilbo's door by a sly and curious Gandalf.

I was drawn to wizards as a neuro-queer kid because they held out the possibility of neurological and narratological difference. Their minds were magic and made me believe that my queer mind could be magic too. Wizards also have a kind of asynchronous relationship with the world, since they understand both an epic context—beyond the personal—as well as an individual sense of being. Gandalf learns to love the hobbits individually, but also needs to see beyond them, to a fate they can scarcely understand. In her book *How Soon Is Now?*, medievalist Carolyn Dinshaw talks about a sort of queer and slippery time within the many realms of medievalism: they include "different time frames or temporal systems colliding in a single moment of *now*" (5). The kind of anachronism that's visible in amateur medievalist performances can "linger at moments of pleasure" (22), and I'd argue that all of Tolkien's wizards—but especially Gandalf—share this form of queer temporality: belonging while simultaneously not. Gandalf's celebrated outsiderness seemed like a mirror to my own experiences, as I tried to reason with social conventions that, quite often, were designed to make me feel like an alien. In *Autistic Disturbances*, Julia Miele Rodas describes neurodivergent language as "language hacking, the joyful breaking down and retooling of conventional language in ways that defamiliarize and implicitly critique seemingly seamless and intuitive communicative practice" (8). I would argue that the songs in *The Hobbit* and *The Lord of the Rings*, Gandalf's sarcastic asides, and even the weaving together of ancient languages represent a kind of neuroqueer rhetoric.

Wizards can't help but think differently. T.H. White's Merlyn has no platitudes for Wart—he's always unflinchingly honest. When they're about to be eaten by a giant and Wart hopes that it was all worth it, Merlyn observes, cuttingly: "I don't think it was [worth it] at all" (304). This line always makes me laugh—it's so gleefully grim. Later, when Wart asks him for advice on how to survive a world without magic, Merlyn delivers a fierce screed that has nothing to do with ethics or prophecy. He commands Wart to find things out:

> You may grow old and trembling in your anatomies, you may lie awake at night listening to the disorder of your veins, you may miss your only love and lose your moneys to a monster, you may see the world about you devastated by evil lunatics, or know your honour trampled in the sewer of baser minds. There is only one thing for it then—to learn. Learn why the world wags and what wags it [319].

Wizards want to know what wags the world. Merlyn's comment about "a world devastated by evil lunatics" is resonant in its timelessness. But the core of this advice is the need to decode all the things that animate the world and make it confusing at the same time. Physical infirmity, loss of love—these things can't be controlled. But we can keep reading. Like Gandalf, we can keep learning about pipeweed and Hobbit lore and the lost history of the Palantír and the proper use of fireworks and how to plan a burglary. When I say that I wanted to be a wizard as a kid, what I really wanted was the spell that would make sense of the world. *If I learn everything, maybe I'll figure out the world, and it won't be able to destroy me.* But Gandalf also chooses to be vulnerable and frail—a lone robed figure moving through Mirkwood—because, yes, the world is hard, but it's also where all the learning is.

Gandalf was one of my long-standing wizard crushes, but not the first. The first was a warlock from the *Fighting Fantasy* series of gaming books, written and illustrated by Steve Jackson and Ian Livingston. I was eight years old and would build a nest for myself on the floor of the Coles bookstore in the mall where my mom worked. I hadn't yet learned the real distinction between bookstores and libraries, so I treated them as interchangeable spaces. The staff didn't seem to mind. I can still recall those vivid green covers, nestled in black and gold plastic bags that I clutched in my sweaty hands. The fantasy section of the bookstore was one of the only places where I felt okay. Often androgynous and surrounded by haloes of power, the wizards in those gaming books felt relatably queer to me. There was a warlock named Zagore: he had a goatee and wore a single glove that looked suspiciously like something from Michael Jackson's closet (it was the 1980s). I'd play our meeting over and over, choosing every possibility, as if we were on a medieval date. I wanted to know what was in a warlock's mind. Once I had my own mountain and army of golems, what was there to long for? I wondered if Gandalf thought about this, in spare moments, while smoking his deliberately anachronistic pipe.

There was also Raistlin Majere, from the *Dragonlance* novels by Margaret Weis and Tracy Hickman. He'd sacrificed his physical health for power—a trade I would have gladly approved as a kid—and he had golden hourglass pupils that saw death everywhere. While Gandalf's humor was gentle with a subtle edge of steel at times, Raistlin was a Juvenalian satirist, constantly tossing barbs at his brother Caramon. I liked that he was angry and chronically ill. It showed me a different kind of wizardly masculinity. There's a moment in *Dragons of Autumn Twilight* when the gully dwarf Bupu—a figure of comic relief—cries because she's grown attached to Raistlin and doesn't want to leave him. Instead of making a caustic joke, we're told that "a look of infinite tenderness touched Raistlin's face, a look no one in this world would ever see. He reached out and stroked Bupu's coarse hair, knowing what it felt like to be weak" (265). Wizards like Gandalf and Raistlin provided subtle queer models that place them outside of traditional masculinity. Like Tolkien himself, they were shy at times, awkward, students of human behavior who always felt at a remove.

Wizards aren't generally known for their romantic inclinations, fighting skills, or conventional beauty. Their power tends to place them at a remove from the social world. That distance—often shaded by a kind of sadness—is something that I related to as a kid. Like a lot of teens on the spectrum, I had a difficult time socializing and understanding the "rules" that my allistic friends seemed to grasp with relative ease. I was also a queer kid, which meant that I had these two secrets crashing around, always threatening to expose me. There was a singularity to wizards that I found encouraging: they were always themselves. Often misunderstood, even a little feared, they were part of the story but also outside of the story, in some way. The ability to control one's narrative was attractive. So was the ability to hide in plain sight, which was something I'd been practicing from an early age.

I wrote my dissertation on the queer role of the wizard in medievalist fantasy novels. In particular, I focused on characters who were sad, anxious, or otherwise socially awkward. At parties, I said I was writing about gay, depressed wizards—a description that usually ended the conversation. Every dissertation has a chapter that doesn't fit anywhere, a thorn in the writer's side that never really goes away. For me, it was a chapter on wizardry and drag culture. I tried to publish it, but the response was not enthusiastic. One reader report scolded me for failing to respect Gandalf as a character (because I'd suggested he might be queer). The reader called the argument "silly" and reminded me that the character was "a member of an angelic order," and so beyond any sort of reproach. What it boiled down to was that I didn't respect wizards. Ten years later, I'm still failing to respect them, still messing with their reputation. That challenge always struck me as an example of straight male privilege. *Wizards belong to us.* In a way, much of my scholarship has been invested in disproving this. As a kid, I chose wizardry because it seemed like the only position that would accommodate my contradictions, fears, and desires.

The first time playing *Dungeons & Dragons*, I created an Elf wizard by design. He was physically weak (only a couple of hit points), but fast and smart. I would have been in my early teens, and I liked the idea of a character who was doubly other—not just a weird magic-user but also belonging to a non-human species. I didn't feel particularly human at the time, and I wanted my character to reflect that. I survived a single battle before succumbing to an Orc's axe. Nobody was surprised. Wizards are smart, but soft. They need knights to protect them, healers to patch them up, thieves to watch their back. Wizards require a whole team just to get through the world, in much the same way as kids with anxiety and depression have to assemble a support system to advocate for them in an ableist world. The 1980 D&D Player's Handbook notes a fundamental contradiction within the character-type of the wizard: "They are possibly the most fearsome of all character classes when high levels of ability are finally attained. Survival to that point can be a problem" (Gygax, 25). How do you keep a wizard alive? It was a question I often asked myself. Gandalf is also deceptively soft, but secretly strong—hiding their majesty.

Gandalf begins *The Hobbit* by scratching a rune—their name rune—on the pristine surface of Bilbo's round door. As openings go, it's direct. A wizard doesn't just knock. They carve themselves into the fiber of a person's life. Tolkien's wizards are angelic beings who don't go to a wizarding school like Hogwarts, or the devil's *scholomance* hidden behind the setting sun. We presume, from *The Silmarillion*, that they've always known how to be wizards—they have to be themselves. Yet Gandalf also takes on human desires (literal greyness) before being resurrected as Gandalf the

White. In both *The Hobbit* and *The Lord of the Rings*, Gandalf revels both in Human and Hobbit inventions: pipeweed (invented by hobbits, according to Merry), fireworks, cakes, hospitality, song. These embodied pleasures reveal Gandalf's love for sensation—a euphoria in touching, tasting, and existing as a being whose magic places them in a state of joyous transition.

Like Merlin, Gandalf also has an expansive view of the past and future. Peter Goodrich notes of the Arthurian Merlin figure: "It is as if he can step outside the conventional reality of the narrative world and re-enter it anywhere he desires" (12). Gandalf is the same. They have a kind of magical queer-view mirror, like T.H. White's Merlyn from *The Sword in the Stone*, who saw everything back-to-front and was only ever confused by the present. Gandalf always seems to be watching the action unfold, never hurried, never startled, except by the One Ring itself, and its capacity to stir unspoken desires. But Gandalf is also unique: Frank Riga notes that the wizard is "by no means a carbon copy of previous exemplars" (22). Drawing upon Arthurian tradition, while forging a distinct path, Gandalf presents a model of transformation for readers. I've maintained in a number of academic texts that this epic foresight confers a particular kind of sadness. A wizardly sense of non-belonging. To many, the wizard's loneliness feels like home.

Gandalf begins *The Lord of the Rings* as a doddering old mage, the very epitome of the absent-minded conjuror (similar to T.H. White's acerbic Merlyn in his *Once and Future King* epic), only to end the series as a legendary figure. Once they don the white robes, Gandalf describes themselves as dangerous. But as Gandalf the Gray, they appear as a kind of gentle scholar and wanderer. They are the only wizard who chooses to study hobbits: "An obscure branch of knowledge, but full of surprises" (*FR*, I, ii, 47). Hobbits are their queer theory, essentially. Gandalf is strong but fragile, clear but vague, studying world-shaking prophecies while reading about the daily ephemera of Hobbit-lore. They are a contradiction, a sigil, the very stylized sign that they carve on Bilbo's door. I think what I appreciated first about Gandalf was this sense of play. They love fireworks—a very human invention—and in the first chapters of *Fellowship*, those fireworks appear as benign magic. Gandalf entertains their favorite people with an act of fire and artifice: fiery green trees that open "like a whole spring unfolding in a moment" (*The Fellowship of the Ring* [*FR*] 1, i, 27).

T.H. White's Merlyn takes a similar delight in human ingenuity and weirdness. His magic is often performative: he sings, dances, and revels in his epic duel with Madame Mim (who also takes a literally delicious pleasure in her plans to eat poor Wart). All of these magic-users take incredible, almost dangerous pleasure in their magic. White describes Merlyn as "a singular spectacle," and as Wart takes in the wizard's odd appearance, he remarks upon "[his] flowing gown with fur tippets which had the signs of the zodiac embroidered all over it…[queer] crosses, leaves of trees, bones and birds and animals and a planetarium whose stars shone like bits of looking glass with the sun on them" (43). Gandalf, Merlyn, and Mim belong to a queer family of wizards who don't simply use magic for a higher purpose. They enjoy the power.

But Gandalf can also be prickly. That is part of what makes them relatable. There's a popular Twitter meme with Gandalf wearing sunglasses (which magically slide over their face), with the text: *deal with it*. This is my Gandalf: a bit camp, a bit tired, a bit over it. Wizards live their life in an epic register, and it is all the more annoying to deal with Hobbit micro-aggressions, tedious questions, and the little insecurities and selfish acts that accumulate to form Tolkien's metaphor of draconic greed. In *Fellowship*, when Frodo asks Gandalf how qualified they are to explain the workings of the One Ring, Gandalf tells him dismissively that "I am not going to give an account of all my doings to you" (*FR*, I, ii, 55). This is perhaps the first instance of Gandalf casting shade—though not the last. I will come back to one of my favorite moments in *Fellowship*, just before the Balrog, when Gandalf simply wants to smoke and be left alone.

Gandalf's queerness is hard to define. As an immortal demi-god, they have no real need for a traditional romantic relationship. We can read them along the LGBTQ+ spectrum, and their fraught relationship with Saruman could easily be the echo of a past romance (made more plausible by Gandalf's own interest in the mortal pleasures of Middle-earth). In his essay on medieval sexualities in *The Lord of the Rings*, Christopher Vaccaro notes that "Gandalf signifies hope and encouragement" (98) as they try to change Saruman's path. In spite of exiling Saruman, Gandalf "continues to hope" for their "friend's reform" (99). It's difficult to know how Istari love one another. For ace/aromantic readers, Gandalf's asexuality can also be empowering. Queer readers can also spin stories of a past romance between both wizards. Magic destabilizes romance in all kinds of interesting ways.

In a 2002 interview with *The Guardian*, Ian McKellen makes Gandalf's queerness canonical: "I was suggesting to Peter [Jackson] yesterday that he should insert some love interest for Gandalf in a later [movie]. He suggested Galadriel…[I] said, no, I was thinking more of someone like Legolas" (Ferguson). Many fans would probably argue that Legolas is already in a committed relationship with Gimli, which I also stan. But would an overt queer relationship make Gandalf a more empowering figure for LGBTQ+ readers? Only if we define queerness within the space of an erotic relationship, which is, frankly, limiting and incorrect. Readers don't need to be told that they aren't queer until they've had sex; instead, they need to be shown queerness as a delicate texture of possibilities and feelings that don't necessarily conform to one act or one desire. This subtle queerness is, in a sense, more medieval, as it recalls the passionate letters of Alcuin to Strabo, the knights who were buried together as a symbol of transformative friendship, and the complex queer intimacies that we see across medieval literature. Gandalf doesn't have to be dating Saruman to be queer. That said, in my mind, they will probably always be bitter exes who couldn't agree on the same narrative.

In *The Two Towers* (*TT*), when the company confronts Gandalf the White for the first time (after his transformation), Gandalf seems confused by their old name: "Yes, that was the name. I was Gandalf" (*TT*, III, v, 484). This act of re-naming might resonate for trans and non-binary readers—Gandalf becomes Mithrandir (was always Mithrandir), but neither forgets nor repudiates who they were read as before. When the hobbits ask Gandalf about their relationship with Saruman, the reply only adds to the wizard's sense of lovely multiplicity: "Saruman as he should have been" (*TT*, III, v, 484). The wizard contains multitudes: Gandalf & Mithrandir & Saruman. The reality of a non-binary wizard like Gandalf is something akin to casting a spell of protection over trans and non-binary readers. They are able to see in Gandalf what José Muñoz calls a horizon of queer possibility or future "[that] is still forming, or in many crucial ways formless" (29). This always-arriving queerness forms a survivable future, as well as a queer medievalist past where readers can see themselves in wizards' robes. Like Gandalf, queerness is never a binary, but rather a spell, without beginning or end.

Gandalf is also willful. The wizard leaves at unexpected moments, and fights in unpredictable ways (such as throwing their voice to distract trolls in *The Hobbit*). In her book *Willful Subjects*, Sara Ahmed talks about the figure of the willful child in children's literature as "one who insists on getting her own way, who comes to you with her own explanations of what it is that she is doing" (21). Though Ahmed's discussion is focused on girlhood, I'd like to extend it to a kind of non-binary willfulness: the feeling of continually trying to break out of singularity while people keep placing you in a gendered box. Gandalf's willfulness shows not just through moments of defiance—like the episode of the Balrog below—but in the flashes of irritation and wit-bombs that I've described above. Ahmed notes that willfulness also "might be what we do when we are judged as being *not*, as not meeting the criteria for being human, for instance" (15). This behavior links back to Remi Yergeau's previous discussion of what counts as rhetorical among neurotypical writers and speakers. Gandalf shows us that a wizard zags, a wizard talks back, a wizard has thorns. This willful wizard can serve as a model of neuro-atypicality for a variety of readers who also don't conform to binary ways of thinking.

As Gandalf faces the Balrog on the Bridge of Khazad-dûm, fire meets fire, shadow collides with shadow. This meme-worthy moment is immortalized on Twitter—Gandalf screaming defiance at the Flame of Udûn. But what we rarely see is their death-drop, the dance between them, as they fall, transform, and embrace in the dark: "We fought far under the living earth, where time is not counted. Ever he clutched me" (*TT*, III, v, 490–91). The Christian implications of the fall are just as powerful, here, as the queer implications of this gorgeous, fiery comet that they become. The Balrogs, after all, are fallen angels: beings like Gandalf (Maiar) who fell with Melkor: "The scourges of fire" (*The Silmarillion* [*S*], "Valaquenta," 23). The Balrog is also a multiplicity who contains different names, different flames. Tolkien's Catholicism infuses the *LotR* mythology, and as a medievalist, he depicts the fall as something with many meanings, perhaps the most significant of which is that of fallibility.

The primary lesson of *Sir Gawain and the Green Knight* (*SGGK*), also translated by Tolkien, after all, is: *humans fail*. Gawain makes all the wrong decisions in this romance, and when he does face the Green Knight, he's visibly scared. In his essay on *SGGK*, Tolkien concedes that Gawain's "'perfection' is made more human and more credible…[by] the small flaw" (*The Monsters and the Critics, and Other Essays* [*M&C*], 97). We fail and fumble in the dark. We get scared, we have bad takes, we choose wrong, we fall apart. We shrink our necks from the Green Knight's axe. But when the court of Camelot laughs at Gawain's "nick," the laughter is merciful. It's a recognition of shared frailty, of scars that we all have, and shouldn't hide. Gandalf also makes mistakes, fails to see things, and perhaps holds onto hope past the point of reason. That makes them "human and more credible."

Before the fall—before Gandalf and the Balrog make their own fireworks—there's a moment of camp and serenity that's probably my favorite moment in all of *LotR*. Gandalf is cranky and tired, but can't quite figure out why. Then, a breakthrough: "'I need smoke! I have not tasted it since the morning before the snowstorm.'" (*FR*, II, iv, 306). Like a nervous poet or performer about to go on stage, Gandalf needs a smoke. A colleague, Jeet Heer, pointed out to me that Gandalf's pipeweed is a deliberate anachronism—Tolkien playing with medievalism and its sense of being out-of-time. This reminds me of Carolyn Dinshaw's same queerly atemporal character of medievalism. Since "the medieval" is never monolithic, medievalism is always a bit queer, always slyly welcoming. Even Tolkien, the professional medievalist, encodes this delightful anachronism in his work.

One of the things I love most of all about this small moment in an epic text is the simple fact that Gandalf is addicted to smoking. Wizards may be out of time, but they can still participate in a series of fascinating failures. And this moment leads to the fire-lit image of a wizard bowed over, trying to nurse a flame: "A dark glimpse of the old wizard huddled on the floor, shielding a glowing chip in his gnarled hands between his knees" (*FR*, II, iv, 306). The smoke, the ember, the flame, the shadow—who can tell them apart? The burning cherry in Gandalf's pipe, like that ash from the cigarette that never quite drops, the night-light of a wizard's staff, becomes Pippin's dream of kinship and love. Gandalf is looking out for them. But Gandalf is also as vulnerable as T.H. White's Merlyn when he tells Wart that all his transformative magic has dried up. Wizards need protecting too, as we've already noted. They need to feel smoke in their lungs and weed on their fingers. They need to tend all kinds of fire.

Gandalf's heavy-lidded eyes see the destiny of the hobbits before they recognize it themselves. Merlin also thought differently, queerly. In Robert de Boron (Robert)'s *Grail* cycle, Merlin is the child of a demon and a mortal woman. As a toddler, he's already talking about destiny and defending his mother in court. His dual lineage gives him knowledge of both the past and the future: "The child inherited knowledge of the past from the Enemy, and, in addition, knowledge of things to come was bequeathed to him by God. It was up to him which way he inclined" (55). Like Gandalf, Merlin needs to make impossible choices about what to do with celestial power. Robert's Merlin calls himself "a figure of secrecy" (62), and goes on to say sorry (not sorry) for his lack of sociability: "You must understand," he says to Pendragon, "that I sometimes need to be away from people...[however] much you may desire my company, don't be upset when I leave you" (84). In these earlier Arthurian stories, Merlin is often configured as a socially anxious person, often struggling with what we'd now call PTSD involvement in intractable wars. This also resonates with neurodivergent readers, who might see their own minds—their own fragilities, differences, and strengths—mirrored by a complex character like Merlin.

Gandalf insists upon similar departures in *The Hobbit*, and though these are for the purpose of the greater mission, we can also see them as instances of multi-tasking and being on wizard's time. What fascinates me most about Robert's Merlin—who was loosely derived from the Merlin in Geoffrey of Monmouth's *Life of Merlin*—is his pervasive need to be alone. Monmouth probably derived his wizard from earlier Welsh poetry about a wild man living in the woods. Lancelot also goes mad in the *Vulgate* cycle, so madness and Arthuriana go hand in hand. But Robert's Merlin seems to express more of a delicacy when it comes to worldly interaction. We might just as easily read his retiring nature as the strategy of someone who is easily overwhelmed—someone who flees to the woods in order to escape the sensory overload of court. Wizards think differently, after all. T.H. White's Merlyn tells Wart that he "was born at the wrong end of time, and I have to live *backwards* from in front, while surrounded by a lot of people living forwards from behind" (53). This backsight makes him wary of all human interactions, and perhaps this is true of all wizards. Certainly, the metaphor of being on the "wrong planet," or at the "wrong end of time," is something keenly understood by neurodivergent readers who also get sensorily overwhelmed.

This brings me back to the image of Gandalf smoking, alone, apart from the Fellowship yet still within sight of them. Like Merlin, Gandalf needs these moments of queer solitude in order to be all the various things They have always been. Wizards are in a queer time slipstream, both in the world and simultaneously apart from it. Gandalf, Merlin, and Raistlin all offered me a series of fluid perspectives that were radically different from heroic masculinity of the warrior. When I think of Gandalf, I always think of that pipe smoke, queer by its very inclusion within a medievalist world that wasn't yet colonizing tobacco. Gandalf as smoke and fire, shedding gender like a gray garment. Allowed to die and be reborn as someone entirely different, yet still loved and accepted. In a contemporary world that demonizes transition and aims incalculable harm at trans kids and adults, wizards invite us to smoke and slough off our skins, to think differently, and hover just outside of the light, beautiful and ill-defined spirits of our own making.

Works Cited

Ahmed, Sara. *Willful Subjects*. Duke UP, 2014.
Chance, Jane. *Tolkien, Self and Other*. Palgrave Macmillan, 2016.
De Boron, Robert. *Merlin and the Grail*. Boydell and Brewer, 2008.
Dinshaw, Carolyn. *How Soon Is Now?* Duke UP, 2012.
Ferguson, Euan. "A World Under His Spell." Interview with Sir Ian McKellen. *The Guardian*, 17 Feb. 2002, film.guardian.co.Uk/lordoftherings/news/0,11016,652303,00.html.
Goodrich, Peter H. *Merlin (Arthurian Characters and Themes)*. Routledge, 2003.
Gygax, Gary. *Dungeons & Dragons Player's Handbook*. TSR, 1980.
Jackson, Steve, and Ian Livingston. *The Warlock of Firetop Mountain*. Puffin, 1985.
Muñoz, José Esteban. *Cruising Utopia*. NYU Press, 2009.
Pacheco, Derek. "'Funny Queer Fits': Masculinity and Desire in J.R.R, Tolkien's *The Hobbit*." *Children's Literature Association Quarterly*, vol. 46, no 3, 2021, pp. 263–82.
Riga, Frank P. "Gandalf and Merlin: J.R.R. Tolkien's Adoption and Transformation of a Literary Tradition," *Mythlore*, vol. 27, no. 1, article 5, 2008, pp. 21–44, dc.swosu.edu/mythlore/vol27/iss1/5.
Rodas, Julia Miele. *Autistic Disturbances*. U of Michigan Press, 2019.
Sir Gawain and the Green Knight, Pearl, and Sir Orfeo. Translated by J.R.R. Tolkien, Allen & Unwin, 1975.
Tolkien, J.R.R. *The Hobbit*. Houghton Mifflin, 2012.
_____. *The Lord of the Rings*. 2nd ed., 3 vols. Illustrated by Alan Lee, Houghton Mifflin, 2002.
_____. *The Monsters and the Critics and Other Essays*. HarperCollins, 2007.
_____. *Unfinished Tales: Of Númenor and Middle-earth*, edited by Christopher Tolkien, Houghton Mifflin, 1980.

Vaccaro, Christopher. "'Morning Stars of a Setting World': Alain de Lille's *De Planctu Naturae* and Tolkien's Legendarium as Neo-Platonic Mythopoeia." *Mythlore*, vol. 36, no. 1, Fall 2017, pp. 81–102, dc.swosu.edu/mythlore/vol36/iss1/6/.
Walker, Nick. "Neuroqueer: An Introduction." *Neurocosmopolitanism*, neuroqueer.com.
Weis, Margaret, and Tracy Hickman. *Dragons of Autumn Twilight*. TSR, 1984.
White, T.H. *The Sword in the Stone*. HarperCollins, 2008.
Wynne Jones, Diana. *Reflections: On the Magic of Writing*. Greenwillow, 2012.
Yergeau, M. Remi. *Authoring Autism*. Duke UP, 2018.

The End Is Queer
Cleanness *and Tolkien's Apocalyptic Landscape*

STEPHEN YANDELL

An apocalyptic weight hangs over J.R.R. Tolkien's legendarium, barreling over the landscape of Arda from its inception. This weight emerged not simply as Eru sang Eä into existence (*The Silmarillion* [*S*] 16), but as Tolkien began composing his earliest Middle-earth text in 1914, "The Voyage of Earendel, the Evening Star" (*The Book of Lost Tales II* [*LT* II] 267). The weight continues to descend as each moral fall unfolds. From Melkor's initial challenge of Eru and theft of the Silmarils to Fëanor's oath and the Kinslaying, the threat of world-ending cataclysm remains pervasive. For Tolkien, however, apocalypticism has little to do with an imminent end though he does predict for Middle-earth a final battle, the *Dagor Dagorath* (*S* 44). Rather, Tolkien's fiction revels in the lives of individuals coping with a world of ongoing apocalypticism, one marked by surveillance, suspicion, and sterility. Because Middle-earth begins its decline immediately, each successive generation is forced to make moral choices while confronting increasingly weakened accomplishments, fading joys, and diminishing people. Ultimately, individuals must learn to fight "the long defeat," as Galadriel laments (*The Fellowship of the Ring* [*FR*], II, vii, 376).

Tolkien's life-long interest in the apocalyptic grew from multiple sources, including religious beliefs, mythical texts, and personal experiences; but no text offered him a greater model than the late fourteenth-century poem *Cleanness*, also known as *Purity*. This text by the anonymous *Pearl*-poet highlights a series of apocalyptic Biblical tales, each of which provides Tolkien with key themes, plot points, and narrativizing techniques that he employs throughout his writings. However, the greatest challenge to Tolkien in his engagement with *Cleanness* lay in its disturbingly deep-rooted homophobia. Undergirding the poem is a core belief that no sin is more damnable than same-sex physical intimacy. This is part of a moralizing ideology that got attached to many apocalyptic tales in the first century and reached a zenith in the late Middle Ages.

In this essay I argue that Tolkien uses his legendarium not simply as a kind of theological sandbox in which to play with difficult moral concepts, including the homophobia promoted by the *Pearl*-poet, but as a way of repudiating that same homophobia which Tolkien knew to have come from unskilled translation, bad theology, and misdirected moral messaging. The legendarium offers him a forum in which to queer *Cleanness*, a text that arguably had already queered its Biblical source material. By embracing apocalypticism's inherent liminality, Tolkien challenges a breadth of simplistic binaries and naïve categories constructed by the *Pearl*-poet. In reimagining *Cleanness*'s three central narratives, Tolkien not only grounds the stories in an alternative moral code, he reveals, in the end, a queerness in God, in humanity, and in sign systems generally. All three prove queerer than any boxes that have been desperately crafted over the centuries to contain them.

"Revealing" queerness is tricky work, of course, as is identifying moments when an author is doing it. For that reason this essay invokes a somewhat flexible lexical sphere of queer. At its heart, queerness challenges straight, mainstream positions. Queer strategies of reading and writing then employ that subversion, allowing Tolkien to reimagine a series of well-known narratives (those of Noah, Lot, and Belshazzar) that for centuries have bolstered the mainstream's most homophobic messages. As Alexander Doty says, "Queerness has been set up to challenge and break apart conventional categories.... [It signifies] a range of non-straight expression in, or in response to mass culture" (vx–xvi). As David Halperin writes, "Queer is by definition whatever is at odds with the normal, the legitimate, the dominant" (62). Harry Benshoff offers an equally useful definition in his study *Monsters in the Closet*: "queer" is not simply the abnormal, but "is what opposes the binary definition and proscriptions of a patriarchal heterosexism" (4). All of these proscriptions are precisely what Tolkien finds in *Cleanness*.

In challenging centuries of homophobia tied to *Cleanness*'s apocalypses, Tolkien thus straddles a queer analytical line that both empowers and challenges textual meaning. This follows a practice Kay Turner and Pauline Greenhill find embedded inside queer theory—a call for "responsibly irresponsible analysis" (13). Tolkien both admires and admonishes the *Pearl*-poet as he reworks source material in ways that are simultaneously responsible and irresponsible. His in-depth knowledge of *Cleanness* and the Hebrew scriptures also situates him perfectly for performing a range of queer work, since "[q]ueer positions, queer readings, and queer pleasures are part of a reception space that stands simultaneously beside and within that created by heterosexual and straight positions" (Doty 15).

Apocalyptic Queerness

While apocalyptic themes appear to some extent in all of J.R.R. Tolkien's writings, they also lie at the heart of his legendarium. Gunnar Urang argues in *Shadows of Heaven* that the apocalyptic subject is foundational to *The Lord of the Rings*: "[w]hat chiefly concerns us ... is the End toward which we move. The theme is eschatology, the occurrences with which our known world comes to its end. The sense of an end broods over all of the story" (158). Apocalyptic images were part of Tolkien's earliest creative writing. His first framework for the *Silmarillion* tales, in fact, follows a model taken directly from Revelation: John of Patmos, the author of the Bible's apocalyptic book, is said to have traveled to a remote island, was offered divine visions, and was charged with writing down the revelatory narratives. Like John, Eriol the mariner finds himself on the island of Tol Eressëa, is offered a series of fantastic visions in the Cottage of Lost Play, and ultimately serves as scribe of these tales for his divine hosts (*The Book of Lost Tales I* [*LT* I] 14). And like John's stories, Eriol's include desolate landscapes, fiery destructions of cities, chained-up Satan figures, and shining cities on hills. These are all features that Richard Emmerson labels the "grammar of apocalypse imagery" (300).

The primary source for Tolkien's apocalypticism appears to be his Catholic upbringing and identity. As he notes in 1956, "I am a Christian, and indeed a Roman Catholic, so that I do not expect 'history' to be anything but a 'long defeat'—though it contains (and in a legend may contain more clearly and movingly) some samples or glimpses of final victory" (*Letters 2* #195, 368). Tolkien suggests to his son Christopher in 1945 that crucial to any understanding of the present, fallen world is an acknowledgment of Eden, posed in Christianity as the antithesis of apocalypse:

> certainly there was an Eden on this very unhappy earth. We all long for it, and we are constantly glimpsing it.... We shall never recover it, ... [but] I suppose that ... the whole human race (as each individual) is free not to rise again but to go to perdition and carry out the Fall to its bitter bottom [*Letter 2* #96, 158–9].

As Tolkien developed his legendarium, he imagined dozens of apocalyptic narratives that followed common Biblical patterns. The flood of Noah, the destruction of Sodom, and the fall of Babylon all find their place in Tolkien's foundational myths, including the sinking of Beleriand, the fall of Númenor, and the destruction of cities like Gondolin.

Tolkien was fascinated with all sorts of myths that described apocalypses, especially flood stories, and this obsession appears throughout his writings. Tolkien recalled, "I have what some might call an Atlantis complex.... I mean the terrible recurrent dream (beginning with memory) of the Great Wave, towering up, and coming in ineluctably over the trees and green fields" (*Letters 2* #163, 311). His dream of flooding also took multiple forms. He noted that that the rising water might appear "either coming out of the quiet sea, or coming in towering over the green inlands. It still occurs occasionally, though now exorcized by writing about it. It always ends by surrender, and I awake gasping out of deep water" (*Letters 2* #257, 486–7). We see this particular strain of apocalypticism in his descriptions of the sinking of Beleriand and Númenor.

Because apocalyptic themes run throughout Tolkien's legendarium, it is unsurprising that a breadth of scholarship in the field exists. Research on Tolkien and apocalypticism tends to fall into three main categories: scholarship that scrutinizes key apocalyptic features in the legendarium, works that suggest specific mythic and literary sources for apocalyptic themes, and those that offer psychoanalytical explanations for Tolkien's apocalypticism. The first of these categories is the broadest, pointing to multiple apocalyptic features that dominate the legendarium. In "Aspects of the Fall in *The Silmarillion*" Eric Schweicher points to a "whole panoply" of falls that create an apocalyptic atmosphere for Tolkien (167). These falls include some by Melkor (his challenges to Eru's music, destruction of the Two Trees, and theft of the Silmarils, for example) and some by the Elves (their refusal of the call to Valinor, swearing of the Oath of Fëanor, and participation in the Kinslaying). Nevertheless, Tolkien's moral message remains consistent according to Schweicher: pride leads inevitably to downfall, and the repetition of these falls "do[es] not lessen the gravity of their consequences" (170).

Several scholars acknowledge that characters may be redeemed in Tolkien's world, but neither they nor Middle-earth ever returns to a prelapsarian state. John Marino points to a series of end-times features in *The Lord of the Rings*. Tolkien is obsessed with threats of an approaching apocalypses, he argues, because they are tied to the past; and in *The Lord of the Rings*, "the past is quite present throughout the narrative" (Marino 181). Sauron, the Ring, the Nazgûl, and even Gandalf and Elrond are vital links to the past, and all contribute to an inevitable movement toward threatening ends (Marino 170). Many scholars in this category approach Tolkien's apocalypticism as a spiritual condition through which Tolkien highlights humanity's greatest challenge, standing up bravely in the face of a bleak world on the edge of defeat. Mark Doyle argues that dystopian themes increase the poignancy of the legendarium, allowing Tolkien to "speak more clearly to his readers' ... misgivings about their current culture" (3).

A second group of apocalyptic research focuses specifically on the literary and mythic sources that influenced Tolkien. Edward Risden points to T.S. Eliot's "The Waste Land," for example, as a key source for Tolkien's apocalyptic landscapes. Eliot's response to post-war devastation resonated deeply with Tolkien and offered him a model for championing what Tolkien saw as a crucial decision for humanity, the choice to "persistently resist despair" (58). The epic-like scenarios that Tolkien found so moving in stories of heroes like Beowulf also point to frightening, bleak endings; however, they "allow a means of choice by which we may most likely persist through difficult and even horrifying times, best show kindness and compassion, and leave something ... worthwhile" (Risden 58).

According to this second group of scholars, Tolkien's passion for the apocalyptic is bound to his broad familiarity with myth. Bradley Birzer's "'The Last Battle' as a Johannine Ragnarök" identifies the book of Revelation and the Norse Ragnarök as particularly rich sources for the legendarium. A. Keith Kelly and Michael Livingston argue that Atlantis, Babel, and the book of Revelation provide Tolkien with meaningful end-times sources for anchoring the legendarium; each includes a city whose pride led to the downfall of a civilization (87, 99). They also find several models that contribute to a figure like Frodo who is willing to sacrifice his life in the midst of a crumbling apocalyptic world. Kelly and Livingston point to medieval texts Tolkien knew well, including *Cursor Mundi*, *The Pricke of Conscience*, *The Parlement of the Thre Ages*, and the English Chester Mystery Plays (99–100). Tom Emanuel more recently makes a case for the book of Jeremiah as a prime source for Tolkien. This prophetic book from the Hebrew scriptures, he argues, helps explain a tragedy that has befallen Yahweh's chosen people. With its focus on failures by leadership and increased oppression of the poor, Jeremiah's narrative mimics the fall of Númenor and offers "a better fit for the *Akallabêth*" than any other proposed literary source (7).

A third group of scholars suggests that Tolkien's interest in the apocalypse is best understood through a psychoanalytic lens. Trauma in Tolkien's life specifically, they argue, offers the most effective insight into the apocalyptic. John Rosegrant finds that the apocalyptic genre offers a literary form through which Tolkien could deal with the pain of losing his father. Rosegrant poses the connection as tentative but ultimately argues that Tolkien's apocalyptic "dream of the ineluctable wave appears to have symbolized an intrapsychic conflict over hubris that he developed in response to the trauma of his father's death" (149–50). Similarly, in "The Art of Eternal Disaster: Tolkien's Apocalypse and the Road to Healing," Megan Fontenot explores the complex relationship between stories, personal trauma, and apocalypse. She points to Tolkien's claims in "On Fairy-stories" as central for our understanding of apocalyptic imagery. Tolkien found the joy that readers get from a good story to be possible only because it contains a memory of the Fall (92–3). Pointing to Tolkien's recurring dream of drowning, Fontenot finds that all of Tolkien's texts are revelatory, and the ecstasy gained from his stories "leads inevitably to apocalypse"; and this ecstasy is simultaneously "the method by which the memory of the apocalypse is purged" (105). Despite this broad scholarly interest in the apocalypse, in none of these three categories have scholars explored connections with *Cleanness*.

Tolkien and the Pearl-poet

Next to the *Beowulf*-poet, perhaps no other author had as great an impact on J.R.R. Tolkien as the *Pearl*-poet. As a medievalist, Tolkien knew well all four poems that most scholars, including Tolkien, ascribe to this author: *Pearl, Cleanness, Patience,* and *Sir Gawain and the Green Knight* (1980, note 3). The poems come to us in a single surviving manuscript, the British Library's MS Cotton Nero A.x. (art. 3). Scholars merely speculate on the degree of training this anonymous poet must have had in ecclesiastical, legal, and other matters, but ultimately they agree on a few facts: he was a contemporary of Chaucer writing around 1375, and he lived in England's northwest Midlands area.[1]

The *Pearl*-poet's works served as foundational material for Tolkien's lectures on medieval literature at the University of Leeds and at Oxford's Pembroke and Merton Colleges; we know he held multiple copies of the texts in his personal library; and Tolkien composed scholarly essays analyzing them. As Tom Shippey notes, "Tolkien had the [*Pearl*]-poet in mind for at least fifty years" (213). Two of the poems, *Sir Gawain and the Green Knight* and *Pearl*, Tolkien references most often in his letters, but he also knew the content of *Patience* particularly well, having offered a partial translation of Jonah for the Jerusalem Bible. Tolkien describes his appreciation of the *Pearl*-poet in "Form and Purpose," included in E.V. Gordon's 1953 edition of *Pearl*, and that appreciation can be seen in Tolkien's extensive commentaries surrounding his translations of *Pearl* and *Sir Gawain and the Green Knight*. Scholars point to various storytelling interests that Tolkien shared with the *Pearl*-poet, including a use of vivid, sensory descriptions and a love of food and feasting. Like the *Beowulf*-poet, the *Pearl*-poet also provided Tolkien with a model for the unsuccessful hero figure; Frodo, like the girdle-accepting Gawain, successfully perseveres to the end of his quest while remaining ultimately unable to complete it.

However, it is Tolkien's and the *Pearl*-poet's shared passion for the apocalyptic, I argue, that forges their strongest bond. While Tolkien draws on a range of biblical, classical, and medieval sources in developing his apocalyptic themes, no text offers him a more energetic presentation of the apocalyptic than *Cleanness*. This fourteenth-century, roughly eighteen-hundred-line, sermon is the second longest poem we ascribe to the *Pearl*-Poet, and it moves through a series of gripping narratives in order to champion the virtue of cleanness. The poem opens by retelling a parable from the book of Matthew of the wedding feast, followed by the stories of Satan's and Adam's downfalls. *Cleanness* then moves into the meat of its project, retelling three apocalyptic narratives from Hebrew scripture that highlight the civilization-ending ramifications of unclean behavior: Noah's flood (based on Genesis 6:1–9:1), the destruction of Sodom (from Genesis 18:1–19:28), and Belshazzar's feast (a retelling of Daniel 5:1–30). *Cleanness* is unique amongst medieval literature in linking these three tales of apocalyptic wrath.

Cleanness offers many of the same dramatic, effective storytelling techniques displayed so effectively in *Gawain*, *Pearl*, and *Patience*, including emotionally developed characters and carefully crafted tension. The poet's compelling style makes *Cleanness* arguably one of the most spectacular examples of late-medieval storytelling; no text matches the ferocity of its apocalypticism. Why *Cleanness* has been wholly overlooked in Tolkien scholarship is thus not easily answered. Despite the huge amount of research on Tolkien's apocalypticism and an equally large corpus of scholarship on Tolkien and the *Pearl*-poet, scholars are virtually silent on the topic of Tolkien and *Cleanness*. This poem gets overlooked for all sorts of reasons, certainly more often than the other three. Some have argued *Cleanness* has been avoided because it is the most didactic of the poet's works, clumsy in its storytelling. However, the primary reason for its being handled gingerly is its robust homophobia. Even as the poem's drownings, surveillance, barren landscapes, and coded messages provided Tolkien with invaluable storytelling components, its rabid homophobia has continued to be read as obsessive and off-putting for multiple generations of readers.

In *Cleanness*'s biblical narratives the *Pearl*-poet celebrates God's angry, watchful personality; and divine judgment is marked consistently and inevitably a result of homosexual behavior. Sexual immorality is coded in the poem primarily as "filth," a term used eighteen times: the God "Who's flung every filth very far from His heart / Cannot bear that a blemished body be near!" (Finch lines 31–32). The poet also makes clear that same-sex intimacy stands as humanity's most egregious affront to God: "But in truth not one text ever told me that God / Ever punished a part of His Precious works, / ... Nor was half so hastily heated with wrath, / Nor so suddenly set upon seeking revenge / As He punished impurity, practiced by fools" (Finch lines 197–202). And while the *Pearl*-poet follows twelve or thirteen centuries of tradition of reading the stories of Noah, Sodom, and Belshazzar as anti-queer, it is worth noting that the poem's anti-filth language fuels a misreading of Hebrew scriptures that continues to have ramifications today.[2]

Of course, homophobia tied to apocalyptic stories is not unique to *Cleanness*, nor is homophobia in the late Middle Ages; however, there is perhaps no medieval narrative poem that champions its homophobia as fervently as *Cleanness*. Its homophobia has been noted by many scholars. A.V.C. Schmidt identifies the most energizing theme of the poem as its "intensity of the poet's 'homophobia' as it would now be commonly regarded" (109). Charlotte Morse finds evidence of the bias in the poet's rearrangement of details from his Genesis source material; while the Genesis author points to the mating of the sons of God with the daughters of men as a primary sin of the antediluvian world, the bedrock of defiance that leads to humanity's sins against nature, the *Pearl*-poet names same-sex carnality as the first and most significant incarnation of the world's refusal of the divine command to "increase and multiply" (lines 153–4).

Here, then, lay a dilemma for Tolkien, who held such a deep admiration for the poet's work in *Sir Gawain and the Green Knight* (*SGGK*). *Cleanness* offered him versions of apocalyptic stories far more exciting than what was offered in the Bible, but Tolkien also recognized that theological nuance was a limitation of the poet: "He ... had an interest in theology, and some knowledge of it, though an amateur knowledge perhaps rather than a professional" (*SGGK* xv). While building his legendarium over the decades, Tolkien employed Middle-earth as a landscape on which to rehabilitate *Cleanness*'s three central narratives and restore theological readings that predated a specific strain of first-century homophobia.

Even today the apocalyptic genre remains associated with queerness for multiple reasons. Queer behavior is seen as invoking end-times judgment, and mainstream society can be made to feel uneasy by being moved into shifting, apocalyptic spaces. According to Mark Simpson, the unsettling feeling associated with an apocalyptic world is not simply the result of queerness, but synonymous with queerness: "The 'queer world' ... [is] a world put out of order, out of sorts, out of joint; a world of queasy dislocation and general indeterminacy" (22). For centuries, punishment for queer behavior has also been tied to society-ending cataclysm. Lee Edelman suggests in *No Future: Queer Theory and the Death Drive* that disease, isolation, and lack of reproductive options all contribute to society's move toward an end-times death spiral (9, 13, 17). Consequently, queerness is viewed as destabilizing not simply queer identities, but also queer futures; and humanity's understanding of queers, death, and the end of society remain inexorably connected.

The act of Tolkien's queering entails celebrating some aspects of *Cleanness* while probing other aspects more critically. This ambivalent embrace allows him to address the poem's core homophobia while not simply rejecting the poem outright, as most scholars both before and after Tolkien have done. Although Tolkien appears to challenge the poet's biased reading of his source material, no simple, binary split exists between a straight reading and queer reading of Biblical apocalyptic narratives. Such challenges to mainstream readings necessarily open a schism in which queerness enters, and this in turn offers readers a "site of resistance," as bell hooks reminds us (153). Tolkien's entire legendarium thus serves as an immensely valuable exegetical space. Here readers are able to understand more fully the queer complexities of the divine, of humanity, and of sign systems.

Queering Cleanness

Creating a legendarium allowed Tolkien to, among other things, reimagine key elements of the three main apocalyptic Biblical narratives that constitute *Cleanness*. The first of the poet's stories, the narrative of Noah's flood, is particularly problematic in its presentation of the divine. The *Pearl*-poet poses God as the primary character in his version of the tale, a fundamentally knowable character whose spoiled temperament displays a relatable range of human emotions. These are features the Genesis author merely hints at while simultaneously tempering his description with images of divine compassion. *Cleanness*'s God laments ever having made humans and becomes enraged when faced with their uncleanness. The *Pearl*-poet also devotes more than three times the words of the *Genesis* author to describe God's anger and the world-ending flood.

Tolkien casts the god of his legendarium, Eru, in a very different position. Tolkien refuses to allow his God to be pinned down in simplistic boxes created by humanity, and Eru's aloofness prevents him from being understood in human terms. In the *Ainulindalë*, for example, Eru displays no negative emotions even as chaos arises; he simply smiles (*S* 5). Eru is a supremely divine figure who remains in complete control of both his actions and his emotions. Tolkien is adamant in revealing only a minimal amount of emotion by Eru when faced with a challenge to power in the *Ainulindalë*. Eru calmly weaves even the most uproarious music from Melkor into "its own solemn pattern" (*S* 5). Similarly, Eru explains to Melkor that no theme can emerge that does not ultimately have its source in Eru himself. Any disruption ultimately becomes a tool in creating even greater, unimaginable beauty (*S* 6).

In contrast the *Pearl*-poet's God displays some of humanity's worst features, responding to events with childish, relatable, and ultimately simplistic emotions. In *Cleanness*, God's love for what the poet poses as natural means that God cannot help but be incensed by anything unnatural. Elizabeth Keiser notes in *Courtly Desire and Medieval Homophobia* that, faced with homosexual behavior, God in *Cleanness* is so "thoroughly distraught and so beyond himself that he forgets his noble qualities. Indeed, in venting his wrath that has invaded his very heart ... [he acts] instead like a man possessed by madness" (43).

Tolkien continues to queer a version of God offered in *Cleanness* by challenging any simplistic boundaries associated with the divine. Eru's aloofness ultimately prevents him from being contained in a human model. Even as Tolkien adopts language from the *Pearl*-poet's destructive scenes that adds incredible energy to his storytelling, he downplays agency from Eru for any acts of destruction. Additionally Tolkien recasts seemingly negative natural forces as productive; harsh cold and fire become beautiful mist, rain, and frost in Eä (*S* 9). In those scenarios where the world is damaged, Eru remains unassailably distant. Instead, Morgoth's fighting is repeatedly posed as the primary cause for damage to Beleriand. And because the Valar serve as regents for Eru in their rule over Arda, they call to Eru when Ar-Pharazôn's Númenórean fleet challenges the ban of the Valar, and Men are at risk of hurting themselves. Consequently, in Tolkien's flood narratives Eru is cast as savior of Valinor to a far greater extent than punisher of Númenor, whose destruction emerges as an unfortunate consequence. Noah's story of survival also becomes a key element of Tolkien's apocalyptic retellings, as we see when Elendil and his sons save those who have been faithful to Eru and create a "Naochian situation" (*Letters 2* #156, 303).

Tolkien thus offers a queered version of the divine, one that cannot fit into tidy categories of human emotions. The *Pearl*-poet fills the text of *Cleanness* with multiple aspects of surveillance, all of which are tied to the divine: for God there is "no secret so small He can't see it with ease.... He's the great, searching God.... And he sees into secrets, the seat of desire" (Finch lines 588–592). However, Tolkien poses Eru as a different kind of God, transferring onto the character of Sauron an array of negative qualities ascribed to God in *Cleanness*. In the legendarium the act of surveillance is cast inevitably as negative. It is Sauron who is cast as self-absorbed. It is Sauron who acts with vindictive anger and surveils with paranoia. Sauron serves for Tolkien as that divine figure who amplifies humanity's worst features. As Gandalf reminds the Fellowship, Sauron "had watched us, and had long prepared against our stroke.... Soon I became aware that spies of many sorts ... were gathered round the Shire" (*FR*, II, ii, 268).

The destructive work of God in *Cleanness* is shown by the *Pearl*-poet to result in a sterile landscape: "Thus the Dead Sea it's dubbed, darkened and grim; / The death that that was done there endures evermore.... What has life never lives very long in that sea.... Nothing green there can grow: neither grass nor plants. / If a body were brought to be buried, it would / Never sink in that stagnant, vast sea" (Finch lines 1020–30). In order to maintain distance between God and human understanding, Tolkien actively separates Eru from any negative aspects of creation. In the legendarium desolate landscapes are the result not of divine wrath, but of the concentrated efforts by figures like of Morgoth and Sauron. Mordor, we are told, "was a dying land.... And here things still grew, harsh, twisted, bitter, struggling for life" (*The Return of the King* [*RK*], VI, ii, 956). Similarly, the marshes outside of Mordor where the Battle of Dagorlad was fought are described with similar qualities: "It was dreary and wearisome. Cold clammy winter still held sway in this forsaken country. The only green was the scum of livid weed on the dark greasy surfaces of the sullen waters....'" (*The Two Towers* [*TT*], IV, ii, 651–2).

Tolkien borrows narrative techniques from *Cleanness* to take advantage of the *Pearl*-poet's skill at building empathy. For example, the poet creates dramatic tension by offering details of individuals struggling to survive as floodwaters rise. His sensationalized focus allows readers to wallow in their punishment, reminding readers of how angry God can become and why such punishments are warranted:

> Many fled from the flood, tried to find a safe place.
> Many women ran wildly and wailing, young babes....
> Though the highest of heights was heavy with rain,
> Still the folk there flocked in their fear and their dread....
> But confusion increased; the Creator's mercy
> With His pity had passed for the people he loathed.
> When the flood to his feet had finally swelled,
> Each sinner was certain he'd suffer his death.
> In that flood every friend joined a friend to embrace,
> To endure there his doom and to die arm in arm.
> Lovers took leave of their loves; they must part.
> All had ended forever; they would ever be sundered.
> Thus no flesh, when forty days finally had passed,
> Was left stirring; that strong flood had struck down all life [Finch lines 377–404].

However, in Genesis, source for the *Pearl*-poet, readers are given only a quick description of the tragic flood: "Every living thing that moved on land perished—birds, livestock, wild animals, all the creatures that swarm over the earth, and all mankind" (*New Oxford Annotated Bible* Genesis 7:21).

The Genesis author is also succinct in describing the fall of the city of Sodom: "Then the Lord rained down burning sulfur on Sodom and Gomorrah—from the Lord out of the heavens. Thus he overthrew those cities and the entire plain, destroying all those living in the cities—and also the vegetation in the land" (Genesis 19: 25–25). The *Pearl*-poet models for Tolkien a much more exciting account, using the horror of God's wrath to drive the narrative:

Then God, in His anger, began in the sky
To awaken the wildest of winds with His call;....
The folk were afraid as [searing rain] fell from the sky.....
[The city's] inhabitants, helpless, were harrowed with fear
When they saw no escape from destruction and death.
They clamored and called with such crying laments
That the clouds were cloven, and Christ would have wept!....
All the doomed were now damned; all were drowned by that time [Finch lines 947–989].

It is from these sensationalized accounts, ones the *Pearl*-poet himself changes from his Biblical sources, that Tolkien borrows and queers. We see Tolkien's use of the poet's sensationalized descriptions throughout his narration of the destruction of Númenor. Like the poet, Tolkien focuses on individuals, but he builds empathy for individuals rather than legitimizing any kind of divine wrath:

and the sky reeled, and the hills slid, and Númenor went down into the sea, with all its children and its wives and its maidens and its ladies proud; and all its gardens and its halls and its towers, its tombs and its riches, and its jewels and its webs and its things painted and carven and its lore; they vanished forever.... Too late [Tar-Míriel] strove to ascend the steep ways of the Meneltarma to the holy place; for the waters overtook her, and her cry was lost in the roaring of the wind [S 279].

Tolkien's act of queering the divine allows him to focus attention on the valuable human drama while disconnecting active agency from God.

Tolkien also poses a God beyond humanity's understanding by reminding readers that all descriptions of Eru in the legendarium have been related through non-divine sources. In "Myths Transformed" Tolkien explains that all stories of Eru and the Ainur were passed down by Elves of the First Age, none of whom were in direct contact with the Valar; this means that the stories were necessarily "blended and confused with…. Mannish myths and cosmic ideas" (*Morgoth's Ring* [*Morgoth*] 373). For Tolkien stories of the divine are inevitably and necessarily incomplete, and he reinforces for readers the idea that non-divine narrators can never fully capture the complex, and ultimately queer, nature of the divine.

The second apocalyptic story in *Cleanness*, the demise of Sodom, is another key narrative that Tolkien reimagines in multiple ways throughout the legendarium; and each version helps him offer a queer version of humanity. When Tolkien writes of communities coming under attack, including Nargothrond, Númenor, and Minas Tirth, he follows a Sodomitic blueprint: a city's growing wickedness leads to its downfall. However, the sin he poses as worthy of destruction is radically different from the one obsessed over by the *Pearl*-poet. In the legendarium communities are condemned for having abandoned hospitality and for refusing to show empathy toward others. Bree has grown increasingly paranoid of outsiders, for example (*FR*, I, ix, 167), and Gandalf laments the growing insularity of Minas Tirith (*FR*, II, ii, 269).

Although the *Pearl*-poet's homophobic perspective was commonly shared theology in the fourteenth century, Tolkien knew well that such a reading ignored Hebrew scripture's own, earliest commentaries on the story of Sodom. Ezekiel offers exegesis that surely would have been familiar to Tolkien: "Now this was the sin of your sister Sodom: She and her daughters were arrogant, overfed and unconcerned; they did not help the poor and needy" (*New Oxford Annotated Bible*, Ezek. 16.49). A parallel version of the Sodom story also exists in Joshua, narrating the destruction of Jericho (*New Oxford Annotated Bible*, Josh. 6). In this sister-tale, the city's people are revealed as inhospitable, and a prostitute is shown to be spared specifically because of her hospitality.

Although the apocalyptic world has long been tied to queerness, the connections between same-sex desire and world-ending destruction grew particularly noticeable after the first century. Over a short period of time, texts explaining Sodom's story shifted from a focus on the city's "greed, nastiness, and lack of hospitality" to same-sex intimacy (Hoffman 261). John Boswell traces this critical move from the first century onward, when a homophobic reading of Sodom began taking hold amongst theologians. A "Christian revulsion against Hellenistic hedonism" (206) created a culture in which the church became hostile against anything sexual, and this culminated, Boswell argues, in exactly the period during which the *Pearl*-poet writes (97). The late Middle Ages begins a period he calls The Rise of Intolerance (269), and European societies became "bent on restraining, contracting, protecting limiting, and excluding" (Boswell 270).

One of the most troubling aspects of theology in *Cleanness* is its depiction of humans, something Tolkien reimagines by queering humanity. Humanity is posed in *Cleanness* through a lens of unbending binaries: an individual is either worthy of God's somewhat mitigated wrath (as we are shown in the stories of Satan and Adam) or his radically unmitigated wrath, as we see in the stories of Noah, Lot, and Belshazzar. However, it is in the poet's opening lines, a retelling of the parable of the New Testament wedding feast, that the poet offers a particularly troubling rigidity. The lord's feast in the tale is presented as something to be shared by all, nobles and commoners, wealthy and poor. Calls to the feast, we are told explicitly, represent all of humanity being invited to approach the divine, and anyone arriving with good intentions is welcome.

However, the parable takes a dark turn (as we see in Matthew's original) when a figure shows up in filthy clothes. Here the metaphor of "all are welcome" crashes into an impenetrable category of "filthy," and the poet leans into the tale's retributive violence. The man arriving in filthy clothes holds an inherently filthy identity, and attendance at the feast (that is, salvation) remains simply unavailable. The man dressed in rags is taken outside, beaten, and thrown in the dungeon: "Baliff, now bind at his back both his hands, / Fix fast on his feet fetters of iron, / Stick him in the stocks, and stow him away / In my deepest of dungeons where dwells biting grief, / Where weeping and woe, endless wailing and pain / Live together—until he is taught how to dress!" (Finch lines 155–160).

While championing acceptance for many, the *Pearl*-poet ultimately poses filthy feast-goers in essentialist terms, much like the queer-behaving figures he describes throughout *Cleanness*. In contrast, Tolkien queers this presentation of humanity and subverts its troubling theological underpinnings. Sodom's sin is inhospitality, and Tolkien reminds readers frequently that this is perhaps humanity's greatest spiritual failing. All of Tolkien's narratives insist that people are more complex, queerer than anything the poet proposes. Humans are revealed by Tolkien as incapable of being contained in strict binaries, and the virtue of showing hospitality, empathy, mercy, and forgiveness is championed throughout the legendarium. We see this in the best treatment toward characters like Gollum, Wormtongue, Saruman, and even Morgoth. Inhospitality for Tolkien is also more complex than simply showing someone unkindness. Instead, inhospitality embodies a collection of sins that drive people inward rather than outward toward the societies in which they belong. These are the same human failings that Hrothgar preaches against in *Beowulf*: greed, pride, and envy (*Beowulf* lines 1758–1768; Chance 263).

Cleanness's final tale of apocalypse, that of Belshazzar's feast, comes from chapter five in the book of Daniel and centers on the fall of King Belshazzar. Having desecrated the temple vessels stolen from Jerusalem,

Belshazzar must contend with an inscrutable four-word message scrawled by a detached hand on the wall above him. Only the prophet Daniel is able to read the "writing on the wall," and this interpretive act proves a marker of his moral cleanness. In the poem Daniel probes at least three levels of complexity in the message before declaring to Belshazzar its meaning. First, Daniel shows he is literate by understanding that *mene, mene, tekel upharsin* are Aramaic words. Second, he shows that he understands their literal meaning: "numbered, numbered, weighed, divided." And thirdly, he offers to the king the prophetic implications of the words: Belshazzar's kingdom had been numbered in its days, it had been weighed and found lacking, and God was about to divide Babylon between the Medes and Persians, who the king soon learns will bring his downfall when they arrive the same night (Finch lines 1531–1740).

Unfortunately, the *Pearl*-poet's presentation of the tale reinforces several naïve premises: that language is stable, sign systems are fixed, and words are ultimately knowable by the proper reader. A wall-inscribed message may have multiple layers, and narrative tension depends on this complexity, but the inherent integrity of language is never in doubt for the *Pearl*-poet. In *Cleanness* language comes from God and is always, necessarily whole. A text simply requires a skilled, moral reader to render its message accurately. Any misunderstanding in the interpretive process grows out of a reader and has nothing to do with language.

The tale of the proverbial "writing on the wall" was of course familiar to Tolkien, but his life-long training in linguistics also meant that he understood the poet's presentation of sign systems, and of human language specifically, to be wildly inaccurate. As countless examples of wordplay in Tolkien reveal,[3] language is multi-valent, shifting, and queer. Therefore, readers should not be surprised to discover that Tolkien wanted to explore his own versions of the moment of Belshazzar's dilemma over a wall inscription. The most notable reimagining of this tale occurs in the early chapters of *The Lord of the Rings*, soon after the Fellowship leaves Rivendell. As Gandalf and the company attempt to enter the Mines of Moria, they are offered an equally inscrutable four-word message on a stone wall, the Dwarf Narvi's West Gate inscription: "Speak friend and enter" (*FR*, II, iv, 322). This writing confounds everyone in the Fellowship and is one that Tolkien spent a great deal of time thinking about, revising, and drawing. Next to his maps of Middle-earth and attempts at book-cover art for *The Lord of the Rings*, no single subject was drawn by Tolkien more frequently than his drawings of Durin's Doors, as far as we know from the extant artwork (Hammond and Scull 66–71).

Tolkien's version of the writing-on-the-wall episode revels in the queerness of language. Rather than questioning the skills of a reader (in this case, even the wisest of the Fellowship's party is stumped by the message), the episode reminds all readers, including the Fellowship, of the inherent slipperiness of language. Tolkien shapes his narrative to remind us that the skill of a reader is of minor importance compared to the inherent ambiguity of sign systems.

Linguistic mutability is revealed particularly well in Durin's Doors and plays out for Tolkien on at least nine separate levels. Although Daniel knows he has been given a message from God, Gandalf, when confronted with Narvi's words, is unsure what he even faces. This represents a first level of linguistic queerness: the text's genre. "Speak, friend, and enter" may be a riddle, a command, a warning, or a greeting (*FR*, II, iv, 322). Second, we are reminded that the specific language in which the wall verse is written proves challenging for most of the characters. Only some in the Fellowship know Sindarin or can even recognize the source language as Elvish. Third, it remains unclear how much language change has occurred since the creation of the wall; or, more broadly, how much change may take place in any Quenya sentence before it may be deemed Sindarin—or what transforms Quenya on its route to any new dialect. For the purposes of his own translation from the Book of Westmarch, Tolkien presents the writing to us as English, or perhaps as Westron. The writing system we are shown (by illustration) is Tengwar, but the text is also offered to readers through Roman letters. All five of these linguistic categories thus appeal to boundaries while simultaneously reminding us language is boundary-defying and queer.

The words on Durin's Doors also highlight four additional linguistic fields. The single-sentence inscription reveals a queerness of verbs: "speak" can function both intransitively and transitively. Does one simply speak (as a friend—taking no object) or speak a specific text, like the word "friend"? The verse reminds us of the queerness of nouns: does "friend" here take an accusative case? Or as a direct address does it take the vocative case? Modern-English word forms no longer mark a distinction in case (as retained in a few pronouns), but Tolkien the philologist understood well the history of the words. The punctuation of the sentence is also queerly ambiguous. The heart of our misunderstanding of the sentence, in fact, lies in a lack of orthographic markers communicating lexical function: should "friend" be offset with commas to clarify its use as direct address or be placed in quotation marks to mark it as a specific word to be spoken? Finally, as a form of contractual language, the verse cannot help but function queerly: must one intend to speak the word "friend" to get the door to work? Could an individual say the word in a different language and have the door open? Could one say the word sarcastically, or say the word casually while passing by, or use the word deceptively while not really being a friend? The exact felicitous conditions are never articulated, but a range of possibilities begins circulating in a reader's mind as soon as the inscription is introduced.

Tolkien provides us no clearer answer to these questions than do Durin's Doors. Instead, Tolkien's reimagining of *Cleanness*'s tale of Belshazzar reminds us that sign systems—like humanity, and like divinity—reside in messy, boundary-defying, queer space. Unlike the *Pearl*-poet's version, Tolkien's writing on the wall challenges tidy boundaries and clear answers. Like his understanding of God and humans, language for Tolkien isn't a binary; it is inherently ambiguous, even for the most skilled readers.

In borrowing from *Cleanness* and the apocalyptic genre, Tolkien cannot help but invoke many of its tropes. However, Tolkien's best challenge to *Cleanness*'s homophobia lies in his championing of an alternative moral code, one grounded in the original Biblical apocalyptic stories: the call to offer hospitality to the outsider. This emerges in the legendarium as a queer ethic, actively countering mainstream homophobia. It also counters a multi-century call to punish homosexual behavior by wiping entire communities off the earth. Eschewing greed, pride, and jealousy proves the most telling determination of character in the legendarium, above all else. The virtue originally championed in the Sodom story, hospitality, along with empathy and forgiveness, are also rooted in perhaps the most fundamental challenge to fixed boundaries, a questioning of the distinction between insider and outsider.

Tolkien's queering of *Cleanness* consists of rejecting the poem's rabid homophobia while posing God, humanity, and sign systems as things refusing to be bound in ways proposed by the *Pearl*-poet and by a well-established mainstream. Tolkien instead champions a queer ethic. It is this alternative moral code, the ability to challenge the fixedness of insider and outsider by offering hospitality, that determines one's moral cleanness. And by queering the poem, Tolkien also contributes to queering the medieval apocalyptic genre broadly. What emerges is a more complex understanding of the relationship between divinity, humanity, and the world of signs in which they live. We come to see that Arda is not apocalyptic because it is queer, as *Cleanness* might suggest. Rather, Tolkien's world rises to triumphal queerness because it is apocalyptic.

NOTES

1. The *Pearl*-poet's works are written in a West-Midlands dialect of Middle English; however, quotations will be offered in this essay as Modern-English translations from Casey Finch.

2. In February 2024, Oklahoma State Senator Tom Woods defended a series of anti-

LGBTQ bills at a public forum in Tahlequah: "We are a religious state and we are going to fight to keep that filth out of the state of Oklahoma because we are a Christian state— we are a moral state" (Bryan). Similarly, North Carolina's Lt. Gov. Mark Robinson in June 2021 called LGBTQ issues "filth" during a church presentation (Lau).

3. See Tolkien's use of wordplay through *The Hobbit* and "Farmer Giles of Ham," for example.

WORKS CITED

Andrew, Malcolm, and Ronald Waldron, eds. *The Poems of the Pearl Manuscript*. U of California P, 1982.
Benshoff, Harry M. *Monsters in the Closet: Homosexuality and the Horror Film*. Manchester UP, 1997.
Beowulf: A New Verse Translation. Translated by Seamus Heaney, W.W. Norton, 2001.
Birzer, Bradley J. "The 'Last Battle' as a Johannine Ragnarök: Tolkien and the Universal." *The Ring and the Cross: Christianity and the Writings of J.R.R. Tolkien*, edited by Paul E. Kerry, Fairleigh Dickinson UP, 2011, pp. 259–82.
Boswell, John. *Christianity, Social Tolerance, and Homosexuality: Gay People in Western Europe from the Beginning of the Christian Era to the Fourteenth Century*. U of Chicago P, 1981.
Bryan, Max. "State Senator Calls LGBTQ+ People 'filth' When Asked About Death of Nonbinary Student." *Public Radio Tulsa*, 23 Feb. 2024, publicradiotulsa.org/local-regional/2024-02-23/state-senator-calls-lgbtq-people-filth-when-asked-about-death-of-nonbinary-student.
Chance, Jane. "Grendel's Mother as Epic Anti-Type of the Virgin and Queen." *Interpretations of* Beowulf, edited by R.D. Fulk, Indiana UP, 1991, pp. 251–263.
The Complete Works of the Pearl Poet. Translated by Casey Finch, U of California P, 1993.
Doty, Alexander. *Making Things Perfectly Queer: Interpreting Mass Culture*. U of Minnesota P, 1993.
Doyle, Mark. *Utopian and Dystopian Themes in Tolkien's Legendarium*. Lexington Books, 2020.
Edelman, Lee. *No Future: Queer Theory and the Death Drive*. Duke UP, 2004.
Emanuel, Tom. "By the Waters of Anduin We Lay Down and Wept: Tolkien's *Akallabêth* and the Prophetic Imagination." *Mallorn*, vol. 64, Winter 2023, pp. 6–13.
Emmerson, Richard K. "The Apocalypse in Medieval Culture." *The Apocalypse in the Middle Ages*, edited by Richard K. Emmerson and Bernard McGinn, Cornell UP, 1992, pp. 293–332.
Fontenot, Megan N. "The Art of Eternal Disaster: Tolkien's Apocalypse and the Road to Healing." *Tolkien Studies*, vol.16, 2019, pp. 91–109.
Hammond, Wayne G., and Christina Scull. *The Art of* The Lord of the Rings *by J.R.R. Tolkien*. Houghton Mifflin Harcourt, 2015.
Harding, Nancy. "Queer Theory." *Key Concepts in Critical Management Studies*, edited by Mark Tadajewski et al, SAGE P, 2011, pp. 198–201.
Hoffman, Joel M. *The Bible Doesn't Say That: Biblical Mistranslations, Misconception, and Other Misunderstandings*. St. Martin's P, 2016.
hooks, bell. *Yearning: Race, Gender, and Cultural Politics*. South End P, 1990.
Keiser, Elizabeth B. *Courtly Desire and Medieval Homophobia: The Legitimation of Sexual Pleasure in* Cleanness *and Its Contexts*. Yale UP, 1997.
Kelly, A. Keith, and Michael Livingston. "'A Far Green Country': Tolkien, Paradise, and the End of All Things in Medieval Literature." *Mythlore*, vol. 27, no. 3, article 3, pp. 83–102, dc.swosu.edu/mythlore/vol27/iss3/13.
Kirsch, Jonathan. *A History of the End of the World: How the Most Controversial Book in the Bible Changed the Course of Western Civilization*. HarperOne, 2006.
Lau, Sam. "Human Rights Campaign Equality Votes PAC Slams North Carolina's Mark Robinson and His Agenda of Anti-Equality Hate." *Human Rights Campaign*, 3 Mar.

2024, hrc.org/press-releases/human-rights-campaign-equality-votes-pac-slams-north-carolinas-mark-robinson-and-his-agenda-of-anti-equality-hate.
Marino, John B. "The Presence of the Past in *The Lord of the Rings*." *Tolkien in the New Century: Essays in Honor of Tom Shippey*, edited by John Wm. Houghton et al., McFarland, 2014, pp. 169–81.
Moorman, Charles. *The Works of the* Gawain*-Poet*. UP of Mississippi, 1977.
Morse, Charlotte C. *The Pattern of Judgment in the* Queste *and* Cleanness. U of Missouri P, 1978.
The New Oxford Annotated Bible: New Revised Standard Version with the Apocrypha. Michael D. Coogan, editor, Oxford UP, 2018.
Pearl. Translated and edited by E.V. Gordon, J.R.R. Tolkien, and Ida Gordon. Clarendon P, 1953.
Risden, Edward L. "Middle-earth and the Waste Land: Greenwood, Apocalypse, and Post-War Resolution." *Tolkien in the New Century: Essays in Honor of Tom Shippey*, edited by John Wm. Houghton et al., McFarland, 2014, pp. 57–64.
Rosegrant, John. "From the Ineluctable Wave to the Realization of Imagined Wonder: Tolkien's Transformation of Psychic Pain Into Art." *Mythlore*, vol. 35, no. 2, article 9, 2017, pp. 133–51, dc.swosu.edu/mythlore/vol35/iss2/9.
Schmidt, A.V.C. "*Kynde Craft* and the *Play of Paramorez*: Natural and Unnatural Love in *Purity*." *Genres, Themes and Images in English Literature*, edited by Piero Boitani and Anna Torti, Gunter Narr Verlag, 1988, pp. 105–24.
Schweicher, Eric. "Aspects of the Fall in *The Silmarillion*." *Mallorn* 33, 1995, pp. 167–71. Rpt. *Mythlore*, vol. 21, no. 2, article 26, 1996, pp. 167–71, dc.swosu.edu/mythlore/vol21/iss2/26.
Shippey, Tom. "Tolkien and the *Gawain*-poet." *Mythlore*, 21.2, Winter 1996, 213–19.
Simpson, Mark. *It's a Queer World*. Vintage, 1996.
Sir Gawain and the Green Knight, Pearl, and Sir Orfeo. Translated by J.R.R. Tolkien, Ballantine, 1980.
Spearing, A.C. *The* Gawain*-Poet: A Critical Study*. Cambridge UP, 1970.
Stanbury, Sarah. *Seeing the* Gawain*-Poet: Description and the Act of Perception*. U of Pennsylvania P, 1991.
Tolkien, J.R.R. *The Book of Lost Tales Part One*, edited by Christopher Tolkien, Houghton Mifflin, 1984. The History of Middle-earth, vol. 1.
———. *The Book of Lost Tales Part Two*, edited by Christopher Tolkien, Houghton Mifflin, 1984. The History of Middle-earth, vol. 2.
———. *Farmer Giles of Ham: Anniversary Edition*, edited by Christina Scull and Wayne G. Hammond, Houghton Mifflin, 1999.
———. *The Hobbit*. Houghton Mifflin, 2007.
———. *The Letters of J.R.R. Tolkien*, edited by Humphrey Carpenter, assisted by Christopher Tolkien, Revised and Expanded ed., HarperCollins, 2023.
———. *The Lord of the Rings*. Unwin, 1988.
———. *Morgoth's Ring: The Later Silmarillion Part One*, Houghton Mifflin, 1993. The History of Middle-earth, vol. 10.
———. *The Silmarillion*, edited by Christopher Tolkien, Houghton Mifflin, 1977.
Tolkien, J.R.R., and E.V. Gordon, editors. *Sir Gawain and the Green Knight*. 2nd ed., Clarendon P, 1972.
Turner, Kay, and Pauline Greenhill. "Once Upon a Queer Time." *Transgressive Tales: Queering the Grimms*, edited by Kay Turner and Pauline Greenhill, Wayne State UP, 2012, pp. 1–24.
Urang, Gunnar. *Shadows of Heaven: Religion and Fantasy in the Writing of C.S. Lewis, Charles Williams, and J.R.R. Tolkien*. United Church P, 1971.
Wytenbroak, J.R. "Apocalyptic Vision in *The Lord of the Rings*." *Mythlore*, vol. 14, no. 4, article 2, 1988, pp. 7–12, dc.swosu.edu/mythlore/vol14/iss4/2.
Zimmerman, Bonnie. "Perverse Reading: The Lesbian Appropriation of Literature." *Sexual Practice, Textual Theory: Lesbian Cultural Criticism*, edited by Susan J. Wolfe and Julia Penelope, Blackwell, 1993, pp. 135–149.

Part II

Queer Intersections

Mother or Other

Tolkien's Shelob and the "Monstrous-Feminine"[1]

Sara Brown

J.R.R. Tolkien's menacing character of Shelob, the great arachnid who inhabits Torech Ungol, embodies the ultimate danger that faces Frodo on his journey to destroy the Ring of Power. Just as, metaphorically, the Ring threatens to consume Frodo and render him bodiless in the physical world, so Shelob threatens actual consumption of Frodo's physical body in her quest for self-nourishment. Her actions, in combination with the language that Tolkien uses to describe her, present Shelob as repulsive and horrific, designating her as Other in the tradition of female characters like Grendel's mother. More, Shelob is the monstrous-feminine who is queer in her representation of a maternal figure that is both masculine and sadistic. It is as a Masculine Mother, queering the gendered act of motherhood, that Shelob is at her most disruptive and subversive.

Previous scholarship has often addressed Shelob's character and examined her presence in the text from one (or more) of three perspectives. First are those readings of Shelob that label her an aberrant sexual being, noting her abjection and her monstrous "Otherness" (Armitt; Craig; Lionarons; Partridge; Smol; Ray; Miller and Miller). Of these, only Armitt and Miller and Miller make the connection with Barbara Creed's 1993 discussion of the "monstrous-feminine" that challenges the kyriarchal norms upon which this essay will draw. Other studies have explored Tolkien's creative process in the evolution of Shelob's character, tying this to Primary World mythology and literature (Abbott; Chance 2004; Donovan; Klinger; Lauro; Lionarons; Nagel). For example, Jane Chance suggests that Tolkien's inspiration for Shelob may have been the figure of Sin in Milton's *Paradise Lost* (2004, 215), while Mac Fenwick and Joe Abbot link Shelob with Grendel's mother, although neither points out that, unlike

Shelob, she does love her child. Perhaps the most popular focus has been on the oppositional relationship between Shelob and Galadriel (Burke; Burns; Craig; Donovan; Fenwick; Goselin; Grant; Petty; Sly). While some of these scholars use a specifically Jungian lens to examine this dichotomy (Goselin; Grant), Leslie Donovan draws upon Old Norse and Old English narratives to position the two characters as opposing malevolent and benevolent aspects of what Donovan refers to as the "Valkyrie Reflex." This inclination to regard Shelob as functioning mostly as an antithesis to Galadriel, rather than as an important character in her own right, reduces this powerful, fascinating, monstrous female character to merely an obstacle to the progress of Frodo and Sam on their quest, stripping her of her agency.

Up to this point, there has been little engagement with Shelob's "Otherness," specifically her "queerness" as a female character who is not only outside the norm, but also subverts the norm entirely, particularly in her role as mother. Non-normative presentations of gender in *The Lord of the Rings* have previously been addressed; for example, in "Mimetic Patterns of Masculinity or Just Another Fantasy Book," Beatriz Domínguez Ruíz employs Judith Butler's theoretical framework on gender fluidity to examine presentations of masculinity in Tolkien's work. However, Ruíz focuses mostly on the male characters, considering the ways in which their gender performance is less polarized than might be expected of a work from this time (138). Apart from a brief mention of Éowyn (139), Ruíz does not touch on the kind of "masculine femininity" performed by characters like Shelob: a gap in the scholarship that this essay aims to address. Working with an understanding of queerness as "any nonnormative expression of gender, including those connected with straightness" (Doty 6), a gender performance that "demarcates not a positivity but a positionality vis-à-vis the normative" (Halperin 62), this essay considers Shelob via third-wave feminist scholarship that proposes a recognition of multiple genders and sexualities, the fluidity of gender performance, and an opposition to binary gender characterization.

A major influence on this essay is Julia Kristeva's theory of abjection as a state of human existence in which identity is continually being created. The desire to construct an individual identity informs the relationship with what Kristeva identifies in *Powers of Horror* as the ("abject mother"); as the "child" of this maternal figure, Kristeva explains, we are attracted to her and repelled at the same time (12–13). It is this figure of the abject mother that provides the link between the concept of abjection and a queering of femininity that is strongly suggested in a reading of Shelob whose voracious appetites include the consumption of her own offspring. While Shelob is certainly a representation of the abject feminine in general, it is in her role as a monstrous mother that her abjection is most fully developed. As this essay will argue, though, Shelob's transgressions may be abject, but her gender non-conformity is also queer.

Shelob's monstrosity also leads to descriptions of her as "Other" in the sense of being "unnatural" (see Donovan 241, 242). The socially-constructed notions of "natural" and "unnatural" are biased concepts that come under interrogation in this essay. At different periods in history, "science" and "science experts" have theorized and conceptualized the relationship between humans and nature, embedding these ideas in our understanding of the world. The label of "unnatural" has morphed from an understanding of something simply not occurring in nature to being an epithet aimed at anything that stands outside of an accepted norm. Such norms have often been constructed with the notion of heavily persuading those on the "inside" not to venture to the "outside"; what awaits transgressors is rejection at best, revulsion at worst. This norm is what underlies much of the language around Shelob: she is monstrous, repulsive, and unnatural—terms that have, historically, been applied to women who do not conform as they threaten a perceived "natural order," in which men dominate women and, as an extension of this, control the world around them. The natural world may also be included here, as it is commonly referred to in feminized terms such as "Mother Nature," but regarded through a masculinized lens that demands total dominion and a reduction of nature to merely a resource to be used at will.[2] This being the case, it becomes apparent that a labelling of Shelob as not only monstrous-feminine but also a grotesque maternal figure may be a result of the effect of these culturally-embedded ideas.

My reading of Shelob therefore also draws on theorists such as Butler and Halberstam to offer a specific interpretive lens that encompasses social expectations of the maternal body and complicates the traditional good/evil binary. Shelob should not necessarily be identified as female simply because she is a mother; one does not, after all, need to be female to be a mother, as gender is not tied to the physical body. Such fluidity is possible if Shelob is read via Butler's concept of gender as being an unstable identity: the gendered act of motherhood can be observed, but a performance of dominance, aggression, and violence is equally evident. The comparisons between Shelob and Grendel's mother may therefore seem justified, but I suggest that there is more to be found by analyzing the differences between them than the similarities. To this end, this essay is moving beyond previous scholarship by considering Shelob as a representation of what Creed has termed the "monstrous-feminine," examining Shelob's presentation as not only identified as female, but also as more specifically maternal, queering this gendered space. In addition, Halberstam's concept of female masculinity enables a wider discussion of Shelob as monstrous-feminine: I propose that Shelob is performing a nonnormative expression of gender, in which her actions demonstrate a modern femininity that draws on traditionally masculine power structures.[3] I aim, therefore, to offer a consideration of Shelob that extends beyond her designation of "monstrous," and thus allow for a perception of this character as a powerful creature in her own right, who complicates both femininities and masculinities.

Shelob may be depicted in the text as being arachnid in form, but her femininity, and, more particularly, her role as mother, however grotesquely presented, is unavoidable. The concept of "mother" as a symbol of nurturing is widely accepted; usually seen as a performance of femininity, the ideal "mother" is the caring and supportive figure who enables the "child," with loving encouragement, to become whatever or whoever they are destined to be. Kristeva argues that the bond between mother and child is more complex as the mother nurtures the child so that she herself may be nurtured; Shelob thus presents a horrific imitation of this model. Tolkien's description of her consumption of blood, "bloated and grown fat with endless brooding on her feasts," creates several grotesque associations, including the murder of her own children, as implied by the word "brooding" (*The Two Towers* [*TT*], IV, ix, 707). Here, the reader is confronted with seemingly irrefutable evidence of Shelob's role as the monstrous, abject mother, as the "desirable and terrifying, nourishing and murderous, fascinating and abject inside of the maternal body" (Kristeva 54). By injecting Frodo with her poison, Shelob "feeds" Frodo with a bodily fluid that is drawn from within her. She wraps Frodo in material extracted from her own body, swaddling him in her web, setting him aside so that he may nurture *her* later. She is the "devouring mother" (Kristeva 54) who has mated with and then slain her own offspring, possibly then consuming them to complete the circle of nourishment. These associations define her firstly as parasitic, with Shelob like a louse that lives solely on the blood of its victims; secondly, she is demonic, sucking blood like the vampire and thus draining the life force of her victims. Thirdly, she is abject. With its connection to the idea of suckling, the sucking is, as Lucie Armitt points out, "an explicit articulation of her role as the bad mother" (100) with the implication that this suckling is far from the nourishing care that is commonly expected of a mother.

Within Tolkien's description of Shelob there lies a twisted perversion of the feminine. Grotesque yet recognizably female, "her huge swollen body, a vast bloated bag, swaying and sagging between her legs" both mesmerizes and repels us (*TT*, IV, ix, 709). The description of her body resonates with images of the pregnant female, thus emphasizing Shelob's status as the abject mother, a twisted perversion of the feminine. Her belly emits a foul stench that increases our sense of disgust and our fascinated horror, particularly as this stench appears to be so powerful that it is almost enough to overcome Sam by itself. The combination of this smell and the physical description of Shelob's lower body as being "black, blotched with livid marks" indicates, as Armitt asserts, that it is this part of Shelob's body in particular "that is associated most clearly with a kind of putrefying abjection" (*TT*, IV, ix, 709; Armitt 98). Tolkien's language paints Shelob as a diseased female whose very existence endangers the male (in this case both Frodo and Sam) with first infection, then consumption, in a threat to male sexuality that has been previously explored by scholars such as Barbara Partridge in her well-known essay "No Sex Please—We're Hobbits: The Construction of Female Sexuality in *The Lord of the Rings*."[4]

Shelob's physicality is under interrogation, though; on the page, her shape seems to shift between the arachnid form of first impression and something even more monstrous and disturbing. Tolkien does not create a fixed description of Shelob's physical shape; his use of the more distanced nuance of simile in the phrase "[m]ost like a spider she was" (*TT*, IV, ix, 709), reinforced by the equally ambivalent description "an evil thing in spider-form" (*TT*, IV, ix, 707) projects a blurred boundary between forms that is emphasized by Sam's vision of her as the "most loathly *shape* that he had ever beheld" (*TT*, IV, ix, my emphasis). Neither a humanoid nor merely a spider, she is the great, bloated, archaic mother who Creed, in her work on the monstrous-feminine figure in horror films, associates with "the voracious maw, the mysterious black hole ... which threatens to give birth to equally horrific offspring as well as threatening to incorporate everything in its path" (63). Tolkien's language invites revulsion as the reader's response; here, Shelob is unequivocally a monster, but her ambiguous form enhances this impression.

Shelob's sexuality also comes under scrutiny as the sexual slurs embedded in her description and her actions make evident. In a letter to his son Michael, Tolkien asserts that women's indulgence in sex alone is alien to their nature (*Letters 2* #43, 66–74). In his essay "Queer Lodgings: Gender and Sexuality in *The Lord of the Rings*," David Craig argues that Shelob therefore "represents these thoughts taken to their limit, a female sexuality run rampant" (Craig 13). Such an interpretation plays into a reading of characters like Shelob, or Ungoliant, or even Lobelia Sackville-Baggins, as representations of an inversion of the natural order—signifying the world being turned upside down.[5] If Shelob is a part of the natural world, then perhaps she is what Kristine Larsen, in her critique of the prevailing misogynistic characterization of nature, refers to as "nature as feminine chaos that must be tamed" (97). Tolkien's use of language in his description of Shelob implies that he envisages the reader feeling repulsed by her actions and thus rejecting her femininity. The feminist counter argument to this expectation on Tolkien's part, though, is that feminine agency is historically challenging, even repellant, for men. Shelob embodies a powerful, voracious female sexuality that is both terrifying and compelling; her appetites and desires must therefore be resisted by naming her "monstrous" and representing her as Other.

Judgment of Shelob's behavior and actions therefore depends on whether Tolkien's assertion that Shelob is a monster is accepted. Understanding her via Creed's framework of the monstrous-feminine that threatens order and stability (49), the reader is invited to view Shelob as occupying an abject space, rather than being subject or object, and then denounce her for doing so. Shelob never speaks for herself, so she may only be judged by her actions—but by whose standards is she judged? Her performance as a powerful "monstrous female" highlights the immediate danger to the hobbits, but it is her wider crimes, incest, illegitimacy, and infanticide, "all crimes pertaining to sex" (Craig 13), that appear to condemn her. A performance of female masculinity is not synonymous with the rejection of maternity, though; Galadriel and Melian are all examples of heteronormative female characters who embody the modern queer understanding of female masculinity yet also, through their normative sexualities, marriages, and production of children, pose no threat to the institution of motherhood.

Complicating the binary of good vs. evil, Shelob's methods of feeding—capturing live prey, paralyzing them, then storing them in her web—may seem repulsive to a human but are perfectly natural behaviors for a spider. Recalling that "natural" is a contested notion, reading this scene without those biases offers a different perspective. When Shelob hunts Frodo and Sam, it should be remembered that the hobbits are intruding on and violating her space: they are legitimate prey, and she is hungry. The horror comes from the emotional connection to the hobbits, built over the course of the narrative, and because they are only in Shelob's lair due to the machinations and treachery of Gollum. This episode taps into the evolutionary human instinct to fear a predator, as well as a very common human response to an arachnoid figure, although it should be remembered that such arachnophobia is only true in certain cultures.[6] Why is Shelob abject? She is outside society; she is "Other" because of *how* and on *what* she feeds. Tolkien's description of her demands that we turn away but, at the same time, we are drawn to her, per Kristeva, in horrified fascination. She does not nurture; her fixation is solely on nurturing and nourishing herself, at the expense of others. Her actions in mating with then killing her own offspring thus combines incest with violence; this fact alone invites the reader to condemn her. Filial cannibalism, though, is a natural phenomenon that occurs in a significant number of species from mammals to insects and is often done for sound biological and evolutionary reasons. In her article "Why Some Animals Eat Their Offspring," Andrea Thompson explains the behavior as seemingly unthinkable but having many benefits. Citing the 2011 study by Michael Bonsall and Hope Klug, which concludes that filial cannibalism is a behavior driven by multiple factors, including resource management (1345), Thompson concludes that maternal cannibalization actually increases the rate of development of the eggs, thus promoting survival of the young as well as husbanding resources. Her findings, echoed in many similar studies, offer an alternative understanding of Shelob's behavior that, whilst repugnant to humans, is a common phenomenon in the natural world.

Shelob may occupy an abject space, but any judgment of her as "monstrous" is also a reflection of how female beings who do not conform to human social expectations, or who do not behave in what is generally accepted to be "correct" maternal fashion, are judged in kyriarchal spaces; that is to say, those based on domination/submission and oppression. Reading Shelob via Kristeva, then, a compelling connection may be drawn between Shelob's abjection and her femininity. Lionarons argues that "spiders have long been a symbol for the kind of dark, insatiable female sexuality that devours the male" (10). The passage in which Frodo and Sam together with Gollum (each perhaps functioning as surrogate children) travel through Shelob's lair resonates with imagery of the monstrous mother. According to Anna Smol, "Frodo and Sam's journey into Shelob's lair through dark tunnels to face a female embodiment of primitive appetites which threatens to consume them could also be read in Kristevan terms as a regression into an archaic maternal space from which the subject has to separate in order to survive" (60n53). Combining these two arguments by Lionarons and Smol offers sufficient evidence to read Shelob's spidery maternal body as consistently reading within the recent cultural imaginary as threatening and abject. Indeed, Shelob's transgressive appetite and non-conformational performance of femininity are also entirely queer.

Both Shelob and Galadriel are compelling examples of a different kind of femininity that is antithetical to a traditional understanding of gender performance and gender roles. A fascinating fluidity exists in gender performance in Tolkien's works, as some of the male characters appear to subvert masculine traditional norms by doing what is usually ascribed as women's work. As some scholars have noted, most chores traditionally tended to by women are almost exclusively performed in *The Lord of the Rings* by male characters, such as the cooking (Sam), the running of baths (Merry and Fatty Bolger), and the tending of wounds (Aragorn and

Elrond), thus permitting a more flexible understanding of gender roles in the text and moving us away from a binary understanding of gender performance (Green; Craig; Crowe). However, it should be noted that it is the fluidity of *masculinity* that has been observed here, but apparently not the fluidity of *femininity*, which appears to remain bound by social mores and thus more liable to condemnation.

To understand this idea of gender fluidity further, the presentation of Shelob may be approached via Halberstam's theory of female masculinity. Halberstam's argument, that there are many types of masculinity and that what masculinity *is* need not be tied only to the male body, reveals that the female is equally capable of masculinity if it is understood as separate from biological gender, and that biological females also participate in the construction of masculinity. The problem arises when female masculinity is not recognized socially and is labelled somehow deviant. Noting here Butler's discussion in *Gender Trouble* on construction of gender (179), alongside Ruíz's framing of gender performance as a construct influenced by socio-cultural and historical context (135), I propose that Shelob challenges and subverts gender norms traditionally ascribed as female. Shelob's body performs the functions of a female, but her actions indicate more masculinity than femininity, thus queering her gender identity.

Shelob's performance of gender as a masculine female embodying masculine qualities is used as a reason to label her a monster, a descriptor Tolkien uses three times in the space of two pages (*TT*, IV, ix, 710; *TT*, IV, x, 711); this language emphasizes how a masculine female may automatically be designated both monstrous and abject. "Monstrous" is an appellation that addresses the ways in which a female character subverts or challenges gender norms and, by extension, certain social expectations. Shelob is both sexually deviant and sexually predatory, and she simply does not conform to cultural and historical notions of femininity, certainly not those with which Tolkien would have been most familiar. Language like "monstrous" is part of the mechanism for controlling female bodies, through condemnation of any behavior deemed non-normative. To be the monstrous-feminine, therefore, is to be judged vis-à-vis a heteronormative context in which binary notions of gender hold sway. Instead, Shelob may present as one gender, but she performs (*pace* Butler) as another, which lends her enviable strength and power. She is then condemned for this transgression.

As noted earlier, Shelob has sometimes been compared to another fictional female often depicted as a grotesque, a figure of revulsion: Grendel's mother. Similarities between the characters are apparent: both epitomize Creed's description of the figure of the monstrous-feminine, lusting after flesh and blood as murderous, twisted versions of the "maternal." While there are many other monstrous-feminine characters throughout world literature and mythology, perhaps none is more relevant to Tolkien scholarship, given Tolkien's close connection with the *Beowulf* text in his academic life. For those scholars who do examine the parallels between the two, the consensus is that the connection lies in their monstrosity. For example, Donovan names Shelob "the obverse valkyrie aspect, which is typified by baleful, vengeful, destructive female figures such as Grendel's mother," connecting her to the figure of the malevolent valkyrie and stating that "the excessive strength of such valkyries is portrayed generally as monstrous in its inversion of medieval ideals of femininity," the sole such representation in *The Lord of the Rings* (229; 241). Donovan argues that this singularity highlights Shelob's monstrous nature (as opposed to characters such as Galadriel, Éowyn, and Arwen), especially in her "unnaturalness" but Donovan's overall argument is on how Shelob serves as a narrative counterweight to Galadriel (239–41). Fenwick recognizes more of the links between Shelob and Grendel's mother, finding structural similarities in how and where these two characters occur in their respective narratives but, again, the focus is on how both characters are monsters; focusing on the similarities between Shelob and Grendel's mother does not take account of the possibility that there are significant differences that this essay addresses.

Like Shelob, Grendel's mother is depicted as a monster; she is also queer in that she, like her son, occupies a marginal position, is socially ostracized, and acts upon desires that are transgressive. Just as for Shelob, specific language is used to emphasize her aberrant behavior; like Shelob, Grendel's mother illustrates the ways in which transgressive female characters are "punished" via the medium of language. An additional layer of queerness is added by conflicts in the translation of the term used to describe her—"aglæcwif"—another example of how such characters transgress easy classification. The word "aglæcwif," found in line 1259a, is at the heart of debate about the nature of Grendel's mother, and much depends on the translator and the translation that is used. For example, in Seamus Heaney's popular version, "aglæcwif" is translated as "monstrous hell-bride" (89). This understanding of the term reflects the 1922 publication of *Beowulf and the Fight at Finnsburg* by Frederick Klaeber; in his glossary, he translates "aglæcwif" as "wretch, or monster of a woman," with aglæca/æglæca defined as "monster, demon fiend" when referring to Grendel, Grendel's mother, or the dragon but as "warrior, hero" when referring to the character of Beowulf (Klaeber 347). This disparity is echoed in other translations, including "monster-woman" (Chickering), "monstrous ogress" (Alexander), "monster of a woman" (Gummere) and "monstrous hag" (Kennedy).

Translating "aglæcwif" in this way seems to play into notions of socially acceptable norms of femininity—to transgress these boundaries is to have language turned against you—but it is also now much disputed. Scholars such as Sherman Kuhn, Eric Stanley, Christine Alfano, Melinda Menzer, and Maria Dahvana Headley all emphasize the "warrior" definition of the word "aglæca" and offer less pejorative translations such as "female warrior" (Kuhn 218) or "a woman, a human female, who is also aglæca" (Menzer 2). Tolkien, who is closely associated with the poem, has his own translation that seems to fall somewhere between the two, describing her as "ogress, fierce destroyer in the form of woman" (Tolkien 2014, 49). This marking of Grendel's mother as "fierce" but removing the descriptor of "monstrous" does, at least, tone down some of the derogatory language, but she remains Other in her designation as "ogress."

For both Shelob and Grendel's mother, their maternal selves are central to their depiction as monstrous, although their presentations of maternity are different. For example, Grendel's mother is described as having "yrmþe gemunde" (remembered her misery), which Heaney translates as "brooded on her wrongs," thus homing in on the reason for her distress (line 1259). Not only does this description resonate with Shelob's "brooding on her feasts" (*TT*, IV, ix, 707), but it is worth observing the play on words here, a' "brood" may also be understood to mean "offspring." The brood in question for Grendel's mother is, of course, Grendel himself, whose murder at the hands of Beowulf is the main "wrong" over which she "broods." For Shelob, the word is even more significant in this context as her "brood," her offspring, were also her mates and her victims, on whose flesh she feasted. Here is one significant difference between these two characters, then. Although Grendel's mother is depicted as the monstrous maternal, her love for her child is evident in the poem. Both Kiernan and Chance (2019) note that Grendel's mother is, in fact, avenging the death of her only son and, though in mourning, is responding to his murder in the same way as any man in such a tale might be expected to act. If, as Carol J. Clover argues, "it is incumbent upon the woman to urge vengeance and it is incumbent upon the man to take it" when she asserts that social power lay behind the construction of gender in early northern Europe (145), then Grendel's mother transgresses this norm by taking vengeance herself. It is significant, though, that she is condemned for her actions when it would have been not merely acceptable, but even expected, for a man to perform this role.

The analogy with Grendel's mother is useful to a consideration of Shelob's queerness. Shelob is similarly condemned for her "monstrosity" in her actions, such as when she seeks to capture the hobbits so that she may consume them. She does not "perform" as expected of a female—she is neither caring nor nurturing and seeks to fulfil only her own desires for herself—and stands truly outside social norms as a mother. When the hobbits intrude upon what is her territory, she hunts them so that she may eat; while her behavior is an instinct for all living creatures, the reader's response is determined by a combination of support for the hobbits that has been built up over the previous seven hundred pages and Tolkien's use of language to describe Shelob. Amplifying the language used for Grendel's mother, the language that surrounds Shelob is unequivocal in its depiction of her as monstrous. Tolkien's choice of words (*TT*, IV, ix, 704–709) is designed to elicit that shudder of revulsion that leads to rejection; the slurs on Shelob's femininity are deliberately constructed to increase our revulsion, are expected to render her more horrific, more repulsive and, thus, more abject.

It is therefore apparent that, while Shelob is certainly a representation of the abject feminine in general, it is in her role as a monstrous mother that her abjection is most fully developed. Shelob is what Creed describes as "the oral sadistic mother" (54), who sucks the blood, and therefore the life force, of her victims, whom she has fed with secretions from her own body. These acts reveal Shelob as the queer mother who does not perform "mothering" in a traditional, socially understood way. Recalling Kristeva's definition of true abjection as "what disturbs identity, system, and order ... borders, positions, rules. The in-between, the ambiguous, the composite" (4), Shelob's presentation as "mother" is, perhaps, the most disturbing and challenging aspect of her character. Therefore, using my understanding of a queerness that challenges social expectations of the maternal body, I read Shelob as queering the maternal, calling into question the heteronormative and socially accepted understanding of motherhood by performing this function in a way that is diametrically opposite the norm, yet still, undeniably, performing that function.

If gender may be read as performative, then Shelob's actions construct an image of a powerful modern femininity that draws on masculine power structures (assuming an understanding of gender as fluid rather than fixed, as constructed rather than biological). As noted earlier, many of Tolkien's male characters may also be read as challenging or subverting traditional norms of masculinity by performing. Recognizing this fluidity is significant in understanding Shelob's non-normative performance of gender. Viewing this powerful female figure through both feminist and queer theory offers a wider understanding of her personality and motivations in *The Lord of the Rings*. Instead of perceiving Shelob merely as a monstrous-feminine, which limits her to binary classification of gender, we should see Shelob as a female who is also performing traditionally masculine traits of strength and aggression, consequently constructing a formidable femininity. An alternative understanding of Shelob as more than merely an obstacle in the path of Frodo and Sam, and as more complex than simply a foil to Galadriel, is now possible: she is also a powerful, transgressive, queer mother whose desires and appetites take no account of patriarchal social norms.

To ascribe the label of monstrous-feminine to sexual promiscuity or perceived sexual deviancy, therefore, is to indulge in gender essentialism and heteronormativity while also ignoring the fact that different representations of masculinity may be read throughout Tolkien's Middle-earth legendarium. To label Shelob as monstrous because she complicates traditional understandings of femininity is reductive and ignores her inherent queerness. We cannot disregard the queer maternal as, like her Orc victims, she takes up Frodo like a child, wrapping him up and "feeding" him, even while her abject queerness is disturbing as she poisons Frodo with the intent to eat him. While her violent maternal body horrifies us, Shelob is a symbol of masculine femininity; she interrogates the boundaries between the feminine and the masculine and, hence, queerly dismantles the gender binary. She is both Mother and Other, queer in her representation of a masculine (and sadistic) motherhood, and it is as a Masculine Mother that this compelling figure is at her most disruptive and subversive.

Notes

1. A 2022 presentation titled "Monstrous Feminine, Deviant Mother: Tolkien's Shelob and the Grotesque Maternal," which was an early version of this chapter was published in *The Journal of Tolkien Research* in 2024.

2. For a thorough exploration of how Tolkien's depiction of the natural world sits alongside an understanding of the inherent historical biases of scientific thought, see Larsen, "Medieval Organicism or Modern Feminist Science? Bombadil, Elves, and Mother Nature."

3. I am indebted to Robin Anne Reid's discussion of Halberstam's second-generation queer theory of *Female Masculinity* in her essay "Light (noun, 1) or Light (Adjective, 14b)? Female Bodies and Femininities in *The Lord of the Rings*." Reid explains Halberstam's argument of "the need to consider gender as being constructed socially, in part through language, and not as contingent upon the body, allowing for female participation in the construction and performance of masculinity" (107), which sheds a new light on the consideration of Shelob as monstrous-feminine.

4. Brenda Partridge's work, which reads the scene between Sam and Shelob through a feminist, Freudian-psychoanalytical optic, does not form part of this essay, but I would draw attention to how, despite the extensive criticism it has since faced, the essay provides useful context for early scholarship on Shelob's transgressive nature. See Robin Anne Reid, "The History of Scholarship on Female Characters." Reid points out that, beyond the Freudian interpretations of this scene:

> a number of Partridge's other points have been developed in later Tolkien criticism—the closeness of the homosocial male friendships in Tolkien's life, the patterns of chivalric and modern warfare, and the relationships of Sam and Frodo relating to Tolkien's World War I experiences among them." (18 note 10)

She also notes that that she now believes Partridge's essay to be more nuanced than it has hitherto been allowed.

5. See Amy Amendt-Raduege's essay "Revising Lobelia" for a compelling take on Lobelia Sackville-Baggins as a marginalized woman who seems to be subverting accepted gender norms, yet is actually responding to social demands and the concerns of family. It is easy to categorize Lobelia as a deeply unpleasant termagant; Amendt-Raduege offers a thought-provoking counterpoint.

6. See Wigington for information on some of the American Indian cultures that venerate the spider as a goddess figure, as do some Wiccan, Pagan, and Neopagan groups who see the spider as powerful and/or a symbol of the Goddess's energy.

Works Cited

Abbott, Joe. "Tolkien's Monsters: Concept and Function in *The Lord of the Rings*, II: Shelob the Great." *Mythlore*, vol. 16, no. 2, article 3, 1989, pp. 51–9, dc.swosu.edu/mythlore/vol16/iss3/8.
Alexander, Michael. *Beowulf: A Verse Translation*. Penguin, 1973.
Alfano, C. "The Issue of Feminine Monstrosity: A Re-evaluation of Grendel's Mother." *Comitatus: A Journal of Medieval and Renaissance Studies* vol. 23, iss. 1, 1992, pp. 1–16.
Amendt-Raduege, Amy. "Revising Lobelia." *Tolkien and Alterity*, edited by Christopher Vaccaro and Yvette Kisor, Palgrave Macmillan, 2017, pp. 77–93.
Armitt, Lucie. *Fantasy Fiction: An Introduction*. Continuum, 2005.
de Beauvoir, Simone. *The Second Sex*. Translated and edited by H.M. Parshley, Jonathan Cape, 1949. Rpt. Vintage Books, 1974.
Beowulf. Translated by Frances B. Gummere, Red and Black Publishers, 2007.
Beowulf: A Dual-Language Edition. Translated by Howell D. Chickering, Anchor, 2006.
Beowulf: A New Translation. Translated by Maria Dahvana Headley, Farrar, Straus and Giroux, 2020.
Beowulf: A New Translation. Translated by Seamus Heaney, W.W. Norton & Company, 2000.
Beowulf: A Translation and Commentary Together with Sellic Spell. Translated by J.R.R. Tolkien, edited by Christopher Tolkien, HarperCollins, 2014.
Beowulf, the Oldest English Epic. Translated by Charles W. Kennedy, Oxford UP, 1940.
Bonsall, M.B., and H. Klug. "Effects of Among-offspring Relatedness on the Origins and Evolution of Parental Care and Filial Cannibalism." *Journal of Evolutionary Biology*, vol. 24, iss. 6, 2011, pp. 1335–50.
Brown, Sara. "Monstrous Feminine, Deviant Mother: Tolkien's Shelob and the Grotesque Maternal." *Journal of Tolkien Research*, vol. 20, iss. 2, article 9, 2024, scholar.valpo.edu/journaloftolkienresearch/vol20/iss2/9/.
Burke, Jessica. "Fear and Horror: Monsters in Tolkien and *Beowulf*." *The Mirror Crack'd: Fear and Horror in J.R.R. Tolkien's Major Works*, edited by Lynn Forest-Hill, Cambridge Scholars Publishing, 2008, pp. 15–52.
Burns, Marjorie. "Spiders and Evil Red Eyes: The Shadow Sides of Gandalf and Galadriel." *J.R.R. Tolkien's* The Lord of the Rings—*New Edition, Bloom's Modern Critical Interpretations:* edited by Harold Bloom, 2008, pp. 69–99. Bloom's Literary Criticism.
Butler, Judith. *Gender Trouble. Feminism and the Subversion of Identity*. Routledge, 1999.
_____. *Undoing Gender*. Routledge, 2004.
Chance, Jane. "*The Lord of the Rings*: Tolkien's Epic." *Understanding* The Lord of the Rings: *The Best of Tolkien's Criticism*, edited by Rose A. Zimbardo and Neil D. Isaacs, Houghton Mifflin, 2004, pp. 195–232.
_____. "Reading Grendel's Mother." *New Readings on Women and Early Medieval English Literature and Culture*, edited by Helene Scheck and Christine E., ARC Humanities P, 2019, Cross-Disciplinary Studies in Honor of Helen Damico, pp. 209–226.
_____. *Tolkien, Self and Other: "This Queer Creature."* Palgrave, 2016.
Clover, Carol J. "The Germanic Context of the Unferþ Episode." *Speculum*, vol. 55, no. 3, 1980, pp. 444–68.
Craig, David M. "'Queer Lodgings': Gender and Sexuality in *The Lord of the Rings*."

Mallorn, vol. 38, Jan. 2001, pp. 11–18, journals.tolkiensociety.org/mallorn/article/view/145/139. Rpt. "Queer Lodgings: Gender and Sexuality in *The Lord of the Rings*—Reprinted with a New Introduction by the Author." *Mallorn, Vol.* 61, 2020, pp. 20–29.
Creed, Barbara. "Horror and the Monstrous-Feminine: An Imaginary Abjection." *Screen*, vol 27, iss. 1, 1986, pp. 44–70.
Crowe, Edith L. "Power in Arda: Sources, Uses and Misuses," *Mythlore*, vol. 21, no. 2, article 40, 1996, pp. 272–77, dc.swosu.edu/mythlore/vol21/iss2/40. Rpt. *Perilous and Fair: Women in the Works and Life of J.R.R. Tolkien*, edited by Janet Brennan Croft and Leslie Donovan. Mythopoeic P, 2015, pp. 136–49.
Donovan, Leslie A. "The Valkyrie Reflex in J.R.R. Tolkien's *The Lord of the Rings*: Galadriel, Shelob, Éowyn, and Arwen." *Tolkien the Medievalist*, edited by Jane Chance, Routledge, 2003, pp. 106–32. Rpt. *Perilous and Fair: Women in the Works and Life of J.R.R. Tolkien*, edited by Janet Brennan Croft and Leslie Donovan. Mythopoeic P, 2015, pp. 221–257.
Doty, Alexander. *Flaming Classics: Queering the Film Canon*. Routledge, 2010.
The Lord of the Rings: The Fellowship of the Ring. Directed by Peter Jackson, New Line Cinema, 2001.
Fenwick, Mac. "Breastplates of Silk: Homeric Women in *The Lord of the Rings*." *Mythlore*, vol. 21, no. 3, article 4,1996, pp. 17–23; 51, dc.swosu.edu/mythlore/vol21/iss3/4.
Foster, Hal. "Obscene, Abject, Traumatic." *October*, vol. 78, Autumn 1996, pp. 107–124.
Goselin, Peter Damien. "Two Faces of Eve: Galadriel and Shelob as Anima Figures." *Mythlore*, vol. 6, no. 3, article 1, 1979, pp. 3–4; 28, dc.swosu.edu/mythlore/vol6/iss3/1.
Grant, Patrick. "Tolkien: Archetype and Word." *Understanding The Lord of the Rings: The Best of Tolkien Criticism*, edited by Rose A. Zimbardo and Neil D. Isaacs, Houghton Mifflin, 2004, pp. 163–82.
Green, William H. "'Where's Mama?' the Construction of the Feminine in *The Hobbit*." *The Lion and the Unicorn*, vol. 22, no. 2, 1998, pp. 188–95, doi.org/10.1353/uni.1998.0024.
Halberstam, Jack. *Female Masculinity*. Duke UP, 1998.
Halperin, David. *Saint Foucault: Towards a Gay Hagiography*. Oxford UP, 1997.
Kiernan, Kevin S. "Grendel's Heroic Mother." *Geardagum 6: Essays on Old English Language and Literature*, 1984, pp. 13–33.
Klaeber, Frederick. *Beowulf and the Fight at Finnsburg*, D.C. Heath & Co., 1922.
Klinger, Judith. "Hidden Paths of Time: March 13th and the Riddles of Shelob's Lair." *Tolkien and Modernity 2*, edited by Thomas Honegger and Frank Weinreich, Walking Tree, 2006, pp. 143–209. Cormarë Series No. 10.
Kristeva, Julia. *Powers of Horror: An Essay on Abjection*. Translated by Leon S. Roudiez, Columbia UP, 1982.
Kuhn, Sherman M. "Old English Aglæca-Middle Irish Olach." *Linguistic Method: Essays in Honor of Herbert Penzl*, edited by Irmengard Rauch and Gerald F. Carr, Mouton Publishers, 1979, pp. 213–30.
Larsen, Kristine. "Medieval Organicism or Modern Feminist Science? Bombadil, Elves, and Mother Nature." *Tolkien and Alterity*, edited by Christopher Vaccaro and Yvette Kisor, Palgrave Macmillan, 2017, pp. 95–110.
Lauro, Reno E. "Of Spiders and Light: Hope, Action and Medieval Aesthetics in the Horrors of Shelob's Lair." *The Mirror Crack'd: Fear and Horror in J.R.R. Tolkien's Major Works*, edited by Lynn Forest-Hill, Cambridge Scholars Publishing, 2008, pp. 53–79.
Lionarons, Joyce Tally. "Of Spiders and Elves," *Mythlore*, vol. 31, no. 3, article 2, 2013, pp. 5–13, dc.swosu.edu/mythlore/vol31/iss3/2.
Menzer, Melinda J. "Aglæcwif (*Beowulf* 1259a): Implications for -Wif Compounds, Grendel's Mother, and Other Aglæcan." *English Language Notes*, vol. 34, iss.1, September 1996, pp. 1–6.
Miller, T.S., and Elizabeth Miller. "Tolkien and Rape: Sexual Terror, Sexual Violence, and the Woman's Body in Middle-earth." *Extrapolation*, vol. 62, no. 2, June 2021, pp. 133–156.
Nagel, Rainer. "Shelob and Her Kin: The Evolution of Tolkien's Spiders." *The Mirror Crack'd: Fear and Horror in J.R.R. Tolkien's Major Works*, edited by Lynn Forest-Hill, Cambridge Scholars Publishing, 2008, pp. 81–92.
Partridge, Brenda. "No Sex Please—We're Hobbits: The Construction of Female Sexuality

in *The Lord of the Rings.*" *J.R.R. Tolkien: This Far Land*, edited by Robert Giddings, Vision, 198, pp. 179–197.

Petty, Anne. *One Ring to Bind Them All: Tolkien's Mythology*, U of Alabama P, 1979.

Ray, Stella M. "Constructions of Gender and Sexualities in J.R.R. Tolkien's *The Silmarillion* and *The Lord of the Rings*." 2010, Texas A&M University–Commerce, PhD Dissertation.

Reid, Robin Anne. "The History of Scholarship on Female Characters" *Perilous and Fair: Women in the Life and Works of J.R.R. Tolkien*, edited by Janet Brennan Croft and Leslie A. Donovan, Mythopoeic P, 2015, pp. 13–40.

———. "Light (noun, 1) or Light (Adjective, 14b)? Female Bodies and Femininities in *The Lord of the Rings*." Vaccaro, pp. 98–118.

Ruíz, Beatriz Domínguez. "Mimetic Patterns of Masculinity or Just Another Fantasy Book." *Atenea*, vol. 28, no. 2, 2008, pp. 135–44.

Simons, M.A. *Beauvoir and the Second Sex: Feminism, Race and the Origins of Existentialism*, Rowman and Littlefield, 1999.

Sly, Debbie. "Weaving Nets of Gloom: "Darkness Profound" in Tolkien and Milton." *J.R.R. Tolkien and His Literary Devices: Views of Middle-earth*, edited by George Clark and Daniel Timmons, Greenwood P, 2000, pp. 109–119.

Smol, Anna "Frodo's Body: Liminality and the Experience of War." Vaccaro, pp. 39–62.

Stanley, Eric G. "Two Old English Poetic Phrases Insufficiently Understood for Literary Criticism." *Old English Poetry: Essays on Style*, edited by D.G. Calder, U of California P, 1979.

Thompson, Andrea. "Why Some Animals Eat Their Offspring." *Live Science*, 14 Nov. 2007, livescience.com/2053-animals-eat-offspring.html.

Tolkien, J.R.R. *The Letters of J.R.R. Tolkien*, edited by Humphrey Carpenter, assisted by Christopher Tolkien, Revised and Expanded ed., HarperCollins, 2023.

———. *The Lord of the Rings*. HarperCollins, 1995.

———. *The Silmarillion*. HarperCollins, 1992.

Vaccaro, Christopher, editor. *The Body in Tolkien's Legendarium: Essays on Middle-earth Corporeality*, McFarland, 2013.

Wigington, Patti. "Spider Mythology and Folklore." *Learn Religions*, 23 Dec. 2018, learnreligions.com/spider-mythology-and-folklore-2562730.

Éowyn and/or Dernhelm
Reading Éowyn's (Trans)Masculine Disguise

GAVIN FOSTER

One of the most famous scenes in J.R.R. Tolkien's *The Lord of the Rings* is when Éowyn reveals herself to the Witch-king at the Battle of the Pelennor Fields, laughing, "no living man am I!" (*The Return of the King* [*RK*] V, vi, 841) before raising her sword and shield against the enemy. It is no wonder that the scene has been taken up by feminist fans and scholars alike for its shining depiction of a female hero. However, less commonly discussed is Tolkien's depiction of Éowyn before she removes her disguise—while she is still Dernhelm. The following essay considers Tolkien's representation of gender performativity in his construction of Dernhelm.[1] While I do not intend to suggest that Éowyn is necessarily trans-coded, or identifies as a man, I do suggest that her disguise substantively blurs the boundaries between masculinity and femininity, and that said blurring may be usefully read through the perspectives of transgender theorists such as Jay Prosser, Jack Halberstam, and Susan Stryker. Ultimately, my goal is to demonstrate how an introduction of these new lenses might provide further insight into the way gender and gender performance function in Tolkien's works.[2]

When I discuss gender performativity, I am largely referring to gender performativity as theorized by Judith Butler—the notion that gender is a repetition of signifiers, being "an 'act,' as it were, that is open to splittings, self-parody, self-criticism, and those hyperbolic expressions of 'the national' that, in their very exaggeration, reveal its fundamentally phantasmic status" (200). However, I will also draw on Jay Prosser's conversation with Butler in "Judith Butler: Queer Feminism, Transgender, and the Transubstantiation of Sex." Prosser argues that Butler's *Gender Trouble* allows for the creation of the syllogism, "transgender = gender performativity = queer = subversive" (37). He notes that, regardless of authorial intent, *Gender Trouble* produces "the belief that Butler's theory of gender was both radically voluntarist and antimaterialist: that its argument was that gender, like a set of clothes in a drag act, could be donned and doffed at will, that gender is drag" (Prosser 37), culminating in "the effective appropriation of transgender by queer" (39), queer being defined as pure theory, rather than as a human identity. This appropriation is troubling for Prosser because it erases the intentionally non-performative lived experiences of many transgender, gender non-conforming, and queer people. Prosser's work continuously reasserts the idea that the transgender body is not just a concept to be mobilized. While some people certainly engage in modes of gender-crossing for their subversive effects, queer subversion is not the overarching goal of all gender-crossings (Prosser 39). Gender-crossings can simply be a form of "realness" or naturalization—fulfillments of the gendered lives of transgender people.[3]

It is useful to make such a distinction in reading Éowyn's disguise because, while she certainly performs masculinity as Dernhelm, Tolkien's rhetorical choices surrounding that disguise naturalize it in a way that most drag performances are not naturalized. While drag is subversive due to its visible blurring of masculinity and femininity, Éowyn's disguise is subversive due to the duality of its (in)visibility. Tolkien offers hints concerning Dernhelm's original identity, but these hints are only accessible to the reader; other characters never doubt his maleness. I read the paradoxical legitimacy afforded to Dernhelm's maleness subversively as it exists in conversation with the character's femaleness.

As part of an analysis of race and gender in Tolkien, John Miller briefly discusses Éowyn; however, his reading of her character contradicts my own. Miller argues that Éowyn's unwillingness to remain confined to the home "is represented almost as a kind of madness" (147–48), as evidenced by the way that Merry shivers upon first seeing Dernhelm's hopelessly battle-ready expression (*RK*, V, iii, 803) and Gandalf's commentary on Éowyn's deteriorating psyche following the battle of Pelennor Fields (*RK*, V, viii, 867). Ultimately, Miller concludes that Éowyn is characterized as "a woman who yearns to wander, does so, is gravely wounded as a result, and upon healing acquiesces to her conventional, stationary gender role, turning her attentions to more conventional feminine and stationary pursuits" (148). While this argument is certainly compelling, it also depends on the notion that Éowyn can only ever engage with the world as a woman. Merry's shiver upon "seeing her disguised as a man heading off to battle" (Miller 148) can only represent a womanly madness if Merry does, in fact, see a woman disguised as a man. If he sees a man, as I will suggest he does, he must be unsettled by another aspect of the scene. Likewise, Gandalf's assertion retroactively genders Éowyn's disguise as feminine; if Gandalf presumes that Éowyn experiences a form of madness centered around her female identity, he erases Dernhelm's potentially masculine experiences.

David Craig and Robin Anne Reid's queer readings of Éowyn more closely align with my own. In "Queer Lodgings," Craig explains Tolkien's struggle in constructing Éowyn's gender. Craig compares different versions of Éowyn in Tolkien's drafts that are collected in *The History of Middle-earth* (*HoMe*), to argue that Tolkien did not intend to create a feminist character when he wrote her. Tolkien was not celebrating women's liberation by sending Éowyn to battle. Rather, her actions were "the product of a deeply troubled and unhappy mind" (Craig 23). In setting up this anti-feminist approach, though, Tolkien invites a queer approach. As Craig states, Éowyn has to "become a 'man' and overturn the natural gender roles" (23). Reid notes a similarly unintentional lean towards queerness in Tolkien's writing of Éowyn, arguing that she makes "queer" choices according to the norms of Rohirrim culture, especially as she moves across space in ways other female characters cannot and cross-dresses in the final battle (111).

While acting as Dernhelm, Éowyn performs masculinity in a multi-layered way, her female identity being paradoxically both present and invisible. As previously stated, Tolkien offers numerous not-so-subtle suggestions pertaining to her femininity, making it present to the reader, but these suggestions do not undercut other characters' constructions of her disguise as being fundamentally male. In illustrating this point, it will be useful to examine Dernhelm's introduction, which is narrated through Merry's perspective. Dernhelm glances at Merry, and Merry perceives him to be "[a] young man [...] less in height and girth than most" (*RK*, V, iii, 802–803). Here, Tolkien highlights Dernhelm's femininity in noting that his stature is different than that of other warriors; however, this does not change the fact that Merry ultimately recognizes him as being a man. Dernhelm's masculinity takes precedence in this passage, and this is furthered by Merry's reading of Dernhelm's expression: that of someone who is hopeless and driven towards death (*RK*, V, iii, 803). The other men in line have "stern and unmoved faces" (*RK*, V, iii, 803), but Dernhelm's face is the sternest of all. Such sternness may begin to align Dernhelm with Tolkien's theory of bleak northern heroism, which he defines in "Ofermod," his companion essay to "The Homecoming of Beorhtnoth Beorhthelm's Son."

Tolkien defines the Old English "northern heroic spirit" as a motivation that is "of gold and an alloy" (*Tree and Leaf* [*T&L*] 144). He imagines an "unalloyed" form would be powerful enough to "direct a man to endure even death unflinching, when necessary" (*T&L* 144), while also acknowledging that, in action, the motivating forces of warriors would be much more complicated. The primary examples that Tolkien uses to illustrate his concept of the more realistic, "alloyed" form of heroism, then, are Beorhtnoth, Beowulf, and Sir Gawain. In each of these men, Tolkien explains, "[an] element of pride [...] [drives] a man beyond the bleak heroic to excess—to chivalry" (*T&L* 144). And, while his conception of heroism remains inherently bleak, he proceeds to identify the men who fight subordinate to a ruling power as being the closest to exemplifying "unalloyed" heroism. In discussing the "Battle of Maldon" warriors, Tolkien writes, "Their part was to endure and die, and not to question" (*T&L* 148). Heroic action itself is not inherently gendered in this passage, as anyone might intend to unquestioningly "endure and die" for their master. Nonetheless, I posit that the traditional masculinity of the "Maldon" warriors, as ideal characterizations of such heroic action, lends itself to broader associations of northern heroism with masculinity. Tolkien's chosen heroic figures, both "alloyed" and potentially "unalloyed," are figures whose heroism has been explicitly tied to their masculinity.

This connection between heroism and masculinity is perhaps why, when Tolkien scholars have analyzed Tolkien's own characters through his definition of northern heroism, they have focused on his male characters. Alexander Bruce begins a contemporary conversation by suggesting that Gandalf's fall at the Bridge of Khazad-dûm mirrors Beorhtnoth's fall in "Maldon" (150). He explains that Gandalf's challenge to the Balrog mirrors Beorhtnoth's challenge to the Vikings, and Gandalf "holds off the Balrog's first attack, as the three Anglo-Saxon defenders held off the Vikings" (Bruce 153). However, for Bruce, this is where a connection between the two characters is severed. Following the Balrog's first attack, Tolkien uses Gandalf as a means "to 'correct' the behaviour of the self-serving Byrthnoth through the actions of the less self-centered Gandalf" (150). Gandalf "personally stands his ground and saves the party by destroying the bridge and casting the Balrog into the abyss—though he himself is unwillingly dragged down in the process" (Bruce 153), rather than exhibiting excessive pride and endangering his companions. Bruce takes a similar stance in describing Aragorn's heroism, explaining that it is amended when Aragorn makes the choice "to lead his reduced forces right to the very gates of Mordor expecting death but not defeat, for he knows he is giving Frodo more time to destroy the Ring" (156). As well, Bruce briefly notes that Éowyn and Merry's fight against the Witch-king might constitute northern heroism (156), potentially challenging the foregrounding of men in discussions of Tolkien's theory, though he does not further this argument in light of gendered constructions/performances. These arguments mark the creation of the formula that future Tolkien scholars will use in analyzing Tolkien's use of "northern heroic spirit" in his own fiction. There remains a general consensus that, when Tolkien employs northern heroic qualities, he often does so in critique of "alloyed" heroism—the type of excessive pride that drove Beorhtnoth.

Mary R. Bowman cites Bruce as inspiration for her article on "northern heroic spirit" in Tolkien's fiction (91) and pushes his analysis further in a few ways. First, she notes the link between Old English heroism and the Rohirrim people, suggesting that, if they have songs that reference Old English elegies, it is not unthinkable that Old English battle poetry and, therefore, literary "northern heroic spirit" would be part of their culture (Bowman 94). Second, while she mentions other male characters, she uses Sam as a primary case study for northern heroism in *The Lord of the Rings*. In considering the aftermath of Frodo's attack by Shelob, Bowman argues that the options Sam weighs, like suicide and revenge, "are comparable to the flight of the sons of Odda: doing what serves the individual interest at others' expense" (101). Sam is made heroic because he ultimately continues on his quest, being focused on "his 'purpose and duty'—repetitively so" (Bowman 101). Bowman continues, "[Sam's] choice also transcends the appeal of personal glory remembered in a song, making a pointed contrast with Byrthnoth himself" (102). In the same manner as Bruce argues that Tolkien's "northern heroic characters" are a means to amend flawed heroism, Bowman sees Sam as a figure onto which Tolkien constructs an idealized form of northern heroism.

While I agree that Sam is a heroic figure, I do question the extent to which he exemplifies "northern heroic spirit." He seems to straddle the line between northern heroism and a more modern form of heroism. This ambiguity is because Sam's narrative trajectory lacks some of the essential bleakness that Tolkien associates with "northern heroic spirit." While northern heroic figures meet their ends in darkness, Tolkien's Hobbits are not so constricted, and their heroism often appears to be located in their resistance to darkness—their constant ability to keep moving forward. No better place is this represented than in the following passage, as Bilbo slowly creeps towards Smaug: "Going on from there was the bravest thing he ever did. [...] He fought the real battle in the tunnel alone, before he ever saw the vast danger that lay in wait" (*The Hobbit* [H] 249). Bilbo's heroism does not arise from his ability to fight, and very likely die, for "some object of will" (*T&L* 144) or moral necessity. Instead, it arises from his ability to fight fear rising within himself and continue on in spite of himself. Sam's heroism is much the same. For example, when Sam thinks that he has lost Frodo at Cirith Ungol, and that his journey has been in vain, his main challenge is to overcome the darkness consuming his mind. He sings a song (in ballad form, distinct from the alliterative verse of the Rohirrim) to combat that darkness, trying to find the strength to continue his journey (*RK*, VI, i, 908–909). He fights against emotional ruin, rather than physical ruin.

Tolkien's characterization of Dernhelm, on the other hand, is wholly northern heroic—like his characterizations of Gandalf or Thorin. When Tolkien "corrects" northern heroism in his depiction of Gandalf on the bridge, that depiction remains inherently bleak. While Gandalf saves his companions, he himself plummets to what readers then assume is his death. Tolkien presents a similar bleakness in his correction of Thorin's heroism. At the end of *The Hobbit*, Thorin displays bravery in battle, being willing to die for the safety of his companions, and he verbally amends his previous "chivalry," or excess, moving beyond selfish desires (*H* 333). However, because he must die in the same moment that his redemption occurs, his heroism—even if potentially "unalloyed"—remains bleak. For Tolkien, the presence of "northern heroic spirit" necessitates the possibility of a tragic end. Dernhelm, then, is an ideal characterization of "northern heroic spirit" in a few ways. His masculinity aligns him with the male heroes that both Tolkien and Tolkien scholars have referenced in exploring the theory. As well, in having a stern, death-seeking expression, Dernhelm embodies the core quality of the warriors Tolkien describes; he would "endure even death unflinching" to achieve that which he deems necessary.

Likewise, it is significant that Dernhelm is of the Rohirrim, who Tolkien constructs through an Old English framework. Tom Shippey argues that "[w]ith one admitted exception [that they have horses] the Riders of Rohan resemble the Anglo-Saxons down to minute details" (106). Their language is Old English and, in it, "[t]hey preserve the sonority, the sadness, the feelings for violent opposites […] integrated [from Old English into] the Rider's language and culture" (Shippey 114) as well as preserving the alliterative meter of Old English poetry. Expanding these ideas, Jorge Luis Bueno Alonso notes that the language and culture of Rohan demonstrate the influence of "the elegiac tone, the memories of the pleasures of life in the *comitatus*, the social values of life in the mead-hall, the banquets, the symbols of past glories, the transience of life, etc." (24) of Anglo-Saxon language and culture. The Rohirrim also participate in Anglo-Saxon battle culture through both their courageous dedication to battle and their "calls to battle" (Bueno Alonso 24), as when Théoden calls the Riders to rise (*RK*, V, vi, 838) before leading them to fight.

Théoden, himself, fulfills the role of an Old English "god cyning" (*Beowulf* 11), or "good king," in many ways. These connections are also noted by Michael R. Kightley, who draws on Shippey's argument that "The King of the Golden Hall" chapter of *The Lord of the Rings* is "calqued on *Beowulf*" (112). Kightley explains that Tolkien's use of calquing leads to a sense that likenesses to *Beowulf* "act as signposts, creating a signaling effect that resonates throughout the entirety of the chapter, even as the similarities progressively fade into differences" (119). The purpose of this, he argues, is to "maneuver the reader into interpreting the main characters of the second half of the chapter primarily in terms of their counterparts in *Beowulf*, beginning with Théoden and Hrothgar" (Kightley 119). So, when Gandalf and company approach the golden hall, Tolkien is at the same time writing Beowulf's first glimpse of Hrothgar's golden hall.[4] And, by integrating Dernhelm into this culture, Tolkien furthers a connection between Dernhelm and masculine northern heroism.

Yet, the dichotomy of Éowyn's masculine/feminine disguise only grows as Tolkien develops Dernhelm's character. In Dernhelm's first conversation with Merry, Tolkien twice mentions the softness of his voice (*RK*, V, iii, 804). He also alludes to Merry's previous meeting with Éowyn. Dernhelm tells Merry to ride with him to Mundburg, and Merry replies that he does not know his name, to which Dernhelm says, "Do you not? [...] Then call me Dernhelm" (*RK*, V, iii, 804). This brief moment of questioning, while not enough to deconstruct Dernhelm's identity for the characters in the text, signals to readers that his identity may not be as it seems. Then, as in Dernhelm's introductory passage, Tolkien once again highlights his femininity and masculinity within a single sentence. He calls Dernhelm, "less in weight than many men, though lithe and well-knit" (*RK*, V, iii, 804). I argue that the combination of these moments works to feminize the character, operating in stark contrast to what comes next. At the outset of the chapter following Dernhelm's introduction, Tolkien shifts from hinting at the character's femininity to representing him as being wholly masculine. And, as Dernhelm comes to be recognized as male by his peers, he is fit with traditionally masculine pronouns and a new social framework for engaging with men.

Relatively little in Tolkien studies has been written on gender affirmation and pronoun usage from a literary perspective, especially in reference to transmasculine (and potentially related) identities. However, these discussions have been quite active in psychological, sociological, and medical spheres, and their contents can quite easily function in an interdisciplinary sense. Jae M. Sevelius, et al. define gender affirmation as a largely social process, explaining that both cisgender and transgender people experience social affirmation processes, though the term "gender affirmation" tends to be associated with transgender people because their gender identities are more commonly disaffirmed (2). Said disaffirmation can include "being misgendered (e.g., addressed in a way that is inconsistent with one's gender identity) through incorrect pronoun usage" (Sevelius, et al. 2), having gendered titles (ex. "sir" or "ma'am"), or gendered compliments (ex. "handsome" versus "pretty") inappropriately applied, among a number of additional possibilities. Sevelius, et al. also note that, while the term "preferred pronoun" has come into common usage, it is not accurately reflective of many people's gendered experiences. They explain, "transgender communities and their advocates have increasingly emphasized that pronoun use goes beyond 'preference,' since 'preference' implies that using the correct pronoun is simply 'preferred' by the person and therefore optional" (Sevelius, et al. 2). The terminology ignores both how fundamentally intertwined pronouns can be with a person's sense of self and how potential "disrespectful, harmful, and even unsafe" (Sevelius, et al. 2) it can be to address someone using incorrect pronouns.

These definitions are expanded in studies like that of Kristina Howansky, et al., who unpack the nuance behind the misgendering of transgender people. They recognize that "some people might challenge a transgender woman or man's identity by referring to them with the pronouns associated with their sex assigned at birth" (Howansky, et al. 2), while other people "might challenge their identity by referring to them with gender-neutral/non-binary pronouns or by abstaining from pronoun use entirely when they would not refrain from pronoun use when describing a cisgender woman or man" (Howansky, et al. 2). Howansky, et al. define such an abstention from pronoun use as "degendering" (2) and explicitly recognize intentional degendering as a discriminatory act. In studying degendering through a series of social experiments, then, Howansky, et al. have determined that, rather than emerging as a result of ignorance towards transgender people, degendering "is more likely to represent identity denial stemming from negative biases towards transgender individuals" (11). And, interestingly, "[p]roviding pronouns only resulted in less degendering towards transgender women (not men) and did not result in any less misgendering" (Howansky, et al. 11). These findings on degendering and misgendering can be usefully applied to Tolkien's pronoun usage for Dernhelm.

While it may seem a minute detail, the pronouns that Tolkien chooses to refer to Dernhelm lay the groundwork for how readers might perceive the character. If Tolkien were to have continued using "she" and "her" in describing Dernhelm, as he uses for Éowyn, he would have immediately delegitimized the character's disguise. Readers would know that Dernhelm was simply a woman playing a man which, while still interestingly performative, would not as substantially blur the boundaries between masculinity and femininity. But, Tolkien does not highlight Dernhelm's femininity in such an overt way. Instead, he chooses to forego the use of any pronouns on Dernhelm's first introduction, degendering the character for rhetorical effect, rather than as a malicious, discriminatory, or ignorant practice. Aligning with his hints about Dernhelm's feminine physicality, for the duration of "The Muster of Rohan," Tolkien uses phrases like "the glance" or "the eyes" (*RK*, V, iii, 803) to avoid phrases like "his/her glance" or "his/her eyes." This choice is offset by Tolkien's frequent pronoun usage for Merry in the same passage (*RK*, V, iii, 803), subtly signaling that something is different about Dernhelm's gender identity.

Then, as the disguise develops, Tolkien allows readers to imagine Dernhelm like the other men in each scene. At the beginning of "The Ride of the Rohirrim," Merry reflects negatively on his decision to ride with Dernhelm, thinking, "he never spoke to anyone" (*RK*, V, v, 830). Now, like the other men in each scene, Dernhelm uses he/him pronouns. Descriptions of his speech and actions are structurally indistinguishable from those of other male characters. This comment, in combination with Merry's sense that there is an understanding between Dernhelm and the commanding Marshal, Elfhelm (*RK*, V, v, 830), cements Dernhelm's masculine identity in opposition to previous allusions to his femininity. In cementing Dernhelm's masculinity, then, Tolkien is able to begin shifting the social framework in which the character operates.

Éowyn is Théoden's niece, but, as Dernhelm, his relationship to Théoden is that of a retainer to his lord. Tolkien highlights Dernhelm's loyalty to Théoden in battle in describing the riding order of the Rohirrim; Dernhelm rides near the back of the king's guard, remaining close to the king even when Elfhelm's company is positioned further away (*RK*, V, viii, 837). This closeness is only heightened when Théoden falls in battle, and Tolkien notes that Dernhelm stays by his side weeping because of how much he loved his lord (*RK*, V, vi, 840). Like the men who stick fearlessly by their lords in Tolkien's Old English references, Dernhelm is intrinsically bound to Théoden.

However, Dernhelm's masculine social role is increasingly interesting if he retains his family lineage—if his gender identity shifts, but he remains related to Théoden. In "Totemic Reflexes in Tolkien's Middle-earth," Yvette Kisor traces the imprints of shamanism in Tolkien's works, citing the work of Stephen Glosecki on "shamanic and totemic reflexes" (Kisor 129) in Old English culture as inspiration for her own project. She writes:

> These related terms refer to the residue of an older culture that remained in the Germanic cultures of history and record. Things like the prominence of the avunculate (the tie between the mother's brother and sister's son) and the prevalence of animal imagery, according to Glosecki, point to an earlier culture that was matrilineal and totemic [Kisor 129].

The role of the sister's son is especially important to a reading of Tolkien.

Of primary relevance to my own argument is Kisor's reading of the Rohirrim, "who feature cultural traces similar to those detected by Glosecki in poems like *Beowulf*: not intact matrilineal structure but reflexes of it" (134). In Tolkien's construction of the Rohirrim:

> The prominence of the avunculate reflects not a current political reality but a trace of one, preserved in the frequency of the MoBr-SiSo pairs (mother's brother-sister's son), the affectionate nature of such bonds, and the presence of language to describe these familial relationships [Kisor 134].

According to Kisor, this is best exemplified in *The Lord of the Rings* through Théoden's relationships to Éomer and Éowyn. She writes:

> Théoden consistently [refers] to Éomer as his sister-son and Éowyn as his sister-daughter [...] demonstrating language that singles out that familial relationship, and among the characters of Rohan the trio of Théoden, Éomer, and Éowyn is not only the most prominent, but the most affectionate [134].

Kisor lists a few examples of these interactions, not expanding on their contents in the span of her article. Here, however, it will be necessary to examine one scene in detail.

Éowyn is introduced as Théoden's sister-daughter before Tolkien describes her more wholly (*The Two Towers* [*TT*], III, vi, 515). He makes Éowyn's role as sister-daughter the most important part of her character—before her personality, before her physical appearance, Tolkien chooses to highlight her culturally significant relationship to Théoden. And, Tolkien signals considerable affection through this relationship. Théoden tells Éowyn not to fear and, in return, Éowyn looks upon him with a great deal of emotional depth. From her introductory passage, it is clear that she cares deeply about Théoden, even as her gaze contains some degree of coldness—her "cool pity" never turns to cool detachment (*TT*, III, vi, 515). Therefore, if Dernhelm is already bound to Théoden under the role of a retainer to his lord, he would be even more so carrying with him the emotional depth of a sister-son relationship. Not only would he maintain the existing closeness demonstrated by Théoden and Éowyn, but he would also carry the masculine, military implications of the bond as in the relationship between Beowulf and Wiglaf, further nuancing Théoden's defeat. The emotional intensity of the scene is significantly heighted by the simultaneous existence of these usually incompatible gendered feelings in one embodied experience.

At the height of these gendered significations, however, Tolkien once again switches his characterization of Dernhelm. Almost immediately following Théoden's defeat, Éowyn sheds her disguise to fight the Witch-king. This moment marks the instance where Éowyn should naturally revert back to a more concrete feminine identity, having progressed beyond the need for her disguise. Tolkien signals this change where he writes, "her bright hair, released from its bonds, gleamed with pale gold" (*RK*, V, vi, 841). This passage accomplishes three things. First, it draws the reader back to Éowyn's introduction through its focus on her golden hair which, in both passages, serves as a marker for her femininity. Second, it switches the character's pronouns back to their feminine versions. And, third, it constructs Dernhelm's masculinity as restrictive while Éowyn's femininity is made a necessary part of her heroism. The masculine disguise that Éowyn takes as she enters the battlefield is a "bond" for her hair—her hair operating metonymically for her femininity—and she cannot physically engage in battle until her femininity is recognized.

Yet, interestingly, this seemingly complete shift in gendered categorization does not mark the end of Éowyn's complex gender performance. I suggest that the paradox of Dernhelm's simultaneously masculine and feminine identity only reaches its peak following the oft-discussed removal of Éowyn's disguise. It is only in the following passage that Tolkien brings the two identities together, experimenting with their potential to co-exist. Merry recognizes Dernhelm's hopeless expression in Éowyn, thinking, "Éowyn it was, and Dernhelm also" (*RK*, V, vi, 841). In this moment Éowyn and Dernhelm are quite literally made one and the same. And, given Tolkien's dual characterizations of Éowyn as feminine and Dernhelm as masculine, this suggests that, at least for a moment, the character embodies both male and female gender significations.[5]

This interplay of gender significations is quickly overwritten by Merry's new assessment of Éowyn. While Éowyn still embodies the bleakness of Tolkien's "northern heroic spirit" that was identified in Dernhelm, Merry's new understanding of Éowyn as a woman changes his assessment of this bleakness. He thinks, "She should not die, so fair, so desperate" (*RK*, V, vi, 841), suggesting that the role of the hero is fundamentally different for a man than a woman. But despite the overwriting of Éowyn's co-existence with Dernhelm, the moment of gender duality is worth examining through a few queer theoretical lenses.

To read gender duality effectively, I want to foreground theories which lean into the challenges offered by transgender studies, rather than those which ultimately rely on readings of transness and gender non-conformity as adjacent to (or as a subsets of) sexuality. Jack Halberstam's "Transgender Butch" is all about such challenges.[6] The paradox of Éowyn's masculine/feminine disguise mirrors Halberstam's complication of a "masculine continuum," which would assume that bodies can be identified on a scale from androgynous to a binary transmasculine identity—the later being a more "serious" version of the former (294–295). The difference between androgynous identities, like those of butch lesbians, does not exist wholly separate from transmasculine identities. In real life, gender identities and modes of presentation are not always distinct and easily read. Halberstam cites Jordy Jones, a transmasculine performance artist, saying:

> Not everyone who experiences gender dysphoria experiences it in the same way, and not everyone deals with it in the same way. Not all transgendered individuals take hormones, and not everyone who takes hormones is transgendered. I have a (genetically female) friend who identifies as male and passes perfectly. He's never had a shot. I certainly know dykes who are butcher than I could ever be, but who wouldn't consider identifying as anything other than women [qtd. in Halberstam 469].

Much of the terminology in this passage is now long outdated given that it was published in 1998, but its core point stands strong. As Halberstam puts it, "Jones's understanding of transgender variability produces an almost fractal model of cross-gender identifications that can never return to the binary models of before and after, or transsexual and nontranssexual, or butch and FTM" (470). Jones breaks down the notion that every form of gender non-conformity must be distinct, that every form of gender non-conformity should be easily recognized and chartable—he makes space for nuanced, and even paradoxical, identities. Theories like this offer context for how identities like Éowyn/Dernhelm's might exist and how we might write about them, purposefully acknowledging and sitting with their paradoxical nature.

Halberstam continues his argument against a masculine continuum by arguing that "[a]t the transgender end of the spectrum, the continuum model miscalculates the relation between bodily alternation and degree of masculinity; at the butch end, the continuum model makes it seem as if butchness is sometimes just an early stage of transsexual aspiration" (471). Regardless of where an individual might be placed within such a model, their identities undergo some degree of misrepresentation or invalidation. Much like Prosser's rejection of the potentially appropriative, inaccurate views that emerge from the way Butler theorizes gender performativity in *Gender Trouble*, for Halberstam, the truth of lived experiences cannot be represented statically.

Such variation in lived experiences might be exemplified within the term "FTM" (female to male). While Halberstam primarily uses "FTM" to describe transgender men, the transmasculine community has now largely rejected the term. As Halberstam argues, "'FTM' names a radical shift in both identity and body base within the context of transsexuality" (468). But, in naming that shift, the term contains both the previous and current identities of the people it seeks to describe. To be "FTM" is to always be tied to femininity, even in completely reconstructing oneself to escape femininity. Halberstam alludes to this issue:

> Some of those transgender people who retain the label "FTM" (rather than becoming "men") have mastectomies and hysterectomies and take testosterone on a regular basis and are quite satisfied with the male secondary

characteristics that such treatments produce. These transgender subjects are not attempting to slide seamlessly into manhood, and their retention of the FTM label suggests the emergence of a new gender position marked by this term [473].

However, Halberstam does not delve into the difficult nature the term's construction, instead focusing on how the very existence of a transgender label differentiates its subject from cisgender people.

Despite its imperfect application to the transmasculine community, the term "FTM" might be usefully repurposed to describe Éowyn's disguise. In becoming Dernhelm, Éowyn quite literally transitions from female to male. The language that Tolkien uses to describe her, focalized through both Merry and the narrator, undergoes a shift from the feminine, to the degendered, to the masculine. Yet, within the masculine identity, there remain hints of the feminine and, within the feminine identity, there remain hints of the masculine. As in the term "FTM," the feminine and masculine are always intertwined. I also find the term useful for the legitimacy it might afford Dernhelm's maleness. While it is not the same as transgender maleness—a maleness that is a reflection of the fundamentally non-female internal self—it is more than drag. While still tied to the female, the male is an identity in itself.

This sequence of analysis becomes a bit more complicated as Éowyn socially transitions back to femininity. Is she then MTF, as separate from FTM? Or, is she FTMTF, representing a full range of gendered identities? Are these labels able to do the work of legitimizing her male and female identities, or do they simply overwrite each other?

Of immediate relevance is Susan Stryker's argument for the inherently disruptive nature of transgender studies, even within queer theory:

> If queer theory was born of the union of sexuality studies and feminism, transgender studies can be considered queer theory's evil twin: it has the same parentage but willfully disrupts the privileged family narratives that favor sexual identity labels (like *gay, lesbian, bisexual*, and *heterosexual*) over the gender categories (like *man* and *woman*) that enable desire to take shape and find its aim [212].

Transgender studies and, consequently, the application of transgender studies to our readings of texts across literary fields, remains contentious. But, should it be able to function beyond its construction as monstrous (Stryker 213)—beyond the constructed circumstances that also constitute its necessary erasure, or existence "in the shadow of queer theory" (Stryker 214)—transgender studies contains massive potential. As Stryker argues, transgender studies "has the potential to address emerging problems in the critical study of gender and sexuality, identity, embodiment, and desire in ways that gay, lesbian, and queer studies have not always successfully managed" (214). Therefore, transgender studies offers a means through which to articulate Tolkien's construction of Dernhelm, which points to a complexity of gender signification where masculinity and femininity simultaneously, perhaps transgressively, co-exist.

In examining Tolkien's rhetorical construction of Dernhelm's gender/gender performativity, and in reading the character through the lens of transgender theorists like Prosser, Halberstam, and Stryker, I hope to have opened a new window through which we might view Tolkien's works. As I have argued, Tolkien's use of traditionally male pronouns for Dernhelm and his integration of Dernhelm into a masculine social framework legitimize the character's male identity beyond that of a more typical crossdressing character. Yet, even in doing so, Tolkien retains hints of Dernhelm femininity. When Dernhelm is introduced, his female identity is foreshadowed and, when he fully assumes a male identity, that identity is quickly subverted by Éowyn's return. This crossing makes Éowyn one of the most interestingly gendered characters across the legendarium, being able to exist (however briefly) under both female and male signifiers. As transgender studies increasingly functions as "a point of departure for a lively conversation" (Stryker 215), it offers a means through which to articulate bodies and performances which are rebellious, mutable, and paradoxical. And, I suggest that, in becoming Dernhelm—in making a gendered transition "there and back again"—Éowyn's characterization is perhaps more rebellious than previous discussion has recognized.

Notes

1. For an additional reading of Éowyn's queerness, see Sara Brown's "'Éowyn it was, and Dernhelm also': Reading the 'Wild Shieldmaiden Through a Queer Lens'" which was published after the completion of my essay, but before its publication. Our approaches are similar, although we apply different theories and arrive at different conclusions.

2. For duration of this essay, I will be using "Dernhelm" to refer to the character under discussion in disguise and "Éowyn" to refer to the character out of disguise. I do this both to mirror how Tolkien writes the character in *The Lord of the Rings* and for clarity's sake. Likewise, as Tolkien uses traditionally masculine (he/him) pronouns for Dernhelm, I will be adopting the same approach to my discussion of the character.

3. For additional scholarship on transgender realities, articulated through fanfiction, see the essay by Cordeliah G. Logsdon in this volume (201–14): "'What care I for the hands of a king?': Tolkien Fanfiction and Narratives of the Transgender Self."

4. Additional references to Old English literature/culture include Théoden's relationship with his sister-son (Éomer), which mirrors, that of Beowulf and Wiglaf, his decision to personally lead his men into battle (even in his old age), his participation in the Old English boasting tradition (ex. Beowulf's swimming contest), etc.

5. For additional scholarship on gender non-conforming characters, see the essay in this volume by Danna Petersen-Deeprose (107–22): "'Something Mighty Queer': Destabilizing Gender, Intimacy and Family in Tolkien's Legendarium."

6. For a reading of Shelob through the lenses of Butler and Halberstam, see the essay

in this volume by Sara Brown (77–91): "Mother or Other: Tolkien's Shelob and the 'Monstrous-Feminine.'"

Works Cited

Bowman, Mary R. "Refining the Gold: Tolkien, the Battle of Maldon, and the Northern Theory of Courage." *Tolkien Studies*, vol. 7, 2010, pp. 91–115.

Brown, Sara. "'Éowyn It Was, and Dernhelm Also': Reading the 'Wild Shieldmaiden Through a Queer Lens." *Journal of Tolkien Research*, vol. 18, no. 2, article 4, 2023, scholar.valpo.edu/journaloftolkienresearch/vol18/iss2/4/.

Bruce, Alexander M. "Maldon and Moria: On Byrhtnoth, Gandalf, and Heroism in *The Lord of the Rings*." *Mythlore*, vol. 26, no. 1, article 11, 2007, p. 149–59, dc.swosu.edu/mythlore/vol26/iss1/11/.

Bueno Alonso, Jorge Luis. "'Eotheod' Anglo-Saxons of the Plains: Rohan as the Old English Culture in J.R.R. Tolkien's *The Lord of the Rings*." *Anuario De Investigación En Literatura Infantil Y Juvenil*, vol. 2, 2004, pp. 21–35.

Butler, Judith. *Gender Trouble*. Routledge, 2006.

Chance, Jane. *Tolkien, Self and Other: "This Queer Creature."* Palgrave Macmillan, 2016.

Craig, David M. "'Queer Lodgings': Gender and Sexuality in *The Lord of the Rings*." *Mallorn*, vol. 38, Jan. 2001, pp. 11–18, journals.tolkiensociety.org/mallorn/article/view/145/139. Rpt. "Queer Lodgings: Gender and Sexuality in *The Lord of the Rings*—Reprinted with a New Introduction by the Author." *Mallorn*, Vol. 61, 2020, pp. 20–29.

Domínguez Ruiz, Beatriz. "J.R.R. Tolkien's Construction of Multiple Masculinities in *The Lord of the Rings*." *Odisea*, no. 16, 2015, pp. 23–38.

Halberstam, Jack (Judith). "Transgender Butch: Butch/FTM Border Wars and the Masculine Continuum." *GLQ: A Journal of Lesbian and Gay Studies*, vol. 4, no. 2, 1998, pp. 287–310.

Howansky, Kristina, et al. "Him, Her, Them, or None: Misgendering and Degendering of Transgender Individuals." *Psychology and Sexuality*, 2021, pp. 1–15.

Kightley, Michael R. "Heorot or Meduseld?: Tolkien's Use of *Beowulf* in 'The King of the Golden Hall.'" *Mythlore*, vol. 24, no. 3, article 8, 2006, pp. 119–134, dc.swosu.edu/mythlore/vol24/iss3/8.

Kisor, Yvette. "Totemic Reflexes in Tolkien's Middle-earth," *Mythlore*, vol. 28, no. 3, article 9, 2010, dc.swosu.edu/mythlore/vol28/iss3/9.

Liuzza, R.M. *Beowulf*. 2nd ed., Broadview P, 2013.

Miller, John. "Mapping Gender in Middle-earth." *Mythlore*, vol. 34, no. 2, article 9, 2016, pp. 133–152, dc.swosu.edu/mythlore/vol34/iss2/9.

Pacheco, Derek. "'Funny Queer Fits': Masculinity and Desire in J.R.R. Tolkien's *The Hobbit*." *Children's Literature Association Quarterly*, vol. 46, no. 3, 2021, pp. 263–282.

Prosser, Jay. "Judith Butler: Queer Feminism, Transgender, and the Transubstantiation of Sex." *The Routledge Queer Studies Reader*, edited by Donald E. Hall and Annamarie Jagose, Routledge, 2013, pp. 445–63.

Reid, Robin Anne. "Light (noun, 1) or Light (adjective, 14b)? Female Bodies and Femininities in *The Lord of the Rings*." *The Body in Tolkien's Legendarium: Essays on Middle-earth Corporeality*, edited by Christopher Vaccaro, McFarland, 2013, pp. 98–118.

Sevelius, Jae M., et al. "Gender Affirmation Through Correct Pronoun Usage: Development and Validation of the Transgender Women's Importance of Pronouns (TW-IP) Scale." *International Journal of Environmental Research and Public Health*, vol. 17, no. 24, 2020, pp. 1–13.

Shippey, T.A. *The Road to Middle-Earth*. Allen & Unwin, 1982.

Stryker, Susan. "Transgender Studies: Queer Theory's Evil Twin." *GLQ*, vol. 10, no. 2, 2004, pp. 212–215.

Tolkien, J.R.R. *The Hobbit*. HarperCollins, 2006.

_____. *The Lord of the Rings*. HarperCollins, 2007.

_____. *Tree and Leaf*. HarperCollins, 2001.

"Something Mighty Queer"

Destabilizing Gender, Intimacy and Family in Tolkien's Legendarium[1]

Danna Petersen-Deeprose

This essay offers a queer reading of gender, relationships, and family units in Tolkien's Middle-earth stories. It is, however, first necessary to explain what exactly I mean when I use the word "queer." When I talk about queerness, I do not specifically mean same-gender sex or romance, although those are of course included. Those forms of queerness are one facet of the broader, more ideological lens that I mean to employ. Lewis Seifert states that "[i]n the broadest sense, *queer* involves the questioning of dominant forms of social and political relationships while deliberately resisting any prescription of what those relationships should look like" (16). I would argue that throughout his Middle-earth stories, Tolkien does exactly that: he pushes and questions forms of relationships, as well as ideologies of gender, without ever prescribing idealized models of either, suggesting the existence of multiple, equally valid ways of experiencing gender, sexuality, intimacy, and family. From the invented races, which do not experience physical sexual difference the same way humans do and sometimes experience gender on an internal level completely separate from the bodily, to the intensely intimate same-sex relationships that blur the lines between platonic, romantic, and erotic, to the non-marital partnerships and unconventional family units that shatter ideals of a nuclear family, Tolkien's world and characters are frequently and consistently queer.

There can be no doubt that Tolkien does present heterosexual marriage in a positive light, fail to depict any explicit homosexuality, and, in some ways, uphold traditional gender ideologies. At the same time, however, both *The Lord of the Rings* and the other stories in the surrounding legendarium include an incredible number of characters who defy heteronormative expectations and entire peoples who present gender and sex in ways that conform neither with the idea of a strict gender binary nor with contemporary Western ideologies of gender presentation and biological sexual difference.

Depictions of Gender

Contemporary Western culture has strict ideologies of gender that our entire social system works to uphold. Women are expected to look, present, and behave in particular ways, and men in others; and those who do not conform to these conventions are often punished: see, for example, the multiple cases of cisgender women who have been harassed in public bathrooms because they do not look traditionally feminine enough (Lopez; Letters Editor; Wiggins). Mainstream fiction also frequently serves to reinforce these ideologies by presenting women and men in ways that uphold those standards.

Conversely, Tolkien's Middle-earth stories present a multitude of different ways of embodying gender. In his article "Mapping Gender in Middle-earth," John Miller posits that there are "different ways of being masculine suggested by the characteristics of the different 'races' of Middle-earth.... The other races of Middle-earth represent alternatives to the version of masculinity embodied in the race of Men" (136). I agree with Miller, and I would further argue that Tolkien's world-building also provides alternative versions of femininity.

Tolkien's non-normative approach to gender is perhaps most evident in the beards of Dwarf women. In the real world, although there are cisgender women who grow beards, facial hair is still seen as a mark of maleness and masculinity. In Tolkien's world, this is immediately subverted by the fact that all Dwarves grow beards, regardless of gender (*The War of the Jewels* [*WJ*] 205). Tolkien also notes that Dwarf women are almost indistinguishable from Dwarf men (*WJ* 205, 211). Similarly, the Elves also display a surprising lack of sexual difference. They do not grow beards at all, whether they are male or female.[2] Regardless of sex, they wear their hair long,[3] and elaborate hairstyles appear to be normative: see, for example, Fingon, who "wore his long dark hair in great plaits braided with gold" (*The Peoples of Middle-earth* [*Peoples*] 345) and the Wood-Elves of Mirkwood, whose "gleaming hair [is] twined with flowers" (*The Hobbit* [*H*], viii, 191). It might be tempting to claim that the sturdy, bearded Dwarves are universally masculine while the beautiful, smooth-cheeked, long-haired Elves are universally feminine, but those terms cannot even be applied to these peoples who have fundamentally different experiences of sexual difference and gender presentation.

Hobbits are also presented as androgynous to a certain degree. Regardless of sex, they have high voices and beardless faces, and within Hobbit culture, masculinity and femininity are not presented as altogether distinct. Bilbo Baggins, when we first meet him in his comfortable Hobbit-hole, is doing a fine job of performing the masculinity expected of a Hobbit, and that masculinity includes lots of pantries (*H*, i, 12) stocked with cakes that he bakes himself (20), along with "whole rooms devoted to clothes" (12). The Hobbit ideal of masculinity is decidedly domestic and appears to include no physical prowess. Adventures, while not respectable, seem to be offered and decried with equal opportunity, or at least they were in the past: Bilbo's mother, but not his father, had adventures in her youth (13), and Gandalf was known to spirit off both "lads and lasses ... into the Blue for mad adventures" (17). Although Hobbits do evidently have an idea of a gender binary, and the only Hobbit women we ever meet are in traditionally feminine roles, its power over them is unclear. When a Gondor guard refers to Pippin as a man, he indignantly replies, "Man! Indeed not! I am a hobbit" (*The Return of the King* [*RK*], V, i, 8). This rejection of the label "man" is particularly important when we note the prophecy that no "living man" can hinder the Witch-king (*RK*, V, vi, 129). He is killed by Éowyn/Dernhelm and Merry—neither of whom is a man. Here we have two different ideas of what it means to be a man: species and gender. Dernhelm and Merry might each call the other a man, but neither would identify as such. The Rohirrim want to leave behind everyone not-man, but it is specifically the not-men, maybe-men, depending-on-definition-men who defeat the lord of the Nazgûl.

Certain of Tolkien's invented races disrupt gender essentialism on an even deeper level than just their physical attributes. In both the Elves and the Ainur, he explores the idea that biological sex and gender identity are separate: "*fëar* [spirits] of the Elves are of their nature male and female, and not their *hrondor* [bodies] only" (*Morgoth's Ring* [*Morgoth*] 227). By making it clear that gender lies not in the body, Tolkien breaks with gender essentialism and leaves open the possibility of transgender Elves. I would argue that the phrasing male *and* female, not male *or* female, also allows the possibility of non-binary and intersex Elves. In fact, in one of his earliest Elven languages, Tolkien created the word "gwegwin" to mean "hermaphrodite" ("The Gnomish Lexicon" 44). Evidently, he did imagine intersex Elves and deliberately included them in his language, eschewing with a biological sexual binary.

The Ainur, meanwhile, are essentially bodiless, although they can take on a physical form if they choose, and they have an innate, internal, non-bodily sense of gender. If they choose to take on a physical body, then they "take upon them forms some as of male and some as of female; for that difference of temper they had even from their beginning, and it is but bodied forth in the choice of each, not made by the choice" (*The Silmarillion* [*S*] 11). They can take any shape they choose, or no shape at all, and are not bound by any sexual binary. For example, the Vala Yavanna at times takes the form of a woman, "but at times she takes other shapes. Some there are who have seen her standing like a tree under heaven" (*S* 18). There is endless possibility of Ainur whose "temper" is non-binary or fluid, and as with Elves, this separation of gender from biology leaves open those possibilities.

Even among races that seem, on the surface, to inhabit gender in blatantly traditional ways, the truth is more complex. The Orcs, for example, are consistently presented as hypermasculine and are associated, though obliquely, with sexual violence (Chance, 290). This characterization casts light on the intersection between ideologies of gender and ideologies of race. When Orcs are described, they are "sallow," "swarthy," or "black," and their features are racist caricatures; note, for example, the tracker described as "black-skinned, with wide and snuffling nostrils" (*RK*, VI, ii, 237).[4] The ways Orcs are gendered align very closely with real-world stereotypes of racialized, and particularly Black, men: they are dangerous, sexualized, and above all violently hypermasculine.[5]

Yet I would argue that for Orcs, like for Tolkien's other invented peoples, gender is more complex than it first appears. Despite the seemingly universal masculinity of the Orcs, there must be Orc women. Tolkien notes that Orcs "multipl[y] after the manner of the Children of Ilúvatar" (*S* 47) and stated in a letter that "[t]here must have been orc-women" ("Letter to Mrs. Munby"). So where are they? Certainly when Mordor empties of Orcs towards the end of *The Return of the King*, it does not appear that half of them remain behind to wait for the menfolk to return from battle. Either the women are kept somewhere completely separate, far away from the legions of Orcs who have been living in and around Mordor, or else they have been there the whole time, unrecognized by the narrators. Orcs are referred to sometimes as "he" and sometimes as "it," indicating narrative uncertainty about which pronouns are appropriate. Is it not possible that all Orcs, much like Dwarves, appear masculine to those of other species?

There is evidence of narrative unreliability regarding the Orcs in other areas. The characters appear to view them as universally evil, but there are aspects of the narrative that belie that. The few glimpses we see of Orc culture demonstrate a more nuanced picture, particularly the conversation between Shagrat and Gorbag at the end of *The Two Towers* (*TT*).[6] The two Orcs do not want to serve Sauron, and they know that no matter which side wins the war, they are going to suffer (*TT*, IV, x, 433). Similarly, the Orcs of Moria are loyal to neither Sauron nor Saruman and refuse to follow their orders, motivated instead by a desire to avenge for their slaughtered kin (*TT*, IV, iii, 48–49). Likewise, in *The Hobbit*, Bolg leads his people to the Battle of Five Armies to avenge his father (xvii, 336). Orcs, like all the other peoples of Middle-earth, evidently have families they care for. Yet the heroes of the narrative do not treat them like another sentient race with emotions, culture, and society deserving of life and respect; rather, they are killed with impunity and hunted like animals. There are evidently gaps between how the heroes view Orcs and the experience of the Orcs themselves, and the gender ambiguity is one clear sign of this, highlighting the ways that perceptions of gender can influence and be influenced by perceptions of race, and how both can influence perceived morality. Tolkien has provided openings into a more sensitive and layered understanding of Orcs, though he never fully explores them.[7] Orcs thus present yet another alternative relationship with gender—one that is so foreign as to be abhorrent to the biased narrators, but is ultimately full of potential for readers.

There is, of course, one race in Middle-earth that is presented as having an extremely rigid and essentialist sex and gender binary: the Ents and Entwives. Each group appears to have distinct characteristics that are universal for the entire gender, at least according to Treebeard. Besides that, the female Ents are completely absent, and there appears to have been no contact between Ents and Entwives for thousands of years. It is important to remember, however, that they were originally sundered specifically because they adhered so very firmly to distinct gender roles. There was not a single Entwife who chose to go wandering instead of planting gardens, and (to our knowledge) not a single Ent who chose to stay with them. Ernelle Fife argues that:

> Because the Ents and Entwives are separated ... neither can withstand evil ... the Ents and Entwives lose their lands because they no longer combine forces to protect them.... Perhaps if the Entwives were still part of this story, the story would have been a different one. Perhaps Ents and Entwives would have already defeated Saruman, or at least limited his evil influences [150].

This strict division of gender, and strict assignment of personality traits based solely on sex, is a tragedy. As Edith Crowe points out in her landmark essay "Power in Arda," Tolkien "recognizes the interdependence of male and female, and suggests repeatedly that to ignore one at the expense of the other is a grave mistake which at the very least diminishes the individual and at the worst can lead to disaster for both the individual and society" (273–74). The fate of the Ents and Entwives can therefore be read as a warning against gender essentialism.

Taken as a whole, Tolkien's invented races dismantle the idea of a rigid gender binary. To contemporary Western culture, a Dwarf woman with a beard would seem gender-non-conforming, but within her own culture she isn't at all; likewise, an Elven man with long hair, smooth cheeks, and jewelry is performing his gender perfectly, within his race and culture. In Tolkien's world, sex and gender are separate categories, and there are countless ways of embodying each.

Depictions of Sexuality

Just as Tolkien presents multiple models of gender, he also engages with alternative approaches to sexuality that challenge compulsory heterosexuality. Although there is no explicit homosexuality, we must remember Alexander Doty's assertion that "[i]t is arrogant to insist that all non-blatantly queer-coded characters must be read as straight—especially in cases … where all we have is narrative silence on the subject of certain characters' sexuality" (12). There is a great deal of narrative silence surrounding sex and sexuality in Tolkien's works, but there are several same-sex relationships that defy heterosexual expectations regardless of whether or not we read them as erotic. Notably, these relationships exist among both protagonists and antagonists. I want to begin this section by acknowledging one male character who develops intense bonds with other male characters in ways that are predatory, manipulative, and altogether disruptive to the world order: Sauron.

Sauron's trajectory as a villain begins when he is seduced by an even more powerful male figure:

> In the beginning of Arda Melkor seduced [Sauron] to his allegiance, and he became the greatest and most trusted of the servants of the Enemy, and the most perilous, for he could assume many forms, and for long if he willed he could still appear noble and beautiful [*S* 341].

Sauron comes to serve Morgoth, whom he "adore[s]" (*Morgoth* 420), with obsessive devotion that lasts even after Morgoth's overthrow. In *The Return of the King*, Gandalf says that Sauron is "but a servant or emissary" (*RK*, V, ix, 178), implying that Sauron continues to act as a servant of Morgoth more than six thousand years after the latter's defeat. Morgoth's original seduction eventually turns Sauron himself into a seducer who lures other male characters into evil (and more explicitly queer) relationships.

In the Second Age, Sauron becomes a clear example of the archetypal queer villain. He demonstrates a pattern of taking on a fair body and seducing powerful male figures to achieve his ends:

While Sauron is described as both "the greatest" and "the most perilous" of Morgoth's servants, this peril comes from the way "he could assume many forms," especially those of beauty and nobility. In other words, Sauron is dangerous mainly because he can manipulate his appearance, speech, and intentions in ways that conceal his true purpose, thus carrying on the tradition of seduction that Morgoth initiated with him [Alberto 8].

This behavior begins in earnest upon Morgoth's defeat, when Sauron is apprehended by the Maia Eönwë. Instead of attempting to continue fighting, Sauron chooses a different method to win his freedom: "When Thangorodrim was broken and Morgoth overthrown, Sauron put on his fair hue again and did obeisance to Eönwë" (*S* 241). This strategy establishes the modus operandi that we will see from Sauron throughout the Second Age: he does not succeed through strength of arms, but rather by taking on a beautiful form and flattering a powerful male figure.

I would argue that Sauron's relationships with both Celebrimbor and Ar-Pharazôn are openly coded as homoerotic. When he seduces the Elves of Eregion, including Celebrimbor, he does so by taking on "the fairest form that he could contrive" (*Unfinished Tales* [*UT*] 236). Then, when Celebrimbor learns the truth about Sauron's intentions, he hides the Rings of Power, and Sauron kills him: "In black anger [Sauron] turned back to battle; and bearing as a banner Celebrimbor's body hung upon a pole, shot though with Orc-arrows" (*UT* 238). This image of a male figure strung up and pierced full of arrows is clear Saint Sebastian iconography.

Saint Sebastian is a Christian martyr who was tied to a pole and shot through with arrows. The image of the near-naked saint pierced by arrows, which is a staple of Christian art, became a well-recognized symbol of male homosexuality, and "[w]ith impassioned if veiled enthusiasm, late–Victorian writers ... submitted to images of St. Sebastian as a coded means of articulating same-sex desire" (Kaye 291). The parallels with Celebrimbor are self-evident. He is beguiled by a fair male figure who shares dangerous secrets, and he ends up on a pole, shot through with arrows. As a Catholic, Tolkien would have known the iconography, and as a distinguished scholar of the arts, it is likely that he would have understood the cultural significance thereof.

Sauron goes on to seduce the human king Ar-Pharazôn, assuming a fair form once again and allowing Ar-Pharazôn to take him captive: "Sauron was not in fact overthrown personally: his 'captivity' was voluntary" (*Morgoth* 404). Using this beautiful body, he "seduces the King" (*RK*, "Appendix B," 450), to great success: "Ar-Pharazôn, being besotted ... hearkened to Sauron; and he began to ponder in his heart how he might make war upon the Valar" (*S* 329). This language, especially directly following the overt use of Saint Sebastian iconography, is heavily erotically coded.

As he is the main villain of *LotR* and an important villain in Tolkien's later writing about the First and Second Ages of Arda, for Sauron to be so blatantly queer-coded does, in many ways, reinforce homophobic ideologies. But like the gendering of Orcs and Ents, Sauron's queerness is more nuanced than it first appears. He is a villainous character, but his queerness is not always depicted as such. His ability to "admire" Morgoth is described as "a shadow of good" within him (*Morgoth* 398), and his time in Eregion is the closest he comes to redemption, as he works with the Elves in a genuine attempt to heal the world. Tolkien emphasized that at that point in time, Sauron possessed "fair motives: the reorganizing and rehabilitation of the ruin of Middle-earth" (*Letters 1*, Letter #131).

Moreover, Sauron's coded queerness, present primarily in texts that Tolkien did not complete and publish in his lifetime, must be read in balance with the more positive depictions of same-sex intimacy in his published works—the most obvious being that between Frodo Baggins and Samwise Gamgee. Their relationship is deeply intimate, both emotionally and physically, and involves hand-holding, kissing, and sleeping in each other's arms. It is in fact explicitly depicted as a form of pair bonding when Sam defends Frodo against Shelob like "some desperate small creature ... that stands above its fallen mate" (*TT*, IV, x, 420). Whether or not we read the relationship between Frodo and Sam as erotic, there exists between them a deep love and tenderness that is often manifest through physical intimacy. This topic has been discussed at length by other scholars (Craig, Smol, Vaccaro, among others), so I will not beleaguer the point. Instead, I would like to call on Audre Lorde's seminal essay "Uses of the Erotic," which explores the power and possibility of multiple, fluid types of intimacy and passion that are not reduced to or dependent on sex, celebrating "the power which comes from sharing deeply any pursuit with another person" because "[t]he sharing of joy, whether physical, emotional, psychic, or intellectual, forms a bridge between the sharers" (89). What we see between Frodo and Sam is precisely this deep intimacy that does not rely on sex for meaning (though it can leave open the possibility of sex, as Lorde's conception of the erotic can, but does not necessarily, fuel sexual desire).

Despite the lack of explicit homosexuality, Tolkien presented same-sex characters engaged in deeply emotionally and physically intimate relationships that blur the lines of the platonic, amorous, and erotic. For Tolkien, there are multiple ways of experiencing intimacy, and it is not constrained to the realm of the heteronormative. As David Craig argues, "The intimacy and love between Frodo and Sam is the moral and emotional heart of the story which is capable of saving the world from evil" (17).

Same-sex intimacy is one of the most identifiable ways of disrupting normative ideologies of sexuality, but it is far from the only one. Throughout his writing, Tolkien consistently undermines compulsory amatonormativity—that is, the "assumptions that a central, exclusive, amorous relationship is normal for humans, in that it is a universally shared goal, and that such a relationship is normative, in that it *should* be aimed at in preference to other relationship types" (Brake 88). This phenomenon is widespread in Western culture, but that is not exclusively the case in Middle-earth. Many of Tolkien's heroes have no interest in sexual or romantic pair bonding at all. By making this lack of interest in marriage such a fundamental part of his world, and by frequently presenting it in a positive light, Tolkien obliquely criticizes compulsory amatonormativity. As with gender, there is in Tolkien no default way of approaching marriage and relationships.

The queerness of Tolkien's heroes begins with his first published novel, *The Hobbit*. Notably, although Bilbo brings home treasure from his adventures, he does not bring home a bride. As Derek Pacheco notes, this "ending is a happy one, but it is not the sort of fairytale ending we are trained to expect" (263). Nor is it an ending that the other Hobbits expect or understand: in the very first version of "A Long-Expected Party," the narrator states that Bilbo's neighbors "would have been less surprised if he had come back with a wife" (*The Return of the Shadow* 17). As he does not, he finds that he has "lost his reputation" and is "held by all the hobbits of the neighborhood to be 'queer'" (*H*, xix, 363). Yet Bilbo is "quite content" (363), remaining unpartnered and spending his fortune on "the pleasures of queer, that is, non-heteronormative, non-familial, excess" (Pacheco 263). By remaining unmarried, Bilbo disrupts the cisheteronormative culture of the Shire, which is characterized by "large families" amid which Bilbo and Frodo are "as bachelors very exceptional" (*The Fellowship of the Ring* [*FR*], "Concerning Hobbits," 9).

Likewise, in *The Silmarillion*, Haleth, chief of the Haladin, refuses to wed (*S* 170). Unlike Bilbo's, her decision is left uncriticized. Her nephew becomes the next chief, and her lack of a direct heir never has negative repercussions for her or for her people. Even among the Valar, marriage is not an option chosen by all. Both Ulmo and Nienna remain unpartnered, and this is not presented as a source of surprise or disruption. They are both forces of good, untainted by any evil: Ulmo is the Vala who most aids the Elves during their long war with Melkor, while Nienna collaborates with Yavanna to make the Two Trees, and "all those who wait in Mandos cry to her, for she brings strength to the spirit and turns sorrow to wisdom" (19). For the Valar, unlike for Hobbits, remaining unpartnered is not negative or destabilizing. The same is true of Dwarves, for whom marriage is in fact very uncommon: "save their kings and chieftains few Dwarves ever wed" (*Jewels* 205).[8]

Tolkien's writing can certainly not be read as anti-marriage, but it can be read as anti-*compulsory* marriage. Beyond providing examples of characters who do not desire marriage, Tolkien also demonstrates the wide-scale negative repercussions that compulsory amatonormativity can have. Tar-Ancalimë, the first Ruling Queen of Númenor, is one such example. Ancalimë's father Aldarion shows great reluctance to marry. He undergoes extreme pressure from his father, Tar-Meneldur, until he finally agrees to wed Erendis. Rosenthal notes that "[o]nce they are engaged, Meneldur is astonished that Aldarion waits for three years and more, implying criticism of his son's lack of libido" (Rosenthal 41). Aldarion's lack of interest in marriage is seen as strange and disruptive in his culture, much like Bilbo's is in the Shire. And after their eventual marriage, Aldarion's feelings and desires do not change: he is still more interested in voyaging than he is in his wife, and he leaves for long stretches of time. This traveling leads Erendis to withdraw from the court and live exclusively among women, refusing to spend the night with Aldarion when he finally does come to visit (*UT* 197).

Their daughter, Ancalimë, learns in turn from her mother that "[a]ll things were made for [men]'s service ... women for their body's need, or if fair to adorn their table and hearth" (*UT* 207). As a result, she, like her father, is extremely reluctant to marry, which "wreaks political havoc" (Rosenthal 41). Eventually she does consent to wed, because she needs to produce an heir, but she scorns her husband and forbids her maidservants to marry. This culture that insists on marriage and demands a legitimate biological heir leads to both Aldarion and Ancalimë entering into unhappy, unwanted marriages. The strife between Aldarion and his wife and Ancalimë and her husband cause political instability, destabilizing the monarchy and the society at large. To demand that people, even leaders or deities, seek marriage and biological children against their will is presented as dangerous and disruptive through generations in Tolkien's stories, while those who choose not to marry—even if it means leaving no direct heir—are celebrated.

Non-Normative Family Units

This celebration of those who remain voluntarily unpartnered is perhaps clearest in the non-conventional families that flourish in Tolkien's writing. Aldarion and Ancalimë are both made to marry because of the need to produce an heir. Bilbo, on the other hand, avoids this problem by making a family for himself, one that is by Shire standards—and contemporary Western standards—non-normative: he adopts an heir. This choice is controversial, given that Hobbits place a great deal of importance on blood relationships (*FR*, "Concerning Hobbits," 10). It is certainly seen as controversial by the other Hobbits, and the opening pages of *The Fellowship of the Ring* are devoted to a discussion in the local pub about Bilbo's adoption of Frodo, whether or not Frodo really counts as a Baggins, and how it must have been a terrible shock for Bilbo's would-be biological heirs, the Sackville-Bagginses. But ultimately this disruption is positive, because Bilbo's non-normative adoptive family of bachelors is the only reason the Ring is destroyed.

One of the key structures upholding compulsory cishetero amatonormativity is the heterosexual nuclear family. Seifert notes that:

> As forms of resistance to the heteronormative order, queer genders and sexualities aim to destabilize the binaries (such as masculine-feminine, heterosexual-homosexual, dominant-submissive, active-passive) that are so central to upholding normative categories. Queer erotic and affective relationships also contest the privilege granted to the nuclear heterosexual family unit and seek to expand the spectrum of relational arrangements. If there are no such things as a natural gender and a natural sexuality, then affective and kinship relationships are likewise not determined by any natural order [16].

As seen above, pursuit of life partnership is not the default in Middle-earth. Even when it is present, however, it does not necessarily take place between two sexual and romantic partners. Throughout the stories in the legendarium, Tolkien presents multiple options of family structures and partnerships.

Upon Frodo and Sam's return to the Shire, their intimacy evolves to include Rose Cotton. When Frodo asks Sam to move into Bag End with him, Sam feels "torn in two" at the prospect of choosing between Frodo and Rose (*RK*, VI, ix, 370). He assumes that any family arrangement he pursues must be with a single partner. Frodo, however, immediately suggests that the three of them live together. Why should we, as readers, assume that the emotional and physical intimacy that grew between Frodo and Sam on their quest has ended simply because a third person joins their family? If they want to live together, surely that is an indication that they want to continue that intimacy. Nor does Rose appear to have any objections to this arrangement—indeed, Sam notes that both he and Rose decided together to name their first child "Frodo" in his honor (*RK*, VI, ix, 371). When they ultimately decide against that name because the baby is a girl, Frodo is the one who names her, specifically choosing "a flower name like Rose," a moment that indicates not only how integrated he is in their family but also his respect for Sam's wife. This sentiment is reinforced by the fact that Frodo makes them his heirs and chooses the names for their next four children as well (*RK*, VI, ix, 376).

Ultimately, Frodo cannot remain in the Shire, and Sam does not feel that he can leave yet, but he is heartbroken when Frodo departs—and, as we learn in the appendices, he eventually does follow Frodo across the sea (*RK*, "Appendix B," 470). I do not mean to subordinate Sam's love for Rose and the family that he builds with her, but rather to demonstrate that this relationship, between Frodo and Sam and all three of them, whether or not it includes sex, transcends any concept of heterosexual amatonormativity and presents a beautiful model of a nontraditional family unit.

This type of non-normative family appears repeatedly: Beleg's unfailing devotion to Túrin; Maedhros and Maglor, brothers raising foundling children; Beorn with his family of animal companions; the list goes on. Perhaps the most obvious other example is Legolas and Gimli's non-marital partnership. Following the destruction of the Ring, the two remain together for the rest of their lives and share their cultures with each other, visiting both the Glittering Caves and Fangorn Forest together (*RK*, VI, vi, 309). Ultimately, Gimli is said to have gone with Legolas across the sea, a decision attributed to the "great love" that has developed between them (*RK*, "Appendix A," III, 447). Appendix A notes that "[i]f this is true, then it is strange indeed: that a Dwarf should be willing to leave Middle-earth for any love, or that the Eldar should receive him." The strangeness is perhaps understated. Gimli is mortal, and mortals are not allowed to enter the realm beyond the sea. The only exceptions to that rule have been the Ringbearers, because of the burden they bore and the service they rendered, and Tuor, who is allowed only because he marries an Elf (*S* 294). We do not see between Legolas and Gimli the physical tenderness that exists between Frodo and Sam, but we do see them elevate friendship to the level usually reserved for romance: lifelong partnership and mutual commitment that stretches beyond the edges of the world and into immortality.[9]

A footnote in *The Nature of Middle-earth* (*Nature*) specifically discusses the relationship between friendship and marital love among Elves, explaining that in Quenya (one of Tolkien's invented Elven languages), there is no distinction between friendship and romantic or sexual love:

> *Love*, which Men might call "friendship" … is represented by √*mel*. This was primarily a motion of inclination of the *fëa* [spirit], and therefore could occur between persons of the same sex or different sexes.… Such persons were often called *melotorni* "love-brothers" and *meletheldi* "love-sisters."
>
> The "desire" for marriage and bodily union was represented by √*yer*; but this element was … seldom used except to describe occasions of its dominance

in the process of courting and marriage. The feelings of lovers desiring marriage, and of husband and wife, were usually described by √*mel*. This "love" remained, of course, permanent after the satisfaction of √*yer* [20, note 2].

Tolkien thus draws no distinction between love between friends and love between spouses. Sexual desire is held apart, but romantic and platonic love appear to be one and the same, and √*mel* between Elves of the same gender is such an important part of the culture that there are specific Quenya words to describe it.[10] Assuming that these concepts are known also to Sylvan and Sindarin Elves, Legolas's love for Gimli is unusual not for its intensity or for the gender of its recipient, but only because it exists between an Elf and a Dwarf rather than between two Elves. Likewise, Beleg's love for Túrin and the devotion between Fingon and Maedhros are not exceptional. This type non-marital love is integral to culture, history, and plot in the legendarium. It is, for Tolkien, simply another way of existing and relating to others, not inferior to marital love and the nuclear family, but equally valid and equally important to the history of Middle-earth.

Conclusion

Ultimately, Tolkien's fiction is filled with queer relationships and characters, as well as a complicated approach to gender and sex that leaves space for transgender, non-binary, and intersex characters. He presents a myriad of different ways of experiencing gender, sexuality, and family—sometimes cast as positive, sometimes negative, but always complicated and subjective. What we might read as gender nonconformity is, in many ways, normative in Middle-earth, and relationships that we might call non-normative are integral to the redemption of the world.

Although the end of *The Lord of the Rings* can seem to reinforce compulsory heteronormativity, with so many characters being shuffled into heterosexual marriages in a way that sometimes seems arbitrary, the compulsory nature is undermined by Frodo's family with Sam and Rose and by Legolas and Gimli's partnership, and by other characters who remain unpartnered. And though many of the Elves, with their beautiful gender ambiguity, are leaving Middle-earth, the Dwarves and Hobbits remain. So while on the surface Tolkien's fiction can reinforce gender norms and compulsory cishetero amatonormativity, beneath the surface, it in fact destabilizes both. In Arda, Tolkien has envisioned a world with a wide range of diverse sexual, romantic, familial, and gender categories.

Notes

1. An earlier version of this essay was presented at the 2021 Tolkien Society Summer Seminar and published in their seminar proceedings, and a shortened version was published in *Amon Hen* journal in 2021.
2. There are rare examples of Elves with beards, but they are extremely uncommon. Only two are ever mentioned by name: Círdan and Mahtan.
3. Nowhere is it stated that every single Elf has long hair. However, there is not a single instance of an Elf being described with short hair; many male Elves have long hair that is described in detail, and when they are described in the collective, attention is frequently drawn to their long hair. Note, for example, the description of the Teleri Elves who "walk in the waves upon the shore with their long hair gleaming like foam" (*Morgoth* 178) and the comment that "Finwë (and Miriel) had long dark hair, so had Fëanor and all the Noldor" (*Nature* 186).
4. For a list of sources about racism in Tolkien studies see Robin Anne Reid's bibliographic essay and online supplement.
5. See Slatton and Spates for additional research on these stereotypes.
6. For a more detailed discussion, see Robert T. Tally's essay, "Let Us Now Praise Famous Orcs."
7. See *Morgoth*, "Myths Transformed" for Tolkien's dilemma about how Orcs fit into his created moral system.
8. Ty Rosenthal argues that "[c]haracters who do not desire marriage and/or sex, even though they might, such as Boromir and Frodo, have something wrong with them" (36), and it is true that those who fall under the influence of the Ring all seem disinterested in marriage. The sheer number of characters who were not affected by the Ring but also lack interest in marriage, however, belies this argument. There is no indictment of Haleth, Nienna, or Yavanna, nor of Gandalf, Legolas, or Gimli. It is, in Tolkien's world, a neutral choice.
9. The appendix also states that "it is said that Gimli went also out of desire to see again the beauty of Galadriel" (*RK*, "Appendix A," III, 447), which offers a more heteronormative explanation. No admiration of a lady's beauty, however, can negate the queerness of this partnership.
10. Since the publication of *The Nature of Middle-earth* in 2023, this topic has been discussed at length in internet fandom spaces. See, for example, Mercury Natis's 2023 blog post which argues that by giving these terms "proper elvish linguistic signifiers," Tolkien has established them as "commonplace in Elvish culture and definitive."

Works Cited

Alberto, Maria. "'It had been his virtue, and therefore also the cause of his fall': Seduction as a Mythopoeic Accounting for Evil in Tolkien's Work." *Mythlore*, vol. 35, no. 2, 2017, pp. 63–80, dc.swosu.edu/mythlore/vol35/iss2/5.
Brake, Elizabeth. *Minimizing Marriage: Marriage, Morality, and the Law*. Oxford UP, 2012.
Chance, Jane. *Tolkien, Self and Other: "This Queer Creature."* Palgrave Macmillan, 2017.
Craig, David M. "'Queer Lodgings': Gender and Sexuality in *The Lord of the Rings*." *Mallorn*, vol. 38, Jan. 2001, pp. 11–18, journals.tolkiensociety.org/mallorn/article/view/145/139. Rpt. "Queer Lodgings: Gender and Sexuality in *The Lord of the Rings*—Reprinted with a New Introduction by the Author." *Mallorn*, vol. 61, 2020, pp. 20–29.
Crowe, Edith L. "Power in Arda: Sources, Uses and Misuses," *Mythlore*, vol. 21, no. 2, article 40, 1996, pp. 272–77, dc.swosu.edu/mythlore/vol21/iss2/40. Rpt. *Perilous and Fair: Women in the Works and Life of J.R.R. Tolkien*, edited by Janet Brennan Croft and Leslie Donovan. Mythopoeic P, 2015, pp. 136–49.
Doty, Alexander. *Flaming Classics: Queering the Film Canon*. Routledge, 2010.
Fife, Ernelle. "Wise Warriors in Tolkien, Lewis, and Rowling." *Mythlore*, vol. 35, no. 2, 2017, pp. 147–63, dc.swosu.edu/mythlore/vol25/iss1/11.

Kaye, Richard A. "'Determined Raptures': St. Sebastian and the Victorian Discourse of Decadence." *Victorian Literature and Culture*, vol. 27, no. 1, 1999, pp. 269–303.

"Letter to Mrs. Munby." Tolkien Gateway, 2014, tolkiengateway.net/wiki/Mrs._Munby_21_October_1963.

Letters Editor. "I'm a Biological Woman—Why Am I Questioned in the Women's Toilets?" *Metro*, 8 Aug. 2023, metro.co.uk/2023/08/08/im-a-biological-woman-why-am-i-questioned-in-the-womens-toilets-19301301

Lopez, German. "Women Are Getting Harassed in Bathrooms Because of Anti-Transgender Hysteria." *Vox*, 9 May 2016, vox.com/2016/5/18/11690234/women-bathrooms-harassment.

Lorde, Audre. "The Uses of the Erotic: The Erotic as Power." *Sister Outsider*, Penguin Books, 2020, pp. 53–59.

Miller, John. "Mapping Gender in Middle-earth." *Mythlore*, vol. 24, no. 2, 2016, pp. 133–52, dc.swosu.edu/mythlore/vol34/iss2/9.

Natis, Mercury. "Let's Go, Meletheldi, Let's Go! Revisiting a Footnote, Analyzing Tolkien's Description of Same-Sex Love in Nature of Middle-earth." *Partners in Making and Delight*, 20 Aug. 2023, anditsfolkarequeerer.substack.com/p/lets-go-meletheldi-lets-go.

Pacheco, Derek. "'Funny Queer Fits': Masculinity and Desire in J.R.R. Tolkien's *The Hobbit*." *Children's Literature Association Quarterly*, vol. 46, no. 3, 2021, pp. 263–282.

Petersen-Deeprose, Danna. "'Something Mighty Queer': Destabilizing Cishetero Amatonormativity in the Works of Tolkien." *Amon Hen*, no. 290, 2021, 12–16.

———. "'Something Mighty Queer': Destabilizing Cishetero Amatonormativity in the Works of Tolkien." *Tolkien and Diversity: Proceedings of the Tolkien Society Summer Seminar*, edited by Will Sherwood, Luna Press Publishing, 2023, 119–140.

Reid, Robin Anne. "Race in Tolkien Studies: A Bibliographic Essay." *Tolkien and Alterity*, edited by Christopher Vaccaro and Yvette Kisor, Palgrave, 2017, pp. 33–74.

———. "Scholarship on Racisms and 'Tolkien': An Ever-Expanding Bibliography." *Writing from Ithilien*, 9 Mar. 2023, robinareid.substack.com/p/scholarship-on-racisms-and-tolkien.

Rosenthal, Ty. "Warm Beds Are Good: Sex and *Libid.o* in Tolkien's Writing." *Mallorn: The Journal of the Tolkien Society*, vol. 42, 2004, pp. 35–42.

Seifert, Lewis C. "Introduction: Queer(Ing) Fairy Tales." *Marvels & Tales*, vol. 29, no. 1, 2015, pp. 15–20.

Slatton, Brittany C., and Kamesha Spates, editors. *Hyper Sexual, Hyper Masculine? Gender, Race and Sexuality in the Identities of Contemporary Black Men*. Taylor & Francis, 2016.

Smol, Anna. "'Oh…oh…Frodo!': Readings of Male Intimacy in *The Lord of the Rings*." *Modern Fiction Studies*, J.R.R. Tolkien Special Issue, guest editor Shaun F.D. Hughes, vol. 50, no. 4, 2004, pp. 949–79, doi.org/10.1353/mfs.2005.0010.

Tally, Robert T., Jr. "Let Us Now Praise Famous Orcs: Simple Humanity in Tolkien's Inhuman Creatures." *Mythlore*, vol. 29, no. 1, article 3, 2010, pp. 17–28, dc.swosu.edu/mythlore/vol29/iss1/3.

Tolkien, J.R.R. *The Fellowship of the Ring*. HarperCollins, 1999.

———. "The Gnomish Lexicon." *Parma Eldalamberon* no. 11, edited by Christopher Gilson et al, Mythopoeic Society, 1995, pp. 17–75.

———. *The Hobbit*. HarperCollins, 1998.

———. *The Letters of J.R.R. Tolkien*, edited by Humphrey Carpenter, assisted by Christopher Tolkien, e-book ed., HarperCollins, 2012.

———. *Morgoth's Ring*, edited by Christopher Tolkien, HarperCollins, 1995.

———. *The Nature of Middle-earth*, edited by Carl F. Hostetter, HarperCollins, 2023.

———. *The Peoples of Middle-earth*, edited by Christopher Tolkien, Allen & Unwin, 1996. The History of Middle-earth, vol. 12.

———. *The Return of the King*. HarperCollins, 1999.

———. *The Return of the Shadow*, edited by Christopher Tolkien, HarperCollins, 1988. The History of Middle-earth, vol. 6.

———. *The Silmarillion*, edited by Christopher Tolkien, HarperCollins, 1999.

———. *The Two Towers*. HarperCollins, 1999.

———. *Unfinished Tales: Of Númenor and Middle-earth*, edited by Christopher Tolkien, Unwin, 1990.
———. *The War of the Jewels: The Later Silmarillion, Part Two*, edited by Christopher Tolkien, HarperCollins, 1994. The History of Middle-earth, vol. 8.
Vaccaro, Christopher. "'Dyrne Langað': Secret Longing and Homo-Amory in *Beowulf* and J.R.R. Tolkien's *The Lord of the Rings*." *Journal of Tolkien Research*, vol. 6, iss. 1, article 6, 2018, scholar.valpo.edu/journaloftolkienresearch/vol6/iss1/6.
Wiggins, Christopher. "Cis Woman Confronted by Police Officers in Arizona Walmart Restroom for Looking Too Masculine Speaks Out (Exclusive)." *Advocate*, 28 Feb. 2025, advocate.com/news/lesbian-mistaken-transgender-arizona-walmart.

Part III

Intra-Male Queerness

"For he would take no wife"
Surface Reading, Eärnur and the Queering of the Unmarried Male in The Lord of the Rings

Nicholas Birns

This essay is largely devoted to Eärnur, the king of Gondor and the last descendant of Anárion who dies in single combat with the Witch-king of Angmar in Third Age 2050. I argue that Eärnur fails to recognize his queerness for what it is and thus foregrounds the queerness of the other unmarried males in Middle-earth. Eärnur becomes obsessed with the Witch-king, as an opponent, while failing to reproduce and provide heirs for a Gondor that desperately needs them. Unmarried, and sexually unattached, he becomes fixated on his male opponent. Eärnur's queerness is not latent, but rather manifest. It is part of what Best and Marcus call "the truth to which a text bears witness" (1). This is a truth that is textually evident, but which has been "rendered invisible" by heteronormative practices of reading (1). Instead of a queer reading focusing on what the text "does not say," Best and Marcus focus on "the truth to which a text bears witness" (1). Although perhaps not explicit in Tolkien's text, I will argue that Eärnur's queerness is apparent there. In turn, Eärnur's story plays an important role in the history not just of kingship in Middle-earth but also in the history of dynastic lineages, mixtures and differentiations between people, and thus racial representation. Eärnur, solitary yet at the center of so many representations of identities in Third Age Middle-earth, is a figure very present in the narrative of Tolkien's text, but whose significance needs to be fully elucidated.

Eärnur's story is part of *The Lord of the Rings*, as published in 1955, in an appendix, but in the book, nonetheless. Though Tolkien relegates the core of the story to an appendix, it is referred to enough in the main narrative to be clearly significant for the story. For Best and Marcus, attention to the surface has special relevance to the analysis of queer texts, as often queer valences that are manifest on the surface of texts tend to be scanted in favor of allegedly deeper readings that end up anchoring a heteronormative sensibility. Best and Marcus argue that female friendship in Victorian novels is often dismissed just because readers assumed Victorian plots wanted to "eliminate lesbian desire" (7). Similarly, queerness in Tolkien may be hidden by the lures of allegedly "deeper" meanings that Best and Marcus warn may divert readers from the queer surface and tug at their latent heteronormative prejudices. Thus the apparent queerness of Eärnur escapes notice.

Best and Marcus, in calling attention to textual instances that are "evident, perceptible, apprehensible," (9), that are "not hidden nor hiding" (9), are asking readers to bear witness to queer characters like Eärnur. Tolkien's carefully wrought world presents just this sort of openly presented complexity. Eärnur is a little-known and little-discussed character. But Eärnur is present in the text just as the other characters are, even if not as frequently. Best and Marcus warn against a "symptomatic reading" (1) that privileges reading meanings into texts over meanings that are already present, what is not there over what is apparent. Characters like Eärnur, who feature mainly in Appendix A, tend not to be emphasized. To put Eärnur and the queer problems he poses on the same level as Bilbo, Frodo, and Boromir is to challenge heteropatriarchal hierarchies that would deign to determine what is central and what is peripheral. It also underscores how Eärnur foregrounds the most visible sign of the queerness of all the above-named characters: their not engaging in heterosexual reproduction and thus not having any heir.

Valerie Rohy has written of the way the film adaptation of *The Lord of the Rings* raises the specter of negatively portrayed queerness in order to distance the reader from the positively portrayed same-sex relationships depicted in Tolkien's narrative (2004). Eärnur, I will argue, embodies this split within one body. Eärnur's crisis is not just a personal but also a dynastic one. For the rulers of Gondor, dynasty, and the reproductivity underlying dynasty, are paramount. This valuing of heirs also reveals the relevance of dynastic models in exposing where compulsory heterosexuality cannot delineate what transpires in Tolkien's imagined history.

Tolkien critics have noted that there is more than one path to masculinity that one can take in Middle-earth. Jane Chance refers to the "self-abnegation and generosity" (118) of Bilbo, although she qualifies this by noting that the Ring eventually impinges on this generosity. Steven Brett Carter speaks of the "possibility of gaining honor and glory" (100) that characters such as Boromir seek. This point is also more than applicable to Eärnur, who dies in an honorable but foolhardy way.

The tragic and conflicted nature of Eärnur's behavior—not reproducing but fixating on the Witch-king as opponent—best emerges in contrast with Bilbo and Frodo and in comparison to Boromir. Eärnur undoes himself, by being, to use the title of John Mulgan's 1939 novel, *Man Alone*. In Tolkien's day, a posture of Man Alone flourished among white male writers, particularly those who had seen action in or witnessed war. But the spirit of Man Alone, as James Bennett points out, was widespread in the English-speaking world in the aftermath of World War I. This was a masculinity defined as a result of witnessing the horrors of trench warfare. Such a masculinity exuded a simultaneous attraction to and revulsion of a world without women and the female principle, a harsh, male-only world of the trenches. The trope of *Man Alone* shows frightened, closeted men recoiling from such affection. Zoë Jaques contrasts a masculinity "celebrated in acts of violence" (98) that occasionally manifests itself in Tolkien's work. Yet this is more than offset by a far more emphasized masculinity of "compassion and companionship" (98). The first sort of masculinity is still manifest in Tolkien's work, and is represented no more poignantly than by Eärnur, a man whose sexually undeclared and unattached stance informs his fixation on fighting and vengeance.

How would someone in Tolkien's era have understood the phenomenon of the unmarried adult male? Hugh Montefiore, the Anglican Bishop of Tolkien's hometown, Birmingham, England, in the 1980s, said that men "usually remain unmarried for three reasons: either because they cannot afford to marry or there are no girls to marry ... or because it is inexpedient for them to marry in the light of their vocation ... or because they are homosexual in nature..." (109). Poverty and a lack of available females do not seem to be issues for Tolkien's characters. Although the vast range of Tolkien's characters will render any sort of generalization not fully adequate, in broad measure, there are two kinds of unmarried males among the diminutive Hobbits and the big Númenórean men. One is typified by Bilbo and Frodo. They are each a Man Alone, but in a constructive and nurturing way that sets off the warrior rigidity of Boromir and Eärnur. Bilbo and Frodo fall into Montefiore's category of not marrying out of a vocation, even if here it is an aesthetic and moral vocation. They take no wife and have no children because their interests go beyond the normally Hobbitish ones of hearth, home, and inn. They are aesthetes, caring for art and beauty. Gandalf picks Bilbo, in part, because he is unmarried; Bilbo's not having settled down meant he was saving himself for some more unorthodox life journey. "Already growing a bit queer" (*Unfinished Tales* [*UT*] 323), and still a bachelor in midlife, Bilbo is ripe for a different kind of experience. Bilbo's unmarried curiosity is a direct contrast with Boromir and Eärnur, whose unmarried status is bound up with their war-born incuriosity. The unmarried masculinity of the two warriors, Boromir and Eärnur, has no connection to the aesthetic and is only altruistic, at best, in a narrow military way.

That neither Bilbo nor Frodo marries has implications for the Bagginses' succession, differentiating it from the crisis-ridden succession dramas of Gondor exemplified in the nonreproductivity of Boromir and Eärnur. Bilbo, and then Frodo, are contested by their rivals, the Sackville-Bagginses. Frodo, selling Bag End and then leaving the Shire, leaves to the Sackville-Bagginses the lordship of their family, although by this time Otho, the original Sackville-Baggins claimant, is dead. His wife Lobelia is the one who most fervently presses the Sackville-Baggins' claim (see Amendt-Raduege). But the position of the head is now—given the patriarchal nature of Shire inheritance-laws— held by her son, Lotho. Lotho is a gentlehobbit of mature years. No one who aspires to be Chief of the Shire would want to be seen as immature or incomplete. Yet he has never taken a wife and has no more heirs than Frodo does.

This Baggins' nonreproductivity leaves the very future of the name "Baggins" in doubt. Frodo, after he goes over Sea, leaves Bag End to Sam— leaving him to have the life of achievement and the role of *paterfamilias* Frodo can never have. But Sam does not change his name to Baggins and does not become the head of the Baggins family. As Tolkien points out, in *The Letters of J.R.R. Tolkien* (*Letters 1*), Letter #214 (394–8), the headship of the Baggins family passes to Ponto Baggins II, thus separating name and property. As David Cannadine points out, Britain held on to the practice of entailing estates, which meant that the property was always to be associated with the male line bearing the same surname, in a way that was "not the case in most of Europe" (20). Frodo's non-reproductive reality thus occasions a crisis in lineage.

Frodo, reflective and kind, is the polar opposite of the aggressive, warlike Eärnur in character and demeanor. In both cases, though, they leave no successor. Bilbo and Frodo represent a queerness that is comfortable with itself and does not, unlike the Gondorian warriors, seek to suppress queer affect within traditional scripts of aggressive masculinity. Edith L. Crowe contends that Tolkien depicts "attitudes toward power" (137) that are compatible with an anti-patriarchal stance. Bilbo and Frodo, for example, forsake power by leaving the Shire and their possessions, and do so without leaving a blood heir. Bilbo and Frodo are both great lovers of their *collateral* relatives. As Jane Chance points out, it is Bilbo's and Frodo's cultivation of an informal network of relatives, friends, and associates through the Shire that enables the Shire to resist Lotho (and ultimately Saruman) (116). Frodo loves not just Sam but also, after their marriage,

Rosie and their children. Frodo conjures a queer succession. The queerness of Bilbo and Frodo is thus an enabling, avuncular queerness, an eccentricity that allows the next generation to emerge. The queerness of Boromir and his Gondorian predecessor, Eärnur, is of a very different stripe.

Strong Body and Hot Mood

These characters belong to another type of queerness in Tolkien, and, in particular, another type of *Man Alone*. This type is that of the male warrior. Boromir is described as "a man after the sort of King Eärnur of old, taking no wife and delighting chiefly in arms" (*The Return of the King* [*RK*], "Appendix A," I, iv, 1083). The man whom Boromir is compared to, King Eärnur, is also described as a solitary warrior. "He was a man of strong body and hot mood, but he would take no wife, for his only pleasure was in fighting" (*RK*, "Appendix A," I, iv, 1083). Both figures are great fighters and leaders. But those traits are connected to their personal aloofness, their lack of interest or participation in heterosexual reproduction, and—most unlike Bilbo and Frodo—their disregard for the future.

Boromir and Eärnur fall into Montefiore's first category of unmarried males. Their warrior vocation seemingly forestalls their marrying. But they fall even more apparently into his second category. They evince no special attraction to women. They are solitaries. Boromir is the oldest son and heir of the Steward of Gondor. He is the pride of his father. But he was a man who took "no wife" and delighted "chiefly in arms." He was a brave warrior, but cared little for lore, "save the tales of old battles." (*RK*, "Appendix A," I, iv, 1089). Even his long journey to Rivendell is done completely alone, without even a servant.

Boromir's younger brother, Faramir, at times seems the more nonnormative. To trope on Jack Halberstam's idea of female masculinity, Faramir evinces a kind of male femininity. This femininity is manifested in a disinclination towards the assigned gender role prescribed to him. Halberstam speaks of the "excessive conventional femininity associated with female heterosexuality" (268). Boromir exudes an analogous excessive conventional masculinity. Denethor thinks Boromir is the manlier man, saying he was not a "wizard's pupil" (*RK*, V, iv, 86) like Faramir. Denethor intensifies his paternal affection such that it nearly swerves into incestuous queerness.

As long as Denethor is alive, neither Boromir nor Faramir marries women. But, after Denethor dies, Faramir feels he can operate within heterosexual canons. Faramir's courtship of Éowyn can, I would argue, occur only after Boromir and Denethor are gone. Denethor prefers the queer son,

Boromir, to the more heteronormative Faramir. Gandalf says that the blood of Númenor "runs nearly true" (*RK*, V, ii, 993) in Denethor and Faramir but not so much in Boromir. Gandalf has been understood as saying that Boromir is a narrowly militaristic Middleman, barbarian more than Dúnadain. But though Boromir at first might seem an ideal of conventional virility, in reality, his situation is very different. Saying, for instance, that not just that Boromir takes no wife but that he takes no wife after the manner of Eärnur is ostentatiously associating him with the queer.

The queer in Middle-earth is evaluated differently in different ideological contexts. Rohy has differentiated between the sterile proliferation of Saruman's Man-Orc hybrids and the reproductivity of the Sam-Rosie couple (2004). Though queerness is solicited, according to Rohy, in the same-sex affect in the relationship of Frodo and Sam, it is also made distant by associating it with Saruman's mechanical reproduction of Orcs (2004). Queerness is welcomed in a specific sentimental avatar but demonized as a general principle. Boromir is martial and non-reproductive like the Orcs are. But he is so not by manufacture, but by endemic disposition. Furthermore, Boromir's queerness is not simply destructive, but neither is it benign and altruistic like that of the Bagginses. Rohy's differentiation between the sentimental queerness of the hobbits and the anathematizing queerness of Saruman shows Boromir and Denethor in just the third position they are concerning the struggle between good and evil. Frodo seeks to overthrow Sauron. Saruman seeks to abet and, to some degree, restrain him. Denethor and Boromir oppose Sauron. But they do not hope to win, or the only victory they can think of winning is through an armed force that is playing Sauron's game. As Valerie Rohy puts it, "an attenuated heterosexuality is not akin to the absence of sexuality" (2004, 928) and Boromir's warrior manhood attenuates heterosexuality as it leads him to not marry and not have children (Rohy, 2017). Boromir's non-reproductivity is linked to the sterility of arms and a warrior ethos that can see no end beyond itself. Anna Smol says Tolkien emphasizes the "interdependence of masculinity and femininity" (234) in the characters he portrays most positively. Boromir, by his loner masculinity, falls out of the gender mainstream in Tolkien by hiding his feminine side so much.

Denethor is reproductive himself. Yet Denethor embodies in his love for his son Boromir's warrior masculinity an affiliation with the queer "no future" that Lee Edelman has asserted in the challenge of heteronormative reproduction. If there is a "reproductive mandate inherent in the logic of futurism itself" (117), this logic is even stronger in the case of a ruling dynasty. But this mandate is defied by Boromir, and by Denethor in his love for Boromir. Boromir cannot manufacture orc-human hybrids as Saruman does. But he also cannot stand aside and let others father people, as can Frodo with respect to Sam. Frodo uses the prospect of "no future" to traverse realms of beauty and to succor his friends. Boromir's life, though, is simply war, and more war.

If Boromir had possessed a boon companion, a Patroclus figure, a comrade in arms, his affect might be more overtly queer. But Tolkien gave him no such comrade, not even a loyal servant who would share Boromir's arduous trip from Gondor to Imladris. Indeed, Boromir's social conduct does not fit into a relationship like that of Frodo and Sam or Gimli and Legolas, in which, as Yvette Kisor points out, readers can see queer affect (24). For Boromir, the problem is a lack of investment. He is solitary and seemingly unattached beyond his family of origin. Boromir's only close relationships seem to be with his father and brother. Boromir is forty when the action of *The Lord of the Rings* begins. This is an age at which marriage would be expected even for a longer-lived Númenórean. Indeed, given his elderly father, Boromir's marriage is needed to secure an heir to Gondor. Dynastic marriage is one of the few cases where reproduction is more of a motive than sexual desire. Yet the way royal marriage unharnesses reproductivity from erotic pleasure also lends royal marriage an inherently queer aspect. Moreover, Tolkien needs the line of Anárion, and then the line of the Stewards, to lie fallow, for Aragorn to regenerate the polities of Gondor and Arnor. But this means Aragorn's reproductive heterosexuality is enabled by sundry anterior queernesses.

This is seen in the way the line of Isildur—Aragorn's line—goes directly from father to son uninterrupted, while the ruling line of Gondor—the house of Anárion—is interrupted several times as the kingship passes to nephews or other collateral relatives. Aragorn's line is more credible because it is less interrupted. But even a line passing directly from father to son requires the presence of female reproductivity. The breaks in the Gondorian line underscore how the dynastic requirement for biological reproduction requires men to relate sexually to women. Thus the "no future" line of Anárion overtly articulates the queer logic which the patriarchal succession of Isildur seeks to repress through reproduction. The Baggins' line in the Shire finds a queer solution to this conundrum that allows a future. The Gondor men, though, are trapped between the marital and the marital. They are laden with anxiety that men who are good at being martial are not so proficient at being heterosexually marital. Will warriors squander their society's future?

Narrative Failure, Representational Triumph

Eärnur only becomes King because his father, the general Eärnil, is the most eligible royal left after the disastrous death of King Ondoher and his sons in Third Age 1944. Eärnil has managed to sire Eärnur. But Eärnur does not produce an heir: Tolkien, in discussing why Eärnur did not marry, posits taking a wife as a matter of pleasure, not of dynastic duty. But dynastic duty is what, in a strictly kingly sense, should have been foremost in Eärnur's mind. Eärnur's father, after all, has claimed the throne despite there being an alternative through the female line. His rival Arvedui was the husband of Ondoher's daughter Fíriel and, as Isildur's heir in the North, himself had a right to the throne through that descent. But descent through the male line prevailed. Eärnur's father became king against the protests of Arvedui who points out that in the old country, Númenor, descent through the female was allowed. But Arvedui answers his own protest, as male descent prevailed because of emergency wartime conditions. And both Eärnur's father and Eärnur himself are, consummately, warriors. This warrior identity did not mean they inevitably renounced marriage. Eärnur might have not wanted a wife. But he might have taken one even if not been drawn to her sexually and never had any children. Eärnur's not taking a wife is not just one of whim but one of dynastic irresponsibility.

As long as his father was alive, Eärnur could be his brash and heedless self. But when he ascends the throne in 2043, he is the last of his dynasty. Indeed, his line is defined by its not being perpetuated. Miryam Librán-Moreno has pointed to the relevance of the history of Gondor of the childlessness of the Byzantine Emperor Basil II who gave up "wine and women" to remain unmarried "his whole life" (30). The example of Edward the Confessor, who sired no children and thus precipitated a succession crisis which brought on the Norman Conquest of 1066, would have been even closer to Tolkien's professional work even though Edward's temperament was much more like Faramir's than Boromir's. Tolkien was able to draw upon these historical kings to examine the problems in succession brought on by a male not adhering to society's reproductive mandates. When Denethor tells Gandalf that he is Steward of the House of Anárion, Denethor is saying he serves the house that did not reproduce. Since Boromir is likened to Eärnur, Denethor is also tracing his son's abstention from heterosexuality. Conversely, the House of Isildur, despite being dispossessed and in exile for a millennium, has, as its one asset, its continual heterosexual reproduction. That Denethor says this just before his suicide, and—what he thinks to be—the extinction of his line further aligns the House of Anárion with nonreproductivity.

Eärnur, the last of Anárion's line, cannot resist the siren call of the Witch-king of Angmar, now ensconced in Minas Morgul. This is noteworthy, as it could well be said that any humiliation Eärnur experienced in his earlier confrontation with the Witch-king was not due to any lack of martial prowess on the Gondorian's part. Indeed, Eärnur would have fought the Witch-king up North had his horse been willing. But Eärnur did not take the easy way out and blame his horse. Instead, he saw his defeat as a personal embarrassment, which he spent seventy years brooding over, until his father passes away. As long as Eärnil is alive, the crisis is forestalled. But as soon as his father dies, Eärnur's male warrior identity, and his uneasy obsession with a male Other, becomes blatant. He can hold it off no longer. Indeed, here seems almost an obsession on Eärnur's part with the Witch-king. This might be seen as coming out of repressed homosexual desire. The entire posture Eärnur assumes concerning the Witch-king—warrior, shield, and protector of Gondor, perpetually on guard and vigilant—reflects gender anxiety. Eärnur is so afraid of having his masculinity questioned that he holds his realm itself in the tight yet fragile grip of his being *Man Alone*.

Gondor assumes a guarded male defensiveness in Eärnur's lifetime, with Minas Anor, the Tower of the Sun, being renamed Minas Tirith, the Tower of Guard. Minas Ithil, the sun-fortress's moon counterpart, has been taken over by the Witch-king, becoming Minas Morgul. The sun-fortress has lost its moon-counterpart. This is analogous to the way that, after Arvedui, only the House of Anárion—a name that connotes the sun—remains, the House of Isildur, a name deriving from the moon, having been overthrown by the Witch-king. Furthermore, the house of the Moon has been denied its claim to Gondorian rule by the installation of Eärnur's father. This leaves only the Sun, Minas Tirith (Minas Anor), and the House of Anárion, of which Eärnur is the last representative. They are both perpetually on guard: proud yet vulnerable. Christopher Vaccaro has noted that the medieval thinker Alain de Lille linked pride with sodomy as traits to be "anathematized" (129). The men of Gondor are only defensively proud, not offensively proud like Saruman in his lust for power. Yet the proud posture of the Tower of Guard is visibly, on the surface, very analogous to how the masculinity of Denethor, Boromir, and, before them, Eärnur, is on guard against any probing of its vulnerability. The Tower, as a symbol, reflects these men: stern, aloof, vigilant, prominent, and isolated.

Like Boromir, Eärnur is never depicted as having a sexual relationship of any sort. Yet his fixation on the Witch-king seems as much a displaced homosexual crush as a fixation on vengeance. Eärnur personalizes his struggle with the Witch-king. He does not see it as in fact what it is, a particular incarnation of the struggle of good against evil. The Witch-king and even Sauron himself represent a particular manifestation of evil. To become overly fixated, as Eärnur does, on the embodiment of the representative is to fall prey to a failure of abstraction which is nearly tantamount to the sexual. Boromir's *metanoia*, his "victory" (*TT*, III, i,

404) after his fatal wounding by the Orcs may lie not just in repentance for trying to seize the Ring, but in understanding that his desire for military prowess, and the defense of Gondor as such, is selfish. Rohy speculates that the Ring represents a certain failure of sexuality to fully disclose itself (2017, 118). Boromir's desire for the Ring—or his inability to master his desire for it, as achieved by wiser men—may be also indicative of Boromir's failure to stray outside the garrison of his militaristic defensiveness. The same could be said of his city. Minas Tirith seems gendered as masculine. It is said of Finduilas, Boromir's mother and Denethor's wife, that "she withered in the guarded city" (*RK*, "Appendix A," iv, 336). Finduilas's withering occurred even though her husband loved her as much as he could manage. The city seems nearly empty of children, with a low birth rate. Most obviously, Minas Tirith, Minas Anor, is the sun without the moon; masculinity without femininity (or, if one follows Yvette Kisor's argument about the genders of the Sun and Moon in Germanic languages, femininity without masculinity [see Kisor 2004, 212]). Minas Tirith is the city of the sun, city of guard. With the loss of Minas Ithil to the enemy, it lacks the complementarity of the moon. This is an external symptom of the city possessing an androgyny it cannot overtly acknowledge.

Gondor has race issues as well as gender issues. Appendix A to *The Lord of The Rings*, parts iii and iv, which chronicles the histories of the North and South Kingdoms after Elendil, presents, visibly and on the surface, a dizzying array of peoples and identities. The three major problems of Gondor's history all have to do with the mixture, with the question of how to at once continue the bloodline of Anárion and keep it racially pure. King Eldacar's mother is Vidumavi from Rhovanion, home of a people less culturally and socially prestigious to them but still related to them ethnically. Many Gondor aristocrats rebelled against Eldacar because they saw his noble blood as diluted. Even though Eldacar eventually vanquished his rivals in the Kin-strife and regained his throne, to the end of Eldacar's years in Osgiliath, there were surely commoners who whispered of him as "Vinitharya,"—his Wilderland name. Then there are the Kin-strife rebels and their descendants in Umbar. These rebels are of undoubted Númenórean blood, as Tolkien emphasizes in Letter #347 (*Letters 1*, 470–2). Yet they represent a fundamental principle of division. This division does not truly display racial heterogeneity. As Fimi points out, the Rohirrim (and their relatives, the Rhovanion men) are elevated "to the status of Middle Men" (148). It would have been very different if Eldacar's father had married a woman of the Haradrim. Yet the presence of the Haradrim nearby in the narrative, as the people ruled by the Kin-strife rebels, raises this unrealized specter of heterogeneity.

When Arvedui's claim to Gondor was refused in TA 1944, this refusal was based on the Northern realm's remoteness and marginality. Yet it was also premised on the line of Isildur having become, through long separation, "Other." Eärnil bases his kingship on a refusal of difference. When his son Eärnur succeeds him, his monarchy is built on this refusal, a refusal so immobilizing that it means the end of any kingship in Gondor for a thousand years. Eärnur's distant non-Gondor ancestry is northern and "white." The descent of his ancestors' Kin-strife rivals, Angamaitë and Sangahyando, is pure Númenórean (as Tolkien points out in Letter #347 [*Letters 1* 470–2]). But to manifest their Númenórean purity, the latter have had to flee to the south, the land of the darker-skinned Haradrim, with whom they took refuge and whose soldiers they co-opted to serve in their armies. But there is no actual racial mixture. Indeed, the visible and tantalizing spectacle of (unrealized) racial crossing is blocked by guarded white male defensiveness.

Eärnur is only king because the Gondor elite has rejected Arvedui. They see Arvedui's Northern descent as somehow not noble. Gondor's rejection of Aevedui's claims is notwithstanding the reality that, by inheritance and his marriage to Ondoher's daughter, Arvedui is just as if not more entitled to the throne. Arvedui is thereby Othered. He takes refuge from the Witch-king in the collapse of the kingdom of Arthedain in 1974, with indigenous people named the Lossoth. Arvedui lives for a short time in harmony and mutual assistance with them. The Lossoth feel pity for Arvedui even though they fear the Witch-king.

The Lossoth feel empathy with the exiled Dúnedain, and there is some sense of communication. Arvedui even gives the heirloom of his house, the Ring of Barahir, to the Lossoth, recognizing that they are kin enough to receive this ancient symbol of humanity. Arvedui seeks sanctuary with the Lossoth, and Arvedui is able to, if admittedly only temporarily, recognize the racial diversity of Middle-earth. Even though Arvedui dies because he did not take the advice of the Lossoth, he at least engages with them. Eärnur, conversely, can only fight the dark from a rigid position of white masculinity which falls prey to the dark safe sleep because it is so on guard against any sort of gender or racial identity that is not monolithically white, male, or heterosexual. If Eärnur had been in Arvedui's place, he might well have met the same tragic end. A hypothetical death of Eärnur in the freezing North could have been for the same reason for refusing to trust the wisdom of the Lossoth when it came to the natural environment. Rather, being more of a Man Alone than Arvedui might have been not just a military but a sexual crisis. This is not to say that Eärnur—had he, not Arvedui, been the one fleeting to the ice-bay of Forochel—would have pursued a realized sexual relationship with a Lossoth man. Yet even the sort of tentative intercultural dialogue undertaken by Arvedui might have dilated Eärnur's masculinity enough for him to escape his grim fate. Eärnur would have avoided this because to befriend a Lossoth man might have made him desire that man.

Tolkien has Arvedui, who tragically dies after siring a son, be the one to have some dialogue across racial boundaries. Eärnur, conversely, tragically dies without having a son, and has no benign encounters across cultural lines. Eärnur is ostensibly solitary, queer, and white, yet obsessed with the Witch-king in a way that makes his self-expression dyadic, not truly solitary. If Eärnur had been in Arvedui's place, he might not have undertaken a sexual relationship with a Lossoth man. But experience with the Lossoth might have dilated the proud tower of Eärnur's white masculinity at least enough to keep him from falling in love/hate with an evil monster. Arvedui is individually named. Whereas the Lossoth who help him are collective and anonymous, Eärnur is named. But his abstention from heterosexuality does not dare speak its name. Racial difference is named. But it is not individualized in this world as the people analogous to non–Western peoples are only collectives. Sexual difference, conversely, is individualized but not named, as it is displayed in individual terms by people like Eärnur who are given no group identity, are not a class of people.

The genealogies of the royal houses of Gondor and Arnor display problems of racialized identity. Tolkien makes clear that Arvedui is of purer Númenórean descent than Eärnur. This sets up an aspect of Aragorn's claim to the throne. Yet Tolkien also shows Arvedui was better able to (briefly) acknowledge the multiracial reality of Middle-earth than his rival Eärnur. It would have been more seamless, or at least more gratifying, to see Eärnur, the nonreproductive man, be also the one who interrogated racial barriers, not the reproductive Arvedui. Yet individuality in Appendix A seems to vary directly with the assignment of racial Otherness. The peoples of Middle-earth who are represented as non-white—the Lossoth, Haradrim, Easterlings—may be looked down on, but they have no problem declaring their identity overtly. They are acknowledged and named, even if Othered. Conversely, while individuals such as Frodo, Boromir, Bilbo, and Eärnur are identifiable as queer, they are only eccentric individuals with no group identity. There is no chance for them to speak their queerness. Whiteness contrasts itself overtly with other races. But heterosexual masculinity is blocked from speaking to its queer others. This paradox also pertains to the world of Tolkien's England. The shock of Mohandas K. Gandhi to the British mainstream was that in him a people presumed, by the colonialist mentality, a faceless mass gained an individual voice. But the shock of Oscar Wilde to the British mainstream was that an individual acknowledged as such was associated with a collective practice of dissident sexuality. In both Tolkien's twentieth century and that of his created Third Age, whiteness acknowledged other races but tried to de-individuate them. In turn, straightness acknowledged queer individuals but quailed from noting the practice of their queerness.

Bilbo and Frodo's abstention from heterosexual norms enables them to show the Shire a more unconventional face so that it can be preserved. If, as Christopher Vaccaro and Yvette Kisor argue, the evil characters in Tolkien's world are defined by "a rejection of difference" (5), Bilbo and Frodo foster difference through their mentorship of Sam Gamgee. In doing this, they shake up the class structure of the Shire. A hundred years after Sauron's fall, there are still Tooks and Brandybucks on top of the Shire's power structures, but there are also Gardners and Fairbairns and Cottons who owe their social eminence to Sam's rise and the unmarried Baggins men's sponsorship of it. Pertinent here is Jes Battis's observation that Hobbits, as compared to the other denizens of Tolkien's world, have both "social mobility" and "ambivalent subjectivity" (908). Thus Bilbo and Frodo's queer altruism has within it the seeds of Sam's progeny. Judith Butler says of Hegel's thought, "kinship is a precondition for the emergence of the state" (20). The early Fourth Age Shire, with Sam as mayor, is a state that has emerged precisely through this queered kinship transfer from the Baggins family to Sam's family. In contrast, the cadet Baggins line, the descendants of Ponto II are not depicted as living lives of any great moment in the Shire other than as minor *noblesse*. Butler's critique, which argues Hegel was too eager to leave kinship structures behind when he constructed a dyad of individual and society, leads to the appreciation of this queer transfer as a revised and more inclusive kinship network. This network is neither of the individual nor the state. This inclusive queer transfer enables new blood, Sam's blood, to come to the fore. Eärnur, on the other hand, can be as generous to anyone not his blood-kin, as Frodo is to Sam, giving up all he has and transferring it. The Stewards do inherit the rule of Gondor. But they do not do so because Eärnur relinquishes it to them. They take up the reins in his catastrophic absence after he leaves for single queerly-defined combat and never returns.

Anna Smol characterizes altruistic masculinity as a "critique of traditional masculine roles." This altruistic masculinity occupies "a space of internal and spiritual heroism" (234). Bilbo, who gives up Bag End for his kinsman, though not his son, and Frodo, who gives up the Shire for people unrelated to him by blood, exemplify this modern heroism. Eärnur, the direct counterpoint to this, makes just the mistakes Frodo does not. Again, this may seem like asking the character of Eärnur to bear more meaning than someone mentioned so inconspicuously in the text can. But Eärnur is overtly mentioned and is apparent in the text, not just in the Appendices but in the main narrative. It is the crown of Eärnur that Faramir uses in Aragorn's coronation. Indeed, Appendix A indicates that the state of Gondor as seen at the beginning of *The Return of the King* is a consequence of the events of Eärnur's life and reign. As a philologist, Tolkien knew that minor details and references mattered in a text and mattered to its readers, something true not just for *Beowulf* but, more widely, for the Bible and Homer. Best and Marcus's surface reading is an exemplary methodology with which to read these texts. This methodology has already produced productive results in terms of queer criticism, such as Vaccaro's reading of the quite apparent love between Beowulf and Hrothgar.

Eärnur may fail on the battlefield. But in the text, his character succeeds in being enunciated, on the surface, as queer. Or we could say that Tolkien succeeds in enunciating him as such. Eärnur's opposition to the Witch-king becomes an obsession that ensnares him in the end. On a more abstract level, hyper-aggressive masculinity hides a submissive masochism. For Eärnur, his hatred of the Witch-king becomes his major emotional attachment. Indeed, albeit in a very occult way, it emerges as a form of love.

Queer solitude can bottle up desires that when released veer into the uncontrollable and loathsome. Tolkien makes clear that for the Baggins males, being unmarried is a self-sacrificial form of deliverance. Yet for the Gondorian warriors, it is a proud isolation which, especially in the case of Eärnur, dooms them. Dismaying Eärnur's failure, however, Tolkien succeeds in making Eärnur's sexuality apparent, on the surface of the text. The nooks and crannies of Tolkien's feigned histories may be arcane. But they are not invariably heteronormative. Eärnur is an overtly queer figure. His overt presence in Tolkien's world queers the nature of its representation. Eärnur's failure in narrative terms is, nonetheless, on Tolkien's part, a triumph in the representation of queerness.

Works Cited

Amendt-Raduege, Amy. "Revising Lobelia." Vaccaro and Kisor, pp. 77–93.
Battis, Jes. "Gazing Upon Sauron: Hobbits, Elves, and the Queering of the Postcolonial Optic." *MFS Modern Fiction Studies*, guest editor Shaun F.D. Hughes, vol. 50, no. 4, 2004, pp. 908–26, doi.org/10.1353/mfs.2005.0001.
Bennett, James. "Man Alone and Men Together: Maurice Shadbolt, William Malone and Chunuk Bair." *Journal of New Zealand Studies*, vol. 13, 2012, pp. 46–61.
Best, Stephen, and Sharon Marcus. "Surface Reading: An Introduction," *Representations*, vol. 108, no. 1, Fall 2009, pp. 1–21.
Butler, Judith. *Antigone's Claim: Kinship Between Life and Death*. Columbia UP, 2002.
Cannadine, David. *The Decline and Fall of the British Aristocracy*, Doubleday, 1999.
Carter, Steven Brett. "Faramir and the Heroic Ideal of the Twentieth Century; Or, How Aragorn Died at the Somme," *Mythlore*, vol. 30, no. 3, article 6, 2012, pp. 89–102, dc.swosu.edu/mythlore/vol30/iss3/6.

Chance, Jane. "Power and Knowledge in Tolkien: The Problem of Difference in 'The Birthday Party.'" *Mythlore*, vol. 21, no. 2, article 19, 1996, pp. 115–20, dc.swosu.edu/mythlore/vol21/iss2/19.
Croft, Janet Brennan. *War and the Works of J.R.R. Tolkien*. Greenwood, 2004.
Crowe, Edith L. "Power in Arda: Sources, Uses and Misuses," *Mythlore*, vol. 21, no. 2, article 40, 1996, pp. 272–77, dc.swosu.edu/mythlore/vol21/iss2/40. Rpt. *Perilous and Fair: Women in the Works and Life of J.R.R. Tolkien*, edited by Janet Brennan Croft and Leslie Donovan. Mythopoeic P, 2015, pp. 136–49.
Edelman, Lee. *No Future: Queer Theory and the Death Drive*. Duke UP, 2004.
Fimi, Dimitra. "'Come Sing Ye Light Fairy Things Tripping So Gay': Victorian Fairies and the Early Work of J.R.R. Tolkien," *Working with English: Medieval and Modern Language, Literature*, and *Drama*, vol. 2, 2005, pp. 10–26.
Halberstam, Jack. *Female Masculinity*. Duke UP, 1998.
Jaques, Zoë. "'There and Back Again': The Gendered Journey of Tolkien's Hobbits." *J.R.R. Tolkien*, edited by Peter Hunt, Palgrave Macmillan, 2013, pp. 88–105. New Casebooks.
Kisor, Yvette L. "Elves (and Hobbits) Always Refer to the Sun as She": Some Notes on a Note in Tolkien's *The Lord of the Rings*." *Tolkien Studies*, vol. 4, 2007, pp. 212–222.
Librán-Moreno, Miryam. "Byzantium: New Rome: Goths, Langobards, and Byzantines in *The Lord of the Rings*." *Tolkien and the Study of His Sources*, edited by Jason Fisher, McFarland, 2011, pp. 84–115.
Montefiore, H.W. "Jesus, the Revelation of God," in *Christ for Us Today: Papers Read at the Conference of Modern Churchmen*, Somerville College, Oxford, July 1967, edited by Norman Pittenger, SCM P, 1968, p. 109.
Mulgan, John. *Man Alone*. Selwyn and Blount, 1939.
Rohy, Valerie. "Cinema, Sexuality, and Mechanical Reproduction," Vaccaro and Kisor, pp. 111–22.
———. "On Fairy Stories." *MFS: Modern Fiction Studies*, J.R.R. Tolkien Special Issue, guest editor Shaun F.D. Hughes, vol. 50, no. 4, 2004, pp. 927–48.
Smol, Anna. "Gender in Tolkien's Works." *J.R.R. Tolkien Encyclopedia: Scholarship and Critical Assessment*, edited by Michael D.C. Drout, 2007, pp. 233–35.
Tolkien, J.R.R. *The Letters of J.R.R. Tolkien*, edited by Humphrey Carpenter, assisted by Christopher Tolkien, Houghton Mifflin, 2000.
———. *The Return of the King*. Boston. Houghton Mifflin, 1965.
———. *The Silmarillion*, edited by Christopher Tolkien, 2nd ed., Houghton Mifflin, 2001.
———. *The Two Towers*. Houghton Mifflin, 1965.
———. *Unfinished Tales: Of Númenor and Middle-earth*, edited by Christopher Tolkien, Houghton Mifflin, 1980.
Tyler, J.E.A. *The Tolkien Companion*. St Martin's P, 1976.
Vaccaro, Christopher. "Saruman's Sodomitic Resonances: Alain de Lille's *De Planctu Naturae* and J.R.R. Tolkien's *The Lord of the Rings*." Vaccaro and Kisor, pp. 123–47.
Vaccaro, Christopher, and Yvette Kisor. *Tolkien and Alterity*. Palgrave Macmillan, 2017.

"Bending over with naked blade"

The Erotics of Suffering and Male-Male Penetration in Tolkien's Legendarium[1]

ZACHARY CLIFTON ENGLEDOW

Sexuality and its presence (or lack thereof) is often a criticism Tolkien's works have faced since their release. As noted by Anna Smol, *The Lord of the Rings* has been described by literary critics as "childish" for its handling of romance and women (949–50). However, readers are often struck by the intense expressions of romantic and erotic desires between men. After slaying his friend, the Elf Beleg, Túrin cries, "O Death dark-handed, draw thou near me/if remorse may move thee, from mourning loosed/crush me conquered to his cold bosom!" (*The Lays of Beleriand* [*Lays*] lines 1351–53). These intense expressions of desire and love inform my own queer investigation into desire, pleasure, and sexuality in Tolkien, and in Túrin and Beleg's relationship specifically. While much scholarly attention has been given to Frodo and Sam, and in general to *The Lord of the Rings*, I would like to focus on the relationship between Túrin and Beleg and consider the queer potentialities inherent in Tolkien's constant revision and re-figuring of their relationship throughout his legendarium. Through a consideration of both queer Tolkien scholarship and queer medieval scholarship on sexuality, I hope to demonstrate that Tolkien presents a queer romance, one predicated upon the pleasures of hanging onto a damaged identity in which failure, trauma, and shame bind bodies together through time and even beyond narrative frameworks. This association with failure and other darker affects does not mean queer desire cannot be achieved or becomes impossible, but rather that Tolkien opens his readers up to new and often disorienting modes of desire and pleasure that exceeds erotic figurations beyond just simple categories of "heterosexual" or "homosexual."

Overall, my goal in this essay is to build upon the work of queer Tolkien scholarship and medieval theories of sexuality to create a compelling case study that addresses Karma Lochrie's argument that "[h]eterosexuality did not exist in the Middle Ages," meaning that, unlike in today's culture, there was no system of (sexual) identity in which bodies, desires, and culture cohere into a stable sexual subjectivity (2014, 37). As the trends in both queer Tolkien studies and of Tolkien's queer medievalism suggest, desire and sexuality in Tolkien are fraught with moments of unintelligibility but also passionate expressions of intimacy, proximity, and perhaps, even perversity between men. In discussions of Tolkien's portrayal of sexuality and desire, there is often an unquestioned acceptance of heterosexuality as a stable category of identity and eroticism within Middle-earth among critics and scholars alike. In contrast to queerness, heterosexual desire and relationships become represented as a universal fact without the same level of scrutiny or questioning that queer desires and relationships undergo in Tolkien's works. Yet, I cannot help but wonder, as Lochrie argues for the Middle Ages, does heterosexuality even exist in Middle-earth?

By asking this question, I do not mean to suggest that there is no heterosexual sex happening in Middle-earth, but that there is no evidence to suggest sexuality in Tolkien is a stable marker of discreet sexual subjectivities like "heterosexual" or "homosexual." While Christopher Vaccaro's conception of "homoamory" in Tolkien begins to move away from a strict hetero/homo binary interpretation of Tolkien's male relationships, I would like to further his argument and consider the full implications of heterosexuality as not a fundamental component of reading eroticism and desire in Tolkien's legendarium (1–2).[2] The movement away from heteronormativity as an organizing principle opens up the potentially queer aspects of Tolkien's works. Queerness, as defined by Alexander Doty, can describe "complex circumstances in texts, spectators, and production that resist easy categorization but that definitely escape or defy the heteronormative" (7). My use of queer aligns with Doty's definition, inasmuch as I argue that queerness exceeds straightforward binary definitions. I also further argue that heterosexuality does not constitute a significant system of identification or subjectivity in the legendarium.

Before turning to Túrin and Beleg's relationship and its various iterations across Tolkien's legendarium, I will briefly sketch an overview of queer Tolkien and medieval scholarship on sexuality and desire that dislodge heteronormativity's privilege in defining the legendarium's scripts of eroticism and sexuality. Early critics of Tolkien's *The Fellowship of the Ring* (since this was the only volume of Tolkien's trilogy that was available), considered its treatment of gender and sexuality as nonexistent or infantile. However, queer scholarship published in the recent years has done much to complicate the ways in which sexuality and desire can be approached in Tolkien's works. As Yvette Kisor takes note of in her overview of queer Tolkien criticism, two critical camps have emerged in queer Tolkien studies: "queer as sexuality" and "queer as generic difference/alterity" (18). My essay falls within the first camp and explicitly engages with Valerie Rohy's "On Fairy Stories," in which she argues that queerness does exist within Tolkien's *The Lord of The Rings* and considers how the impossibility of queer desires becomes a "scapegoat for the failure of all sexual relations" (944). However, as Rohy asserts, queer theoretical readings should resist legitimizing discourses and instead insist on queerness's impossibility. In this way, queer readings of Tolkien should own "the lack, the incompletion, the failure" that queerness signifies to ultimately liberate all forms of eroticism and sexual relations from heteronormative fantasies of "wholeness, completion, and accomplishment" (Rohy 945). While my work operates within Rohy's framework, I also address Kisor's suggestion to explore queerness beyond *The Lord of the Rings*. Despite clear parallels to medieval masculinity as well as their queer potentiality, there are not yet any queer readings that consider Túrin and Beleg's relationship in light of both queerness and medievalism (Kisor 26).[3] In this way, my analysis explores how queerness is central to Tolkien's portrayal of sexuality and eroticism within his legendarium, drawing from medieval and modern systems of desire and sexuality to mix them in often disorienting and pleasurable ways.

Disorientations: Suspending Desire, Imagining Pleasures

Medieval systems of desire alongside Tolkien seemingly present straightforward lines in terms of eroticism and pleasure. Superficially, medieval system of desire, such as courtly love, appear to correspond to heterosexuality since heterosexual romantic love became idealized in medieval romances and other courtly fictions. However, as Karma Lochrie argues, courtly love does not operate like modern heterosexuality or heteronormativity. She concludes that "[n]ot only are heterosexual love and sex secondary to male homosociality in the cultural hierarchy," they are also placed in tension within the predominance of male-male intimacies and relationships, particularly since sexual desire became increasingly associated with women, irrationality, and excess ("Heterosexuality" 56). Overall, medieval systems of desire were derived from male homosociality and did not emphasize procreative sexuality as a unifying norm, which means that heterosexual romantic love and sex did not attain the political, literary, or social dimensions often afforded to modern heterosexuality within heteronormative discourses. While Tolkien denies that courtly love structures any forms of desire within *The Lord of The Rings*, Rohy contends that Tolkien does deploy its logic to represent queerness. "It is homosexuality," she argues, "not heterosexuality, that *The Lord of the Rings* most accurately observes the conventions of courtly love as a relation structured and enabled by its own prohibition" (940). Similar to Lochrie's categorization of courtly love, Tolkien's deployment of its conventions acknowledges the possibility for queer relations to exist in his privileging of male homosociality and his eroticization of bodies through their perceived nobility rather than sexual difference.

Thus, courtly love becomes one avenue for exploring Tolkien's deployment of queerness across his legendarium as it focuses on similar medieval visual economies that encourage homoerotic identification. These medieval visual economies, as Richard Zeikowitz explores, present the sublime male body as a site of imaginative possibility in which men can explore the vulnerability of their bodies and emotions toward each other. Male readers, or other knights in romance, could either experience pleasure in their submission to a highly idealized male body, or find that same idealized body under their control (Zeikowitz 74–6). Even as courtly and chivalric texts attempt to situate knighthood as immune to erotic disruption, eroticism between men could not be fully disentangled from oaths of brotherhood as they encouraged men to find their "mirror image not through heterosexual contact with a woman, but through a homosocial union with a man whose body reflects his own" (Pugh 75). In this way, courtly love does not necessarily signify heterosexuality but rather is an economy of desire that privileges male desire as well as the desirability of the male body through an eroticized male-male gaze.

These erotic scenarios between men, which are at once normative (in a medieval context), but potentially homoerotic, reveal the limitations of modern ideals of eroticism. As Lochrie contends, "The limitations of our categories and terminologies for understanding desire and eroticism are as prohibitive in the present as they are for recognizing eroticisms of the past" (2005, xvii). Following Lochrie, we should also ask what counts as potentially erotic in Tolkien. If boar guts and green girdles in *Sir Gawain and the Green Knight*, as Lochrie points out, can be seen as tokens of desire and eroticism, what fetishes can be read in Tolkien through a medieval sensibility of porous boundaries, intense suffering, and even the very dissolution of the body itself? Vaccaro observes that queer Tolkien scholarship faces a challenge when attempting to attach a liberatory eros to Tolkien's works, arguing that even though Tolkien appreciated physical pleasure, he still scrutinized unrestrained sexual desire and pleasure (125). While queer readings can emphasize the liberating force of queer desires and pleasures in their move away from restrictive or oppressive paradigms, medieval desire—and by extension desire in Tolkien—does not always ascribe to this liberatory move but rather inheres around systems of power that seemingly re-inscribe boundaries and occlude pleasures and desires outside the norm.

By regulating queerness through prohibition and impossibility, Tolkien's works are also simultaneously and paradoxically obsessed with pushing bodies and desires to their absolute limits. Even as these bodies become transformed (Gollum), become incorporeal (Ringwraiths), become fragmented (Frodo), they never stop desiring until the absolute limits of the body are reached. Similar to medieval systems of desire, Tolkien's eroticisms do not orient bodies toward a stable fetish of (hetero) sexual desire, allowing for queer imaginings and possibilities to exist, even if those pleasures are suspended, fragmented, or fleeting. As Rohy contends queerness in Tolkien's Middle-earth, "represents desire at its most fatally incomplete and most compellingly alive, its pleasures emerging not *against* but *out of* its failure" (942). In this way, the suspended and failed actions of queerness can be a form of imaginative action insomuch as this suspension and failure allow a reader to question objects and bodies that at first appear to be stable and normal (Burgwinkle and Howie 167). For Tolkien, this means that bodies, desires, and pleasures are always more than what they seem even as they appear to a reader as normative in their use. Likewise, the erotic imaginings as presented by Zeikowitz of the male body in medieval texts demonstrate the degree to which the male body in Tolkien allows the reader to participate in these imagined pleasures even as Tolkien denies them full signification within his work.

Orc-Play: Male-Male Penetration and Sadomasochism in Tolkien's Legendarium

While Túrin and Beleg may not end up together in Tolkien's legendarium, their bodies broken and separated, this does not fully signify a lack of queer desire in Tolkien's works. After all, to be held in suspense is to be denied simple gratification of desires and pleasures, which is perhaps what is the most perverse and queer about Tolkien's works. Even as queer desires and pleasures fail—Túrin and Beleg's relationship seemingly removed from the narrative—the ultimate climax is reserved for the imaginative possibilities that elide easy categories of eroticism. Perhaps, then, the most pleasurable and erotic moments in Tolkien are those that disorient, deny, and suspend bodies and pleasures in a continuous cycle of suffering, degradation, and dissolution. Only by "giving up the body and its limits on what is considered pleasurable, can alternate and ecstatic pleasures be experienced outside the body and even outside text" (Burgwinkle and Howie 174).

As part of the three "Great Tales" of the Elder Days and a significant relationship in Tolkien's earliest drafts of Middle-earth mythology, Túrin Turambar and Beleg Cúthalion's relationship forms the precursor to other homosocial relationships in the expanded legendarium, such as Sam and Frodo, Aragorn and Legolas, and Legolas and Gimli. Set during the First Age (some 6,000 years before the Council of Elrond in *Fellowship*), the story follows the tragedy of Húrin and his family, particularly his son Túrin Turambar. While the events of *The Children of Húrin* all end in tragedy and the eventual death of Húrin, his wife, and his children, the relationship I will focus on is the one between Túrin and his Elven brother-in-arms, Beleg Cúthalion. Túrin's accidental slaying of Beleg under the curse of Morgoth serves as the initial tragedy that structures the rest of the tale and their relationship throughout all extant versions of *The Children of Húrin* carries significant narrative and emotional weight in the tale.

In his preface to the 2007 compilation, Christopher Tolkien acknowledges that the first draft of Children, "Turambar and the Foalókë" (1919), alongside *The Tale of Tinúviel* (1917) and *The Fall of Gondolin* (1916–17), would ultimately serve as the basis for the entire legendarium, including *The Lord of the Rings* (*Children* 7–9). Tolkien later abandoned this collection, called *The Book of Lost Tales*, to compose the alliterative lays, notably "The Lay of the Children of Húrin," sometime around the earlier 1920s. From there, *Children* became a staple in Tolkien's writings leading up to and preceding the publication of *The Hobbit* and *The Lord of the Rings*. Versions of *Children* were included in his 1926 "Sketch of the Mythology," the earliest draft of *The Silmarillion*, which was written as an outline to explain the background of the lays, an abridged version appears in *The Silmarillion*, and another incomplete version, the "Narn I Chîn Húrin," expands on some of the events described in *The Silmarillion* but remains incomplete. Finally, in 2007, Christopher Tolkien utilized the "Narn" and *The Silmarillion* to compile a completed version of the tale with minimum editorial emendations and additions.

Throughout all these versions, intimacy between Túrin and Beleg is fraught with anxiety, suffering, and fantasies of the degraded male body. Much like medieval knights were encouraged to imagine and desire penetration between their bodies within normative chivalric structures, Túrin and Beleg's relationship does rely on the same tension between homosociality and erotic imaginings. Even as Túrin and Beleg seem to adhere to acceptable medieval standards of male homosociality, their relationship is underscored with moments of intimacy, proximity, and perversity that reveal the inherent eroticisms in Tolkien's medievalism, an eroticism that is dependent on shedding the physicality of the body in favor of pleasures and desires that are extreme and push bodies to their very limits, allowing eroticism to be not so neatly contained since it relies on the spectacle of homoerotic encounters through the suffering and degradation of the male body.

For example, one of the most central moments to Túrin's narrative and his first recognition of Morgoth's curse is when he accidentally causes the death of Saeros, one of Thingol's kin. The mutual animosity between Túrin and Saeros is spurred by their constant competition for Thingol's affection and their own military prowess. During a feast, Túrin's unkempt appearance and his proximity to the king prompts Saeros to insult Túrin's masculinity. He taunts, "If the Men of Hithlum are so wild and fell, of what sort are the women of that land? Do they run like the deer clad only in their hair?" (*Children* 87). While the insult is directed toward women, and by extension Túrin's mother, it also carries a subtle dig at Túrin's masculinity. Saeros's insult conflates the bestial as a specifically feminine trait that Túrin displays in his own long, unkempt hair. Saeros's insult also has a sexual connotation, emphasizing the sexual availability of women in both their nudity and in their ability to be hunted like deer, which again can also be directed to Túrin's own penchant for mostly living in the woods rather than in Thingol's court. Saeros's insult then carries specific sodomitical resonances insofar as Túrin's status as a man is questioned as well as his "fell" nature linked to a feminine and animalistic sensuality.

However, this insult primes the narrative for erotic imaginings and regulates homoeroticism to degradation, shame, and violence. As much as Saeros conflates Túrin's wild appearance to feminine sensuality, Saeros's own femininity is highlighted within the scene and also carries sodomitical resonances. Saeros (called Orgof in earlier versions of the tale) is dressed in a "fine raiment" and adorned with "gems and jewels" which emphasizes Saeros's artifice and careful attention to his appearance (*Lays*, lines 458–59). His more feminized appearance also contrasts with Túrin's wild locks and "woodland weeds" (*Lays*, line 445) that know nothing of "gay jewel or golden trinket" (*Lays*, line 447), bolstering Túrin's own masculinity and ruggedness against the bejeweled and "costly" adorned Elf (*Lays*, line 461). However, also in this early version, when Saeros draws out the comb to further intensify his insult, he is described as drawing it out "daintily" (*Lays*, line 480) and the comb is called a "dear treasure" (*Lays*, line 480). Saeros's excessive femininity hints at the specific threat he poses to Túrin's masculinity as his insult sexualizes—or to borrow Zeikowtiz's term—"sodomizes" (106) the competitive homosocial bond between him and Túrin. In this figuration, Saeros's own femininity becomes weaponized and displaced onto Túrin as he attempts to discredit Túrin's position in Thingol's court.

The apparent insult to Túrin's masculinity becomes apparent by Túrin's swift response—he cracks Saeros's skull with a goblet in the *Lays*. However, *Children* presents a prolonged scenario that further intensifies the sodomitical and erotic valences between Saeros's insult. Unlike the *Lays*, where Túrin accidentally slays Saeros out of anger, Saeros attempts to ambush Túrin after the feast because of the insult to his pride. Túrin is then able to best him in combat and "suddenly [throws Saeros] to the ground" and makes him strip, taunting the Elf with his own insult that his clothes will only hinder him and that his hair will have to suffice (*Children* 89). In this moment, Túrin's physicality is highlighted in contrast to Saeros's vulnerability as the Elf can feel "Túrin's great strength" (*Children* 89). The proximity of the degraded and feminized male body actualizes the potential sodomitical and sadomasochistic underpinnings in Túrin's and Saeros's homosocial relationship. As much as Saeros's insult suggests his own desire to see Túrin in a similar degraded position, Túrin enacts the fantasy and reverses the power dynamics that Saeros attempts to construct. While the homoerotic insult sodomizes the competitive homosocial environment of Thingol's court, it also highlights the desirability of both Túrin's body and Saeros's body. Much like a reader of chivalric texts or romance can imagine the perfect idealized masculine body or submit to it, Túrin's physicality is brought to bear against Saeros's degraded and feminized body. Pleasure, paradoxically, then results from the recognition of Túrin's hyper-masculine body and his phallic sword, but also in Saeros's submission to Túrin's masculine display. After stripping him, Túrin then inserts the point of his sword into Saeros's "buttocks," following him "like a hound" (*Children* 89). The penetration between Túrin and Saeros is then an actualized recognition of the sodomitical valence of Saeros's insult. Anal sex, while highly suggestive in Saeros's insult to Túrin, is mobilized as a very real possibility between the two men, while presented as something that is perverse and sadistic.

Moreover, we know that Túrin's actions are seen as transgressive as the witnesses to Saeros's shaming accuse Túrin of "Orc-work" (*Children* 114). In fact, Túrin seems to embrace this collapse in acceptable homosocial standards, shouting, "Orc-work there was; this is only Orc-play," which further suggests the perversity and erotics of this moment (*Children* 114). As Chance argues about the depiction of the Orcs in the Peter Jackson films, they represent a "repressed sexuality, brute animality, and the hypermasculine Other" (91). Vaccaro, too, notes the sodomitical resonances the Orcs invoke in both the film and the books as their sadism and brutishness reflect the inversion of acceptable masculinity and sexuality (132). In this way, Túrin by rehearsing "Orc-play" further disorients desire since *play* suggests his perverse enjoyment of shaming Saeros through the stripping of his body and the penetration of his buttocks. Túrin's Orc-play then disorients desire in Tolkien as his "play" both acknowledges the potential erotics between men and their bodies but also denies it full signification as entirely liberating or positive experience. Through Saeros's degraded subject position, male-male penetration is presented as threatening and emasculating, but also queer as it allows for a transgression between Túrin and Saeros and the boundaries that homosocial bonds are supposed to guard against and prevent. This violent moment does recognize the potential erotics inherent between Saeros and Túrin even as it condemns Túrin's enjoyment of another man's buttocks as the play of Orcs.

Túrin and Beleg's Failed Erotics: Suffering Pleasures, Suspended Penetration

While Túrin and Beleg's homosocial bond is built upon mutual love and affection, it is still fraught with dark and perverse imagery. In a similar manner to Saeros, other men are often jealous of the connection shared between Túrin and Beleg, which also hints at the exclusivity of their relationship in comparison to their other male-male relationships. After he slays Saeros, Túrin flees Thingol's court and becomes an outlaw, eventually leading a band of other exiled men. Along the way, they encounter Mîm, a dwarf, and after one of the outlaws slays one of Mîm's sons, Túrin pledges his and his men's service to Mîm in penance. Both Andróg, a member of Túrin's outlaw band, and Mîm express jealously over Túrin's relationship with Beleg. Andróg and the other outlaws even describe their relationship as a "tryst," perhaps emphasizing a perceived romantic dimension between their relationship and acknowledging their exclusivity (*Children* 139). Mîm even goes so far as to betray Túrin to Morgoth in exchange for, not only money, but that "Beleg be left behind, bound, for [him] to deal with; and that Túrin be let go free" (*Children* 148). In a similar manner to Saeros, Mîm fantasizes about a vulnerable male body, which is also associated with his jealous desire to win another man's affections. However, these are not the only similarities shared between the slippage between acceptable homosocial bonds and the "Orc-play" that Túrin engages in to shame Saeros. Much like the perverse physicality between

Túrin and Saeros represents the breakdown between acceptable male-male intimacy and sodomy, the intimacy between Túrin and Beleg is disorienting because their relationship cannot fully shed the physicality and the erotic penetration between their bodies.

Take, for example, the shared kisses between Túrin and Beleg. While they do not kiss in the 2007 compilation edited by Christopher Tolkien, the earlier 1920s version displays several moments of kissing and intimacy, one kiss is even open-mouthed. In the *Lays*, after slaying Beleg and preparing his body for burial, Túrin "tearless, turning suddenly/on the corse cast him, and kissed the mouth/cold and open, and closed the eyes" (*Lays*, lines 1403–05). While the eroticism here carries a different emotional resonance compared to Túrin's shaming of Saeros, there is still a link between homoeroticism and the degradation of the male body. Upon seeing that he has killed Beleg, Túrin cries, "'O Death dark-handed, draw thou near me/if remorse may move thee, from mourning loosed/crush me conquered to his cold bosom'" (*Lays*, lines 1351–53)! The open-mouthed kiss becomes a moment that recalls Túrin's own longing for Death to conquer him and bind him to Beleg's body. Similar to the perverse pleasures inherent in Saeros's submission, Túrin invites an imagining of his body crushed and conquered by Death in order to be conjoined to another man's body. Degraded and shamed, the clear eroticism in the open-mouthed kiss between Túrin and Beleg is not all that different from the perverse eroticism inherent in Saeros's shaming, in which the suspension of (homo)eroticism becomes an imagined act of violence and submission between two men. After Beleg's death, all Túrin is left with is a visible mark of trauma and loss impressed upon a desire that will continue to affect him, binding him to Beleg at the point of both their lips and eventually a sword.

While the degraded male body is a fantasy object in *Children*, it is also not the only fetish object with erotic signification. The sword Anglachel functions as a fetish object that has highly phallic connotations. The sword known for its black blade becomes a significant fetish object that stands in for Túrin's body. As Cory Rushton argues about medieval fetishes, "the fetish object … begins as a synecdoche for the whole but comes to take on the force of that whole: not merely a symbol, but the object of desire itself…" (86). In this way, Anglachel represents the mobility of the phallus and the inability for queer desires to fully be contained within the narrative. Later in the story after Túrin slays Beleg with Anglachel and decides to wield it as his own sword, the Elves rename Túrin "Mormegil, the Black Sword" (*Children* 97). Inscribed with the signification of Túrin's body, the sword exhibits the same emotional and bodily responses to Beleg's death with the sword even "mourn[ing] for Beleg [like Túrin does]," which reinforces the connection between Túrin and the phallic connotations of Anglachel (*Children* 157). The sword itself becomes a stand-in for the degraded erotic encounter between Túrin and Beleg as well as a marker of Túrin's phallic masculinity. Even as the sword results in death, in sterility, as it connects to other male bodies, it also becomes a point of contact between those bodies and binds them throughout the narrative.

After Túrin discovers that he has impregnated his sister and that she has killed herself, he cries out to the sword, "Will you take Túrin Turambar? Will you slay me swiftly?" To which the sword replies, "Yes, I will drink your blood, that I may forget the blood of Beleg my master [...] I will slay you swiftly" (*Children* 256). Upon hearing this, Túrin sets the hilt on the ground then throws himself on the same point that killed Beleg. While there is certainly an element of auto-eroticism insofar as Túrin penetrates himself, it also serves as a point of connection between him and Beleg. Even after the narrative moves away from their relationship, the sword becomes a fetish that connects them through time. Anglachel as a fetish object enables a return and repetition of the moment of Beleg's death, which then allows for Túrin and Beleg to be joined together bodily even as it is denied and delayed within the actual narrative. After Túrin's death, the blade is magically broken apart, representing the fragmentation of Túrin's body and the sundering of his desire. While it may seem that queer desire fails or is left incomplete in Tolkien, we have to consider the ways in which, through Túrin and Beleg's dissolution, that bodies become paradoxically bound together in the in-between where bodies and desire fail, where the past and the present rupture much like the fragmented pieces of Anglachel.

Conclusion: Re-Mixing the Middle Ages

Desire in Tolkien reminds us of the uncomfortable edges of pleasures that stretch the male body to its very limits through degradation, shame, and vulnerability to penetration and disruption. Thus, only by leaving behind heteronormative figurations of pleasure, can queer failure and shame be read as affective and erotic possibilities that exceed modern comprehension in both Tolkien medieval texts. Throughout *Children*, Tolkien gives us a desire that is beyond a limit, an abandonment of the limits of desire and the body for a seemingly spiritual union that is predicated on male-male penetration, intimacy, and suffering. As Túrin and Beleg grapple with each other, penetrate each other, and kiss each other, their bodies become bounded by a physical intimacy that is so surplus, so excessive in its desire to come together, that it destroys the physical limits of the body and binds their bodies together in a blurring of medieval and modern erotics of queer suffering. We can see how heteronormative and even strictly homosexual categories of desire and sexuality are insufficient when applied to Tolkien's works as male desire itself becomes a disoriented category. While Jane Chance argues that Tolkien, through his re-imagining of the Middle Ages, recovers it "from prejudice, discrimination, selfishness, and insensitivity toward those different from others by means of love and toleration of difference" (246), I propose a different reading.

Tolkien does not "recover" the Middle Ages, but "re-mixes" the Middle Ages, maintaining the tension between bodies, desires, and pleasures within those systems of desire that seemingly re-inscribe normative sexualities or desires, while also pushing those boundaries to their very limit. As Elizabeth Freeman writes, Sadism/Masochism (S/M) "relentlessly physicalizes the encounter with history and thereby contributes to a reparative criticism that takes up the materials of a traumatic past and remixes them in the interests of new possibilities for being and knowing" (144).[4] In this way, Tolkien presents us with a text that remixes the desire of the past and present together, clashing in often painful and distorting ways that open up new avenues of being and pleasure. After all, is it not the point of Tolkien's work to hold on to a promise of a better future even if it is painful, even when it seems to be impossible? Tolkien presents to us a model of desire that disorients and sunders as much as it allows for pleasure and erotic satisfaction. Through an erotics of suffering, shame, and degradation, desire in Tolkien skews and disorients the norm, prompting new modes of desiring (Pugh 215). Even if that desire is painful, even if it fails, desire in Tolkien allows for these sites to be reoriented toward erotic and pleasurable moments that exceed simple categories and allow for a recognition and a recounting of medieval homoeroticisms that still exist as possible (dis)orientations.

Notes

1. I have many people I would like to thank for their invaluable feedback and words of encouragement during the early drafting of this essay. I am grateful to Stephanie L. Batkie, Gregory J. Tolliver, and Joey McMullen for their insightful comments and for reading early versions of this essay. I am also thankful to the editors for their vital feedback and suggestions for revisions.

2. Through the connection of the departure scenes in *Beowulf* and in *The Lord of the Rings*, Vaccaro contends that Tolkien was perhaps influenced by the ambiguous and passionate friendships in *Beowulf*, suggesting homoamory in both *Beowulf* and Tolkien allow male friendships and eros to overlap while leaving the exact nature of the relationship open to interpretation.

3. For additional scholarship on the queer relationship between Túrin and Beleg, particularly in fandom spaces, see the essay in this volume by Maria K. Alberto: "'and stooping he raised Beleg and kissed his mouth: Queering Canon with Tolkien Fanfiction" (189–200).

4. According to Freeman, S/M allows us to encounter the past through affective and erotic modes of desiring that refuse to conform to modern temporalities Rather, S/M engages with cross-temporal play that connects a dominant temporal modality with other historical moments and their temporalities. In this way, S/M allows the body to experience viscerally specific historic moments while also refusing these moments closure with pastness (145).

Works Cited

Burgwinkle, William, and Cary Howie. *Sanctity and Pornography in Medieval Culture: On the Verge*. Manchester UP 2010.
Chance, Jane. "'In the Company of Orcs': Peter Jackson's Queer Tolkien." *Queer Movie Medievalisms*, edited by Kathleen Coye Kelly and Tison Pugh. Ashgate Publishing Company, 2009, pp. 79–96.
_____. *Tolkien, Self and Other: "This Queer Creature."* Palgrave Macmillan, 2016.
Doty, Alexander. *Flaming Classics: Queering the Film Canon*. Routledge, 2000.
Freeman, Elizabeth. *Time Binds: Queer Temporalities, Queer Histories*, 2010.
Kisor, Yvette. "Queer Tolkien: A Bibliographic Essay on Tolkien and Alterity." *Tolkien and Alterity*, edited by Christopher Vaccaro and Yvette Kisor, Palgrave Macmillan, 2017, pp. 17–32.
Lochrie, Karma. "Heterosexuality." *A Cultural History of Sexuality in the Middle Ages*, edited by Ruth Evans, Bloomsbury Academic, 2014, pp. 37–56.
_____. *Heterosyncracies: Female Sexuality When Normal Wasn't*. Minnesota UP, 2005.
Pugh, Tison. *Chaucer's (Anti-) Eroticisms and the Queer Middle Ages*. Ohio UP, 2014.
Rohy, Valerie. "On Fairy Stories." *MFS: Modern Fiction Studies*, J.R.R. Tolkien Special Issue, guest editor Shaun F.D. Hughes, vol. 50, no. 4, 2004, pp. 927–948.
Rushton, Cory. "Sexual Variations." *A Cultural History of Sexuality in the Middle Ages*, edited by Ruth Evans, Bloomsbury Academic, 2014, pp. 81–100.
Smol, Anna. "'Oh…oh…Frodo!': Readings of Male Intimacy in the Lord of the Rings." *Modern Fiction Studies*, J.R.R. Tolkien Special Issue, guest editor Shaun F.D. Hughes, vol. 50, no. 4, 2004, pp. 949–79, doi.org/10.1353/mfs.2005.0010.
Tolkien, J.R.R. *The Children of Húrin*, edited by Christopher Tolkien, Houghton Mifflin Company, 2007.
_____. "The Lay of the Children of Húrin." *The Lays of Beleriand*, edited by Christopher Tolkien Boston, 1985, pp. 3–130. Vol 3. The History of Middle-earth.
Vaccaro, Christopher. "'Dyrne Langað: Secret Longing and Homo-amory in *Beowulf* and Tolkien's *The Lord of the Rings*." *Journal of Tolkien Research*, vol. 6, iss. 1, article 6, 2018, scholar.valpo.edu/journaloftolkienresearch/vol6/iss1/6.
_____. "Saruman's Sodomitical Resonances: Alain de Lille's *Du Planctu Naturae* and J.R.R. Tolkien's *The Lord of the Rings*." *Tolkien and Alterity*, edited by Christopher Vaccaro and Yvette Kisor, Palgrave Macmillan, 2017, pp. 123–47.
Zeikowitz, Richard. *Homoeroticism and Chivalry: Discourses of Same-Sex Desire in the 14th Century*. Palgrave Macmillan, 2003.

Frodo, Sam and the Ring of Power

A Queer Erotic Triangle

CHRISTOPHER CAMERON

David Craig's 2001 essay "'Queer Lodgings': Gender and Sexuality in *The Lord of the Rings*" seems to mark the beginning of queer scholarship of Tolkien's novels. Craig opposes the traditional reading of Frodo and Sam's relationship as an asexual arrangement based on Tolkien's observations of officers with their batmen in World War I and argues for a queer reading of the bond between the companions. This reading highlights a tension between, on the one hand, the entirely plausible explanation for the intimacy between Frodo and Sam as that of a devoted servant to his officer and, on the other, a queer reading of their relationship.[1] By moving beyond this supposed binary tension, this essay explores a reading that relies on a possible *overlap* in the tension beyond an assumption of the two ends of a spectrum. Tolkien, and the Shirefolk, frequently refer to Frodo and Bilbo (both lifelong bachelors) as "queer," but readers can understand "queer" to mean "odd" and to read male intimacy without sexual connotations.[2]

However, this essay makes a case for a queer reading of Tolkien's characters through the application of queer theory and psychoanalysis. For this essay, I understand queer/queerness in the sense employed by Alexander Doty: "to describe non-straight things that are not clearly marked as gay, lesbian, bisexual, transsexual, or transgendered but that seem to suggest or allude to one or more of these categories" (6–7). This understanding is helpful because queerness is still taboo in the novels, as in Tolkien's lifetime and culture, as it is not overtly expressed. This essay explores Frodo and Sam's erotic feelings for each other, building on Carol Bernard's Sedgwickian analysis of Frodo and Sam's relationship as an erotic triangle with

Gollum. I argue that we should position the Ring within that triangle as a fetishized object of libidinal desire.

As Daniel Timmons has effectively argued, there is no explicit homosexual relationship between Frodo and Sam. The two characters are never shown having sex, nor do they directly express a desire to have sex with each other. Any expressions of homoerotic desire in the novel are subtle, avoiding the scrutiny that accompanies taboo. René Girard provides a model for covert, or veiled, expressions of desire: the erotic triangle. According to Girard, the erotic triangle consists of three points (two rivals, one beloved). The two rivals, almost always male, express an erotic desire for the same person, the beloved.

Therefore, each point of the triangle is connected. The beloved is connected to each rival through a bond of "love," and the rivals are connected through the bond of their "rivalry." Eve Kosofsky Sedgwick summarizes Girard's argument as claiming that "in any erotic rivalry, the bond that links the two rivals is as intense and potent as the bond that links either of the rivals to the beloved: that the bonds of 'rivalry' and 'love,' differently as they are experienced, are equally powerful and in many senses equivalent" (Sedgwick 21). This means that as strong as the desire for the beloved is, the rivals have just as much libidinal energy invested in their rivalry with each other as they do in their desire. By calling the bonds equivalent, Girard places no connection in the triangle above another; the rivalry between the two men is just as important as either's desire for the beloved in terms of the purpose of the triangle. The triangle is typically symmetrical in that no link within it is more important than another. Girard also notes many examples in folklore where the choice of the beloved is secondary to the choice of the rival; the beloved is desirable not because of any trait she possesses but simply because the rival desires her. For Girard, the bonds are typically equivalent because the libidinal energy invested in each connection is the same between rivals as between rival and beloved. Therefore, in some instances, the rivalry between the two men is, in fact, the primary bond. Girard's symmetrical triangle provides "cover" for this, however. I use the terms "primary" and "secondary" here to indicate which bond came first, not to suggest that one is more important than the others. This system of one bond providing cover for another means that the overt expression of rivalry for a beloved can function as a surreptitious way to invest libidinal energy in the rival, especially when overt expressions of desire towards the "rival" are impossible. The triangle shifts the location of overt desire to a third party (the beloved) while allowing libidinal investment in the rival.

Eve Kosofsky Sedgwick questions this symmetry. She argues that Girard builds on Freud's Oedipal triangle, which suggests that during childhood development (3–6 years old), the male child and the father compete for the mother's attention. This triangle is asymmetrical for Freud because the father is physically superior, and the child poses no true rivalry for the mother's sexual attention. The child recognizes this power imbalance through castration anxiety as a manifestation of anxiety concerning the father's physical superiority. Girard's theory takes the concept of the libidinal desire triangle and applies it to relationships outside the family. Sedgwick argues that neither Freud nor Girard accounts for the inherent asymmetry created by the power dynamics between male and female characters. For Girard and Freud, the fact that a woman forms one side of the triangle does not upset the symmetry of the bonds (though Freud's triangle does include a power asymmetry in the bond between the two males). Sedgwick argues that Girard and Freud marginalize the female in the triangles "in making the power relationships between men and women appear to be dependent on the power relationship between men" (25). Girard and Freud create a dynamic in which the female point of the triangle is secondary to the bond between the men. In Girard's triangle, rivalry is the primary bond. In Freud's triangle, the male child desires the mother to arrive at the father's role; the mother bond is a means for discovering the male bond. Thus, for Sedgwick, "man uses a woman as a 'conduit of a relationship' in which the true partner is man" (26).[3] This queers the erotic triangle, as the feminine is simply an excuse for the two men to form a bond. Sedgwick understands these triangle theories as queer: they suggest that the feminine point on the triangle exists so that the men can invest erotic energy into each other while maintaining the appearance of heteronormativity.

Frodo and Sam make up two points of an erotic triangle, but the hobbits are without their beloved: the female point on the triangle. Carol A. Bernard argues that Gollum is the third point of the triangle, taking on the role of mediator between Frodo and Sam. For Bernard, Gollum occupies the place of the beloved in the erotic triangle. As both Frodo and Sam invest libidinal energy into Gollum, Frodo as a reformer, and Sam as a guard, they also invest libidinal energy into each other in Bernard's understanding of the Girardian triangle. Girard describes the mediator: "To see the truth of desire is to see the double role, evil and sacred, of the mediator" (81). The mediator cannot be "anything but an obstacle" as that individual (11), though providing an opportunity for covert expressions of desire for the two other individuals, necessarily inhibits overt expressions of desire since desire must be mediated through a third party in them. The comparison to Gollum is obvious: no character better embodies duality than Gollum, who has the alternative personality of Sméagol. Bernard argues convincingly that Gollum should be read as a gender-fluid character; however, I find her reading of Gollum as the third point on the erotic triangle to be less compelling. Bernard explains that:

> most readers see the primary rivalry in the triangle as Gollum and Sam vying for the affection and attention of Frodo. However ... there are aspects of the novel where Tolkien presents Frodo and Gollum as being linked together in opposition to Sam. Gollum, in both cases, is central to Tolkien's description of rivalry and desire. Gollum's presence intensifies the passion between Frodo and Sam; Gollum desires Frodo, and to a lesser degree, Sam. Gollum also thwarts the growing intimacy of Sam and Frodo's relationship, thus causing a disruption in their relationship [109–110].

For Bernard, since Gollum is essential to descriptions of desire and rivalry, and because of his role as a disruptive mediator between Frodo and Sam, he functions as the third point on the triangle. This fits with Girard's understanding of the role of the mediator as that of a disruptor; but if we are to argue, as Bernard does, that the erotic triangle is a means for understanding the queer relationship between Frodo and Sam, then the hobbits occupy the rival roles, and the missing role is that of the beloved. Bernard collapses the role of the beloved and the mediator into the single character of Gollum, but it is more beneficial to see those two roles as separate in this case. Though I agree with Bernard in her characterization of the relationship between Frodo and Sam as a queer relationship mediated through an erotic triangle, I suggest an alternate third point to this triangle. While there are multiple concurrent triangles in play, I argue for an additional way of understanding the character that occupies the point of the beloved in order to create a clearer understanding of that queer relationship.

There are several reasons that I shift the role of Gollum away from Bernard's placement of him as the beloved object. Firstly, the connection between the beloved and the rivals is a bond of ostensible love. Sam feels outright contempt for Gollum, even wishing death upon him. When Faramir threatens to shoot Gollum for trespassing in the forbidden pool, he asks Frodo if he should carry out the execution. Frodo says "no," but Tolkien narrates that Sam wanted to say "yes" (*The Two Towers* [*TT*], IV, vi, 363). Sam never trusts Gollum and shows his feelings to be anything but love for Gollum. Frodo is kinder to the "creature," but it is not accurate to say that he loves or desires him. Frodo is frightened of Gollum's ferocity, disgusted by his appearance so that he will not touch him, and yet he recognizes the terrible toll the Ring took on Gollum as a fellow Ringbearer; he pities him (*TT*, IV, i, 271). This pity is why Frodo pursues a relationship with Gollum, but pity is not love or desire. There is a partial element of desire between the characters as Frodo self-identifies with Gollum because he is a reminder of what Frodo could become, and Frodo reminds Gollum of his desire to be back in the Hobbit community again. However, while critical to understanding their relationship, these desires are not as significant as others in the novel. Frodo also does not have any rivalry with Sam for Gollum's affection. Sam is against any relationship with Gollum and even hopes for his death. We could read Gollum and Sam as rivals for Frodo's affection implying an erotic desire between the two, or even between Frodo and Gollum as both desire the Ring.[4] I argue that such readings do not account for the fact that Gollum's desire for Frodo's favor is actually out of a desire to get closer to and acquire the Ring which Frodo possesses or for the fact that Frodo's investment in Gollum is a pity, not desire. Therefore, though Gollum and his gender fluidity (which I will discuss later) are essential to a queer understanding of Frodo and Sam's relationship, Gollum is not the third point in the erotic triangle.

If Gollum is not the beloved object of desire, the best candidate is the novel's obvious and literal object of desire. The third, feminine point in the erotic triangle is the One Ring itself. The most obvious objection to this claim is that the Ring is an object, not a woman. This is true; the Ring is a feminine object in the novels, and it is common to invest erotic energy into objects. Gergely Nagy argues for an understanding of the Ring as an object of desire in the Lacanian sense of the word, claiming that desire:

> is essentially a *lack*: it is a tension resulting in an action, aimed at something the subject does not possess, but which is sensed as needed, either physically (like food or sleep) or sublimated into symbolic actions towards symbolic objects. These objects are signs that stand in for suppressed objects of desire, objects which for some reason cannot be desired consciously by the subject without too much tension [66].

Since the Ring represents a desire, it also represents a lack. In Lacanian terms, this alignment of the Ring with desire and lack is significant. This understanding of the Ring is helpful because by arguing that the Ring is an object of Lacanian desire, Nagy implicitly aligns the Ring with femininity. After all, Freud understands the female to represent a lack (penis) for the man, which he understands to be a driving force behind erotic desire. Valerie Rohy also understands the Ring to represent a psychoanalytic lack, as she argues:

> The O of Tolkien's Ring also stands for nothing, but in standing for nothing it stands for something: the specific nothingness understood, in Lacan's account, as the lack at the heart of language and subjectivity. In *The Lord of the Rings*, the Ring figures this insufficiency as a gap or void that, meaningless itself, gives meaning to the world around it [931].

Rohy's understanding moves beyond the Lacanian lack, but still positions the Ring as means of "ordering" the world and allowing for things to be "bound together" (932). Rohy might call the reading of the Ring as a lack of phallus crude. Her understanding of the Ring as representing a Lacanian lack does not preclude its existence in an erotic triangle since, I argue, it allows Frodo and Sam to develop their relationship, and within the triangle, the Ring, as Rohy puts it, "binds them" (932).

Bernard also argues that the Ring is a symbol of femininity:

> the Ring, because it is round and offers a hole to place things through, particularly fingers, suggest femininity. Further, because the Ring does no evil outright but merely acts as an incitement to evil, it implies a stereotypical feminine method of doing evil [94n8].

The genital imagery is obvious, especially because Tolkien frequently describes wearers of the Ring with their finger "thrust" through it.[5] The Ring is also feminine because of its indirect method of evil. Understanding the Ring as a feminine object is not a significant point of contention in Tolkien scholarship. However, it is essential to understand how and why this characterization of the object works to understand how its placement within the erotic triangle helps a queer reading of Frodo and Sam's relationship.

The Ring's primary characteristic is the intense desire it inspires in those close to it. Building on Nagy's psychoanalytic feminization of the Ring, Alison Milbank suggests that this desire is fetishistic: "For the fetishist the stocking, the glove, the fur, or the individual body part becomes the focus of sexual desire in so far as it is fixed and separated off from any relation with the whole person or body" (Milbank 34). The fetishized object is something that becomes the focus of erotic desire that is not a person. The Ring is just such an object as it is fetishized by those who desire it. It is also important that, though the Ring is a powerful magical tool to be wielded, those who desire it do not desire it for what they might do with it (there are exceptions, Boromir, notably, but not among characters who actually possess it). They desire it simply to possess it, much like the fetishist does not desire the fetishized object as a means for the erotic desire of the sexual partner but as an end in itself. For Freud, the desire for the fetishized object is a means of mastering maternal sexual power; the mother's lack of a phallus vexes the child. He writes: "the fetish is a substitute for the penis ... for a particular and quite special penis that had been extremely important in early childhood but had later been lost" (5604). The fetish is a compromise between the refusal to accept the mother's lack of a penis and the reality of the mother's lack of a penis.

The fetishized object is a substitute penis that helps ward off the threat of castration represented in the female lacking a phallus. Milbank claims that this means "a deep terror of the female genitals underlies such behavior and the fetish provides a safe substitute for the risky self-giving of the sexual act" (34). The fetishist desires the object because the woman represents the threat of castration. The One Ring is related to the threat of castration; both Frodo and Sauron have the Ring taken from them and their fingers severed in the process. Sauron has the Ring taken by Isildur, who amputates the Lord of Mordor's finger with a sword, and Gollum takes the Ring by biting off Frodo's finger: two symbolic castrations. Milbank convincingly argues for a fetishistic reading of the One Ring, which means two rivals can form a bond with it, making it a viable candidate to fulfil the role of "beloved" in an erotic triangle. To strengthen my argument to replace Gollum with the Ring in Bernard's erotic triangle, I will examine the libidinal investments in the Ring that make up that triangle.

Frodo undoubtedly comes to desire the Ring throughout the novel. Though initially frightened by the Ring's seductive power, he eventually succumbs to it. Slowly, Frodo grows to form a bond of desire with the Ring, culminating in his refusal to destroy it. The reader despairs as Frodo decides not to destroy the Ring after spending most of the novel attempting to do just that. The reason for the refusal is that the lure of the Ring is finally too much for Frodo to overcome. He succumbs to his desire and takes the object for his own. Frodo's libidinal investment in the beloved is clear.

On the other hand, Sam does not have such an evident desire for the Ring. His inability to relate to Frodo's struggle with the temptation of the Ring drives Frodo closer to Gollum, causing Sam to become jealous of the relationship between the two Ringbearers. For most of the novel, Sam's ostensible investment in the Ring is related to assisting Frodo in destroying it rather than a personal desire for the Ring itself. Sam does, however, bear the Ring. After rescuing Frodo from the Orcs in the tower of Cirith Ungol, Sam reveals that after the attack of the spider Shelob, he mistakenly thought Frodo had died, and so he took the Ring from his unconscious body in order to continue the quest. Frodo begins to panic upon his rescue, thinking the enemy has the Ring, but Sam assures him that he has it with him. Sam feels the weight of the Ring and hesitates to give it back to Frodo (*The Return of the King* [RK], VI, i, 220). This momentary hesitation causes Frodo to shout angrily at Sam, calling him a thief, while demanding the Ring back and having a vision of Sam as an Orc. The narrator says Sam's hesitation is because he does not want to burden Frodo, but this is the Ring tempting him to take it for himself. The Ring is cunning and often tempts people to claim it for "noble" reasons. Indeed, this is consistent with the type of desire for the Ring that Sam shows throughout the novel. He wants the Ring and is invested in its fate because it is tied to the fate of Frodo. Sam has a responsibility to serve Frodo, but that relationship allows him to form another type of bond with Frodo. This duty to Frodo is ostensibly to serve the Ringbearer and assist with the quest, but this investment in the fate of the Ring only manifests itself through expressions of devotion to Frodo himself, not Frodo's role in the quest as Ringbearer.

Sam is only present on the quest because he refuses to leave Frodo alone. Three separate times he should have been left behind, and all three times, he manages to keep his place in the Fellowship. When Gandalf first tells Frodo of the Ring, Sam is eavesdropping by Frodo's window and demands to accompany his master on his mission to bring the Ring to Rivendell. Once in Rivendell, the Council of Elrond decides that the Ring must be destroyed and that Frodo shall be the Ringbearer. Sam bursts in on the secret meeting and refuses to be left behind. Finally, during the breaking of the Fellowship, Sam again refuses to be left behind when Frodo attempts to steal away from the group to continue the quest on his own at the breaking of the Fellowship. All three times, Sam says he wants to help with the quest, which suggests an investment in the fate of the Ring, but this bond only forms because it allows him to stay close to Frodo. Though not as obvious and direct, Sam clearly has a libidinal investment in the Ring insofar as the completion of the quest allows him to have a relationship with Frodo.

Sam is less shy about expressing his feelings of devotion and intimacy towards Frodo than Frodo is about expressing his feelings of desire towards Sam. When Frodo has been stabbed and is recovering in the House of Elrond, Sam displays affection upon seeing him for the first time since the injury: "Sam came in. He ran to Frodo and took his left hand, awkwardly and shyly. He stroked it gently and then he blushed and turned hastily away" (*The Fellowship of the Ring* [FR], II, i, 205). This could simply be Sam being very glad that his friend is all right after almost dying, but several aspects of this moment suggest a queer reading. The fact that Tolkien describes taking Frodo's hand as "awkward" suggests that this is not a "normal" interaction, and Sam's shyness suggests a tentativeness about his actions as if he is unsure how it will be received. Upon showing Frodo a gesture of physical intimacy by stroking his hand, Sam blushes, suggesting that he is embarrassed, and turns "hastily away" as if caught doing something wrong. In his concern for Frodo and his relief at seeing him alive and whole, Sam lets slip something that usually would have stayed hidden. This behavior suggests an awkward exchange due to Sam's emotional struggle, unable to express his desire for Frodo and embarrassed at his display of intimacy that betrays his true feelings. Sam's language throughout the novel is also much more apparent regarding his intimacy and devotion toward Frodo. Frodo's feelings are more muted and reserved but still present. This expression of intimacy and subsequent shame does suggest that an erotic triangle is a better way of understanding their relationship. The intimacy is there, but it must be covert, which is why the triangle is a helpful construct for the relationship.

Frodo's most prominent display of intimacy comes from a sleeping position. Though the sleeping positions of the hobbits would seem unintentional on at least one, if not both parties, we do not know whether Frodo and Sam took up these positions before they fell asleep or if they shifted into them once asleep. In any case, Tolkien chooses to represent the hobbits through this description which suggests that the positions are significant to the story. While climbing the stairs of Cirith Ungol, the hobbits and Gollum stop to rest. Gollum slinks off to set a trap for the hobbits, but upon his return, he finds them sleeping together: "Sam sat propped against the stone, his head dropping sideways and his breathing heavy. In his lap lay Frodo's head, drowned deep in sleep; upon his white forehead lay one of Sam's brown hands, and the other lay softly upon his master's breast. Peace was in both their faces" (*TT,* IV, vii, 403). This is a beautiful description of the hobbits at rest, Frodo lying in Sam's lap, allowing Sam to caress his head and chest. This is the most intimate interaction between the hobbits, and it happens away from the view of anyone else; Gollum only stumbles on it accidentally after they have fallen asleep. This is an example of the type of relationship Frodo and Sam might have had if they did not live in a world that placed a taboo on "queerness." The fact that both hobbits are at peace, even as they briefly rest while scaling a cliffside during a war, suggests their most genuine and pure desire is their love for each other. Unable to express this desire in the open, Frodo and Sam instead have the quest to destroy the Ring, which allows them to form a closer, more intimate bond with each other. The Ring provides a safe substitute for taboo homoeroticism. An erotic triangle with the Ring occupying the third point opposite Frodo and Sam makes the most sense in terms of understanding the queer elements of their relationship.

So long as the Ring exists for Frodo and Sam to pour libidinal energy into, they have an acceptable way to express their desire for each other, using the Ring, as Sedgwick would say, as a conduit for their true partnership. The truth of this is striking when the level of intimacy between the two is severely reduced after the destruction of the Ring. The rivalry bond is broken once the beloved is removed from the triangle. There are no openly gay characters in Tolkien's novels, and the characters who are called queer are held in lower regard than more "respectable hobbits" and viewed with suspicion.[6] For example, Bilbo is called "queer" for his un-hobbitlike desire for adventure and journeying beyond the Shire which results in the degradation of his social status within the Shire; he is no longer as respectable as he was before he became queer. There is no space for an openly homosexual relationship in Tolkien's world.

Though I do not wish to stake this argument on the flawed premise of authorial intent, Tolkien's reading of his novel as a "fundamentally religious and Catholic work" (*The Letters of J.R.R. Tolkien* [*Letters 1*] #142, 172) would suggest that, in his understanding of the work, the Christ figure of Frodo is not in a homosexual relationship with Sam or anyone else. With the triangle broken and the cover for their intimate bond broken, Frodo and Sam return to the Shire and, as is to be expected of post-war companions, never again share the same level of intimacy as they did when they were on the quest with the Ring. Sam marries Rosie Cotton, and Frodo lives as a bachelor before leaving Middle-earth, unable to cope with his post-traumatic stress disorder. He leaves everything he owns to Sam and leaves Middle-earth for the symbolic afterlife in the Undying Lands. Sam lingers in the Shire for years before finally sailing across the sea to join Frodo in symbolic death. With no Ring to allow a safe expression of their desire for each other, the hobbits can only be together in death. Given how the hobbits interact with each other and their libidinal investments in the Ring, I argue that Gollum should be replaced with the Ring as the beloved in the erotic triangle. However, this is not to say that Gollum does not play a vital role in a queer reading of Frodo and Sam's relationship.

What is to be made of Gollum's role concerning the erotic triangle? I argue that the Ring serves as a more fitting beloved in the erotic triangle than Gollum, but that does not mean he does not contribute to the dynamic. In the Peter Jackson film adaptation of the novels, Gandalf explains Gollum's psyche and relationship with the Ring to Frodo: "Gollum hates and loves the Ring as he hates and loves himself" (*The Fellowship of the Ring* 01:49:59–01:50:04).

This evokes the mediator role and the dual role of desire, per Girard. Gollum's role in the novel as it relates to the relationship between Frodo and Sam is to demonstrate what happens to the fetishist if left unchecked. Gollum too fetishizes the Ring, but he does not want anyone else. His relationship to the Ring is linear as an end unto itself rather than triangular as a means for a bond with another. Milbank points out a paradox with this kind of fetishism:

> Paradoxically, although the fetish is intended as a means of erotic control—and a means of warding off the castrating female—its importance as the only possible means of erotic pleasure and self-identity of the fetishist renders him in its thrall as if it were a god, in the manner of the totemic religious practice from which Freud took his original concept. This process is most graphically exemplified in the transmutation of the river-hobbit Sméagol into the craven Gollum. Possession of the Ring by the murder of his friend leads to his self-division and alienation, so now he speaks in the third person, in baby talk—"Don't hurt us! Don't let them hurt us, precious!"—while the Ring is now personified and looked to as a source of aid and protection. Like early Native American totemists, Gollum has figuratively placed his soul inside the fetish

for safe-keeping. Without the Ring, therefore, he is torn in two, and, as he replies to Faramir, "no name, no business, no Precious, nothing. Only empty" [*TT*, IV, vi, 335] [Milbank 35–36].

Gollum is so invested in the object of the fetish that losing the object causes a split in his ego, forming two distinct personalities: the cunning and ferocious Gollum and the meek Sméagol. Though the fetish for the Ring is intended as a means to control the erotic female sexual power, which represents the fear of castration, the fetish begins to control Gollum as it is the only means of holding his ego together. This duality is his most famous character trait, and Bernard argues that the splitting of Gollum's ego also entails a duality in terms of gender. Drawing on Milbank's work with gender, Bernard argues that Gollum is related to femininity while Sméagol represents the masculine side of his ego: "Tolkien presents Gollum as having both masculine and feminine characteristics. Thematically, he is linked with all the worst traits of femininity in the novel.... Gollum's form is considered spider-like, a link to Shelob, the ultimate female monster in the novel. And yet, Gollum is male and a hobbit" (Bernard 113–114). Therefore, there is a duality in Gollum represented not only in personality and speech but in gender as well. Gollum flits back and forth between identities, sometimes speaking as Gollum and sometimes speaking as Sméagol. Bernard argues convincingly that Sméagol is a masculine performance, and Gollum is a feminine construction. The loss of the fetishized object caused not only a split ego but a split gender. Gollum/Sméagol represents the existence of two personas and two genders in the same body at this point in the story.

It is Gollum's spider-like qualities that link him to femininity. One of the few female characters in the novel is Shelob, the gigantic evil spider.[7] Milbank suggests that a Freudian understanding of Shelob would have us read her as a "vagina dentata": "According to Freud, her castrating hold is precisely what the sexual fetishist fears, and seeks to control by his possession of the fetishized object" (Milbank 35). Shelob represents castration anxiety which is a large part of the fetishist's desire for the fetishized object. Without the threat of castration, there is no need to fetishize an object in the first place. Shelob reminds the reader of the ever-looming threat of castration that the feminine represents, thus creating the need for a fetishized object like the Ring. The feminine Gollum and the masculine Sméagol are in a constant battle for control over their body, with Gollum eventually winning out and preventing the male side of the ego from exerting any agency over the situation. This is a symbolic castration.

Furthermore, Gollum's spider-like appearance and the connection to the symbolic vagina dentata are apparent when Gollum symbolically castrates Frodo by biting Frodo's finger off. This occurs at a moment when Frodo's finger is penetrating the feminine Ring. This is a symbolic castration at the hands of feminine erotic power, precisely what the fetish is supposed to help the fetishist avoid.

Milbank's paradox of fetishism raises another paradox within the novel. Sméagol's fetish is a means of protecting him from the castrating feminine force, and it is the loss of the fetishized object that splits the ego and creates the feminine alter-ego, which symbolically castrates both Sméagol and later Frodo. This seemingly supports the idea that fetishized object protects against castration since the castrations would not have occurred had Sméagol not lost the Ring; but if he had never possessed the Ring in the first place, then there would not have been a splitting of the ego that leads to the castrations. To resolve this paradox, we must look to the character who fetishizes the Ring but is not symbolically castrated: Sam.

Gollum becomes obsessed with the Ring, possessing it for over five hundred years in his cave before losing it. He is unable to let go of the fetish. He is, as Milbank says, "in its thrall" (35). Frodo also falls victim to the Ring as he cannot destroy it. Again, he is in its thrall. Sam, however, though he hesitates, can give the Ring back to Frodo. Sam is only ever momentarily in the thrall of the fetish. There are two reasons for this. Firstly, Sam simply has not possessed the object long enough for it to take that strong a hold over him. Secondly, Sam is the most upfront about his libidinal investment in the Ring being for the sake of serving Frodo. Since Sam is conscious of his relationship with the Ring as a means for a relationship with Frodo, he is master of the fetish rather than falling in the thrall of the fetishized object as Frodo and Gollum do. Thus, he can avoid castration, unlike Sméagol, who is symbolically castrated through the reduction of his male agency, and Frodo, who is castrated by the Ring's seduction and Gollum's bite. Sam does confront the threat of castration in the form of the erotic feminized, the vagina dentata herself: Shelob. Sam famously does battle with the spider, eventually defeating her. As Brenda Partridge argues effectively, the sexual imagery in the encounter is unmistakable. Shelob is the dominant sexual partner, the woman on top. Shelob's zealous sexual thrust injures her, and the phallic blade saves Sam as she has him underneath her and attempts to crush him, only to impale herself on the sword (*TT*, IV, x, 421).[8] Not only does Sam avoid castration, but he uses the phallic object itself to vanquish the potentially castrating force. Frodo and Gollum are not so lucky as both are castrated because of their unhealthy relationship with the Ring.

Gollum's role in the erotic triangle is to exist outside of it. He is an example of the terrible consequences of unchecked fetishism: the splitting of the ego, gender, and castration of the self. Though fetishism is intended to protect against this castration, ultimately, it is what causes it for the characters of Gollum and Frodo. Only Sam can avoid this fate because he has avoided enthrallment to the fetishized object by maintaining it as a conduit for his relationship with Frodo. Though Bernard's understanding of Gollum's role is vital to understanding a queer erotic triangle with Frodo and Sam is part of the scholarship consensus, using Milbank's understanding of the Ring as a fetishized object, I argue that his role is better understood as outside of that triangle as an example of unchecked fetishism of the Ring.

The queerness of Frodo and Sam's relationship is discernible through understanding the queer erotic triangle, with the fetishized Ring in the beloved position. Though they both experience feelings of intimacy, even potential erotic desire, the overt expression of those feelings and desires would be taboo in Middle-earth. Therefore, the expression of these desires is hidden in the erotic triangle, with both male hobbits investing libidinal energy into the feminine Ring. This is an acceptable, even encouraged, expression of desire that functions as a means for the hobbits to form an equally strong bond with each other without the judgment and persecution that would come with an openly homosexual relationship. The fetishized object serves as a conduit, a safe substitute, for the otherwise risky homoerotic desires. This holds with Freud's theory of castration anxiety as a male child's response to the sight of the female genitalia, as he writes in "Splitting of the Ego in the Process of Defence":

> He created a substitute for the penis which he missed in females ... a fetish. In so doing, it is true that he had disavowed reality, but he had saved his own penis. So long as he was not obliged to acknowledge that females have lost their penis, there was no need for him to believe the threat that had been made against him: he need have no fears for his own penis, so he could proceed with his masturbation undisturbed [Freud 5064].

The fetish allows for the prohibited behavior (homosexuality), for it hides the dreaded site of female castration, yet it can be removed to display that the love object is indeed a woman, after all. In this sense, fetishism is an ideal method of concealing homoerotic desire. Though Gollum might seem a likely candidate to fulfil the role of the feminine due to his gender fluidity, he functions as an example of extreme fetishism and the paradox of using fetish to protect against the threat of castration by female erotic power. Through understanding the role of erotic triangles and fetishism in the novel, there is a case for another decisively queer understanding of Frodo and Sam's relationship.

Notes

1. Anna Smol gives a sophisticated reading of the intimacy of this relationship in her essay, "'Oh ... oh ... Frodo!': Readings of Male Intimacy in *The Lord of the Rings*."
2. See also Yvette Kisor's "'We Could Do with a Bit More Queerness in These Parts': An Analysis of the Queer against the Peculiar, the Odd, and the Strange in *The Lord of the Rings*" on the strong associations between "queer" and "odd," "strange," etc.
3. Sedgwick quotes from Levi-Strauss, p. 115.
4. The Peter Jackson film adaptations accentuate the rivalry between Sam and Gollum.
5. Bernard is obviously reading a finger, in this instance, as a metaphorical phallus engaged in penetrative sex with the Ring, which she reads as "feminized" because it is penetrated. It should be noted that, while this metaphor does make sense, the act of being penetrated does not automatically feminize the Ring, especially if "finger" is read literally rather than metaphorically, as penetration with a finger can also be an intra-male activity.
6. Yvette Kisor has documented Tolkien's varying use of the term "queer" in the novels and has found that he uses the term both in the traditional meaning of "strange" and the secondary meaning of "questionable character," and even that Tolkien anticipates the reclamation of the term by the queer community decades later even if his use of the term is not explicitly to do with sexuality (1–2).
7. For additional scholarship on Shelob and femininity, please see Sara Brown's essay, "Mother or Other: Tolkien's Shelob And The 'Monstrous-Feminine,'" in this volume (77–91).
8. Brenda Partridge covers this very well in "No Sex Please—We're Hobbits: The Construction of Female Sexuality in *The Lord of the Rings*."

Works Cited

Bernard, Carol A. "Gollum: The Fulcrum of Desire in J.R.R. Tolkien's *The Lord of the Rings*." *Dissertation Abstracts International, Section A: The Humanities and Social Sciences*, vol. 66, no. 6, University of Houston, ProQuest, Dec. 2005, UMI Number: 3180550.
Chance, Jane. "'Queer' Hobbits: The Problem of Difference in the Shire." *The Lord of the Rings: The Mythology of Power*. Revised ed., UP of Kentucky, 2001, pp. 26–37
Craig, David M. "'Queer Lodgings': Gender and Sexuality in *The Lord of the Rings*." *Mallorn*, vol. 38, Jan. 2001, pp. 11–18, journals.tolkiensociety.org/mallorn/article/view/145/139. Rpt. "Queer Lodgings: Gender and Sexuality in *The Lord of the Rings*—Reprinted with a New Introduction by the Author." *Mallorn*, vol. 61, 2020, pp. 20–29.
Doty, Alexander. *Flaming Classics: Queering the Film Canon*. Routledge, 2000.
Freud, Sigmund. "Fetishism." *Freud: The Complete Works*, edited by Ivan Smith, 2010, 2000, 2007, 2010, 2011, pp. 4533–38, freudcompleteworks.com/Freud_Complete_Works.pdf.
_____. "Splitting of the Ego in the Process of Defence." *Freud: The Complete Works*, edited by Ivan Smith, 2000, 2007, 2010, 2011, pp. 5060–5064, freudcompleteworks.com/Freud_Complete_Works.pdf.
Girard, René. *Deceit, Desire, and the Novel; Self and Other in Literary Structure*. Johns Hopkins UP, 1965.
Kisor, Yvette. "Queer Tolkien: A Bibliographical Essay on Tolkien and Alterity." *Tolkien and Alterity*, edited by Christopher Vaccaro and Yvette Kisor, Palgrave Macmillan, 2017, pp. 17–32.
_____. "'We Could Do with a Bit More Queerness in These Parts'": An Analysis of the Queer against the Peculiar, the Odd, and the Strange in *The Lord of the Rings*," *Journal of Tolkien Research*, vol. 16, iss. 1, article 4, 2023, scholar.valpo.edu/journaloftolkienresearch/vol16/iss1/4.
Levi-Strauss, Claude. *The Elementary Structures of Kinship*. Beacon, 1969.
The Lord of the Rings: The Fellowship of the Ring. Directed by Peter Jackson. Special extended DVD ed., New Line Home Entertainment, 2004.

Milbank, Alison. "'My Precious': Tolkien's Fetishized Ring." *The Lord of the Rings and Philosophy*, edited by Gregory Bassham and Eric Bronson, Open Court, 2003, pp. 33–46.
Nagy, Gergely. "The 'Lost' Subject of Middle-Earth: The Constitution of the Subject in the Figure of Gollum in *The Lord of the Rings*." *Tolkien Studies*, vol. 3, no. 1, 2006, pp. 57–59.
Partridge, Brenda. "No Sex Please—We're Hobbits: The Construction of Female Sexuality in *The Lord of the Rings*." *J.R.R. Tolkien: This Far Land*, edited by Robert Giddings, Vision P, 1983, pp. 179–97.
Rohy, Valerie. "On Fairy Stories." *MFS: Modern Fiction Studies*, J.R.R. Tolkien Special Issue, guest editor Shaun F.D. Hughes, vol. 50, no. 4, 2004, pp. 927–948.
Sedgwick, Eve Kosofsky. "Gender Asymmetry and Erotic Triangles." *Between Men: English Literature and Male Homosocial Desire*, Columbia UP, 1985.
Smol, Anna. "'Oh...oh...Frodo!': Readings of Male Intimacy in the Lord of the Rings." *Modern Fiction Studies*, J.R.R. Tolkien Special Issue, guest editor Shaun F.D. Hughes, vol. 50, no. 4, 2004, pp. 949–79, doi.org/10.1353/mfs.2005.0010.
Timmons, Daniel. "Hobbit Sex and Sensuality in *The Lord of the Rings*." *Mythlore*, vol. 23, no. 3, article 7, pp. 70–79, 2001, dc.swosu.edu/mythlore/vol23/iss3/7.
Tolkien, J.R.R. *The Letters of J.R.R. Tolkien*, edited by Humphrey Carpenter, assisted by Christopher Tolkien, Houghton Mifflin, 1981.
Tolkien, J.R.R. *The Lord of the Rings*. Allen & Unwin, 1954.

"Saruman [?Pardoned]"

The Queerness of Sex in Tolkien's The Lord of the Rings

CHRISTOPHER VACCARO

> And then suddenly [Saruman] looked touched. "Well, I thank you," he said. 'You do not crow and your kind looks maybe are not feigned. You seem an honest fellow, and maybe you did not come to crow over me. (Tolkien, *The End of the Third Age*, 65)

The nature of Saruman's "Otherness" or rather the *contra natura* nature of his "Otherness" is hard to decipher. It is shifting and allusive, morphing not only throughout *The Lord of the Rings* but also through the course of Tolkien's thought on the subject. Its queerness is defined first by this indeterminacy and last by what it seems to represent to the author and some of his readers. In *Tolkien, Self and Other*, Jane Chance borrows from Stephen Yandell's 2013 IMC conference paper "Niggle, Smith, and Giles: Medieval as Queer" the idea of a "drag persona" in Tolkien's texts and life (Chance, 12). Both scholars explore the cultivation of a primary world "drag persona" "that depends on a tension with private (closeted) desire" (Chance, 12). Chance examines the two predominant sides of Tolkien's identity: "professor and mythologist, a doubling that refracts into many of his own works" (12). Recalling the words of Slavoj Žižek, Chance brings to focus the ways Otherness conceals itself within the familiar: "beneath the neighbor as my *semblant*, my mirror image, there always lurks the unfathomable abyss of radical Otherness, of a monstrous Thing that cannot be gentrified" (qtd. in Chance 4). Chance adds to this Benjamin Saxton's exploration of "oppositional figures" within Tolkien's characters to make her broader argument that Tolkien—like his characters—experienced a queerness of identity in numerous ways

(Saxton, 167).[1] The Gollum/Sméagol doubling is one set of oppositional figures; Gandalf and Saruman is another. And I would suggest another kind of doubling is present in relation to and within Saruman, manifest through a relation to sexualized desire. He is at once an impatient and trapped reformer, one who feels anguish, loneliness, and pain, one worthy of pity, who yearns to be understood but expects rejection. And he is something else, something unnamable and unnerving, something deserving of divine retribution and his gruesome death (his throat is cut by Grima Wormtongue and his body quickly dissolves into hideous rags of flesh). The first of these interior twins garnered at first a mercy from the author; the second did not.

This doubling might coincide with the two sides of Tolkien's own personality following the death of his mother. Carpenter makes the point:

> [I]t made him into two people. He was by nature a cheerful almost irrepressible person with a great zest for life. He loved good talk and physical activity. He had a deep sense of humour and a great capacity for making friends. But from now onwards there was to be a second side, more private but predominant in his diaries and letters. This side of him was capable of bouts of profound despair [34].

Covering Tolkien's contradictory mythopoetic impulses, Verlyn Flieger astutely argues that "so much of the primary evidence—that is to say, his writing—seems to toggle between diametrically opposite positions" (7). She argues not so much for a reconciliation of opposing forces, but for a welcoming of contradiction in Tolkien himself (16). These opposing valences within Tolkien's imagination seem to operate likewise in the indeterminacy of Saruman's future. In this essay, I examine the range of Tolkien's decisions and the depth of abjection within the textual histories in order to ascertain Saruman's deeper and possibly even psychological meanings. At the heart of this issue is mercy and the potential for Saruman's eventual salvation.

In the spring of 1895, a three-year-old John Ronald Reuel Tolkien set foot on English soil, arriving in Birmingham, England, from Bloemfontein, South Africa, with his younger brother Hilary and his mother, Mabel Suffield Tolkien (Carpenter). Within days of his arrival, Oscar Wilde was wrongfully arrested on charges of gross indecency related to sodomy and sentenced to two years of hard labor at Reading Gaol, after which he lived in exile and poverty for the remainder of his short life. The Labouchere Amendment (Amendment 11) of England's Criminal Law Amendment Act (1885) criminalized a broad range of sexual behaviors between men. Books condoning what was considered "gross indecency" such as D.H.

Lawrence's *The Rainbow* (1915) and Radclyffe Hall's *The Well of Loneliness* (1928) were banned, seized, and burned but not before bringing the topic of homosexuality back into public conversation. Book sellers stocking copies of Havelock Ellis' *Sexual Inversion* (1897), an objective study of homosexuality, were prosecuted and threatened with prison. In such a hysterical and homophobic climate, E.M. Forster did not dare publish *Maurice*, a story about men in love; that novel was written in 1914 but published posthumously in 1971. In 1952, the Labouchere Amendment was likewise used to persecute Alan Turing, forcing that computer genius and World War II hero to undergo forced chemical castration; he took his own life in 1954. It would not be until the Sexual Offenses Act of 1967 that same-sex activities were partially decriminalized.[2] In the wake of these events, it would stand to reason that artistic expressions of same-sex love between men (intra-male homoamory) would be trepidatiously composed.[3] Some might even, consciously or unconsciously, erect firm boundaries between what they might perceive to be a "decent" and platonic love and that "indecent" love that, as Lord Alfred Douglas declared, "dare not speak its name" ("Two Loves").

Within England's literati, same-sex love did not instill the same degree of hostility. In fact, groups of artists, art critics, novelists, enthusiasts of Greco-Roman culture, and university faculty were in closer proximity to the subject. The Bloomsbury Group, with the likes of Virginia and Leonard Woolf, Lytton Strachey, and E.M. Forster, tackled the subject directly. The Inklings, with Tolkien, C.S. Lewis, Charles Williams, and Owen Barfield being the most widely recognized, at times addressed and represented same-sex love with Lewis arguing that intra-male love was central to the earliest English cultures. Later testimonial evidence reveals an engagement amongst those in Tolkien's close literary circle with intra-male homoamory that included the sexual.[4] The climate at universities such as Oxford brought "aesthetes" (artistic types) and "hearties" (athletes) together on campuses to share a love of learning. A love of art was more commonly associated with homosexual men; a love of sports, with heterosexual men. Though of course well-educated men defied easy categorization, providing alternative forms of masculinity and manliness. John Garth notes that even among Tolkien's earlier all-male club, the Tea Club, Barrovian Society (T.C.B.S.), there were frustrations—some expressed by Christopher Wiseman—around the more "aesthetic" behavior of the likes of Robert Gilson and Geoffrey Bache Smith. Tolkien and Wiseman made up "the moral wing of the TCBS" (Garth, *Tolkien and the Great War*, 57). In such an environment of intra-male homoamory, clear distinctions between what could be moral and amoral expressions were crucial.

Queerness

Much like Tolkien's Saruman, the "queer" has come to resist essentializing and totalizing definitions and narratives, encouraging indeterminacy. There is no one set definition, but an amalgam of qualifiers, a relevant selection of which I give here. Many theorists focus on the queer's oppositional relationship to normalcy and ideological hegemony, an aspect which will be relevant to Saruman's positioning in the novel. Jack Halberstam argues that queerness designates a powerful and disruptive failure to comply with heteronormative directives: "[q]ueerness offers the promise of failure as a way of life ... but it is up to us whether we choose to make good on that promise in a way that makes a detour around the usual markers of accomplishment and satisfaction" (*Queer Art*, 186). Failure opens up queer pathways of diversification and freedom from heteronormative proscriptions. Halberstam situates the queer in opposition to a heteronormative status quo defining queerness as, "a marker of a politics of sex and gender," that most significantly critiques, "state power and assimilationist goals" (*Trans**, 50). Michael Warner, also resisting what he terms "regimes of the normal," suggests that the queer "gets a critical edge by defining itself against the normal rather than the heterosexual, and normal includes normal business in the academy" (*Queer Planet*, xxvi).

A key feature of the queer as it has been established in earlier theoretical positions is that of its mutability and indeterminacy. The queer revels in its polysemous positionality. Eve Kosofsky Sedgwick provides a satisfyingly etymological origin that is relevant to my argument:

> Queer is a continuing moment, movement, motive—recurrent, eddying, *troublant*. The word "queer" itself means *across*—it comes from the Indo—European root *-twerkw*, which also yields the German *quer* (traverse), Latin *torquere* (to twist), English *athwart*.... Keenly, it is relational and strange [xii].

As such the queer is very much about movement over various terrains and not about stationary positioning. Annemarie Jagose posits that "queer is less an identity than a critique of identity ... it is more accurate to represent it as ceaselessly interrogating both the preconditions of identity and its effects" (131–32). And Donald Hall contends that "to queer" is "to abrade the classifications, to sit athwart conventional categories or traverse several" (13), and as such it links to the mutability of meaning.

Alongside indeterminacy, some theorists re-associate the queer with its sexual valences. In this argument, I am using "queer" to speak to an unapologetic, in-your-face assertiveness regarding the importance of liberated sexuality. I mean to assert the importance of sex as a means to creating and retaining sociality and community within some populations of gay men. In *The Trouble with Normal: Sex, Politics, and the Ethics of Queer Life*, Warner highlights the moral binary operating around sex within contemporary straight and gay communities. There's good sex, which is monogamous, procreative, private, vanilla, and within a relationship, and there is bad sex, which is promiscuous, non-procreative, public, kinky, and casual. Sentimentalized sex is good and dignified. Anonymous and recreational sex is sinful and stigmatized. In contrast, queerness resists such conventional binaries. A powerful thrust of Warner's book comes as a reminder concerning queer culture: "One of its greatest contributions to modern life is the discovery that you can have both: intimacy and casualness; long-term commitment and sex with strangers; romantic love and perverse pleasure" (25–26).[5] In *Making Things Perfectly Queer*, Alexander Doty argues for a radical set of meanings, one that "views the erotically 'marginal' as both (in bell hooks's words) a consciously chosen 'site of resistance' and a 'location of radical openness and possibility'" (2).

Teresa de Lauretis argues cogently that reclaiming the term "queer" so that it is more inclusive of non-normative sexualities is effectuated through the employment of Freud's principle of oscillating drives—sex and death—as described in his "Beyond the Pleasure Principle" (1920). De Lauretis finds this more sexualized queerness in the "heterotopic space" where both these drives thrive and compete. Her intention is to more accurately define the very queerness of sexuality: "For, while we theorize queer sociability and attachment in local and global contexts, we cannot ignore the compulsive, perverse, ungovernable aspects of sexuality that confront us in the public sphere, in the family, in ourselves" (250). De Lauretis finds the full spectrum of sexuality, "the perverse, polymorphous sexuality that is oral, anal, paragenital, nonreproductive, upstream of sex *and* gender differences" to be constituted through one's very attempt to repress it (253).

One pervasive idea within the discourse of queerness is the abject nature of Otherness, which projects what is perceived as undesirable behavior in ourselves unto someone else. This is what Freud might call "the Uncanny" and Jung, "the Shadow" and is akin to Julia Kristeva's term "abject." Kristeva argues that "[t]here looms within abjection, one of those violent, dark revolts of being, directed against a threat that seems to emanate from an exorbitant outside or inside, ejected beyond the scope of the possible, the tolerable, the thinkable" (91). In this vein, the queer exposes the permeability of the self/other boundaries and an individual's method of coping with unwanted (because socially marginalized) traits. The queer engages with alterior bodies, sexualities, and pleasures in order to dehegemonize their normative counterparts.

Queer Tolkien scholarship has a rich history.[6] Yvette Kisor astutely categories and summarizes all the significant arguments in her bibliographic essay in which she concludes that "the idea of difference is central to Tolkien's work and the moral lesson of *The Lord of the Rings* concerns attitudes towards the queer" ("Queer Tolkien," 27). In her invaluable 2023 analysis of the term "queer," Kisor notes that even the most seemingly conservative character like old Gaffer Gamgee is full of surprises in relation to queerness: "Once those he loves and esteems become seen as queer, queerness itself becomes something to value and embrace" ("We Could Do," 4). The term "queer" appears a number of times in *The Lord of the Rings* and while it is often associated with that which is strange, odd, and peculiar (as Kisor has thoughtfully pointed out), its "associations with sexual deviance are potentially earlier and more British than may be generally acknowledged" ("We Could Do," 2).[7] Kisor concludes that while Tolkien "may never have intended a 'modern' reading of the word 'queer,' with its suggestions of difference from the 'norm' of a sexual register," he did go on to establish "a very specific set of resonances for the term that embed it in provincial mistrust, a sense of real outside threat, and places within the ancient natural world that appear foundationally opposed to the ordinary realm of civilization" (21).

Jane Chance and Valerie Rohy speak specifically of Saruman's queerness within the logic of the text. Chance situates Saruman within the sadomasochistic paradigm of the hyper-masculine struggle of wills ("on mastery and the submission of will") that governs many of the narrative's intra-male relations, a "tough love of queer chivalry" (*Tolkien, Self and Other*, 227). Though not explicitly, Chance comes closest here to expressing Saruman's alterior eros, drawn as it is from a competitive relation to other males, an erotically queer relation that reads as sadomasochistic. Yet Chance's focus remains Tolkien's relation to alterity, which sets up a dialectic ultimately resolved through acceptance of difference. In this reading, "the agenda of both Maia Sauron and wizard Saruman is similar: to erase difference, by installing one point of view" (246).

In "Cinema, Sexuality, Mechanical Reproduction," Valerie Rohy brings critical attention to the ways Saruman flips the texts' (both Tolkien's and Jackson's) requirement for a heteronormative futurity through the queer nature of his parthenogenic Orc-breeding project. Rohy employs the foundational work of Guy Hocquenham to expose how Saruman's sterile proliferations are coded as the monstrous inversion of the sentimentalized intra-male love expressed by Frodo and Sam.[8]

Rohy's argument connects with the argument I make in "Saruman's Sodomitic Resonances" about Saruman's likeness to the sodomitic community, marginalized and anathematized, of Alain de Lille's influential *De planctu naturæ*. I analyze the queer nature of Saruman, who—much like Alain's anathematized—is excommunicated from the community of the virtuous through Gandalf's sacerdotal pronouncements. Saruman is associated with a set of stigmatizing vices associated with the medieval concept of *sodomita* (pride, greed, prodigality, lasciviousness; essentially *luxuria*). The category of sodomy was not restricted to sexual activities alone but included a broad range of behaviors. Saruman's sodomitic resonances are easily recognizable from a heteronormative platonic register. His greed, his pride, and his association with brutishly masculine Orcs and his lustful henchman, Wormtongue, all complete a profile of Saruman that fits within a homophobic and medieval Neoplatonic depiction of those anathematized and excommunicated by divine messengers, specifically of those labelled as sodomites. Moreover, I argue that Saruman's erotic queerness (seen most clearly in the brutish animality of his Orcs and the lasciviousness of his henchman) is a repository for a sexuality, which sadly remains unwelcome and repressed.

Negative Attitudes Towards Sexuality

There exists a heteronormative and conservative strain in Tolkien scholarship that takes a judgmental stance toward the tenets of the sexual liberation movement. This stance is in part due to Tolkien's own conservative position towards physical desire as seen in an exemplative letter to Michael Tolkien from March 1941:

> The dislocation of sex-instinct is one of the chief symptoms of the Fall. The world has been going "going to the bad" all down the ages. The various social forms shift, and each new mode has its special dangers: but the "hard spirit of concupiscence" has walked down every street, and sat leering in every house, since Adam fell [*The Letters of J.R.R. Tolkien* (*Letters 1*), #43, 48].

That Tolkien would use the term "concupiscence" is hardly surprising. It has its etymological roots in the Latin Vulgate, and was used by the likes of Chaucer, Gower, and Milton to speak of the power of sexual desire to lead individuals astray. Tolkien often expressed wariness regarding men's weakness in this regard.

Ty Rosenthal comes to conservative conclusions when speaking of Tolkien's mythology. He argues, "It is a vision of a world less stressed by sexual and romantic complications, where desire is both fulfilled and restrained, powerful yet moral; a hint of what might have been, in Tolkien's view, if the world was purer than it is today" (42). Daniel Timmons's "Hobbit Sex and Sensuality in *The Lord of the Rings*" reveals a clear bias against a liberated "queer" sexuality. He writes:

Tolkien has it all in proper perspective. It may be hard to see in a modern or post-modern society that matters of honor, decency, abstinence, and fidelity can still resonate powerfully with readers, while real sexual deviance blights life and literature. As Tolkien has said, if we can catch a "glimpse" of that "vision" of sensual love that stands apart from sexual depravity then perhaps our personal relationships can be fruitful and long-lasting. But one thing appears all too clear: the path of "free love" or heedless lust leads Timmon to degradation and despair. Is that what Tolkien's detractors would have us choose [79].

I cannot speak for detractors of Tolkien, but a number of devoted queer Tolkien fans would certainly choose "free love" (perhaps articulated today through anonymous and recreational sex) all the while remaining decent and ethical participants in our society. And a celebration of liberated sexuality does not lead to despair; rather, it dismantles the good sex/bad sex binary so often normalized.

In Timmons's desire to find what could be called a sensual heteroamory, similar to what I call homoamory, his mental calisthenics require him to foreclose any possibility of erotic love between Frodo and Sam. Timmons states that critics who recognize any erotic register in the novel, "do not distinguish between the spiritual bond between two males and the romantic love between a male and a female" (78). But he provides insufficient evidence as to why we would see the two loves as different. He imagines "the awakening of the male adolescent desire for the feminine" (76), a reading dependent upon an arbitrary heterosexual fantasy.

The bias within some Tolkien scholarship against libidinous desire and liberated sexuality coalesces around the less sentimental queer character of *The Lord of the Rings*, Saruman, who tends to evoke critical language similar to homophobic slurs of the past. One example is the term "pervert," which according to the *Oxford English Dictionary* could—as a noun—refer to "a person who has forsaken a doctrine or system regarded as true for one thought false" (Sense 1) or to "a person whose sexual behaviour or inclinations are regarded as abnormal and unacceptable" (Sense 2). Kayla McKinney Wiggins adopts this language when talking of Saruman:

> Saruman does not hesitate to corrupt and *pervert* those around him in order to achieve his goals of conquest, even going so far as to torture and *pervert* nature to achieve his ends. He destroys the natural beauty of Orthanc, does extreme damage to Fangorn Forest, and breeds a race of half men/half Orcs that are a *perversion* of both species [102, emphasis added].

Nicholas Ozment refers to the magic of the "bent Saruman" when compared to Gandalf's "'white magic,'" which "can be said to have a kinship with the miracles of the saints and prophets or the Hebraic angels" (192). "Bent" and "bender" have likewise been slurs for homosexuals for quite some time; those who are "bent" are not "straight," and so they "pervert" the natural order of things.[9] Very early on, the term "queer" was a spatial term that, as Sara Ahmed reminds us, was then applied to a bent sexuality, one that didn't follow the straight path (67). Of course, there is an important difference between using the verb "pervert" to describe a move away from a normative process and evoking a slang against a sexual minority, and I am not arguing that Wiggins or Ozment are deliberately employing slurs. But there is an interesting correspondence in exactly what is being disparaged in the scholarship on Saruman.

Tolkien's Shifting Rhetoric

There exists such extremes of attitude around the severity of Saruman's crimes and the possibility of his redemption. This indeterminacy emerges from the characters in the storyline but also from Tolkien himself. Tolkien's post–*Lord of the Rings* remarks offer very tepid criticisms of the wizard, seemingly incommensurate with his ultimate and gruesome fate. In his 1954 letter to Naomi Mitchison, Tolkien uses the term "Sarumanism" in reference to the Machiavellian wish for reform through "exercise of power" (*Letters 1* #154, 197).[10] In a draft letter to Michael Straight (dated around January or February 1956), he speaks to the effect of incarnation on the Istari, which left them vulnerable to sin:

> The chief form this would take with them would be impatience, leading to the desire to force others to their own good ends, and so inevitably at last to mere desire to make their own wills effective by any means. To this evil Saruman succumbed. Gandalf did not [*Letters 1* #181, 237].

In both epistles, Tolkien concentrates on Saruman's impatience, a serious flaw that precipitates a greater fall from grace. Yet "impatience" seems such an innocuous term when readers confront the dire effect of Saruman's actions and the terrifying punishment that is to follow.

At a "Hobbit Dinner" in March 1958, Tolkien gave this toast:

> I look East, West, North, and South, and I do not see Sauron; but I see that Saruman has many descendants. We Hobbits have against them no magic weapons. Yet, my gentlehobbits, I give you this toast: To the Hobbits. May they outlast the Sarumans and see spring again in the trees [Carpenter 255].

Here Tolkien uses the terms of sterile productivity (alluded to in Rohy's scholarship) associated with Alain's sodomitic Others to define Saruman as the ancestor of the brood of ills still plaguing the world. If this is the point Tolkien reaches in deciphering the wizard's meaning, it too seems incongruous with his ultimate punishment. So what happened in the writing of *The Lord of the Rings* to make Saruman deserve such a violent death scene? One finds in Tolkien's indispensable drafts and plot sketches evidence of a progression of thought regarding Saruman's ultimate fate that initially accommodates notions of reform, tenderness and gentleness towards the deviating ethos and eros of this queer wizard. Gandalf offers Saruman a pardon of sorts, encouraging him to come down from his tower (*The Two Towers* [*TT*], x, 187). His words are gentle and sincere though he has little hope in Saruman's redemption. Offered gentleness and a viable future, Saruman's response changes.

In Draft A, characters and readers alike glimpse in Saruman's face his precarious position. The italicized section was written by Tolkien on the margin of the page of the draft as additional text:

> A quick cunning look passed over Saruman's face; before he could conceal it, they had a glimpse of mingled fear and relief/hope. cunning. *They saw through the mask the face of a trapped man, that feared both to stay and to leave his refuge. He hesitated.* "To be torn by the savage wood-demons?" he said [*The War of the Ring* (*WR*), 64].[11]

After Gandalf's quick response, Draft A goes on to say, "Saruman's face was for a moment clouded with anger." In the published chapter "The Voice of Saruman," we see subtle shifts. In a moment that rivals the tragic details of Gollum's missed salvation, the scene goes on to reveal Saruman's inner struggle and ultimate recalcitrance:

> A shadow passed over Saruman's face; then it went deathly white. Before he could conceal it, they saw through the mask the anguish of a mind in doubt, loathing to stay and dreading to leave its refuge. For a second he hesitated and no one breathed. Then he spoke and his voice was shrill and cold. Pride and hate were conquering him [*TT*, III, x, 188].[12]

This pride and hate added here sutures Saruman tightly to his fate. The published version gives this description after Gandalf's response: "Saruman's face grew livid, twisted with rage, and a red light was kindled in his eyes" (*TT*, III, x, 188). Again more villainous, more Other.

From A's, "face of a trapped man" to the published, "anguish of a mind," the change does have subtle consequences. A glimpse upon the "face" of the Other encourages a potential sympathy. The phrase "face of a trapped man" elicits more sympathy; it brings the readers within an intimate proximity to the character. Would such sympathy be inappropriate considering his final end? Sadly there is no draft of Gandalf's summons for Saruman to return to the balcony. In the published version, we do have a return to the face, which was "lined and shrunken" (*TT*, III, x, 188).

A goal of this essay is to expose the shifting trajectories regarding Saruman's future. In the earliest plot sketches, Saruman does not die; he lives to express moments of tenderness. In the plot sketch "The Story Foreseen from Moria" Gandalf suggests to Saruman following Sauron's defeat that he "beg from the charitable for a day's digging" (*The Treason of Isengard* [*Treason*], 212) and Tolkien writes on a scrap of paper an additional note that "Saruman becomes a wandering conjuror and trickster" (*Treason* 287).

Likewise, in the sketch "The Story Foreseen from Kormallen," Tolkien considers the plot for the remainder of the novel. There he writes: "They come on Saruman and he is pardoned," envisioning a potentially happy future for the wizard. The final word in the sentence is nearly indecipherable. Christopher Tolkien provides "[?pardoned]" in his notes and admits that the word is almost impossible to read, but concludes that it "can hardly be otherwise." After direct examination of the draft at the Marquette University archives, I concur with his assessment. The letters spelling out "pardoned" do seem to match up to their counterparts elsewhere on the stray leaf.[13]

Let's interrogate this position of our author. The contrast to the published narrative of Saruman's end in *The Return of the King* is striking and tremendously significant. To pardon Saruman would be to reveal the power of mercy and forgiveness and the victory of the virtuous over the wicked. Kindness and generosity offered freely soften the most impenetrable and obstinate of hearts. It presents a willingness to forgive and a deep-seated compassion towards those who have lost their way. One recalls that Frodo forgives even Gollum after all he has done, and he likewise forgives Saruman. But does Tolkien?

Following the defeat of Sauron, the remaining Fellowship encounter Saruman on the road in what will become the chapter "Many Partings." As one might expect of a Christian Neoplatonist narrative, the greedy become bereft of belongings and the proud are made utterly wretched. But again, Gandalf, through divine sanction having effectively excommunicated Saruman from the White Council and the community of wizards, offers the genuine possibility of a pardon. In Draft A, there is evidence that Tolkien was initially open to Saruman's earnest compunction and pardon. Here the company comes upon Saruman, who states "I am seeking a way out of his realm." To which Gandalf first replies, "Then you are going the wrong way [as seems to be your doom], unless you wish to pass into the utter North and there freeze to death." With "as seems to be your doom," the first draft reveals an ominous undercurrent not yet surfaced. Further along in the first draft, Gandalf continues: "Then you have far to go, said Gandalf, and should be going eastward. Yet even so you would have to travel far and find the border of his realm ever marching up behind you." The material following "Gandalf" is then crossed out and replaced with the version appearing in print.¹⁴

Draft A records Saruman's tenderness in response to Merry's generous offer of pipe-weed:

> Mine, mine, yes, and dearly paid for, said Saruman, clutching at the pouch. And *then suddenly he looked touched.* "Well, I thank you," he said. ["You do not crow and your kind looks maybe are not feigned.] You seem an honest fellow, and maybe you did not come to crow over me. I'll tell you something. When you come to the Shire beware of Cosimo, and make haste, or you may go short of leaf" [emphasis added].¹⁵

In turn for Merry's offer, a vulnerable Saruman gives information that might undo the harm his servant Cosimo is doing to the Shire. The moment calls to mind the reciprocity of gift exchanges that forge bonds between previously combative factions. Saruman's participation in the exchange of gifts situates him squarely within the parameters of acceptable social relations. He appears to accept a future of diverse voices and subject positions. This Draft A speech by Saruman is both gift and bridge whereby he might accept difference.¹⁶

As Draft A continues, so does Merry's kindness towards Saruman: "Thank you, … and if you get tired of wandering in the wild come to the Shire." Merry may speak for Tolkien here if only in the wish that the wizard could be saved and not be destroyed by his pride and hatred. Merry's initial reply may have been the germ idea for what later becomes the final placement of Saruman in the Shire.

Interestingly, Tolkien placed a large query mark beside Merry's remarkable display of forgiveness. There is then a break and Tolkien writes Gandalf's line: "Well…. There's not much to be made of him. He is withered altogether," which will make its way more or less to the published version. And with that, it seems Tolkien drifted away from the idea of Saruman's redemption. Draft B provides more or less Saruman's hateful response as we now know it.

In an editorial note, Christopher Tolkien glosses his father's querying mark and makes interesting assumptions about his father's decision making:

> [M]y father marked Merry's reply with a large query, and at once, on the same page, recognizing that the pride, bitterness, and malevolence of Saruman could never be pierced by such a gesture on the part of Merry Brandybuck, he wrote the passage that stands in RK [*The End of the Third Age* 66].

Tolkien's large question mark is a fitting sign of Saruman's indeterminacy; it marks the wizard's queerness, a "queerying" essential to any ontology of the character's being. Confronting issues of redemption and recalcitrance, even the author initially struggled to decide Saruman's fate. Christopher Tolkien's assurance that this understanding came to his father at once is dubious despite the passage that followed on the page, and his gloss effectively shores up what amounts to Saruman's sodomitic identity.

In the published chapter, Gandalf genuinely offers Saruman assistance and remarks on the futility of his present course of actions. Galadriel is also present, and while not as warm as Gandalf, she acknowledges the possibility of a pardon (*RK*, VI, vi, 261). Saruman responds to these invitations only with scorn and derision, which is sustained as he is confronted by the hobbits' generosity and their pity. His following remarks are mean-spirited as he hurls his hatred towards the hobbits who earnestly offer their pipe-weed. He acknowledges that he has been made a beggar and curses them (*RK*, VI, vi, 262).[17] Saruman's covetousness results in his being left a beggar, and he rewards the hobbit's generosity with a curse. There is no acknowledgment by him of his previous wrongdoing, neither via reflection nor compunction. He is not fit for pardoning in this version.

The moral logic of *The Lord of the Rings* nudges characters to their doom. In Saruman's case, such a one who has fallen so far, corrupted by pride, greed, and arrogance, can hardly be pardoned. While it would add to the overall consolation, it would not fit with the novel's ethical underpinnings. Ultimately, Saruman is not pardoned, nor does he ask to be. He is too far gone. Only death and the cold wind of judgment conclude his life. The moral tenor of this Neoplatonist template—much like that of Alain de Lilles—requires an excommunicated figure, one who is condemned and punished.

The last published scene significant to this investigation is that of Saruman's death in "The Scouring of the Shire." Whether Tolkien wished for Saruman to be thought depraved and monstrous or merely tragically impatient, his revisions and emendations force us to conclude that the wizard was too proud and malicious ever to be redeemed. After being excommunicated from the divinely sanctioned White Council, Saruman's tragedy is to fall to great depths. Even at the end, he attempts to murder Frodo, whose response seems to mimic Tolkien's earliest mood. Even now Frodo wishes Saruman no harm and recognizes that he once belonged to a great order. He hopes that the wizard finds a cure for his fallen state. Saruman represents desire and specifically here the desire for death, which Frodo's pacifism has denied him.[18] Does Tolkien feel as Frodo? If so, why continue in this gruesome trajectory?

Saruman's death scene is horrific. Grima Wormtongue jumps upon his back and slits his throat like two thieves in the forest. And this is where Tolkien initially ends the chapter. Draft A and the Fair Copy Draft B have nothing further to say; even the Typescript stops here. In fact, the Galley page ended here too.

A galley page is the last chance for an author to make changes to the manuscript before publication, and to the bottom of the actual Galley page reviewed for the final printing, Tolkien attached a slip of paper on which he carefully penned in the eleventh hour the gruesome events following Saruman's death. This appears to be one of only four times in the galley proofs that Tolkien adds more than a word or two, but nothing is as extensive as this instance. This last minute addition describes the mist rising out of Saruman's body, being driven away by a cold wind of judgment from out of the West. Frodo looks at the body and is horrified when, "the shriveled face became rags of skin *that clung to* a hideous skull."[19]

The affective movement of Saruman's mist is telling: it "looks" to the West, then slumps and sighs after bending away from the wind; it seems now that Saruman was destined to bend and be bent. His physical face is now seen for the last time, comprised of shriveled rags upon "a hideous skull"—the face of death at last revealed. In his "Essay on the Istari" (1954) Tolkien writes, "Saruman was cast down, and utterly humbled, and perished at last by the hand of an oppressed slave; and his spirit went withersoever it was doomed to go, and to Middle-earth, whether naked or embodied, came never back" (*Unfinished Tales* [*UT*] 396).

Conclusions

Concerning Saruman's crimes, I hope to have shown that there was much more going on than his impatience, for which the most ignoble and horrific death seems a much too harsh a punishment. Not even Frodo wishes it upon him even after being attacked by the wizard. But perhaps Tolkien wished to use Saruman at the end as an example of what happens to those who have entirely lost their way and have hardened their hearts to such an extent that they cannot recognize generosity and forgiveness when it is offered. If this authorial intention is accurate (already a dubious activity), this remains a rather severe death for one Tolkien considered pardoning in the early draft material. It may be that Tolkien felt a revulsion for what Saruman came to represent and that this went far deeper than merely the unfortunate impatience of a once great man. Perhaps the foreclosure of a repressed concupiscence that dare not speak its name is at the heart of the novel's logic, even as or perhaps because it clearly celebrates intra-male homoamory.

Tolkien set out to write a therapeutic psychodrama in which monstrous Others are defeated, masculinity and manhood are defined not by sexual urges but by restraint and renunciation, and divine justice is measured out to both the wicked and the good. But in doing so, he rendered more real a representation of a "bad" sexuality simmering just underneath the surface and made it Other. Concerning the production of fantasy, Žižek writes that it, "conceals the horror (of the Real, of death, of what is beyond symbolization), yet at the same time it creates what it purports to conceal, its 'repressed' point of reference" (*Plague*, 7). Tolkien's fantasy is of course constituted through very specific desires; there is the desire that sexual desire be contained. And so an ethics of sexual indulgence, is anathematized and erased.

Contemporary definitions of the queer intersect with notions of fantasy narratives and fanfiction. Doty claims a primacy for queer reception that goes beyond mere subtext. Elizabeth Cowie likewise speaks to the ability of queer subjects to place themselves within the scenes of narrative and imagine erotic possibilities. She broadly argues that a subject may manifest agency by imagine her/himself within scenes of desire (*Representing the Woman*). Queer readings do not comply to (hetero)normative expectations and boundaries; instead, they could at any moment substantiate insubordinate narratives of possibility through moments of personal fantasy, causing ruptures in the previous narrative and eruptions of queer pleasure for the reader.

Given that queer readers must often rely on personal fantasy in order to establish a narrative that better speaks to their own lives, one could step up to Warner's invitation to resist normalized academic decorum in order to imagine here a pardoned Saruman living within the Shire at Merry's invitation. He and his retinue might settle nicely into the community. He might enter into a healthier relationship with Grima, restricted to using his voice only during scenes of consensual S/M role play. His ruffians might establish Sharkey's, a pub of their own, somewhere further in the woods where their late-night carousing would not be a disturbance, providing a refreshing and sexually liberating influence upon their neighbors. And perhaps Frodo stays and spends the remainder of his days with Sam, visited by an intimate number of aesthetically-minded gender-clastic elves.

This insertion of fantasy is not meant to merely amplify a sub-text; it is a potential revision *for* queer readers that could undermine the primacy of the hetero- and homo-normative ending. It might be for the average reader what Roland Barthes might call a "text of bliss," which "imposes a state of loss … discomforts … unsettles the reader's historical, cultural, psychological assumptions, the consistency of his tastes, values, memories, [and] brings to a crisis his relation with language" (Barthes, *Pleasure of the Text*, 14). This to my mind is one purpose of queer criticism.

The fantasy is queer because it resists the good sex/bad sex taxonomy; it is intra-male in its plot because that is the central mode of relations in Tolkien's text. The Christian Neoplatonism of *The Lord of the Rings* invites readers to accept all sorts of alterity, but it does so at the expense of a representation celebrating the full range of human sexuality (if we agree on Saruman's representation as thus). It, in fact, concretizes the normative good sex/bad sex binary. The fate of liberated sex, of innovative and kinky sex, of non-procreative and casual sex, of wild primal Orc sex, is the fate of the anathematized wizard Saruman.

Notes

1. Yandell's paper was later published as "Cruising Faery: Queer Desire in Giles, Niggle, and Smith," Vaccaro and Kisor, pp. 149–79. See also Žižek, "Neighbors and Other Monsters, and Saxton, who highlights the uncanny nature of Saruman, citing Gandalf's statement: "I am Saruman ... as he should have been."

2. While attempts were made to criminalize sex between women, none were successful. Nonetheless, an obscenity trial over Radclyffe Hall's *The Well of Loneliness* led to a ban on that novel in 1928.

3. An attempt to include female "indecent" behavior into the legal code was attempted in the early twenties but was not successful. This essay does not attempt to explore intra-female/lesbian love in relation to Tolkien's artistic and vocational spheres as the important topic deserves fuller treatment than can be given here. But if the semiotics around Saruman can be read as queer, so too can those around Shelob as both are linked to lust, excess, and a monstrous hyper-sexuality. See the essay in this volume, "Mother or Other: Tolkien's Shelob and the 'Monstrous-Feminine,'" by Sara Brown, 77–91.

4. Not to conflate consensual intra-male lovemaking with nonconsensual abuse, evidence exists that some within Tolkien's circle of struggled to find healthy expressions for their sexual and amorous orientations. See Catherine Pepinster's article in *The Guardian*. I bring up this article only to suggest the circulation of homosexual energies within the Tolkien family circle.

5. Warner borrows from the seminal essay by Gayle Rubin, "Thinking Sex: Notes for a Radical Theory of the Politics of Sexuality" (Vance).

6. Further critical inquiries concerning the queer in Tolkien have evolved over some time and include the following: Jane Chance's "Queer Hobbits," "Tough Love," "In the Company of Orcs: Peter Jackson's Queer Tolkien," "Tolkien and the Other: Race and Gender in Middle Earth," and *Tolkien, Self and Other*. See also: Battis, Craig, Rohy ("On Fairy Stories"; "Cinema, Sexuality, Mechanical Reproduction"), Rosenthal, Saxey, Smol, Timmons, Vaccaro ("Homosexuality,"), and Yandell.

7. Using James Tauber's wonderful corpus, *Digital Tolkien Project*, Kisor points out the following: "Forms of the term 'queer' are used sixty times in *The Lord of the Rings*, the vast majority in the first book: forty-three in *The Fellowship of the Ring* (thirty-eight in Book One and five in Book Two), fourteen in *The Two Towers* (eleven in Book Three and three in Book Four), and just three in *The Return of the King* (once in the text itself—Book Six—and twice in the appendices, both in 'Appendix F,' on the names of Bucklanders)" (4).

8. See Hocquenham: "The transmission of homosexuality has something faintly mysterious about it, like the production of desire: a prefect of Police quoted by Gustav Macé defines homosexuals as 'people who, though not procreating, have a marked tendency to multiply'" (109).

9. Tolkien states that the proper function of the Istari was "perverted by Saruman" (*Letters 1*, #144, 180).

10. This idea appears again in Tolkien's "Essay on the Istari" (1954) where we are told

Saruman, "becoming proud and impatient and enamored of power sought to have his own will by force" (*UT* 395.

11. See also J.R.R. Tolkien Collection, Marquette. Voice of Saruman, folder MSS-3/2/7 (FJ/VS I), 35/41. Christopher Tolkien supplies "wood-demons" and I defer to his excellent reading here. I simply cannot make it out.

12. J.R.R. Tolkien Collection, Marquette. Voice of Saruman, folder MSS-3/2/7 (FJ/VS I), 35/41.

13. J.R.R. Tolkien Collection, Marquette University, Department of Special Collections and University Archives, folder 3/9/23: 3 a-b. Christopher Tolkien, *End of Third Age*, 52 and 53.

14. First Draft A.J.R.R. Tolkien Collection, folder 3/18/16 (MP I), 4/12. See also *End of the Third Age* 65.

15. First draft A.J.R.R. Tolkien Collection, folder 3/8/16 (MP I), 5/12. See also *End of the Third Age*, 65.

16. Deidre Dawson makes the Lévinasian argument that language serves to bring Othered subjects together in *The Lord of the Rings*:

> Just as the greatest gift of the Elves, according to Treebeard, was teaching the trees and other beings to speak, so the greatest gift an individual can give her neighbor, the Other, is through *saying*, the act of acknowledging the Other through speech. Speech which is not meant to dominate or assimilate, but which signifies acceptance of a different voice from our own [198].

17. See first fair copy Draft B. See J.R.R. Tolkien Collection, folder 3/8/15 (MPII), 14/18.

18. As seen in the passage where Saruman looks upon Frodo with a bitter respect and hatred (*RK*, VI, vii, 299).

19. J.R.R. Tolkien collection, Scouring of the Shire, folder 3/8/44 , 86/96. See also *The Return of the King*, VI, viii, 300. Italicized words do not make it into the final publication. All quotations from the Tolkien manuscripts at Marquette University are © The Tolkien Estate Limited 2025. Thanks to the Tolkien Estate for permissions to include unpublished phrases. Thanks must go to William Fliss, the Archivist of the Tolkien Archives at Marquette University, for his assistance in locating the other instances of sentences attached to the galley proof. They are as follows: In Taming of Sméagol (a couple of sentences), in The Field of Cormallen (a version of the song of praise), in The Grey Havens (the title page of the Red Book).

WORKS CITED

Ahmed, Sara. *Queer Phenomenology*. Duke UP, 2006.
Barthes, Roland. *The Pleasure of the Text*. Translated by Richard Miller. Hill and Wang, 1975; rpt. 1998.
Battis, Jes. "Gazing Upon Sauron: Hobbits, Elves, and the Queering of the Postcolonial Optic." *MFS Modern Fiction Studies*, vol. 50, no. 4, 2004, pp. 908–26, doi.org/10.1353/mfs.2005.0001.
Carpenter, Humphrey. *J.R.R. Tolkien: A Biography*. Ballantine, 1977.
Chance, Jane. "'In the Company of Orcs': Peter Jackson's Queer Tolkien." *Queer Movie Medievalisms*, edited by Tison Pugh and Kathleen Coyne Kelly, Routledge, 2009, pp. 79–96.
_____. "'Queer' Hobbits: The Problem of Difference in the Shire." *The Lord of the Rings: The Mythology of Power*. Rev. ed., UP of Kentucky, 2001, pp. 26–37.
_____. "Tolkien and the Other: Race and Gender in Middle Earth," *Tolkien's Modern Middle Ages*, edited by Jane Chance and Alfred K. Siewers, Palgrave, 2005, pp. 171–86. The New Middle Ages (series)
_____. *Tolkien, Self and Other: "This Queer Creature."* Palgrave, 2016.
_____. "Tough Love: Teaching the New Medievalisms," *Studies in Medievalism*, vol. 18, ed. Karl Fugelso, Boydell & Brewer, D.S. Brewer, 2009, pp. 76–98.

"Concupiscence, N., Sense 1.a." Oxford English Dictionary, Oxford UP, June 2024, doi.org/10.1093/OED/6692964729.

Cowie, Elizabeth. *Representing the Woman: Cinema and Psychoanalysis*. U of Minnesota P, 1997.

Craig, David M. "'Queer Lodgings': Gender and Sexuality in *The Lord of the Rings*." *Mallorn*, iss. 38, Jan. 2001, pp. 11–18. Rpt. *Mallorn*, iss. 60, Winter 2020, pp. 20–29, journals.tolkiensociety.org/mallorn/article/view/145.

Croft, Janet Brennan, editor. *Tolkien and Shakespeare: Essays on Shared Themes and Languages*. Critical Explorations in Science Fiction and Fantasy 2. Donald E. Palumbo and C.W. Sullivan III, series editors. McFarland, 2007.

Dawson, Deidre. "Language and Alterity," Vaccaro and Kisor, pp. 183–203.

De Lauretis, Teresa. "Queer Texts, Bad Habits, and the Issue of the Future." *GLQ*, vol. 17, iss. 2–3. 2011, pp. 243–63.

Doty, Alexander. *Making Things Perfectly Queer: Interpreting Mass Culture*. U of Minnesota P, 1993.

Douglas, Alfred. "Two Loves." In *Chameleon* (December 1894).

Flieger, Verlyn. "The Arch and the Keystone." *Mythlore*, vol. 38, no. 1, article 3, 2019, pp. 5–17, dc.swosu.edu/mythlore/vol38/iss1/3.

Freud, Sigmund. "Beyond the Pleasure Principle." *The Revised Standard Edition of the Complete Psychological Works of Sigmund Freud*, translated by James Strachey and Mark Solms, vol 18, Rowman & Littlefield, 2024, pp. 7–64.

Garth, John. *Tolkien and the Great War: The Threshold of Middle-earth*. Houghton Mifflin, 2003.

———. *Tolkien at Exeter College: How an Oxford Undergraduate Created Middle-earth*. Exeter College, 2014.

Halberstam, Jack. *The Queer Art of Failure*. Duke UP, 2011.

———. *Trans*: A Quick and Quirky Account of Gender Variability*. U of California P, 2018.

Hall, Donald. *Queer Theories*. Palgrave, 2003.

Helms, Randel. *Tolkien's World*. Houghton Mifflin, 1974.

Hocquenham, Guy. *Homosexual Desire*. Translated by Daniella Dangoor. Duke UP, 1993.

Jagose, Annemarie. *Queer Theory*. New York UP, 1996.

Kisor, Yvette. "Queer Tolkien: A Bibliographical Essay on Tolkien and Alterity." Vaccaro and Kisor, pp. 17–32.

———. "'We Could Do with a Bit More Queerness in These Parts': An Analysis of the Queer against the Peculiar, the Odd, and the Strange in *The Lord of the Rings*." *Journal of Tolkien Research*, vol. 16, iss. 2, article 4, 2023, scholar.valpo.edu/journalof tolkienresearch/vol16/iss1/4/.

Kristeva, Julia. *Powers of Horror*. Translated by Leon Roudiez. Columbia UP, 1982.

Ozment, Nicholas. "Prospero's Books, Gandalf's Staff," Croft, pp. 177–95.

Pepinster, Catherine. "JRR [sic] Tolkien's Son 'sexually Abused by One of Father's Friends." The Observer, *The Guardian*, 28 April 2019, theguardian.com/books/2019/apr/28/jrr-tolkiens-son-claims-sexually-abuse-fathers-friend.

"Pervert, N., Sense 1." Oxford English Dictionary, Oxford UP, September 2024, doi.org/10.1093/OED/4945970961.

"Pervert, N., Sense 2." Oxford English Dictionary, Oxford UP, September 2024, doi.org/10.1093/OED/5556370864.

Rosenthal, Ty. "Warm Beds Are Good: Sex and Libid.o in Tolkien's Writing." *Mallorn*, vol. 42, 2004, pp. 35–42.

Rohy, Valerie. "Cinema, Sexuality, Mechanical Reproduction." Vaccaro and Kisor, pp. 111–22.

———. "On Fairy Stories." *MFS Modern Fiction Studies*, vol. 50, no. 4, 2004, pp. 927–48, doi.org/10.1353/mfs.2005.0009.

Rubin, Gayle. "Thinking Sex: Notes for a Radical Theory of the Politics of Sexuality." In *Culture, Society, and Sexuality: A Reader*, edited by Richard Parker and Peter Aggleton. Routledge, 2014, pp. 143–78.

Saxey, Esther. "Homoeroticism." *Reading* The Lord of the Rings, edited by Robert Eaglestone, Continuum, 2006, pp. 124–37.
Saxton, Benjamin. "Tolkien and Bakhtin on Authorship, Literary Freedom, and Alterity." *Tolkien Studies*, vol. 10, 2013, pp. 167–84.
Sedgwick, Eve Kosofsky. *Tendencies*. Duke UP, 1993.
Smol, Anna. "'Oh. Oh. Frodo!': Readings of Male Intimacy in *The Lord of the Rings*." *MFS Modern Fiction Studies*, vol. 50, no. 4, 2004, pp. 949–79.
Sutton, John William. *Death and Violence in Old and Middle English Literature*. Edwin Mellen P, 2007.
Tauber, James. *Digital Tolkien Project*. digitaltolkien.com/.
Timmons, Daniel. "Hobbit Sex and Sensuality in *The Lord of the Rings*." *Mythlore*, vol. 23, no. 3, article 7, Summer 2001, pp. 70–79, dc.swosu.edu/mythlore/vol23/iss3/7/.
Tolkien, J.R.R. *The End of the Third Age*, edited by Christopher Tolkien, Houghton Mifflin, 1992.
———. *The Fellowship of the Ring*. 2nd ed., Houghton Mifflin, 1987.
———. *The Letters of J.R.R. Tolkien*, edited by Humphrey Carpenter, assisted by Christopher Tolkien, Houghton Mifflin, 1995.
———. *The Return of the King*. 2nd ed., Houghton Mifflin, 1987.
———. *The Treason of Isengard*, edited by Christopher Tolkien, 1989. The History of Middle-earth, vol. 7.
———. *The Two Towers*. 2nd ed., Houghton Mifflin, 1987.
———. *Unfinished Tales: Of Númenor and Middle-earth*, edited by Christopher Tolkien, Houghton Mifflin, 1980.
———. *The War of the Ring*, edited by Christopher Tolkien, Houghton Mifflin, 1990. The History of Middle-earth, vol. 8.
Vaccaro, Christopher. ""Dyrne Langað": Secret Longing and Homo-amory in Beowulf and J.R.R. Tolkien's *The Lord of the Rings*." *Journal of Tolkien Research*, vol. 6, iss. 1, article 6, 2018, scholar.valpo.edu/journaloftolkienresearch/vol6/iss1/6.
———. "Homosexuality." *J.R.R. Tolkien Encyclopedia: Scholarship and Critical Assessment*. Edited by Michael D. C. Drout, Routledge, 2007; 2013, pp. 285–6.
———. "'Morning Stars of a Setting World': Alain de Lille's *De Planctu Naturæ* and Tolkien's Legendarium as Neo-Platonic Mythopoeia." *Mythlore*, vol. 36, iss. 1, article 6, 2017, pp. 81–102, dc.swosu.edu/mythlore/vol36/iss1/6/.
———. "Saruman's Sodomitic Resonances: Alain de Lille's *De Planctu Naturæ* and J.R.R. Tolkien's *The Lord of the Rings*." Vaccaro and Kisor, pp. 123–47.
Vaccaro, Christopher, and Yvette Kisor, editors. *Tolkien and Alterity*. Palgrave, 2017.
Warner, Michael. *Fear of a Queer Planet: Queer Politics and Social Theory*. U of Minnesota P, 1993.
———. *The Trouble with Normal: Sex, Politics, and the Ethics of Queer Life*. Harvard UP, 1999.
Wiggins, Kayla McKinney. "The Person of a Prince: Echoes of *Hamlet* in J.R.R. Tolkien's *The Lord of the Rings*. *Tolkien and Shakespeare: Essays on Shared Themes and Language*, edited by Janet Brennan Croft, pp. 91–109.
Wilson, James. "Cynewulf and Cyneheard: The Falls of Princes." *Papers on Language and Literature* vol. 13, no. 3. Summer 1977, pp. 312–17.
Yandell, Stephen. "Cruising Faery: Queer Desire in Giles, Niggle, and Smith." Vaccaro and Kisor, pp. 149–79.
Žižek, Slavoj. "Neighbors and Other Monsters." *The Neighbor: Three Inquiries in Political Theology*. Edited by Slavoj Žižek, Eric L. Santner, and Kenneth Reinhard, U of Chicago P, 2005.
———. *The Plague of Fantasies*. Verso, 1997.

Part IV

Queer Transformations

"and stooping he raised Beleg and kissed his mouth"

Queering Canon with Tolkien Fanfiction

Maria K. Alberto

The story of the human hero Túrin Turambar is one of what J.R.R. Tolkien called the three "Great Tales" of his Legendarium, which he envisioned underlying and inspiring the larger narrative of Arda. Given their centrality and importance, Tolkien reworked each of the three Great Tales—the lives of Beren and Lúthien and the fall of Gondolin, as well as Túrin's story—multiple times over the course of his own life. This reworking resulted in numerous drafts that his son Christopher Tolkien variously incorporated into the 1977 *Silmarillion*, collected in the *Histories of Middle-earth* from 1983 to 1996, and published in free-standing versions such as *The Children of Húrin* in 2007, *Beren and Lúthien* in 2017, and *The Fall of Gondolin* in 2018. However, this proliferation of drafts for each of the Great Tales also means that particular versions include details, or sometimes even entire events, that the other accounts do not. And in the case of Túrin's story, one of the details that varies among drafts includes what some Tolkien fans have called the "canon kisses," which occur between Túrin and his Elven companion Beleg Cúthalion in two of the five versions of this tale.

Many of the details that remain the same across all versions of Túrin's story already concern Beleg.[1] For instance, readers are shown that the two form a close bond: Beleg first meets Túrin as a young child refugee, then helps mentor and train him, and then serves alongside him as they protect the hidden Elven kingdom of Doriath. Later Beleg also leaves Doriath to follow Túrin when the younger man is banished for supposedly killing a courtier, then "yielding to his love against his wisdom" (*The Children of Hurin* [*Children*] 139), Beleg remains in the wilderness with Túrin and his band of outlaws. Another narrative element that remains consistent across versions is that Túrin eventually kills Beleg by accident while the Elven warrior is trying to rescue him from capture by Orcs.

My essay here takes the kisses between Beleg and Túrin as a starting point from which to, first, theorize the notion of "queering the canon" and then second, to consider what this idea could offer to both personal and scholarly readings of Tolkien, which each must reckon with his vast and multiply-drafted vision of Arda. As the rest of this collection aptly demonstrates, Tolkien's legendarium already constitutes a rich and rewarding site for queer reading(s) and transformative engagement, even when Tolkien scholarship has also questioned how we might arrive at these possibilities, how intentional they were, and what Tolkien himself might have thought of them. Those invested in such inquiries certainly include queer studies scholars and readers interested in queer potentials, but also transformative fans who look to create their own work(s) derived from Middle-earth. While these audiences have certain interests in common, transformative fans and their engagement of Tolkien's corpus evidence a particularly queer means by which we can approach Tolkien's legendarium: as a multiplicitous corpus, this body of work represents an entire canon that can be queered, rather than just the reading practices one brings to it, or else the characters and narratives within it.

Queering, Canon(s) and Queering Canon(s): A Brief Consideration of Terms

Several of the terms and concepts that I invoke in order to make this claim are complex, shifting ones worth revisiting. "Canon," for instance, is a significant yet fraught idea, both for fandom and also, increasingly, for critical studies of popular culture. Meanwhile, the term "queering" stems from a particular milieu, but its deliberate ambiguities and its expansion beyond that initial context also render it complex.

In one of its earliest senses, "canon" describes a definitive set of texts used to set the standards for a category, such as a genre like science fiction or a tradition such as Christian scripture. Movements such as the canon wars of American higher education during the 1980s–90s used this term to either set or interrogate standards of intellectual thought, such as which authors were considered foundational for a liberal arts education, or whether that foundation overly prioritized white men of European descent when in fact literature and cultural productions have always come from a far more diverse range of creators. This use of "canon" to describe high culture was then taken up by fandom, wherein canon came to denote "the collection of texts considered to be the authoritative source for fan creations" (Busse 101). More recently—and increasingly, as transmedia adaptations become more numerous—the term "canon" has been taken up by producers of popular culture texts. In this context, "the canon" comprises the texts that producers proclaim to be telling the official story: so, films may be called canon to a franchise while videogames are not. In each of these usages, though, the use of the word "canon" evokes a sense of authority and knowledge, in order to distinguish between types and delineate their value(s). Put differently, canon is imagined to differentiate high from low, true from apocryphal, authorized from unauthorized, which it does by evaluating and treating these as distinct categories.

Tolkien and his legendarium occupy a complex place in relation to these concepts of canon. For one thing, Tolkien's place within the larger literary canon is still contested—that is, the literary quality of his work has been debated by critics since *The Lord of the Rings* first became popular, and there is still debate about whether to teach his work at the university level, and, if so, then whether as an English author, a modernist, a Catholic author, a World War I or World War II author, and/or a fantasy author. Likewise, Tolkien has also long been hailed as a "father of fantasy," in the sense that successive authors writing in this genre—primarily in English and Anglo-American contexts, but also in other languages and circumstances—have built from, debated, combatted, or departed from his work as a foundational point (Moran 8). In the third sense, fans may read Tolkien's multiplicitous body of work, finding multiple versions of pre–Third Age stories such as the Great Tales and considering these differences in terms of which is "most true"—itself a slippery term that could mean, "closest to authorial intent" or "most sensible within this fictional storyworld" or something else altogether, depending on the person using it. Finally, adaptations such as Jackson's film trilogies, videogames like *Shadow of Mordor*, and the more recent *The Lord of the Rings: The Rings of Power*, have spurred conversations about how much they draw or change from Tolkien's own words, breathing new life into much older, longer-running debates about fidelity in adaptation as, now, questions of canon.

The term "queering" also admits of several definitions. It is generally understood to derive from queer reading, or what Alexander Doty in *Making Things Perfectly Queer* has described as "the recognition and articulation of the complex range of queerness that has been in popular cultural texts and their audiences all along" (16). Notably, new media forms such as games can make queer readings more difficult when new modalities require new methods of reading, or when audiences debate whether meaning is implicit or explicit (Shaw and Persaud par. 1–2). Queering, though, tends to be more active: that is, it seeks not simply to excavate queer meanings from its subject, but also adjust, transform, or revolutionize that subject itself. This approach has been applied to topics ranging from migration (for example, queering borders) to art and music (for example, *Queering the Pitch*, edited by Brett, Wood, and Thomas) as well as cultural and historical figures and their work (for example, queering J.D. Salinger). Simultaneously, there is also a dialogue about whether "queering" is too ambiguous and subsequently, of how to ensure rigor without forcing rigidity; these concerns mirror larger debates over queer studies as a discipline, and even the word "queer" itself, that have recurred since its growing usage in the early 1990s.

These concerns come together in the term I open this essay with, "queering the canon." In one sense, this usage could describe simply pushing to make a cultural or artistic category more inclusive of queer works and perspectives initially marginalized from it. An example of this is Christoph Lorey and John L. Plews's *Queering the Canon*, which seeks to highlight gay German literature, and in doing so, thus challenge the more predominant narrative that heterosexual works and authors constitute the category of renowned German literature. But I am identifying something slightly to the left of this purpose—a practice that will be familiar to many transformative fans, particularly those who write fanfiction. Namely, another possibility for queering the canon is to destabilize how this tool of categorization itself works, rather than simply expanding it or doing queer readings of what is already included in it.

While far from the only example of this practice—or even the only example of it in Tolkien's legendarium—I turn to the kisses of Beleg and Túrin because they offer a paradigmatic case that we can trace and follow. Notable here are how transformative Tolkien fans seek out the kisses in the multiple drafts of the tale, where they locate these gestures, and what they must do in order to remediate them once found.

The Canon Kisses

This particular case of queering the canon begins with a more material set of considerations based on texts. As previously mentioned, there are five versions of this particular Great Tale extant as of this writing. Túrin's story is told in chapter 21 of *The Silmarillion (S)*, "Of Túrin Turambar" (*S* 1977); in "Narn i Hîn Húrin," included in *Unfinished Tales (UT* 1980); in "Turambar and the Foalókë," as included in *The Book of Lost Tales II (LT II* 1984); in "The Lay of the Children of Húrin," as collected in *The Lays of Beleriand (Lays* 1985); and finally, in the standalone *Children of*

Húrin (2007). Beyond the fact that each of these versions may present different details or events, each is also characterized by more technical and functional differences too. Looking at just Túrin's own story, we will find that various versions are in verse or in prose ("The Lay" versus all others); are presented as "finished" or "unfinished"/annotated texts (the *Silmarillion* chapter and *Children* versus "The Lay," "Narn," and "Foalókë"); and may either stand as self-contained narratives or else be located as one smaller part intertwined with other tales within a larger history of Arda ("The Lay," "Foalókë," and *CoH* versus "Narn" and the *Silmarillion* chapter). Then, looking at the material texts themselves, we find that some of these are simpler to find (*The Silmarillion* graces more bookshelf stores than the full *Histories of Middle-earth*); more affordable to collect (I paid over $100 a decade ago for my copy of *HoMe*, which is a box set repackaging the twelve *History of Middle-earth* books into three volumes); and easier to read (the already-dense *HoMe* is also replete with bibliographic materials and multiple drafts that make traditional reading, from one cover to the other, difficult if not impossible).

How transformative Tolkien fans locate the gestures of these "canon kisses," then, entails excavating them from reams of often dense, less-accessible material—or else, learning about them from fellow fans who have done so and then created fanworks based upon that discovery. In Beleg and Túrin's case, this second possibility is especially worth stressing because, unlike other *Silmarillion*-based character pairings, these details of Beleg and Túrin's story are less completely documented in fan-facing texts like online wikis, which otherwise are quite comprehensive and accessible resources dedicated to detailing Tolkien's voluminous canon. This collective excavation and sharing of canon already queers reading practices in various ways: it disrupts typical linear reading practices, focuses upon un-traditional texts, and shares hard-earned knowledge among community members who may lack the textual resources or access to make these discoveries firsthand.

Where transformative Tolkien fans locate these gestures is also telling. Among the five versions listed above, the canon kisses between Beleg and Túrin are found only in two of the unfinished, annotated versions of Túrin's story—the verse "Lay" and the prose "Turambar and the Foalókë," with the latter actually being the earliest version extant. The veiled location and non-normative structure of the two versions that contain these kisses are well worth noting, though delving through and reading them is arguably less queer in and of itself—scholars and fans alike regularly wade out into posthumously-assembled, non-linear, non-narrative texts seeking new insights into narratives or materials of interest.

What transformative Tolkien fans do to remediate the canon kisses once they have been located, though, involves material, thematic, and reiterative practices alike. All of these, I maintain, can be described as various forms of queering, and together they form an example of what I have been calling queering the canon.

Genre is the first important consideration here. Tolkien's legendarium is famously difficult to classify along genre lines: in a much-quoted missive to publisher Milton Waldman Tolkien calls the beginning of *The Silmarillion* "a cosmogonical myth" (*The Letters of J.R.R. Tolkien* [*Letters 1*], #131, 146) and the middle a history that leaves myth to become "more like stories and romances" with the entrance of humankind (#131, 149). He also calls *The Hobbit* a "fairy-story" from this larger whole (#131, 158–9), while *The Lord of the Rings* is a tale of "world politics" in Middle-earth as past events and figures "[come] down from myth and legend" (#131, 160). In scholarly terms, this profusion of genre is echoed by Christopher Vaccaro and Yvette Kisor, who maintain that *The Lord of the Rings* alone "has been called an epic, a romance, and a novel, among other genres. It partakes of older genres at the same time it births a new one, high fantasy" (27). In terms of precedent genres, Tolkien's letter to Waldman also cites Greek, Celtic, Germanic, Scandinavian, and Finnish legend as inspirations for his work overall (144), but claims that tragedy is undeniably the main influence for Túrin's story, as it is a "tragic tale" that is "derived from elements in Sigurd the Volsung, Oedipus, and the Finnish Kullervo" (150).

Reading any version of Túrin's story thus reveals what John Rateliff has called Tolkien "borrowing" and "mixing" elements of specific genres and texts within them in order to create specific structures, signs, stylistic configurations, and other formal characteristics in his own work (144–5). In *Children of Hurin* alone, this impetus results in phrases such as Beleg's "yielding to his love" (139), Túrin's "desire of his heart" (139), and the "tryst" of them meeting (139). Such phrases can certainly be understood as an example of why Richard Mathews calls *The Silmarillion* "an 'epic of return' in the high mimetic mode" (58)—or, alternately, how Tison Pugh has explained that in medieval literature "declarations of love and devotion are [often] revealed to be eloquent displays of manner, etiquette, and, for the most part, non-sexual affections" (25). These dictation choices also describe a relationship that is quasi-feudal, very familiar, and undeniably long-standing, since Beleg has sworn fealty to Túrin's adoptive father figure, Elu Thingol the King of Doriath, and evidences a deep loyalty to Túrin himself; meanwhile, Túrin is attached to Beleg as a protector figure he has known since childhood and a fellow warrior he has fought alongside for years. Together these social bonds and the specific ways they are described in Túrin's story are familiar, even expected, within the genres that Tolkien draws from.

For transformative Tolkien fans to remediate the canon kisses, then, entails relocating descriptions and depictions of their relationship into genre contexts where these gestures are *not* simply what Pugh describes as "manner, etiquette, and, for the most part, non-sexual affections" (25). The possibilities for doing so are numerous, though. Beleg continually describes his relationship with Túrin and his reasons for seeking him as those of his love (*S* 202, 207); elsewhere Túrin has tears in his eyes upon seeing Beleg again, just before Beleg falls into his arms (*Children* 139). Later on, Túrin can take action after threats to the elven princess Finduilas or the human woman Níniel, but when he accidentally kills Beleg he then stays "unmoving and unweeping in the tempest" beside Beleg's body despite the threat of Orcs attacking (*S* 210). Readers are also told that Beleg's death came "at the hand of him whom he most loved; and that grief was graven on the face of Túrin and never faded" (*S* 211–12). The fan practices that I am describing thus recognizes moment of queer potential in order to, later, re-articulate that potential as queer.

The question of genre, and the answer of tragedy and epic, also leads into the initial context of the canon kisses, which is an important second consideration for what transformative Tolkien fans must remediate. In "Lay," after Túrin releases Beleg from his captivity by the outlaws Túrin himself leads, "then he kissed him kindly / comfort speaking" (line 594); then, later in the same version, after Túrin has accidentally killed Beleg, "on the corse [sic] cast him, and kissed the mouth / cold and open, and closed the eyes" (lines 1404–1405). The kiss in "Turambar and the Foalókë" likewise takes place after Beleg's death at Túrin's hands: "and stooping he raised Beleg and kissed his mouth" (*LT II* 80). Readers will have encountered somewhat comparable gestures in *The Lord of the Rings*, where the hobbits and the warriors of Gondor sometimes place kisses to the brow or hands to signify fealty, honor, or grief. In this case, though, Túrin kisses Beleg as a way of showing kindness and providing comfort after Beleg has been held captive, wrongly, by those Túrin commands ("Lay"), and then again in a frenzied grief when Beleg is already dead by his hand ("Lay" UT). These are both instances that speak to a long familiarity—and arguably a deeper, more personal emotion—between these two characters than between their counterparts from *The Lord of the Rings*: this bond is distinct from fealty, even though intertwined with it, and then a grief that is devoid of thanks or honor. Likewise, these kisses may come across with a different sort of poignancy and meaning because they are placed upon the mouth rather than the head or hands.

From genre and initial context, then, we arrive at a third consideration that transformative Tolkien fans must engage and remediate: intent. By invoking the notoriously tricky notion of authorial intent, I do not mean to oversimplify or to echo the common but contested refrain of "but

Tolkien didn't say it was gay." Instead, I point to the previous discussions of genre and context in order to highlight the canon kisses as a question of tragic convention, not sexual orientation. Transformative Tolkien fans are not unaware that they are reading gestures and signs created and intended for a very specific context. So, I maintain, it is what they then do with this awareness that queers it.

As this consideration of Beleg and Túrin's canon kisses demonstrates, then, queering the canon may certainly include queer readings as well as sites of queer potential within a canonical text. For instance Yvette Kisor, looking to future avenues for queer Tolkien scholarship, has identified "[s]trong, devoted male relationships [in] *The Silmarillion*" (24) as important possibilities, and "Beleg's devotion to Túrin" is one of her primary examples (24). However, queering the canon also entails disrupting the category of a canon in the first place. In this case, some transformative Tolkien fans consider the non-normative unfinished drafts on par with more normative finished ones; these fans also pool and share knowledge from these complicated sites with one another and extricate the norms of one genre, context, and understanding of authorial intent in order to relocate specific signs or gestures from their original place into alternative contexts that create new meanings for them.

Having Queered the Canon: Beleg and Túrin Fanfiction

Such instances—and even language—that depict intimacy, familiarity, and tragic circumstances between central male characters are not unique to the tale of Beleg and Túrin, or even to Tolkien's work. Likewise, no matter the text where such examples occur, they often provide fodder for shipping and ships, which respectively describe the fan practice and outcome of "creating new erotic relationships between characters [that are] un-substantiated in the official narratives or source texts, and characterized through fan-authored practices of imagining, rewriting and 'fictioning'" (Parry 127). Thanks to my decade-plus of experience in transformative Tolkien fandom, particularly the corner dedicated to *The Silmarillion*, I can say that Beleg/Túrin is not one of the major "ships" within even Silmarillion fandom, but it has certainly inspired a wealth of transformative fanworks.[2] Moreover, these various fanworks often remediate and re-present particular details or language drawn from various versions of Túrin's tale, sometimes with creator's notes or other paratextual materials identifying the particular source.

For instance, "Love, Not Wisdom" is a short, anonymized work of fanfiction published on the Archive of Our Own (AO3) (Orphan_Account). Of the many possible options, I choose to focus on this piece because it cannot be traced to a particular author, thus preventing any one fan-creator from receiving unexpected, potentially unwanted attention.[3] "Love, Not Wisdom" is set after the second time Beleg returns to Túrin among the outlaws, and the story follows a heated conversation in which Beleg explains to Túrin why he thinks the human outlaws do not trust him, but Túrin rejects Beleg's offer to leave the group. As the fic progresses, Túrin's memories and the characters' dialogue reveals that Beleg and Túrin slept together the first time Beleg appeared, and now Beleg thinks their continuing relationship is hurting Túrin's reputation.

Both the language and the proceedings of "Love, Not Wisdom" reveal a familiarity with their precedents in Tolkien's various versions of Túrin's story. For one thing, it explicitly locates the beginning of their relationship after, as Beleg here puts it, "what happened last time we met; when I came to you with messages from Doriath" (par. 6): as Túrin recollects it, "The memory was still sharp and vivid, of the first night that Beleg had been healed fully—a hand twined in his hair, dragging his head back, hot breath on his ear, Beleg's murmurs and his own cries" (par. 7). Both Beleg's journey and his previous need of healing being referenced here invoke versions of the tale wherein Beleg was captured and tied up by Túrin's outlaw gang—such as the "Lay" version where Túrin kisses Beleg both in apology for his captivity and for comfort following the fact.

Later in this fanfiction, Beleg quietly censures himself for the way Túrin has been raised "wild" and tells Túrin not to call him wise, for Beleg does not feel that way when around the human hero. This turn continues with the passage:

> "Do not blame yourself," Túrin said, a flare of anger rising in him, and would have kissed him again; but Beleg pulled back.
> "I have yielded to love in this matter, as I never had before," he said softly. "You have my heart in a snare, Túrin, and I do not know how to free myself. In the northern marches I sought to forget; but I was maddened by thought of you, and the wilderness seemed painful in its emptiness for the first time" [para. 11–12].

Beleg also continues by cautioning that if their liaison continues, then Túrin will lose his other companions' respect—a warning that canon-savvy readers will recognize as a precursor of both tensions among Túrin's outlaws and later betrayal by Mîm the Petty Dwarf.

Throughout "Love," too, are multiple narratives repurposed right from Tolkien's versions. The kiss of comfort has become the precursor to a romantic and sexual relationship, and Beleg's originally feudal and personal reasons for rejoining Túrin despite the human's outlaw status are now combined with sexual attraction and romantic longing. Likewise, the language of how "Beleg came back to Túrin, yielding to his love against his wisdom" (*Children* 139) is transformed into Beleg's admission that "I have yielded to love in this matter, as I never had before" ("Love, Not Wisdom" par. 12). In these ways, Beleg and Túrin's relationship becomes more than an "ennobling love of men" (Jaeger 26) contextualized through conventions of friendship, courtly love, feudal loyalty, or religious devotion in earlier literary genres. Here, various canons are queered to produce a version wherein Beleg's love of Túrin is romantic and sexual in nature, and fully desired and reciprocated.

Concluding Thoughts

Much excellent scholarship on Tolkien's legendarium has observed its potential for transformative fanfiction, queer practices, or a combination of the two. Megan Abrahamson, for instance, draws important parallels between Tolkien's derivation from older sources and then fanfiction that derives from his corpus; Abrahamson also argues that fanfiction is participating in Tolkien's well-known early conceptualization of his own work as a "cycle" of stories that "other minds and hands" could add to (2). Dawn Walls-Thumma also offers several important perspectives on how fanfiction engages the mytho-historical project of *The Silmarillion* itself, such as by interrogating historical bias or addressing the absence of named women. Likewise, Robin Anne Reid notes that specific kinds of fanfiction derived from Tolkien's work—such as male/male slash or taboo-themed "darkfic"—necessitate "complex relationships between reading and writing practices," often in negotiations of language, performance, and gender (463). The practices identified in each of these strands also often expand upon queer potentials already present in Tolkien canon—that is, sites and possibilities for queerness visible both the texts that Tolkien himself authored, as identified early on by Valerie Rohy and David Craig, as well as in adaptations like Peter Jackson's films, as overviewed by Anna Smol, Jane Chance, and others.

What I hope this essay adds to ongoing conversations about both queering Tolkien and even about "canon" as an organizing structure, then, is a clearer sense of how transformative fans, their works, and their practices operate a higher structural level than previously considered. As demonstrated with the case of Beleg and Túrin, transformative fans may be queering the very canon, as well as practicing queer reading strategies and offering queer works of their own.

Notes

1. For a queer medieval reading of Tolkien's Túrin and Beleg, see the essay in this volume by Zachary Clifton Engledow: "'Bending over with naked blade': The Erotics of Suffering and Male-Male Penetration in Tolkien's Legendarium" (140–52).

2. As of this writing in spring 2025, there are over 330 works on the fanfiction site Archive of Our Own (AO3) that are tagged to show they depict a sexual relationship between Beleg and Túrin, as well as several pages of results featuring Túrin as a central character on The Silmarillion Writers' Guild and a vast quantity of fanart and other works on Tumblr. Conversely, male/male "ships" or character pairings featured in more works on AO3 include Maedhros and Fingon, Melkor and Mairon [Melkor and Sauron], Glorfindel and Erestor, and Celebrimbor and Annatar. I cite these numbers as a quick example, not a representative one, as the latter focus would easily constitute another entire work.

3. The ethics of citing fanworks currently constitute an ongoing conversation in the field of fan studies. Here scholars debate whether to cite works not published for consumption beyond specific in-communities, even if those works are also technically available to everyone online, and especially when such works may deal with sensitive or taboo topics. A full overview is beyond the scope of this essay, but see Sect 4.1 "A Brief Note on Our Methodology" in Sapuridis and Alberto.

Works Cited

Abrahamson, Megan. "J.R.R. Tolkien, Fanfiction, and 'The Freedom of the Reader.'" *Mythlore*, vol. 32, no. 1, 201, dc.swosu.edu/mythlore/vol32/iss1/5.

Brett, Philip, Elizabeth Wood, and Gary C. Thomas, editors. *Queering the Pitch: The New Gay and Lesbian Musicology*. 2nd ed. Routledge, 2007.

Busse, Kristina. *Framing Fan Fiction: Literary and Social Practices in Fan Fiction Communities*. U of Iowa P, 2017.

Craig, David M. "'Queer Lodgings': Gender and Sexuality in *The Lord of the Rings*." *Mallorn*, vol. 38, Jan. 2001, pp. 11–18, journals.tolkiensociety.org/mallorn/article/view/145/139. Rpt. "Queer Lodgings: Gender and Sexuality in *The Lord of the Rings*—Reprinted with a New Introduction by the Author." *Mallorn*, Vol. 61, 2020, pp. 20–29.

Doty, Alexander. 1993. *Making Things Perfectly Queer: Interpreting Mass Culture*. U of Minnesota P, 1993.

Jaeger, C. Stephen. *Ennobling Love: In Search of a Lost Sensibility*. Illustrated ed., U of Pennsylvania P, 1999. The Middle Ages Series.

Kisor, Yvette. "Queer Tolkien: A Bibliographic Essay on Tolkien and Alterity." In *Tolkien and Alterity*, edited by Christopher Vaccaro and Yvette Kisor, Palgrave Macmillan, 2017, pp. 17–32.

Lorey, Christoph, and John L. Plews, editors. *Queering the Canon: Defying Sights in German Literature and Culture*. Camden House, 1998, Studies in German Literature Linguistics and Culture.

Mathews, Richard. *Lightning from a Clear Sky: Tolkien, the Trilogy, and the Silmarillion*. Borgo P, 1978.

McCormack, Una. "Finding Ourselves in the (Un)Mapped Lands: Women's Reparative Readings of *The Lord of the Rings*." *Perilous and Fair: Women in the Works and Life of J.R.R. Tolkien*, edited by Janet Brennan Croft and Leslie A. Donovan, Mythopoeic P, 2015, pp. 309–326

Moran, Patrick. *The Canons of Fantasy: Lands of High Adventure*. Cambridge UP, 2019, Elements in Publishing and Book Culture.

Orphan_Account. "Love, Not Wisdom." *Archive of Our Own*, 27 May 2013, archiveofourown.org/works/820062.

Parry, Owen [owko69]. "'Shipping' (as) Fandom and Art Practice." *Fandom as Methodology: A Sourcebook for Artists and Writers*, edited by Catherine Grant and Kate Random Love, Goldsmiths P, 2019, pp. 127–146.

Pugh, Tison. *Queering Medieval Genres.* Palgrave Macmillan, 2004.
Rateliff, John. "Inside Literature: Tolkien's Explorations of Medieval Genres." *Tolkien in the New Century: Essays in Honor of Tom Shippey,* edited by John Houghton, et al. McFarland, 2014, pp. 133–152.
Reid, Robin Anne. "Thrusts in the Dark: Slashers' Queer Practices." *Extrapolation,* vol. 50, no. 3, 2009, pp. 463–483.
Rohy, Valerie. "On Fairy Stories." *MFS: Modern Fiction Studies,* J.R.R. Tolkien Special Issue, guest editor Shaun F. D. Hughes, vol. 50, no. 4, 2004, pp. 927–948.
Sapuridis, Effie, and Maria K. Alberto. "Self-Insert Fanfiction as Digital Technology of the Self." *Humanities,* special issue of *The Past, Present and Future of Fan-Fiction* edited by Lincoln Geraghty and Bertha Chin, vol. 11, no. 3, 2022, 68, doi.org/10.3390/h11030068.
Shaw, Adrienne, and Christopher J. Persaud. "Beyond Texts: Using Queer Readings to Document LGBTQ Game Content." *First Monday,* vol. 25, no. 8, 24 July 2020, doi.org/10.5210/fm.v25i8.10439.
Smol, Anna. "'Oh…oh…Frodo!': Readings of Male Intimacy in the Lord of the Rings." *Modern Fiction Studies,* J.R.R. Tolkien Special Issue, guest editor Shaun F.D. Hughes, vol. 50, no. 4, 2004, pp. 949–79, doi.org/10.1353/mfs.2005.0010.
Sturgis, Amy H. "Reimagining Rose: Portrayals of Tolkien's Rosie Cotton in Twenty-First Century Fan Fiction." *Mythlore,* vol. 24, no. 3, article 10, 2006, dc.swosu.edu/mythlore/vol24/iss3/10, pp. 165–187.
Tolkien, J.R.R. *The Book of Lost Tales II,* edited by Christopher Tolkien, *The History of Middle-Earth, Part One (History of Middle-earth I),* William Morrow, 2011.
_____. *The Children of Húrin,* edited by Christopher Tolkien, Houghton Mifflin, 2007.
_____. *The Lays of Beleriand,* edited by Christopher Tolkien, Vol. 3, *The History of Middle-earth, The History Of Middle-Earth, Part Two (History of Middle-earth II),* William Morrow, 2011.
_____. *The Letters of J.R.R. Tolkien,* edited by Humphrey Carpenter, assisted by Christopher Tolkien, Houghton Mifflin, 1981.
_____. *The Silmarillion,* edited by Christopher Tolkien, Houghton Mifflin, 1977.
_____. *Unfinished Tales: Of Númenor and Middle-earth,* edited by Christopher Tolkien, Houghton Mifflin, 1980.
Vaccaro, Christopher, and Yvette Kisor. "Introduction." *Tolkien and Alterity,* edited by Christopher Vaccaro and Yvette Kisor. Palgrave Macmillan, 2017, pp. 1–13.
Viars, Karen, and Cait Coker. "Constructing Lothíriel: Rewriting and Rescuing the Women of Middle-Earth [sic] from the Margins," *Mythlore,* vol. 33, no. 2, article 6, 2015, pp. 35–48.
Walls-Thumma, Dawn. "Attainable Vistas: Historical Bias in Tolkien's Legendarium as a Motive for Transformative Fanworks." *Journal of Tolkien Research,* vol. 3, iss. 3, 2016, scholar.valpo.edu/journaloftolkienresearch/vol3/iss3/3.

"What care I for the hands of a king?"

Tolkien Fanfiction and Narratives of the Transgender Self

Cordeliah G. Logsdon

> We hunger for stories, for that is the earth in which we take root.—Anglachel, *Hands of the King*

J.R.R. Tolkien's *The Lord of the Rings* is perhaps one of the most noteworthy examples of a story that has inspired and continues to inspire hunger in a diverse and ever-growing body of readers, serving as a nurturing bit of earth in which those individuals might be enriched, strengthened, uplifted. Indeed, Tolkien's Middle-earth has become nearly synonymous with fantasy itself, serving as inspiration for numerous translations, adaptations, and transformations of Tolkien's fantasy works that each reflects the way we as humans interact with the stories that captivate us via the acts of interpretation and response. Transformative works like fanfiction are a powerful example of how the human impulse to interpretive and responsive engagement results in further creative acts that are subsequent to but no less potent than the source texts from which they proceed. Fanfiction is a celebration of transformation, of expansion, of individual story-telling, a phenomenon of fan engagement with texts that has clear value in terms of human expression and understanding. The fact that there is value in fanfiction and in analyzing it is no longer in dispute, a change that came about in no small part thanks to the efforts of people like Megan Abrahamson. In her article "J.R.R. Tolkien, Fanfiction, and 'The Freedom of the Reader,'" Abrahamson outlines how the value Tolkien places on the freedom of the reader in making meaning from a text requires an acceptance of the possibilities and parameters of transformative works, including fanfiction: that they will exist, and have a right to, and that they serve a function their source texts do not. Not every author could be reasonably construed as taking such a reader-affirming attitude to their own work or to the act of constructing meaning from story; and, though I do not mean to imply that Tolkien is entirely unique, Tolkien-centered fanfiction is distinctly relevant to the work of analyzing fanfiction as a creative phenomenon connected to the human need for story.

Among the fanfiction that has been inspired by Tolkien's Middle-earth, *Hands of the King* by fan author Anglachel is remarkable for the way in which it expands and questions *The Lord of the Rings*. It displays both Anglachel's clear adoration for Tolkien's work and her unflinching critique of many of Tolkien's authorial decisions expressed through well-crafted and compelling authorial decisions of her own. Spanning eighty-five chapters of story (and an additional three of supplemental material), made up of more than 800,000 words, featuring many characters at Tolkien's margins and more of the author's own invention, no one could argue against the claim that Anglachel's story expands the borders of Middle-earth. *Hands of the King* follows the relationship between Denethor and Finduilas from the day they first meet, set by the author in 2974 (Third Age), until shortly after Finduilas' early death, set by Tolkien in 2988 (Third Age), thirty years before the Fellowship sets out from Rivendell in 3018. All of the relevant canon events Tolkien gives in *The Lord of the Rings* are included and more fully developed, such as the births of Boromir and Faramir, Gondor's major military victory against Umbar, the growing threat of Sauron, and the presence of Aragorn and Gandalf in Gondor at this time. The challenge that Anglachel offers in response to Tolkien through her writing is indissolubly tied to her expansion of the story of her two main characters, Finduilas and Denethor precisely because neither of them could be considered main characters of *The Lord of the Rings*.

Within *Hands of the King*, though, Anglachel brings Finduilas and Denethor's voices to life and gives them each a place alongside the many other heroes of Tolkien's world in a way that could never fit within the confines of the original text, thoroughly demonstrating their heroic natures in the process. On the one hand, we have Tolkien's Finduilas of Dol Amroth who is virtually a ghost of the text, deceased for years before the main action begins. Tolkien sums up her life in several neatly recorded dates and a few scant lines that largely extoll her beauty and fragility, all of which are tucked into the appendices of *The Return of the King*. On the other, we have Tolkien's Denethor II, 26th Ruling Steward of Gondor, who is treated most often as an ignoble antagonist, brought directly into the narrative only during the final volume. In Tolkien's terms, Denethor's life is defined primarily by its dramatic end, outlined in a chapter that is often interpreted as a cautionary tale regarding the dangers of foolhardy pride and despair. So, neither Finduilas nor Denethor could possibly be considered among the many heroes of *The Lord the Rings*; simply seeing them as fully humanized characters might even be considered a stretch. They are both undoubtedly heroes within *Hands of the King*, however, and the story of the lives they lead has room for the heroic doings of a whole host of others: military captains, cooks, city officials, sex workers, a tavern owner, a bookseller, and many more. Simply the fact that focus is shifted onto these two characters, one a tragic footnote and the other a dehumanized antagonist, is a transformation of the source text; that their story unfolds in a way that celebrates people and things that a face value reading of Tolkien does not, speaks to the power of fanfiction to subvert.

This transformation, this subversion—made possible through the use of story—is the core impetus of my exploration of *Hands of the King*. This essay builds upon my experience with this piece of fanfiction over the course of the twenty years it has so far played a role in my life. For I have found that finding room to embrace and celebrate queer identities often begins with encountering the queer within stories, whether we originally mark these encounters or stories as queer or not. As was the case for me in regards to numerous stories, perhaps *Hands of the King* most significantly, it is not necessary for the participant in question to even recognize their own queerness in order for this to be true: sometimes stories tell us who we are before we know it ourselves. Throughout the early part of my life, my understanding of gender was impossibly small, the result of being heavily influenced by some of the strictest religious teachings on the subject. I had no idea I was experiencing gender dysphoria. I had never even heard the term. Furthermore, even if it had been explained to me then, I would have been able to conceive of it only as a sinful, worldly lie meant to tempt me from the incontrovertible truth of an immutable divine design. In fact, one of the only reasons my parents considered *The Lord of the Rings* to be an acceptable story for me to engage with in the first place was the Catholic nature of its author, a nature that was thereby posited to automatically create an acceptably orthodox and ultimately harmless fantasy. Neither they nor I suspected that my time in Middle-earth would in fact become a defining part of my ultimate journey out of Catholicism, out of Christianity in general, and into acceptance of myself as a non-binary transgender individual.

When, in adulthood, I began the journey of consciously exploring my gender, I was drawn to reread *Hands of the King* as well. At first, I saw the two as unrelated desires that happened to coincide, explained perhaps by nostalgia. I grew increasingly shocked, though, as both endeavors progressed, to see just how closely related they were, how effortlessly I could recognize and appreciate queer aspects of this story, of these characters,

I had loved long before I could ever have conceived of even recognizing myself as a queer person, let alone responding to that self with love. In fact, the more certain I became that I was finally meeting my true and undeniably transgender self, the more certain I became that Anglachel's Finduilas and Denethor had resonated with me as queer, as transgender, even before I was able to consciously articulate such possibilities. Looking at them anew, Finduilas and Denethor showed me myself, a self I had been all along. Now, I do not mean to imply the connections to a trans experience were the intent of Anglachel as she was writing the story, just as I also would not attempt to argue such connections were the intent of Tolkien with his texts, though they are nonetheless abundant. I mean that in examining why this piece of transformative fiction has so resonated with me, I have been able to understand my gender in new, life-affirming ways. I attribute this in no small part to the fact that *Hands of the King* is a work of fanfiction, and as such is concerned with expanding and challenging an established narrative. This expansion, this challenge, to established narratives of all kinds lies at the heart of what it is to be queer.

Even if at first glance *Hands of the King* tells the story of an apparently cisgendered, heterosexual love, first glances aren't enough to determine the existence of queer identity whether we are speaking of fiction or reality. We can and should discuss the queer in a text that exhibits heterosexual, cisgender and otherwise normative expressions of gender and sexuality, because the presence of that normativity does not belie queer realities. The way Anglachel positions Denethor and Finduilas within *Hands of the King* as its dominant voices, its heroes; the way she fleshes out their stories beyond the possibilities of *The Lord of the Rings* to create fully realized characters who challenge their roles in that source text; and the way the details of their narrative demonstrate the possibilities of constructing ourselves through story, work in concert to definitively put them in a position of queerness, of trans-ness. *Hands of the King* tells a story that celebrates and upholds our drive as humans to use stories creatively, which in turn makes room for non-conformity in one of the most basic parts of our story of self: our gender.

Indeed, gender is one of the most personal and intricate stories we tell about who we are. Whether or not we do so through fanfiction, self-exploration through narrative is an important part of understanding ourselves. For transgender people this is often more complex and crucial. The dominant narratives of our world rarely have room for us, and those that do treat us horribly: we are either nonexistent, predatory, disturbed, or shameful, somehow managing to be both an inherent tragedy and the punchline of cruel comedy. When transgender people make room for ourselves within the narratives we encounter, we make room for ourselves to continue existing, while also proclaiming that we have always existed, in dignity and worth no less than others. Using source texts to understand ourselves is certainly possible, but engaging with transformative works has a particular power because transformative works in and of themselves are often an act of resistance, a celebration of self-interpretation and self-determination, both of which are uniquely crucial efforts for people of trans experience, for people of all sorts of queer identities and/or marginalized genders. So, I am building on an understanding of queerness as existing beyond binaries like cisgender versus transgender or man versus woman because laying aside these binaries is essential to understanding and accurately discussing queer narratives, especially trans narratives, and most especially those that center on non-binary people.

In terms of relevant, published scholarship that deals with Tolkien fanfiction and gender, the work of this essay is unique though not without precedent in the basis of its approach. The work that scholars have done in examining fan authors' treatments of characters who exist at Tolkien's margins (Amy Sturgis with regards to Rosie Cotton, Karen Viars and Cait Coker with Lothíriel, and Una McCormack for a number of characters) has highlighted the important work fans do to confound the function of gender within Tolkien's invented world. Additionally, Weronika Łaszkiewicz speaks to the ways this confounding of gender exists not only in fanfiction but also in Peter Jackson's popular film adaptations. McCormack, Sturgis, Viars and Coker, and Łaszkiewicz center their work around characters they discuss as female without explicitly mentioning other marginalized genders, though inasmuch as they (and the creators of the works they are speaking about) are making room for members of a marginalized gender to be analyzed, their work has implications for the inclusion of the transgender self.

So, I wish to be utterly explicit in my approach: as I make room for Finduilas to be included in this discussion, I do not do so in a way that conceives of her as essentially female, but in a way that positions her as non-binary. I do so because the nature of *Hands of the King* lent itself to such a conception long before I realized it explicitly, and because doing so may help give increased attention to the ways the construct and performance of gender within Middle-earth is interpreted and responded to by fans and scholars alike. And, though he is certainly much more central to the story than his wife, the same wish holds true for Denethor: as I make room for him to be included in this discussion, I do so in a way that positions him as being trans, being non-binary, rather than as being essentially male, not only within Anglachel's fanfiction but within *The Lord of the Rings* as well. The essay by Gavin Foster, "Éowyn and/or Dernhelm: Reading Éowyn's (Trans)Masculine Disguise," in this volume explores how the use of transgender thought to analyze another of Tolkien's central but contested characters, Éowyn, is valuable in terms of gaining further insight into the function of gender as it relates to Tolkien's characters.

My work also builds upon the arguments of published work on Tolkien that demonstrates the active role of the reader in meaning-making engagement with texts via interpretation and response. Dallas John Baker attests that there exists a "privileged reading" of Tolkien which functionally excludes queerness from Middle-earth by presuming heterosexual normativity as a corequisite for existence in a way that interferes with "non-heterosexual or non-gender normative" interpretations (125). This interference does not and should not be upheld as an ultimate exclusion of queerness in Middle-earth, however; Baker clearly demonstrates just how crucial it is that those of Tolkien's readers who make efforts to keep his works alive do so in ways that work against the harmful grain of the privileged reading by leveraging the acts of interpretation and response to move away from silencing gender-centered discussions of Tolkien and move towards embracing them as potentially vital contributions to all readers (130). My hope for this essay—indeed, for this entire book—is that such forward movement in terms of acknowledging and honoring the queer within Middle-earth becomes more fully realized. In terms of making such moves within scholarship, Robin Anne Reid helpfully demonstrates how complicating the ways queer scholarship has functioned in the past will expand the field, positing that moving away from a homosexual/heterosexual binary is the next task of queer scholars (480–81). She notes that fanfiction's mode of telling allows fan authors to perform gender by the formation of texts, of stories; that fanfiction indeed makes it possible for such performance and construction to take place "in an environment which masks the body" and in ways that place the act of discourse above the elements of one's physiology (480). Reid's argument not only has implications for fan authors' explorations of gender, but also for the explorations of those who make up their audience. If fanfiction is a mode of engaging with story by creating story, the work of embodying gender and of attempting to understand it are both inextricably linked to this creative act.

If it is true that "we hunger for stories, for that is the earth in which we take root," as Anglachel says, then that hunger drives us to actions that are both creative and narrative by nature. Certainly, Tolkien's work in creating Middle-earth and the vast sea of all that has been inspired by that creation is a prime example of this hunger at work, of the interpretive, communicative processes by which human beings seek to satisfy that hunger. Within *The Lord of the Rings*, Tolkien displays a habit for using multiple layers of textual creation to achieve the narrative feast that makes Middle-earth come alive. These layers include the central narrative of the novel, the extra-textual and supplemental narratives Tolkien created as part of his wider fantasy work, as well as the narratives Tolkien was interpreting and responding to in being inspired to create this new story of his own. So, within the story that makes up *The Lord of the Rings*, there are multiple, additional stories present, including some which were crafted by Tolkien to serve as in-world histories, legends, and myths. These serve the function of fleshing out Middle-earth while also providing instances in which Tolkien's characters are able to engage with stories they find personally meaningful in the same ways any of us might. The diverse inhabitants of Middle-earth are characters who dwell in a world filled with stories by which they may be seen to build themselves and their understandings.

Within *Hands of the King*, Anglachel builds on Tolkien's habit of using his in-world stories to shape events and characters within her story, characters who Anglachel shows to be actively turning to those stories in order to make sense of their own narratives of self. Anglachel's Finduilas and Denethor engage with the texts of Tolkien's in-world stories that are published in other volumes besides *The Lord of the Rings*, yet exist in conversation with it by Tolkien's design. As we see these two characters engage with the stories of other Tolkienian characters like Beren and Lúthien or Tuor and Idril, we see Finduilas and Denethor demonstrate the very patterns of engagement we as readers so often turn to when encountering stories that resonate with us. In one of the most moving scenes of the story, an original character of the author's invention, Laanga (a wizard much like Gandalf in nature, though with considerably more patience for our heroes), advises Finduilas that when we fashion our experiences into a story to share, even immense grief is more easily carried (Chapter 49). Scenes like this serve not only as insight into Finduilas as a character and her story but also as the potential for insight into our stories, our very selves.

In *Hands of the King*, Denethor and Finduilas both are well-versed in story long before they are able to recognize their mutual love for one another. Their shared love for and use of story is central to what helps their understanding of themselves and each other grow. It is also one of the primary reasons they feel so human, that Anglachel's work is so compelling. One of the most important plot developments centers around Finduilas and Denethor's ongoing engagement with Tolkien's text of "The Lay of Leithian," which exists for them as an important in-world story. This begins when, early in their interactions with one another, Denethor is preparing to leave for battle, and Finduilas, noting his love of old poetry in general, selects a volume from the archives to send off with him as a comfort and talisman of sorts, a well-worn book so small he is able to tuck it in a breast pocket. Unwittingly, she has selected one of his very favorites, a poem he knows much of by heart, the tale of Beren and Lúthien. The excerpts we see within *Hands of the King* are from Tolkien's own telling

208   IV. Queer Transformation

of this story of a mortal and an elf whose love disrupted the mighty, challenged the gods, and reunited them beyond even death. One of the next major scenes is set a few weeks later, as he shares an evening meal with his beloved sister and Finduilas, the first such meal since his return from battle:

> Denethor did not even open the book when he spoke this time. His hands closed tightly around the small volume and he gazed off into an unseen distance.
>
> > *A night there was when winter died;*
> > *then all alone she sang and cried*
> > *and danced until the dawn of spring,*
> > *and chanted some wild magic thing*
> > *that stirred him, till it sudden broke*
> > *the bonds that held him, and he woke*
> > *to madness sweet and brave despair.*
> > [("The Lay of Leithian," canto III, lines 717–23)]
>
> Finduilas wondered if Denethor had meant to speak aloud. He did not seem aware that she and Aiavalë were present. The silence stretched on. She cleared her throat and said, "I must apologize for sending you off with a work you already knew by heart. I had hoped to give you something new to learn."
>
> He gave her a distracted look, still caught in his own thoughts. "But I like this poem" [Chapter 10, emphasis original].

This scene and this poem become a large part of the basis for their growing relationship. It also cements Denethor's use of story as a mode of gaining (or attempting to gain) self-understanding, and Finduilas' response to his methods in ways that will last throughout the work's nearly seventy-five remaining chapters.

When the reader is first made aware that Denethor has realized he is in love with Finduilas (a fact that had been hidden from the reader for several chapters), it is these same lines that come to him, that play through his mind as we see him wrestle with what being in love means given the borders of his life and his current conception of its narrative. This wrestling largely centers on the fact that Anglachel takes Tolkien's placement of Denethor's marriage as occurring notably later in life and explains it by the fact that he has sworn off love and marriage in light of his parents' own disastrous union which was made only for political gain and has resulted in a multitude of sorrows for many, especially Denethor. As he wrestles, we see him remember a few stolen moments from earlier in the story when he had allowed himself to retell his narrative—and himself—in light of Beren and Lúthien's own. The language their story has given Denethor allows him to speak about his love for Finduilas. For it is the words of their tale he repeats aloud to himself, "finally understanding [he has] been in a dream," a Beren ensnared by a Lúthien, thinking "longingly of their dance, when he had been the victor in great battles and small deceptions and she was the most beautiful woman, Lúthien-fair, and had laughed with him and had been glad at his deeds and sorrowful for his wounds and called him friend" (Chapter 12).

Finduilas, still heedless of his love, takes upon herself the task of finding him a new story, not in replacement of the old, beloved poem, but as an addition, something new to encounter. She is the one who first brings another of Tolkien's in-world myths into the tale, finding a matching copy of the story of Tuor and Idril and the Fall of Gondolin (a tale centered on another mortal and elf whose love story played out amidst a tumultuous backdrop of actions between gods, elven-kind, and humanity) to give to Denethor as a gift. He carries these stories near to his heart (both figuratively and quite literally) into many dangers, using them as a shield and source of comfort. These stories guide Denethor throughout the rest of the story (perhaps even more so than these stories can be said to guide Finduilas), even to the very end of *Hands of the King* in fact, when, after Finduilas' untimely death, Denethor reads them ritualistically and repeatedly in his desperate efforts to find a life after the end of their story together (Chapter 85).

The portion of *Hands of the King* that could be characterized as their courtship narrative (which by no means encompasses the whole of Anglachel's work), hinges on their pattern of engagement with story. On the night they finally realize the love they have for one another—in the moment of Finduilas's unexpected confession—we see Denethor utterly unmoored: there was no telling of the tale as he had seen it in his mind that included her love for him. He was under the assumption that she cared for another more worthy, Thorongil, who Denethor and Finduilas have both come to realize has a claim to the throne of Gondor in an earlier chapter when they learned the truth of his identity, that he is Aragorn himself, serving in Gondor at this time in disguise. Anglachel's character of young Aragorn is infatuated with Finduilas, seeing in her a human counterpart to Arwen, whom he is still thinking of as an impossible dream. For his part, Denethor believes his role in the story should be to allow this love between Thorongil and Finduilas to flourish so a great captain (Thorongil/Aragorn) will gain, through a lofty marriage into a wealthy and powerful family (Finduilas's), the political power necessary to reclaim the throne of Gondor in this time of his beloved country's growing instability. And so, he balks at her confession, explaining his self-prescribed inadequacy in the face of Thorongil's own claim.

Finduilas counters by naming herself as Tuor, speaking to Denethor in the language of the stories she knows he loves, saying she "shall do as [her] heart and valor lead [her]." Still he resists: "'Why wouldst thou wish for a darkened creature like myself? The heir of Elendil loves thee, and thou wouldst be queen!'" (Chapter 23). But Finduilas is undaunted, relentless. She reminds him of his own previous words on the subject of stories and fates, imploring him to see her love as not only possible, but real, and not at all hindered by the presence of a more Tolkienian hero (Thorongil/Aragorn), who functions within *Hands of the King* as both more appropriately male and overtly masculine than Denethor. Finduilas counters: "What care I for the hands of a king? In my dreams, I have seen thee crowned with stars, and know what king rules my heart." Though when they part ways that evening, Denethor is still unable to grasp the new room within the narrative she is offering, by the next morning, he has decided to follow her lead, choosing to take that room for himself even before he feels deserving of it.

The story of this kind of love remains an intensely personal and important piece of my conception of self in no small part because I was able to originally experience its queerness as obscured. This is why—even while still in the grip of religiously-enforced gender essentialism—it was able to show me that a different mode of telling, of being, of making room for myself was possible. For if it does nothing else, *Hands of the King* makes room for deep, committed, and complex love to exist between two flawed and beautiful people who exhibit traits beyond normative gendered behavior—people who love each other precisely because of those traits, not in spite of them. Certainly, I understood them first to be a heterosexual couple, not marking any queerness consciously. Unlike the many other such couples I'd encountered in stories, though, I felt something different about them. That difference was born from the way their gender and sexuality are obscured by the text.

That the queerness, the trans-ness, of *Hands of the King* is present partly as a mitigation of non-normative gender expression rather than explicit displays of trans expression is not a detriment to my argument. The text does not show a Denethor and Finduilas who are more explicitly transgender or otherwise queer because Tolkien made no room for such lives to exist explicitly in Middle-earth; and in Anglachel's effort to expand the nature of gender and sexuality within Tolkien's world, she took the approach of operating within canon itself to subvert it. Of course, there are other valuable approaches among fans and fan authors, and many of them choose to write more explicit queer-/trans-ness into their fics. The complex relationship between Tolkien fanfiction, Tolkien fan culture, and Tolkien canon is beyond my scope to fully discuss here but is more deeply explored by the essay in this volume by Maria Alberto: "'and stooping he raised Beleg and kissed his mouth': Queering Canon with Tolkien Fanfiction."

In an essay on the subject of gender and sexuality in Tolkien fanfiction which was my first introduction to queer theory, Anglachel outlines her own approach to Tolkien's text, its surrounding fan culture, and the work of her own fanfiction, as well as the reasons she decided upon her approach. Though the essay is focused on how she did this in preparing to write her series of stories that focus on Frodo and Bilbo, her approach in writing *Hands of the King* came from the same principles. "Writing a Green Sun" details how Anglachel believes a fan author can create in-world believability in discussing modern, real-world concepts, while being mindful not to break the secondary belief of Tolkien's invented world, even if that fan author seeks to challenge aspects of the source text within their own story. Anglachel contends the reason much of Tolkien fanfiction's treatment of sexuality can feel inconsistent or anachronistic is a failure of "presentism," noting that "sexuality is [often] portrayed in modern terms, where there is a polarization and objectification of orientation based on the gender of the selected partner," which she rightly points out is hardly the only way to define queerness (n.p.) In light of her own approach to the concept of queerness and how it is conceived of and expressed by human beings within narrative contexts—something Anglachel clearly has given no small thought to in her work as a fan author—certain textual details of her stories grow even greater in significance. Based on her adherence to this approach out of a wish to create a story of her own within Middle-earth, the lack of overt expressions of queerness based on modern conceptions of gender and sexuality does not mean there is an absence of queerness, only that it will be present in ways consistent with life under Tolkien's "green sun," i.e., the conditions of his secondary world.

The idea that queerness can be present in significant ways yet remain unmarked is hardly new. In fact, it is fully compatible with one of the most common definitions of queer for the purpose of queer scholars, Alexander Doty's fourth and fifth definitions:

> 4. To describe any nonnormative expression of gender, including those connected with straightness.
> 5. To describe non-straight things that are not clearly marked as gay, lesbian, bisexual, transsexual, or transgendered, but that seem to suggest or allude to one or more of these categories, often in a vague, confusing, or incoherent manner [6–7].

Therefore, the places in the narrative where Finduilas takes on the role of Tuor or mirrors Beren (and Denethor by extension is her Idril and Lúthien) display a gender nonconformity that does not disrupt belief in the secondary world, but may still signal to the reader binaries are being broken. For within *Hands of the King*, Finduilas is conceived of as both elf maiden and prince, a title Denethor bestows on her as early as the third chapter and maintains even after he begins to perceive her also as queen;

and, Denethor is both her mannish hero-king and a beautiful, mythic, and fearsome creature, one who memorizes love stories, dreaming of that which he has never known, a sleeping beauty awakened by an act of love.

There are several key ways in which Finduilas specifically is characterized in a queer manner. She is positioned within the narrative as an heir and pupil of her father, though of course it is her younger brother, Imrahil, who will be the next Prince of Dol Amroth in truth. She is often compared to the women of the narrative who exhibit more traditionally feminine traits and found to be lacking them, perhaps most notably by Denethor who says in his contemplation of her, "no one could call Finduilas unlovely; it was only in comparison to her sister that one could fault her," further reflecting "some would think her too tall for a girl, for she was the height of most men, and her figure was still boyish, particularly next to Ivriniel" (Chapter 14). But "some" does not include Denethor, which is perhaps one of the most explicitly queer moments of the narrative.

Additionally, though after marriage Finduilas's political title is "Lady of the White Tower," there are only forty-four places out of more than six thousand times she is referenced by her birth name that her birth name is used in conjunction with "Lady." And of those forty-four times she is called "Lady Finduilas," only seven of them come from Denethor, and all of those are political, public instances. In comparison, Denethor calls her by a special name only he and his sister use for Finduilas, Alquallë, over three hundred times. While a cisgender reader may be quick to interpret this name as merely a nickname, for a transgender reader, the way it functions within the story (even beyond what numbers alone can tell) is a clear allusion to the comfort of a chosen/real name as opposed to the discomfort of a birth-/dead-name. The argument that this is a place of trans-coding within the story is further supported by the scene in which they first meet, another place in the narrative where she stands in stark contrast to the traditional femininity of her sister.

> She offered her hand matter-of-factly.
> "I am pleased to meet you, Lord Denethor." Her handshake was firm and unhurried.
> "The pleasure is mutual, my lady."
> "Finduilas." A correction, given without hesitation [Chapter 1].

Another way Denethor refers to her is also trans-coded. As mentioned above, beginning early on, he names her a prince, and there is no hesitation before she continues their converse, quickly naming him, "fellow prince." Although the term certainly has a gender-neutral application, a transgender reading complicates it: seeing a character presented as both female and referred to as prince is undoubtedly something that speaks to the transgender reader. When their story turns toward the birth of their children, Denethor and Finduilas take up additional narratives that expand and confound gender norms, with Denethor as an instinctual nurturer and careful governess and Finduilas a distant and more reluctant caretaker, preferring political work to child-rearing although both are fierce protectors of their children. For in this, as in all things, they are each other's Beren/Tuor as truly as they are each other's Lúthien/Idril, both of them containing brokenness and beauty, both human and mythic in light of their love for one another, crossing the lines of essential differences between elven and human, male and female that Tolkien placed within Middle-earth. And in doing so, they subvert gendered expectations and confound binaries within our world as well.

For *Hands of the King* clearly allows Denethor and Finduilas something we all need, but that queer people too often suffer, even die, without: a story that has room for the complexity of who we are, that affords us the dignity of our own humanity, that celebrates our heroic parts, even as it does not shy away from our faults. Encountering a narrative that so explicitly makes room for characters that exist in their source text so un-heroically can be revolutionary for those who exist within the dehumanized margins of the real world. As a person of transgender experience, there are many to whom I am now only a tragic footnote vis-à-vis Finduilas. There are many to whom I am a representation of the subversion of divine order, the punishment for which is an eternal death I myself may be blamed for devising, as Denethor, too, represents for so many who engage with *The Lord of the Rings*. But I do not live in those other stories, not anymore. The example of Denethor and Finduilas in *Hands of the King* has been a roadmap of sorts for me: if there is room for them to exist beyond binaries, beyond the margins, beyond divine judgment, might I not make that room for myself, too?

Our conceptions of ourselves are largely built on binaries because our world is largely built on such. We use them to tell stories about who we are and what shape our lives are taking, have taken, could take. When we encounter narratives of identity that display for us something beyond those divisions we have learned, we are expanded, our very conception of what a self can be is expanded. Prevailing narratives of all kinds are challenged by this conceptual expansion; queer theory uses that challenge as a fuel for growth and change. Such growth and change are imperative if the transgender self is to truly find a home in this world over and above the narratives that marginalize, vilify, and condemn. Fanfiction has an important role to play in this work.

For in the face of many kinds of authorities, transformative works—when they are at their best—make room for queer lives as we are allowed to engage with story through the acts of interpretation and response. They allow new modes of understanding, telling, and being ourselves that exceed binaries, doctrines, and legal precedents. They interrogate the fictional to the benefit of the actual, reshaping narratives in consequential ways. They show radical imagination at work, allowing us a glimpse of a world where queerness is heroic, kind, and brave—no matter what other discourse may have led us to believe. They invite us to remember the power and purpose of story in the first place. When we create or consume transformative works, we are engaging in that which magnifies the power of story. We are exercising our right to fantasy, our right to seeing our struggles, our victories, ourselves, mirrored in a story that will move us to overcome, to grow, to be. And as we make space within the text for the characters we hold dear to move more freely, so we make space for ourselves.

I do not care for the hands of a king who is tethered to a narrative that upholds oppressive modes of being. My heart and valor both have led me elsewhere now that story has expanded my understanding of the possible. And in my dreams, I see a world where we are all crowned in the starlight of our own humanity: our own heroes, our own kings.

Works Cited

Abrahamson, Megan B. "J.R.R. Tolkien, Fanfiction, and 'The Freedom of the Reader.'" *Mythlore*, vol. 32, no. 1, article 5, 2013, dc.swosu.edu/mythlore/vol32/iss1/5, pp. 53–72.

Anglachel. *Hands of the King. Rómenna*, romenna.net/story.cfm?stid=2.

———. "Writing a Green Sun." *Rómenna*, romenna.net/story.cfm?stid=8.

Baker, Dallas John. "Writing Back to Tolkien: Gender, Sexuality and Race in High Fantasy." *Recovering History Through Fact and Fiction: Forgotten Lives*, edited by Dallas John Baker, et al., Cambridge Scholars, 2017, pp. 123–133.

Doty, Alexander. *Flaming Classics: Queering the Film Canon*. Routledge, 2000.

Łaszkiewicz, Weronika. "J.R.R. Tolkien's Portrayal of Femininity and Its Transformations in Subsequent Adaptations." *Crossroads: A Journal of English Studies*, vol. 11, no. 4, 2015, pp. 15–28, repozytorium.uwb.edu.pl/jspui/bitstream/11320/5306/1/Crossroads_11_2015_W.Laszkiewicz_JRR_Tolkien%E2%80%99s_portrayal_of_femininity_and_its_transformations_in_subsequent_adaptations.pdf.

McCormack, Una. "Finding Ourselves in the (Un)Mapped Lands: Women's Reparative Readings of *The Lord of the Rings*." *Perilous and Fair: Women in the Works and Life of J.R.R. Tolkien*, edited by Janet Brennan Croft and Leslie A. Donovan, Mythopoeic P, 2015, pp. 309–326

Reid, Robin Anne. "Thrusts in the Dark: Slashers' Queer Practices." *Extrapolation*, vol. 50, no. 3, 2009, pp. 463–483.

Sturgis, Amy H. "Reimagining Rose: Portrayals of Tolkien's Rosie Cotton in Twenty-First Century Fan Fiction." *Mythlore*, vol. 24, no. 3, article 10, 2006, dc.swosu.edu/mythlore/vol24/iss3/10, pp. 165–187.

Tolkien, J.R.R. "The Lay of Leithian." *The Lays of Beleriand*, edited by Christopher Tolkien, Houghton Mifflin, 1985, pp. 183–392. The History of Middle-earth, vol. 3.

Viars, Karen, and Cait Coker. "Constructing Lothíriel: Rewriting and Rescuing the Women of Middle-Earth [sic] from the Margins," *Mythlore*, vol. 33, no. 2, article 6, 2015, pp. 35–48.

Tolkien and Alterity
A Bibliography

Jordan Audas

Definitions

For the purposes of this work, the term "Tolkien" is broadly defined as anything related to J.R.R. Tolkien. One half of this comprehensive perspective includes anything *about* the actual person, such as biographical information, personal or attributed views, the process of creating and writing his academic and literary outputs, and so forth. The other half relates to the literary world he created, such as criticisms and close-text readings of his novels, character interactions and motives, adaptations and transformative works, etc. Similarly, although "Alterity" can be narrowly defined as a state of Otherness relating to aspects of difference, it is broadly defined in this work as aspects of humanity that can be/are marginalized, stigmatized, or discriminated against, such as race, gender, sexuality, etc.

Methods

As part of the planning stage, an unfocused scan was conducted in *Academic Search Premier* and *MLA International Bibliography* to review the volume of available materials related to Tolkien and alterity and identify relevant search terms. "Alterity" keywords in relevant articles were obtained and consolidated to allow for the best and broadest possible outcome. The term "Tolkien" was limited to subject terms to ensure that results did not include all articles present in journals that include Tolkien's name in the title (such *as Mythlore* or *Amon Hen*). Furthermore, to account for the possibility of results not including Tolkien's name, specifically in relation to Jackson's adaptations, for example, "*The Lord of the Rings*" was also included as a search term.

Results

Results include academic essays, periodicals, books, individual book chapters, review articles, dissertations, and conference papers. From 1970–2024, 248 publications were found, with the vast majority (205) being published after 2004 (i.e., 2005 and onwards; post-release of Peter Jackson's filmed adaptations).

Limitations

The results obtained from *ASP* and *MLA* were limited to those available through Mount Saint Vincent's University subscriptions (or through the Novanet consortium request program) during the time period of research. As what is available depends not only on the university's individual subscriptions, but also EBSCO's personal contractual obligations with journals, periodicals, etc., the results obtained are naturally limited to what was available to the user at the specific time period. Furthermore, items that the editors of this collection had personal knowledge about, but were not located in this scan, were added to this bibliography as to present a more comprehensive list. Finally, personal user limitations, which include my inability to read any other language besides English, obviously narrows the available results as well. I have, however, attempted to include those results which have English abstracts, despite any other language the essay may have been written in.

Bibliography by Decade Published

1970–1979

Helms, Randel. "Orc: The Id in Blake and Tolkien." *Literature and Psychology*, vol. 20, no. 1, 1970, pp. 31–35.

Myers, Doris T. "Brave New World: The Status of Women According to Tolkien, Lewis, and Williams." *Cimarron Review*, vol. 17, 1971, pp. 13–19.

1980–1989

Jenkins, Sue. "Love, Loss, and Seeking: Maternal Deprivation and the Quest." *Children's Literature in Education*, vol. 15, no. 2, June 1984, pp. 73–83, doi.org/10.1007/BF01151772.

Partridge, Brenda. "No Sex Please—We're Hobbits: The Construction of Female Sexuality in *The Lord of the Rings*." *J.R.R. Tolkien: This Far Land*, edited by Robert Giddings, Vision; Barnes & Noble, 1983, pp. 179–97.

Rawls, Melanie. "The Feminine Principle in Tolkien." *Mythlore*, vol. 10, no. 4, article 2, 1984, dc.swosu.edu/mythlore/vol10/iss4/2. Rpt. *Perilous and Fair*, edited by Janet Brennan Croft and Leslie Donovan, 2015, pp. 99–117.

Rubey, Daniel. "Identity and Alterity in

the Criticism of J.R.R. Tolkien and D.W. Robertson, Jr." *The Literary Review: An International Journal of Contemporary Writing*, vol. 23, 1980, pp. 577–611.

Rushtoes, Salman. "Colour Prejudice." *Amon Hen*, vol. 99, Sept. 1989, pp. 18–20.

Ryan, J.S. "Oath-Swearing, the Stone of Erech and the Near East of the Ancient World." *Inklings: Jahrbuch Für Literatur Und Ästhetik*, vol. 4, 1986, pp. 107–21.

1990-1999

Critchett, David. "One Ring to Fool Them All, One Ring to Blind Them: The Propaganda of *The Lord of the Rings*." *Extrapolation*, vol. 38, no. 1, Apr. 1997, pp. 36–56, doi.org/10.3828/extr.1997.38.1.36.

Crowe, Edith L. "Power in Arda: Sources, Uses and Misuses," *Mythlore*, vol. 21, no. 2, article 40, 1996, pp. 272–77, dc.swosu.edu/mythlore/vol21/iss2/40. Rpt. *Perilous and Fair*, edited by Janet Brennan Croft and Leslie Donovan, 2015, pp. 136–49.

Doughan, David. "An Ethnically Cleansed Faery? Tolkien and the Matter of Britain." *Mallorn*, iss. 32, Sept. 1995, pp. 21–24.

———. "Tolkien, Sayers, Sex and Gender." *Mythlore*, vol. 21, no. 2, article 53, 1996, pp. 357–59/ dc.swosu.edu/mythlore/vol21/iss2/53.

Drout, Michael D.C. "The Influence of J.R.R. Tolkien's Masculinist Medievalism." *Medieval Feminist Newsletter*, vol. 22, Sept. 1996, pp. 26–27, doi.org/10.17077/1054-1004.1400.

Fenwick, Mac. "Breastplates of Silk: Homeric Women in *The Lord of the Rings*." *Mythlore*, vol. 21, no. 3, article 4, 1996, pp. 17–23; 51, dc.swosu.edu/mythlore/vol21/iss3/4.

Green, William H. "'Where's Mama?' The Construction of the Feminine in *The Hobbit*." *The Lion and the Unicorn*, vol. 22, no. 2, 1998, pp. 188–95, doi.org/10.1353/uni.1998.0024.

Honegger, Thomas. "Éowyn, Aragorn and the Hidden Dangers of Drink." *Inklings: Jahrbuch Für Literatur Und Ästhetik*, vol. 17, 1999, pp. 217–25.

Hopkins, Lisa. "Female Authority Figures in the Works of Tolkien, C.S. Lewis and Charles Williams." *Mythlore*, vol. 21, no. 2, article 55, 1996, pp. 264–66, dc.swosu.edu/mythlore/vol21/iss2/55.

2000-2009

Allington, Daniel. "'How Come Most People Don't See It?': Slashing the *Lord of the Rings*." *Social Semiotics*, vol. 17, no. 1, Mar. 2007, pp. 43–62, ttpes://doi.org/10.1080/10350330601124650.

Baker, Deirdre F. "Musings on Diverse Worlds." *Horn Book Magazine*, vol. 83, no. 1, Jan. 2007, pp. 41–47.

Barnes, Jon. "*Tolkien, Race and Cultural History*." *Times Literary Supplement*, no. 5545, July 2009, p. 27.

Bashir, Nadia, et al. "A Precious Case from Middle Earth." *BMJ*, vol. 329, no. 7480, Dec. 2004, pp. 1435–36, doi.org/10.1136/bmj.329.7480.1435.

Battis, Jes. "Gazing Upon Sauron: Hobbits, Elves, and the Queering of the Postcolonial Optic." *MFS: Modern Fiction Studies*, J.R.R. Tolkien Special Issue, guest editor Shaun F.D. Hughes, vol. 50, no. 4, 2004, pp. 908–26, doi.org/10.1353/mfs.2005.0001.

Benvenuto, Maria Raffaella. "Against Stereotype: Éowyn and Lúthien as 20th-Century Women." *Tolkien and Modernity 1*, edited by Frank Weinreich and Thomas Honegger, Walking Tree, 2006, pp. 31–54.

Bernard, Carol A. "Gollum: The Fulcrum of Desire in J.R.R. Tolkien's *The Lord of the Rings*." *Dissertation Abstracts International, Section A: The Humanities and Social Sciences*, vol. 66, no. 6, University of Houston, ProQuest, Dec. 2005, UMI Number: 3180550.

Brackmann, Rebecca. "'Dwarves Are Not Heroes': Antisemitism and the Dwarves in J.R.R. Tolkien's Writing." *Mythlore*, vol. 28, no. 3, article 7, 2010, pp. 85–106, dc.swosu.edu/mythlore/vol28/iss3/7.

Chance, Jane. "'In the Company of Orcs': Peter Jackson's Queer Tolkien." *Queer Movie Medievalisms*, edited by Kathleen Coyne Kelly and Tison Pugh, Routledge, 2009, pp. 79–96.

———. "Subversive Fantasist: Tolkien on Class Difference." *The Lord of the Rings, 1954-2004: Scholarship in Honor of Rich-*

ard E. Blackwelder, edited by Wayne G. Hammond and Christina Scull, Marquette UP, 2006, pp. 153–68.

———. "Tolkien and the Other: Race and Gender in the Middle Earth." *Tolkien's Modern Middle Ages*, edited by Jane Chance and Alfred K. Siewers, Palgrave Macmillan, 2005, pp. 171–86. The New Middle Ages.

———. "Tolkien's Women (and Men): The Films and the Book." *Mallorn*, iss. 43, July 2005, pp. 30–37.

———. "Tolkien's Women (and Men): The Films and the Book." *Tolkien on Film: Essays on Peter Jackson's* The Lord of the Rings, edited by Janet Brennan Croft, Mythopoeic P, 2004, pp. 175–94.

Chism, Christine. "Charges of Racism." *J.R.R. Tolkien Encyclopedia: Scholarship and Critical Assessment*, edited by Michael D.C. Drout, Routledge, 2007, p. 558.

———. "Race and Ethnicity in Tolkien's Works." *J.R.R Tolkien Encyclopedia: Scholarship and Critical Assessment*, edited by Michael D.C. Drout, Routledge, 2007, pp. 555–6.

Craig, David M. "'Queer Lodgings': Gender and Sexuality in *The Lord of the Rings*." *Mallorn*, vol. 38, Jan. 2001, pp. 11–18, journals.tolkiensociety.org/mallorn/article/view/145/139. Rpt. "Queer Lodgings: Gender and Sexuality in *The Lord of the Rings*—Reprinted with a New Introduction by the Author." *Mallorn*, vol. 61, 2020, pp. 20–29.

Cramer, Zack. "Jewish Influences in Middle-earth." *Mallorn*, iss. 44, Aug. 2006, pp. 9–16.

Dickerson, Matthew. "Finwë and Míriel." *J.R.R. Tolkien Encyclopedia: Scholarship and Critical Assessment*, edited by Michael D.C. Drout, Routledge, 2007, pp. 212–3.

Domínguez Ruiz, Beatriz. "Mimetic Patterns of Masculinity or Just Another Fantasy Book." *Atenea*, vol. 28, no. 2, Dec. 2008, pp. 135–44.

Donovan, Leslie A. "The Valkyrie Reflex in J.R.R. Tolkien's *The Lord of the Rings*: Galadriel, Shelob, Éowyn, and Arwen." *Tolkien the Medievalist*, edited by Jane Chance, Routledge, 2003, pp. 106–32. Rpt. *Perilous and Fair*, edited by Janet Brennan Croft and Leslie Donovan, 2015, pp. 221–57.

Doughan, David. "Tolkien the Fascist?" *Amon Hen*, vol. 207, Sept. 2007, pp. 20–21.

———. "Women, Oxford and Tolkien." *Mallorn*, iss. 45, 2008, pp. 16–20.

Duralde, Alonso. "Gay Guide to the Oscars." *Advocate*, no. 909, Mar. 2004, pp. 49–51.

Elston, M. Melissa. "Xerxes in Drag: Post-9/11 Marginalization and (Mis)Identification in 300." *DisClosure*, vol. 18, Apr. 2009, pp. 58–74.

Enright, Nancy. "Tolkien's Females and the Defining of Power." *Renascence*, vol. 59, no. 2, winter 2007, pp. 93–108. Rpt. *Perilous and Fair*, edited by Janet Brennan Croft and Leslie Donovan, 2015, pp. 118–35.

Fimi, Dimitra. *Tolkien, Race, and Cultural History: From Fairies to Hobbits*. Palgrave Macmillan, 2009.

Firchow, Peter E. "The Politics of Fantasy: *The Hobbit* and Fascism." *Midwest Quarterly*, vol. 50, no. 1, Sept. 2008, pp. 15–31.

Fisher, Jason. "Galadriel." *J.R.R. Tolkien Encyclopedia: Scholarship and Critical Assessment*, edited by Michael D.C. Drout, Routledge, 2007, pp. 227–8.

———. "Goldberry." *J.R.R. Tolkien Encyclopedia: Scholarship and Critical Assessment*, edited by Michael D.C. Drout, Routledge, 2007, pp. 244–6.

———. "Melian." *J.R.R. Tolkien Encyclopedia: Scholarship and Critical Assessment*, edited by Michael D.C. Drout, Routledge, 2007, pp. 412–3.

Fredrick, Candice, and Sam McBride. "Battling the Woman Warrior: Females and Combat in Tolkien and Lewis." *Mythlore*, vol. 25, no. 3, article 4, 2007, p. 29–42, dc.swosu.edu/mythlore/vol25/iss3/4.

Freedman, Carl. "A Note on Marxism and Fantasy." *Historical Materialism*, vol. 10, iss. 4, Jan. 2002, pp. 261–71.

Fuchs, Cynthia. "'Wicked, Tricksy, False': Race, Myth, and Gollum." *From Hobbits to Hollywood: Essays on Peter Jackson's Lord of the Rings*, edited by Ernest Mathijs and Murray Pomerance, Brill, 2006, pp. 249–65.

Gehl, Robert. "Something Is Stirring in the East: Racial Identity, Confronting the 'Other,' and Miscegenation in *Othello* and *The Lord of the Rings*." *Tolkien and Shakespeare: Essays on Shared*

Themes and Language, edited by Janet Brennan Croft, McFarland, 2007, pp. 251–66.

Goldberg, Ruth, and Krin Gabbard. "'What Does the Eye Demand': Sexuality, Forbidden Vision and Embodiment in *The Lord of the Rings*." *From Hobbits to Hollywood: Essays on Peter Jackson's Lord of the Rings*, edited by Ernest Mathijs and Murray Pomerance, Brill, 2006, pp. 265–81.

Hatcher, Melissa McCrory. "Finding Woman's Role in *The Lord of the Rings*." *Mythlore*, vol. 25, no. 3, article 5, 2007, dc.swosu.edu/mythlore/vol25/iss3/5.

Hesser, Katherine. "Éowyn." *J.R.R Tolkien Encyclopedia: Scholarship and Critical Assessment*, edited by Michael D.C. Drout, Routledge, 2007, pp. 168–69.

Hoiem, Elizabeth Massa. "World Creation as Colonization: British Imperialism in "Aldarion and Erendis."" *Tolkien Studies*, vol. 2, 2005, pp. 75–92, doi.org/10.1353/tks.2005.0020.

Hooker, Mark T. "Frodo's Batman." *Tolkien Studies*, vol. 1, 2004, pp. 125–36, doi.org/10.1353/tks.2004.0009.

Houghton, John Wm. "Ungoliant." *J.R.R. Tolkien Encyclopedia: Scholarship and Critical Assessment*, edited by Michael D.C. Drout, Routledge, 2007, pp. 687.

James, Caryn. "Are Women Just Bored of the 'Rings'?" *New York Times*, vol. 153, no. 52704, 21 Dec. 2003, p. 31.

Kaufman, Roger. "*Lord of the Ring* Taps a Gay Archetype." *Gay & Lesbian Review Worldwide*, vol. 10, no. 4, July 2003, p. 31.

Kim, Sue. "Beyond Black and White: Race and Postmodernism in *The Lord of the Rings* Films." *MFS: Modern Fiction Studies*, J.R.R. Tolkien Special Issue, guest editor Shaun F.D. Hughes, vol. 50, no. 4, 2004, pp. 875–907, doi.org/10.1353/mfs.2005.0005.

Kisor, Yvette L. "'Elves (and Hobbits) Always Refer to the Sun as She': Some Notes on a Note in Tolkien's *The Lord of the Rings*." *Tolkien Studies*, vol. 4, 2007, pp. 212–22, doi.org/10.1353/tks.2007.0023.

Klinger, Barbara. "What Do Female Fans Want? Blockbusters, *The Return of the King*, and U.S. Audiences." *Watching the Lord of the Rings: Tolkien's World Audiences*, edited by Martin Barker and Ernest Mathijs, Peter Lang, 2008, pp. 69–82.

Knaus, Christopher. "More White Supremacy? *The Lord of the Rings* as Pro-American Imperialism." *Multicultural Perspectives*, vol. 7, no. 4, Oct. 2005, pp. 54–58, doi.org/10.1207/s15327892mcp0704_9.

Kuipers, Giselinde, and Jeroen de Kloet. "Banal Cosmopolitanism and *The Lord of the Rings*: The Limited Role of National Differences in Global Media Consumption." *Poetics*, vol. 37, no. 2, Apr. 2009, pp. 99–118, doi.org/10.1016/j.poetic.2009.01.002.

Lakowski, Romuald I. "'Perilously Fair': Titania, Galadriel, and the Fairy Queen of Medieval Romance." *Tolkien and Shakespeare: Essays on Shared Themes and Language*, edited by Janet Brennan Croft, McFarland, 2007, pp. 60–78.

Landa, Ishay. "Slaves of the Ring: Tolkien's Political Unconscious," *Historical Materialism*, vol. 10, iss. 4, Jan. 2002, pp. 113–33.

Leibeger, Carol A. "Women in Tolkien's Work." *J.R.R. Tolkien Encyclopedia: Scholarship and Critical Assessment*, edited by Michael D.C. Drout, Routledge, 2007, pp. 710–12.

Libran Moreno, Miryam. "Greek and Latin Amatory Motifs in Éowyn's Portrayal." *Tolkien Studies*, vol. 4, 2007, pp. 73–97, doi.org/10.1353/tks.2007.0025.

McCoy, Sharon D. "'Brothers, I See in Your Eyes the Same Fear': The Transformation of Class Relations in Peter Jackson's *Lord of the Rings* Trilogy." In *Fantasy Fiction Into Film*, edited by Leslie Stratyner and James R. Keller, McFarland, 2007, pp. 55–72.

McFadden, Brian. "Fear of Difference, Fear of Death: The Sigelwara, Tolkien's Swertings, and Racial Difference." *Tolkien's Modern Middle Ages*, edited by Jane Chance and Alfred K. Siewers, Palgrave Macmillan, 2005, pp. 155–69. The New Middle Ages.

McKenna, Elise. "To Sex Up *The Lord of the Rings*: Jackson's Feminine Approach in His 'Sub-Creation.'" *How We Became Middle-earth: A Collection of Essays on The Lord of the Rings*, edited by Adam Lam and Nataliya Oryshchuk, Walking Tree, 2007, pp. 229–37.

McLarty, Lianne. "Masculinity, Whiteness,

and Social Class in *The Lord of the Rings.*" *From Hobbits to Hollywood: Essays on Peter Jackson's* Lord of the Rings, edited by Ernest Mathijs and Murray Pomerance, Brill, 2006, pp. 173–88.

Michel, Laura. "Politically Incorrect: Tolkien, Women, and Feminism." *Tolkien and Modernity 1*, edited by Frank Weinreich and Thomas Honegger, Walking Tree, 2006, pp. 55–76.

Miller, John. "Alternative Masculinities and the 'Dominion of Men' in *The Lord of the Rings.*" *Images of Masculinity in Fantasy Fiction*, edited by Susanne Fendler and Ulrike Horstman, Edwin Mellen P, 2003, pp. 183–203.

Morgan, Gerald. "Medieval Misogyny and Gawain's Outburst Against Women in 'Sir Gawain and the Green Knight.'" *The Modern Language Review*, Vol. 97, No. 2, Apr. 2002, P. 265, Doi.org/10.2307/3736858.

Nelson, Dale. "'Queer, Exciting and Debatable': Tolkien and Shorthouse's John Inglesant." *Mallorn*, iss. 44, Aug. 2006, pp. 27–28.

Neville, Jennifer. "Women." *Reading The Lord of the Rings: New Writings on Tolkien's Trilogy*, edited by Robert Eaglestone, Continuum International Publishing Group, 2006, pp. 101–10.

Nicklas, Pascal. "The Paradox of Racism in Tolkien." *Inklings: Jahrbuch Für Literatur Und Ästhetik*, vol. 21, 2003, pp. 221–35.

Obertino, James. "Barbarians and Imperialism in *Tacitus* and *The Lord of the Rings.*" *Tolkien Studies*, vol. 3, 2006, pp. 117–31, doi.org/10.1353/tks.2006.0026.

Pretorius, David. "Binary Issues and Feminist Issues in *LOTR.*" *Mallorn*, iss. 40, Nov. 2002, pp. 32–38.

Rearick, Anderson. "Why Is the Only Good Orc a Dead Orc? The Dark Face of Racism Examined in Tolkien's World." *MFS: Modern Fiction Studies*, J.R.R. Tolkien Special Issue, guest editor Shaun F.D. Hughes, vol. 50, no. 4, 2004, pp. 861–74, doi.org/10.1353/mfs.2005.0008.

Reid, Robin Anne. "Thrusts in the Dark: Slashers' Queer Practices." *Extrapolation*, vol. 50, no. 3, Jan. 2009, pp. 463–83, doi.org/10.3828/extr.2009.50.3.6.

Ringel, Faye. "Women Fantasists: In the Shadow of the Ring." *J.R.R. Tolkien and His Literary Resonances: Views of middle-earth*, edited by George Clark and Daniel Timmons, Greenwood (Praeger), 2000, pp. 159–71.

Ripley, Aline. "Feminist Readings of Tolkien." *J.R.R. Tolkien Encyclopedia: Scholarship and Critical Assessment*, edited by Michael D.C. Drout, Routledge, 2007, pp. 202–3.

Rohy, Valerie. "On Fairy Stories." *MFS: Modern Fiction Studies*, J.R.R. Tolkien Special Issue, guest editor Shaun F.D. Hughes, vol. 50, no. 4, 2004, pp. 927–48, doi.org/10.1353/mfs.2005.0009.

Rosebury, Brian. "Race in Tolkien Film." *J.R.R. Tolkien Encyclopedia: Scholarship and Critical Assessment*, edited by Michael D.C. Drout, Routledge, 2007, pp. 557.

Rosenthal, Ty. "Warm Beds Are Good: Sex and Libido in Tolkien's Writing." *Mallorn*, iss. 42, Aug. 2004, pp. 35–42.

Ruane, Abigail, and Patrick James. "The International Relations of Middle-earth: Learning from *The Lord of the Rings.*" *Conference Papers—International Studies Association*, 2008 Annual Meeting 2008, pp. 1–38.

Sandoz, Jeff. "Images of Addiction and Recovery in *Lord of the Rings.*" *Annals of the American Psychotherapy Association*, vol. 9, no. 1, spring 2006, pp. 39–42.

Saxey, Esther. "Homoeroticism." *Reading the Lord of the Rings: New Writings on Tolkien's Trilogy*, edited by Robert Eaglestone, Continuum International Publishing Group, 2006, pp. 124–37.

Seaman, Gerald. "Lúthien." *J.R.R. Tolkien Encyclopedia: Scholarship and Critical Assessment*, edited by Michael D.C. Drout, Routledge, 2007, pp. 396–7.

Shippey, Tom. "Noblesse Oblige: Images of Class in Tolkien." *Roots and Branches: Selected Papers on Tolkien*, Walking Tree, 2007, pp. 285–301.

Smith-Rowsey, Daniel. "Whose Middle-earth Is It? Reading *The Lord of the Rings* and New Zealand's New Identity from a Globalized, Post-Colonial Perspective." *How We Became Middle-earth: A Collection of Essays on the Lord of the Rings*, edited by Adam Lam and Nataliya Oryshchuk, Walking Tree, 2007, pp. 129–45.

Smol, Anna. "Gender in Tolkien's Works." *J.R.R. Tolkien Encyclopedia: Scholarship* and *Critical Assessment*, edited by Michael D.C. Drout, Routledge, 2007, pp. 233–5.

———. "'Oh. Oh. Frodo!': Readings of Male Intimacy in *The Lord of the Rings*." *MFS: Modern Fiction Studies*, J.R.R. Tolkien Special Issue, guest editor Shaun F.D. Hughes, vol. 50, no. 4, 2004, pp. 949–79, doi.org/10.1353/mfs.2005.0010.

Thum, Maureen. "The 'Sub-Subcreation' of Galadriel, Arwen, and Éowyn: Women of Power in Tolkien's and Jackson's *The Lord of the Rings*." *Tolkien on Film: Essays on Peter Jackson's* The Lord of the Rings, edited by Janet Brennan Croft, Mythopoeic P, 2004, pp. 231–56.

Timmons, Daniel. "Hobbit Sex and Sensuality in *The Lord of the Rings*." *Mythlore*, vol. 23, no. 3, article 7, 2001, pp. 70–79, dc.swosu.edu/mythlore/vol23/iss3/7.

Tubbs, Patricia. "Juliana." *J.R.R. Tolkien Encyclopedia: Scholarship and Critical Assessment*, edited by Michael D. C. Drout, Routledge, 2007, pp. 313–7.

Vaccaro, Christopher. "Homosexuality." *J.R.R. Tolkien Encyclopedia: Scholarship and Critical Assessment*, edited by Michael D.C. Drout, Routledge, 2007, pp. 285–86.

Vary, Adam B. "Tolkienism." *Advocate*, no. 953, Dec. 2005, p. 61.

Wainwright, Tom. "The Hobbits Versus Hitler." *Times Higher Education Supplement*, no. 1700, July 2005, p. 5.

Watson, Ben. "Fantasy and Judgement: Adorno, Tolkien, Burroughs.'" *Historical Materialism*, vol. 10, iss. 4, 2002, pp. 213–38.

Werber, Niels. "Geo- and Biopolitics of Middle-earth: A German Reading of Tolkien's *The Lord of the Rings*." *New Literary History*, vol. 36, no. 2, 2005, pp. 227–46, doi.org/10.1353/nlh.2005.0039.

Yates, Jessica. "Arwen the Elf-Warrior?" *Amon Hen*, vol. 165, Sept. 2000, pp. 11–15.

Zettersten, Arne. "Ancrene Wisse." *J.R.R. Tolkien Encyclopedia: Scholarship and Critical Assessment*, edited by Michael D. C. Drout, Routledge, 2007, pp. 15–16.

2010–2019

Agan, Cami D. "Lúthien Tinúviel and Bodily Desire in the Lay of Leithian." *Perilous and Fair: Women in the Works and Life of J.R.R. Tolkien*, edited by Janet Brennan Croft and Leslie A. Donovan, Mythopoeic P, 2015, pp. 168–88.

Amendt-Raduege, Amy. "Revising Lobelia." *Tolkien and Alterity*, edited by Christopher Vaccaro and Yvette Kisor, Palgrave Macmillan, 2017, pp. 77–93.

Baker, Dallas John. "Writing Back to Tolkien: Gender, Sexuality and Race in High Fantasy." *Recovering History Through Fact and Fiction: Forgotten Lives*, edited by Dallas John Baker, et al., Cambridge Scholars Publishing, 2017, pp. 123–43.

Bilge, F. Zeynep, and Şebnem Sunar. "Identities Re-Considered/Mythology Re-Written." *Romanian Journal of English Studies*, vol. 8, 2011, pp. 269–78.

Błaskiewicz, Maria. "Tolkien's Queen Women in *The Lord of the Rings*." *"O, What a Tangled Web": Tolkien and Medieval Literature, a View from Poland*, edited by Barbara Kowalik, Walking Tree, 2013, pp. 69–91.

Brazier, P.H. "*Fantasy, Myth and the Measure of Truth: Tales of Pullman, Lewis, Tolkien, MacDonald and Hoffman*. by William Gray and *Tolkien, Race and Cultural History: From Fairies to Hobbits*. by Dimitra Fimi." Book Reviews, *The Heythrop Journal*, vol. 52, no. 6, Nov. 2011, pp. 1076–77, doi.org/10.1111/j.1468-2265.2011.00699_35.x.

Campbell, Lori M. "*Tolkien, Race and Cultural History: From Fairies to Hobbits* (Review)." *MFS: Modern Fiction Studies*, J.R.R. Tolkien Special Issue, guest editor Shaun F. D. Hughes, vol. 57, no. 2, 2011, pp. 355–57, doi.org/10.1353/mfs.2011.0058.

Carter, Susan. "Galadriel and Morgan Le Fey: Tolkien's Redemption of the Lady of the Lacuna," *Mythlore*, vol. 25, no. 3, article 8, 2010, pp. 71–89, dc.swosu.edu/mythlore/vol25/iss3/8.

Chance, Jane. *Tolkien, Self and Other: "This Queer Creature."* Palgrave Macmillan, 2016.

Coker, Cait, and Karen Viars. "Looking for Lothíriel: The Presence of Women in Tolkien Fandom." *The Lord of the Rings*, edited by Lorna Piatti-Farnell, Intellect Books, 2015, pp. 74–82.

Costabile, Giovanni. "'No Englander May Hinder Me': Éowyn the Highland Pipe

Major and Other Highlights of Tolkien's Awareness of Sexual, Class and Ethnic Divisions in Wartime." *"Something Has Gone Crack": New Perspectives on J.R.R. Tolkien in the Great War*, edited by Janet Brennan Croft and Annika Röttinger, Walking Tree, 2019, pp. 357–77.

Croft, Janet Brennan, and Leslie A. Donovan, editors. *Perilous and Fair: Women in the Works and Life of J.R.R. Tolkien*. Mythopoeic P, 2015.

Croggon, Alison. "On Mingled Sorrow and Joy." *Overland*, no. 210, Apr. 2013, pp. 30–31.

Crowe, Edith L. "Power in Arda: Sources, Uses and Misuses," *Perilous and Fair*, edited by Janet Brennan Croft and Leslie Donovan, 2015, pp. 136–49. Rpt. from *Mythlore*, vol. 21, no. 2 article 40, 1996, pp. 272–77, dc.swosu.edu/mythlore/vol21/iss2/40.

Cuntz-Leng, Vera. "Frodo Auf Abwegen: Das Queere Potential Des Aktuellen Fantasykinos." *Zeitschrift Für Fantastikforschung*, vol. 1, 2011, pp. 24–43.

Darvell, Lilian. "'Beautiful and Terrible': The Significance of Galadriel's Hair in *The Lord of the Rings* and *Unfinished Tales*." *Mallorn*, iss. 56, 2015, pp. 22–24.

Dawson, Deidre. "Language, Culture, Environment, and Diversity in *The Lord of the Rings*." *Approaches to Teaching Tolkien's* The Lord of the Rings *and Other Works*, edited by Leslie A. Donovan, Modern Language Association of America, 2015, pp. 157–64.

Donovan, Leslie A. "The Valkyrie Reflex in J.R.R. Tolkien's *The Lord of the Rings*: Galadriel, Shelob, Éowyn, and Arwen." *Perilous and Fair: Women in the Works and Life of J.R.R. Tolkien*, edited by Janet Brennan Croft and Leslie A. Donovan, Mythopoeic P, 2015, pp. 221–57. Rpt. from *Tolkien the Medievalist*, edited by Jane Chance, Routledge, 2003, pp. 106–32.

Downey, Sarah. "Cordial Dislike: Reinventing the Celestial Ladies of Pearl and Purgatorio in Tolkien's Galadriel." *Mythlore*, vol. 29, no. 3, article 8, 2011, pp. 101–17, dc.swosu.edu/mythlore/vol29/iss3/8.

Downs, Jack M. "'Radiant and Terrible': Tolkien's Heroic Women as Correctives to the Romance and Epic Traditions." *A Quest of Her Own: Essays on the Female Hero in Modern Fantasy*, edited by Lori M. Campbell, McFarland, 2014, pp. 55–75.

Duplessis, Nicole M. "On the Shoulders of Humphrey Carpenter: Reconsidering Biographical Representation and Scholarly Perception of Edith Tolkien." *Mythlore*, vol. 37, no. 2, article 4, 2019, pp. 39–74, dc.swosu.edu/mythlore/vol37/iss2/4.

Enright, Nancy. "Tolkien's Females and the Defining of Power." *Perilous and Fair: Women in the Works and Life of J.R.R. Tolkien*, edited by Janet Brennan Croft and Leslie A. Donovan, Mythopoeic P, 2015, pp. 118–35. Rpt. from *Renascence*, vol. 59, no. 2, winter 2007, pp. 93–108.

Filipczak, Dorota. "Éowyn and the Biblical Tradition of a Warrior Woman." *Text Matters*, vol. 7, no. 7, Nov. 2017, pp. 405–15.

Fimi, Dimitra. "Teaching Tolkien and Race: An Inconvenient Combination?" *Approaches to Teaching Tolkien's* The Lord of the Rings *and Other Works*, edited by Leslie A. Donovan, Modern Language Association of America, 2015, pp. 139–144.

Fitzpatrick, Kelly Ann. "(Re)Producing (Neo)Medievalism." *ProQuest Dissertations & Theses Global*, vol. 77, no. 4, State University of New York, Albany ProQuest, Oct. 2016.

Flieger, Verlyn. "The Orcs and the Others: Familiarity as Estrangement in *The Lord of the Rings*." *Tolkien and Alterity*, edited by Christopher Vaccaro and Yvette Kisor, Palgrave Macmillan, 2017, pp. 205–22.

———. "Tolkien, Race and Cultural History: From Fairies to Hobbits. by Dimitra Fimi." *The European Legacy*, vol. 17, no. 3, June 2012, pp. 408–09, doi.org/10.1080/10848770.2012.673348.

———. *Green Suns and Faërie: Essays on J.R.R. Tolkien*. Kent State UP, 2012.

Fündling, Jörg. "'Go Forth, for It Is There!' An Imperialist Battle Cry Behind the Lament for Boromir?" *Music in Tolkien's Work and Beyond*, edited by Julian Eilmann and Friedhelm Schneidewind, Walking Tree, 2019, pp. 111–31.

Gilbert, Felicity. "Mighty Men of War: The Impact of Gender and War in the Work of J.R.R. Tolkien." *"Something Has Gone Crack": New Perspectives on J.R.R.*

Tolkien in the Great War, edited by Janet Brennan Croft and Annika Röttinger, Walking Tree, 2019, pp. 319–43.

Hemmi, Yoko. "Tolkien's *The Lord of the Rings* and His Concept of *Native Language*: Sindarin and British-Welsh." *Tolkien Studies*, vol. 7, 2010, pp. 147–74, doi.org/10.1353/tks.0.0063.

Higgins, Andrew Scott. "'Those Who Cling in Queer Corners to the Forgotten Tongues and Memories of an Elder Day': J.R.R. Tolkien, Finns, and Elves." *Journal of Tolkien Research*, vol. 3, iss. 2, article 2, 2016, scholar.valpo.edu/journaloftolkienresearch/vol3/iss2/2.

Hiley, Margaret. "(Re)Authoring History: Tolkien and Postcolonialism." *Sub-Creating Middle-earth: Constructions of Authorship and the Works of J.R.R. Tolkien*, edited by Judith Klinger and Stephanie Luther, Walking Tree, 2012, pp. 107–25.

House-Thomas, Alyssa. "'Fair as Fay-Woman and Fell-Minded': Tolkien's Guinevere." *The Inklings and King Arthur: J.R.R. Tolkien, Charles Williams, C.S. Lewis, and Owen Barfield on the Matter of Britain*, edited by Sørina Higgins, Apocryphile P, 2017, pp. 333–66.

Inloes, Amina. "Muhammad Abd Al-Rahman (Phillip) Barker: Bridging Cultural Divides Through Fantasy/Science-Fiction Role-Playing Games and Fictional Religion: Muhammad Abd Al-Rahman (Phillip) Barker." *The Muslim World*, vol. 108, no. 3, July 2018, pp. 387–418, doi.org/10.1111/muwo.12225.

Jensen, Anika. "Flowers and Steel: The Necessity of War in Feminist Tolkien Scholarship." *Tolkien Studies*, vol. 16, 2019, pp. 59–72, doi.org/10.1353/tks.2019.0006.

Johannesson, Nils-Lennart. "Bring on the Leprawns." *English Today*, vol. 26, no. 1, Mar. 2010, pp. 60–61, doi.org/10.1017/S0266078409990630.

Kaufman, Roger. "The Amplification and Avoidance of Homosexual Love in the Translation of Tolkien's Work from Books to Films." *The Fantastic Made Visible: Essays on the Adaptation of Science Fiction and Fantasy from Page to Screen*, edited by Matthew Wilhelm Kapell and Ace G. Pilkington, McFarland, 2015, pp. 117–32.

Kightley, Michael R. "Racial Anglo-Saxonisms: From Scholarship to Fiction in England, 1850–1960." *Dissertation Abstracts International, Section A: The Humanities and Social Sciences*, vol. 70, no. 12, University of Western Ontario; ProQuest, June 2010, UMI 4672.

Kisor, Yvette. "Queer Tolkien: A Bibliographical Essay on Tolkien and Alterity." *Tolkien and Alterity*, edited by Christopher Vaccaro and Yvette Kisor, Palgrave Macmillan, 2017, pp. 17–32.

Kroner, Susanne. "'Still Not King'-The Very Secret Diaries: Tolkien Fan Fiction Between Book-Verse and Movie-Verse." *Inklings: Jahrbuch Für Literatur Und Ästhetik*, vol. 28, 2010, pp. 107–17.

LaFontaine, David. "Sex and Subtext in Tolkien's World." *Gay & Lesbian Review Worldwide*, vol. 22, no. 6, Nov. 2015, pp. 14–17.

———. "The Tolkien in Bilbo Baggins." *Gay & Lesbian Review Worldwide*, vol. 23, no. 6, Nov. 2016, pp. 24–28.

Lakowski, Romuald I. "The Fall and Repentance of Galadriel." *Perilous and Fair: Women in the Works and Life of J.R.R. Tolkien*, edited by Janet Brennan Croft and Leslie A. Donovan, Mythopoeic P, 2015, pp. 153–67.

Larini, Gloria. "To Die for Love: Female Archetypes in Tolkien and Euripides." *Tolkien and the Classics*, edited by Roberto Arduini, et al., Walking Tree, 2019, pp. 25–34.

Larsen, Kristine. "Guinevere, Grímhild, and the Corrigan: Witches and Bitches in Tolkien's Medieval Narrative Verse." *Journal of Tolkien Research*, vol. 4, iss. 2, article 8, 2017, scholar.valpo.edu/journaloftolkienresearch/vol4/iss2/8.

———. "Medieval Organicism or Modern Feminist Science? Bombadil, Elves, and Mother Nature." *Tolkien and Alterity*, edited by Christopher Vaccaro and Yvette Kisor, Palgrave Macmillan, 2017, pp. 95–108.

———. "The Power of Pity and Tears: The Evolution of Nienna in the Legendarium." *Perilous and Fair: Women in the Works and Life of J.R.R. Tolkien*, edited by Janet Brennan Croft and Leslie A. Donovan, Mythopoeic P, 2015, pp. 189–203.

Linton, Phoebe C. "Speech and Silence in *The Lord of the Rings*: Medieval Romance and the Transitions of Éowyn." *Perilous and Fair: Women in the Works and Life of J.R.R. Tolkien*, edited by Janet Brennan Croft and Leslie A. Donovan, Mythopoeic P, 2015, pp. 258–80.

Măcineanu, Laura. "Feminine Hypostases in Epic Fantasy: Tolkien, Lewis, Rowling." *Gender Studies*, vol. 14, no. 1, Dec. 2015, pp. 68–82, doi.org/10.1515/genst-2016-0005.

———. "Masculine and Feminine Insights Into the Fantastic World of Elves: J.R.R. Tolkien's *The Lord of the Rings* and Muriel Barbery's *The Life of Elves*." *Gender Studies*, vol. 15, no. 1, Dec. 2016, pp. 270–83, doi.org/10.1515/genst-2017-0018.

Madsen, Catherine. "A Woman of Valour: Éowyn in War and Peace." *Mallorn*, iss. 52, 2011, pp. 28–33.

McCormack, Una. "Finding Ourselves in the (Un)Mapped Lands: Women's Reparative Readings of *The Lord of the Rings*." *Perilous and Fair: Women in the Works and Life of J.R.R. Tolkien*, edited by Janet Brennan Croft and Leslie A. Donovan, Mythopoeic P, 2015, pp. 309–26.

Miesel, Sandra. "Life-Giving Ladies: Women in the Writings of J.R.R. Tolkien." *Light Beyond All Shadow: Religious Experience in Tolkien's Work*, edited by Paul E. Kerry and Sandra Miesel, Fairleigh Dickinson UP, 2011, pp. 139–52.

Miller, John. "Mapping Gender in Middle-earth." *Mythlore*, vol. 34, no. 2, article 9, 2016, dc.swosu.edu/mythlore/vol34/iss2/9.

Mitchell, Philip Irving. "Book Review: *Tolkien, Race, and Cultural History: From Fairies to Hobbits*." *Christianity & Literature*, vol. 59, no. 3, June 2010, pp. 563–65, doi.org/10.1177/014833311005900318.

Molyneux, John. "A Marxist View of Tolkien's Middle Earth." *JohnMolyneux*, 22 Sept. 2011, johnmolyneux.blogspot.com/2011/09/tolkiens-world-marxist-analysis.html. Rpt. *Jacobin*, "Literature / Theory," 11 Jan. 2023, jacobin.com/2023/01/jrr-tolkien-lord-of-the-rings-marxist-critique.

Neidorf, Leonard. "*Beowulf* as Pre-National Epic: Ethnocentrism in the Poem and Its Criticism." *ELH*, vol. 85, no. 4, 2018, pp. 847–75, doi.org/10.1353/elh.2018.0031.

Nicholas, Angela. "Female Descent in J.R.R. Tolkien's Middle-earth Mythology." *Amon Hen*, vol. 252, Mar. 2015, pp. 11–18.

Petzold, Dieter. "'Oo, Those Awful Orcs!': Tolkien's Villains as Protagonists in Recent Fantasy Novels." *Inklings: Jahrbuch Für Literatur Und Ästhetik*, vol. 28, 2010, pp. 76–95.

Phillips, Martin. "*The Lord of the Rings* and Transformations in Socio-Spatial Identity in Aotearoa/New Zealand." *Cinematic Countrysides*, edited by Robert Fish, Manchester UP, 2017, pp. 147–74.

Phillips-Zur-Liden, Vanessa. "Arwen and Edward: Redemption and the Fairy Bride/Groom in the Literary Fairytale." *Mallorn*, iss. 50, 2010, pp. 37–41.

Rateliff, John D. "The Missing Women: J.R.R. Tolkien's Lifelong Support for Women's Education." *Perilous and Fair: Women in the Works and Life of J.R.R. Tolkien*, edited by Janet Brennan Croft and Leslie A. Donovan, Mythopoeic P, 2015, pp. 41–69.

Rawls, Melanie A. "The Feminine Principle in Tolkien." *Perilous and Fair: Women in the Works and Life of J.R.R. Tolkien*, edited by Janet Brennan Croft and Leslie A. Donovan, Mythopoeic P, 2015, pp. 99–117. Rpt. from *Mythlore*, vol. 10, no. 4, article 2, 1984, pp. 5–13, dc.swosu.edu/mythlore/vol10/iss4/2.

Ray, Stella M. "Constructions of Gender and Sexualities in J.R.R. Tolkien's *The Silmarillion* and *The Lord of the Rings*." *Dissertation Abstracts International, Section A: The Humanities and Social Sciences*, vol. 72, no. 4, Texas A&M University, Commerce,; ProQuest, Oct. 2011, UMI 1303.

Rees, Shelley. "Women Students and *The Lord of the Rings*: Showing Them Where They Fit In." *Approaches to Teaching Tolkien's* The Lord of the Rings *and Other Works*, edited by Leslie A. Donovan, Modern Language Association of America, 2015, pp. 150–56.

Reid, Robin Anne. "The History of Scholarship on Female Characters in J.R.R. Tolkien's Legendarium: A Feminist Bibliographic Essay." *Perilous and Fair: Women in the Works and Life of J.R.R. Tolkien*, edited by Janet Brennan Croft and Leslie A. Donovan, Mythopoeic P, 2015, pp. 14–40.

———. "Light (Noun, 1) or Light (Adjective, 14b)? Female Bodies and

Femininities in *The Lord of the Rings.*" *The Body in Tolkien's Legendarium: Essays on Middle-earth Corporeality*, edited by Christopher Vaccaro, McFarland, 2013, pp. 98–118.

———. "Race in Tolkien Studies: A Bibliographic Essay." *Tolkien and Alterity*, edited by Christopher Vaccaro and Yvette Kisor, Palgrave Macmillan, 2017, pp. 33–74.

Rohy, Valerie. "Cinema, Sexuality, Mechanical Reproduction." *Tolkien and Alterity*, edited by Christopher Vaccaro and Yvette Kisor, Palgrave Macmillan, 2017, pp. 111–22.

Ruppo Malone, Irina. "What's Wrong with Medievalism? Tolkien, the Strugatsky Brothers, and the Question of the Ideology of Fantasy." *Journal of the Fantastic in the Arts*, vol. 27, no. 2, 2016, pp. 204–24.

Sanguineti, Barbara. "With Light Step Through the Threshold: Female Characters, the Gothic, and the Meditatio Mortis in Tolkien and Poe." *Tolkien and the Classics*, edited by Roberto Arduini, et al., Walking Tree, 2019, pp. 217–27.

Saxton, Benjamin. "Tolkien and Bakhtin on Authorship, Literary Freedom, and Alterity." *Tolkien Studies*, vol. 10, 2013, pp. 167–83, doi.org/10.1353/tks.2013.0010.

Schroeder, Sharin. "She-Who-Must-Not-Be-Ignored: Gender and Genre in *The Lord of the Rings* and the *Victorian Boys' Book*." *Perilous and Fair: Women in the Works and Life of J.R.R. Tolkien*, edited by Janet Brennan Croft and Leslie A. Donovan, Mythopoeic P, 2015, pp. 70–96.

Simpson, Jacqueline. "*Tolkien, Race and Cultural History: From Fairies to Hobbits*." *Folklore*, vol. 121, no. 1, Apr. 2010, pp. 106–07, doi.org/10.1080/00155870903482098.

Sinex, Margaret. "'Monsterized Saracens,' Tolkien's Haradrim, and Other Medieval 'Fantasy Products.'" *Tolkien Studies*, Vol. 7, 2010, pp. 175–96.

Smith, Melissa A. "At Home and Abroad: Éowyn's Two-Fold Figuring as War Bride in *The Lord of the Rings*." *Perilous and Fair: Women in the Works and Life of J.R.R. Tolkien*, edited by Janet Brennan Croft and Leslie A. Donovan, Mythopoeic P, 2015, pp. 204–17.

Solomons, Sunny. "Tauriel in *The Hobbit: The Desolation of Smaug.*" *Amon Hen*, vol. 246, Mar. 2014, pp. 13–14.

Soloveichik, Meir. "The Secret Jews of *The Hobbit.*" *Commentary*, vol. 142, no. 2, Sept. 2016, pp. 62–66, commentary.org/articles/meir-soloveichik/the-secret-jews-of-the-hobbit.

Thum, Maureen. "Hidden in Plain View: Strategizing Unconventionality in Shakespeare's and Tolkien's Portraits of Women." *Perilous and Fair: Women in the Works and Life of J.R.R. Tolkien*, edited by Janet Brennan Croft and Leslie A. Donovan, Mythopoeic P, 2015, pp. 281–305.

Vaccaro, Christopher. "Saruman's Sodomitic Resonances: Alain de Lille's *De Planctu Naturae* and J.R.R. Tolkien's *The Lord of the Rings*." *Tolkien and Alterity*, edited by Christopher Vaccaro and Yvette Kisor, Palgrave Macmillan, 2017, pp. 123–47.

Vaccaro, Christopher, and Yvette Kisor, editors. *Tolkien and Alterity*. Palgrave Macmillan, 2017.

Viars, Karen, and Cait Coker. "Constructing Lothíriel: Rewriting and Rescuing the Women of Middle-earth from the Margins." *Mythlore*, vol. 33, no. 2, article 6, 2015, pp. 35–48, dc.swosu.edu/mythlore/vol33/iss2/6.

Vinci, Tony M. "Remembering Why We Once Feared the Dark: Reclaiming Humanity Through Fantasy in Guillermo Del Toro's *Hellboy II*." *The Journal of Popular Culture*, vol. 45, no. 5, Oct. 2012, pp. 1041–59, doi.org/10.1111/j.1540-5931.2012.00972.x.

Vink, Renée. "'Jewish' Dwarves: Tolkien and Anti-Semitic Stereotyping." *Tolkien Studies*, vol. 10, 2013, pp. 123–45, doi.org/10.1353/tks.2013.0003.

Vogt-William, Christine. "Brothers in Arms: Death and Hobbit Homosociality in *The Lord of the Rings*." *Inklings: Jahrbuch Für Literatur Und Ästhetik*, vol. 34, 2017, pp. 81–95.

———. "Tolkien's Green Man: The Racialised Cultural Other Within and Green Spaces in *The Lord of the Rings*." *Binding Them All: Interdisciplinary Perspectives on J.R.R. Tolkien and His Works*, edited by Monika Kirner-Ludwig, et al., Walking Tree, 2017, pp. 305–39.

Wallace, Anna. "A Wild Shieldmaiden of the North: Éowyn of Rohan and Old

Norse Literature." *Philament*, vol. 17, Aug. 2011, pp. 23–45.

Walls-Thumma, Dawn M. "Attainable Vistas: Historical Bias in Tolkien's Legendarium as a Motive for Transformative Fanworks." *Journal of Tolkien Research*, vol. 3, iss. 3, 2016, scholar.valpo.edu/journaloftolkienresearch/vol3/iss3/3.

Williams, Rowan. "Master of His Universe." *New Statesman*, vol. 147, no. 5430, Aug. 2018, pp. 40–43.

Williamson, James T. "Emblematic Bodies: Tolkien and the Depiction of Female Physical Presence." *The Body in Tolkien's Legendarium: Essays on Middle-earth Corporeality*, edited by Christopher Vaccaro, McFarland, 2013, pp. 134–56.

Workman, Sarah. "Female Valor Without Renown: Memory, Mourning and Loss at the Center of Middle-earth." *A Quest of Her Own: Essays on the Female Hero in Modern Fantasy*, edited by Lori M. Campbell, McFarland, 2014, pp. 76–93.

Yandell, Stephen. "Cruising Faery: Queer Desire in Giles, Niggle, and Smith." *Tolkien and Alterity*, edited by Christopher Vaccaro and Yvette Kisor, Palgrave Macmillan, 2017, pp. 149–79.

Young, Helen. "Diversity and Difference: Cosmopolitanism and *The Lord of the Rings*." *Journal of the Fantastic in the Arts*, vol. 21, no. 3 [79], 2010, pp. 351–65.

———. "Freedom to Discriminate." *Medievalism and Discrimination*, edited by Karl Fugelso, Boydell & Brewer; D.S. Brewer, 2019, pp. 3–12.

2020–2024

Artamonova, Maria. "Edith Tolkien in the Eye of the Beholder." *Thanks for Typing: Remembering Forgotten Women in History*, edited by Juliana Dresvina, Bloomsbury Academic, 2021.

Battis, Jes. *Thinking Queerly: Medievalism, Wizardry, and Neurodiversity in Young Adult Texts*. De Gruyter, 2021, doi.org/10.1515/9781501515330.

Brown, Sara. "Éowyn It Was, and Dernhelm Also": Reading the 'Wild Shieldmaiden' Through a Queer Lens." *Journal of Tolkien Research*, vol. 18, iss. 2, article 4, 2023, scholar.valpo.edu/journaloftolkienresearch/vol18/iss2/4.

Brown, Sara. "The Tale of 'Aldarion and Erendis': Not Just a Medieval Love Story." *Journal of Tolkien Research*, vol. 18, iss. 1, article 6, scholar.valpo.edu/journaloftolkienresearch/vol18/iss1/6.

Brust, Annie. *Tolkien's Transformative Women: Art in Triptych*. Vernon Press, 2024.

Colvin, Kathryn. "'Her Enchanted Hair': Rossetti, 'Lady Lilith,'" and the Victorian Fascination with Hair as Influences on Tolkien." *Mythlore*, vol. 39, no. 1, article 7, 2020, pp. 133–48, dc.swosu.edu/mythlore/vol39/iss1/7.

Craig, David M. "'Queer Lodgings': Gender and Sexuality in *The Lord of the Rings*." *Mallorn*, vol. 38, Jan. 2001, pp. 11–18, journals.tolkiensociety.org/mallorn/article/view/145/139. Rpt. "Queer Lodgings: Gender and Sexuality in *The Lord of the Rings*—Reprinted with a New Introduction by the Author." *Mallorn*, Vol. 61, 2020, pp. 20–29.

Duarte Rufo, Alline. "A Constituição Do Corpo Pela Alteridade Bakhtiniana: De *O Silmarillion* De J.R.R. Tolkien às Mulheres Negras Brasileiras (The Constitution of the Body by Bakhtinian Alterity: From *The Silmarillion* by J.R.R. Tolkien to Black Brazilian Women)." *Letrônica*, vol. 14, no. esp (sup.), Dec. 2021, pp. 1–11, doi.org/10.15448/1984-4301.2021.s.42468.

Fimi, Dimitra. "*Tolkien, Race, and Racism in Middle-earth* (2022) by Robert Stuart," *Journal of Tolkien Research*, vol. 15, iss. 1, article 3, 2022, scholar.valpo.edu/journaloftolkienresearch/vol15/iss1/3.

Flieger, Verlyn. "Tolkien's Lúthien: From Life to Art to Life as Art," *Mythlore*, vol. 43, no. 1, article 14, 2024, pp. 234–40, dc.swosu.edu/mythlore/vol43/iss1/14.

Frederick, Candice, and Sam McBride. *Women Among the Inklings: Gender, C.S. Lewis, J.R.R. Tolkien, and Charles Williams*, Greenwood, 2021.

Fuller-Shafer, Kelsey A. "Middle-earth's Middleman: Exploring the Contradictory Positionalities of Faramir in J.R.R. Tolkien's 'The Lord of the Rings,'" *Journal of Tolkien Research*, vol. 18, iss. 2, article 7, 2023, scholar.valpo.edu/journaloftolkienresearch/vol18/iss2/7.

Granby, Isobel. "Asexuality and the Baggins Bachelors: Finding My Counterparts in Middle-earth." *Reactor*, 20

April 2020, reactormag.com/asexuality-and-the-baggins-bachelors-finding-my-counterparts-in-middle-earth.

Hansen, Christopher. "The Monstrous Feminine: Ungoliant, Shelob, and Women in Tolkien's Middle-earth," *Crossroads*, no. 34, Nov. 2021, pp. 4–15.

Haydon, Trinity. *Queer Lodgings: The Quest to Find Home Through LGBTQ+ Readings of Middle-earth*. Thesis. Regis University Student Publications (comprehensive collection), 1073, 2023, epublications.regis.edu/theses/1073.

Heierli, Kathrin. "Finding the Feminine in Tolkien." *Amon Hen*, vol. 290, Aug. 2021, p. 17.

Henderson, Dylan L. "'A Bleak, Barren Land': Women and Fertility in the Lord of the Rings." *Mythlore*, vol. 42, no. 1, 2023, article 6, pp. 87–106, dc.swosu.edu/mythlore/vol42/iss1/6/.

Kisor, Yvette. "'The Lay of Aotrou and Itroun': Sexuality, Imagery, and Desire in Tolkien's Works." *Tolkien Studies*, vol. 18, 2021, pp. 19–62, doi.org/10.1353/tks.2021.0005.

———. "'We Could Do with a Bit More Queerness in These Parts': An Analysis of the Queer Against the Peculiar, the Odd, and the Strange in *The Lord of the Rings*." *Journal of Tolkien Research*, vol. 16, iss. 1, article 4, 2023, scholar.valpo.edu/journaloftolkienresearch/vol16/iss1/4.

LaFontaine, David. "The Fellowship of the Tea Club." *Gay & Lesbian Review Worldwide*, vol. 27, no. 4, July 2020, pp. 25–29.

Larsen, Kristine. "Elwing and the Isle of Seabirds: Tolkien's Towers and the Lais of Marie de France." *Journal of Tolkien Research*, Vol. 19, iss. 3, article 4, scholar.valpo.edu/journaloftolkienresearch/vol19/iss3/4.

Mendro, Hannah. "'Wondered at This Change': Queer Potential and Telling Silence in the Relationship of Legolas and Gimli." *Journal of Tolkien Research*, vol. 18, iss. 2, article 8, 2023, scholar.valpo.edu/journaloftolkienresearch/vol18/iss2/.

Miller, T.S., and Elizabeth Miller. "Tolkien and Rape: Sexual Terror, Sexual Violence, and the Woman's Body in Middle-earth." *Extrapolation*, vol. 62, no. 2, June 2021, pp. 133–56, doi.org/10.3828/extr.2021.8.

Mills, Charles W. "The Wretched of Middle-Earth: An Orkish Manifesto." *Southern Journal of Philosophy*, vol. 60, iss. S1, Sept. 2022, pp. 105–35.

Moore, Clare. "Elmar, Aerin, and Aredhel: Female Enslavement in Tolkien's Legendarium," *Mythlore,*, vol. 43, no. 1, article 9, 2024, dc.swosu.edu/mythlore/vol43/iss1/9.

Moore, Clare, and Leah Hagan. "A Bleak, Barren Take: A Response to "Women and Fertility in *The Lord of the Rings*." *Mythlore*, vol. 43, no. 1, article 13, 2024, pp. 227–34, dc.swosu.edu/mythlore/vol43/iss1/13.

Pacheco, Derek. "'Funny Queer Fits': Masculinity and Desire in J.R.R. Tolkien's *The Hobbit*." *Children's Literature Association Quarterly*, vol. 46, no. 3, 2021, pp. 263–82.

Petersen-Deeprose, Danna. "'Something Mighty Queer': Destabilizing Cishetero Amatonormativity in the Works of Tolkien." *Amon Hen*, vol. 290, Aug. 2021, pp. 12–16.

Pridmore, Julie. "Andy Duncan's 'Senator Bilbo': Reflections on J.R.R. Tolkien and Matters of Race." *Scrutiny2*, vol. 26, no. 1, Jan. 2021, pp. 60–75, doi.org/10.1080/18125441.2022.2044374.

Queripel, Rory M. "The Mariner (and His Wife): Queering Aldarion's (A)sexuality," *Journal of Tolkien Research*, vol. 18, iss. 2, article 12, 2023, scholar.valpo.edu/journaloftolkienresearch/vol18/iss2/12.

Reid, Robin A. "Celebrating 'Queer Lodgings.'" *Mallorn*, Iss. 61, 2020, pp. 30–31.

———. "A Queer Atheist Feminist Autist Responds to Donald Williams's 'Keystone or Cornerstone? A Rejoinder to Verlyn Flieger on the Alleged "Conflicting Sides" of Tolkien's Singular Self.'" *Mythlore*, Vol. 40, No. 2, Article 14, 2022, pp. 196–220, Dc.swosu.edu/mythlore/vol40/iss2/14.

———. "Race in J.R.R. Tolkien's *The Lord of the Rings* and in Katherine Addison's *The Goblin Emperor*." *Journal of Tolkien Research*, vol. 15, iss. 2, article 4, 2022, scholar.valpo.edu/journaloftolkienresearch/vol15/iss2/4.

Retakh, Alexander. "The Inconsistencies of Galadriel: The Influence of Earlier Legendarium in *The Lord of the Rings*," *Mythlore*, vol. 43, no. 1, article 11, 2024,

Rios Maldonado, Mariana. *Ethics and the Encounter with the Other in J.R.R. Tolkien's Middle-earth Narratives.* University of Glasgow, PhD thesis, 2024, theses.gla.ac.uk/84320/.

Stuart, Robert. *Tolkien, Race, and Racism in Middle-earth.* Palgrave Macmillan, 2022, doi.org/10.1007/978-3-030-97475-6.f.

Swain, Larry. "Mythic People of Fire and Tolkien's Southern Races in *The Lord of the Rings.*" *The Lord of the Rings by J.R.R. Tolkien,* edited by Robert C. Evans, Salem P, 2022, pp. 257–73.

———. "Tolkien's Alleged Anti-Semitism and the Diaspora." *The Lord of the Rings by J.R.R. Tolkien,* edited by Robert C. Evans, Salem P, 2022, pp. 274–91.

Swank, Kris. "The Deer-Maid Motif in *The Children of Húrin.*" *Journal of Tolkien Research,* vol. 17, iss. 2, article 5, scholar.valpo.edu/journaloftolkienresearch/vol17/iss2/5.

Tally, Robert T., Jr. "Demonizing the Enemy, Literally: Tolkien, Orcs, and the Sense of the World Wars," *Humanities,* vol. 8, no. 54, 2019, War and Literature: Commiserating with the Enemy Issue, doi.org/10.3390/h8010054.

———. "Let Us Now Praise Famous Orcs: Simple Humanity in Tolkien's Inhuman Creatures." *Mythlore,* vol. 29, no. 1, article 3, 2010, pp. 17–28, dc.swosu.edu/mythlore/vol29/iss1/3.

———. "*Tolkien, Race, and Racism in Middle-earth* by Robert Stuart," *Mythlore,* vol. 41, no. 1, article 16, 2022, pp. 253–58, dc.swosu.edu/mythlore/vol41/iss1/16.

Tornikoski, Johanna. *"Bag End's a Queer Place, and Its Folk Are Queerer": Queer Masculinities and Queerness in JRR Tolkien's* The Lord of the Rings. MS thesis. University of Eastern Finland. Itä-Suomen yliopisto, 2024, erepo.uef.fi/bitstream/handle/123456789/32241/urn_nbn_fi_uef-20240806.pdf?sequence=1.

Trenk, Christian S. "'And Each Day After They Did Likewise.' Looking at Life Together as the Fulcrum of Éowyn's and Faramir's Love Story," *Journal of Tolkien Research,* vol. 19, iss. 2, article 2, 2024, scholar.valpo.edu/journaloftolkienresearch/vol19/iss2/2.

Venkatesan, Emily. "A Fallen Woman of Arda: The Battle Over Wills and Desire of Aredhel of Gondolin." *Cities and Strongholds of Middle-earth: Essays on the Habitations of Tolkien's Legendarium,* edited by Cami Agan. Mythopoeic Press, 2024, pp. 41–54.

Vossen, Emma. "There and Back Again." *Feminist Media Histories,* vol. 6, no. 1, Jan. 2020, pp. 37–65, doi.org/10.1525/fmh.2020.6.1.37.

Whyte, Alastair. "Many a Tale of Dread: The Dystopian Interface of Totalitarianism and Colonial Imperialism in the Númenor Narratives of J.R.R. Tolkien." *Journal of Language, Literature and Culture,* vol. 67, no. 2–3, Sept. 2020, pp. 83–96, doi.org/10.1080/20512856.2020.1849943.

About the Contributors

Maria K. **Alberto** is a scholar of literature and new media and member of the tenure-track English faculty at Richland Community College. Her research explores canon(s) and community in popular culture, tabletop roleplaying game texts, and transformative fanworks, as well as queer storytelling on digital platforms. Her recent work can be found in *Transformative Works and Cultures, Convergence,* and *The Journal of Cinema and Media Studies.*

Jordan **Audas** is a project manager at Digital Nova Scotia, the industry association for Nova Scotia's Information and Communications Technology (ICT) and digital technologies sector. Jordan graduated from the Master of Information program at Dalhousie University (2022) and completed his bachelor's degree at Mount Saint Vincent University, majoring in English and graduating with distinction (2020). He is passionate about promoting information distribution and access.

Jes **Battis**, PhD (he/they), teaches literature and creative writing at the University of Regina. Their research and teaching focuses on medievalism, sexuality, and neurodiversity. Jes's monograph, *Thinking Queerly: Medievalism, Wizardry, and Neurodiversity in Young Adult Texts*, was published in 2021 by the Medieval Institute Press at the University of Western Michigan, and shortlisted for the Margaret Wade Labarge Prize in Medieval Studies.

Nicholas **Birns**, PhD (he/him/his), teaches at New York University. His book *The Literary Role of History in the Fiction of J.R.R, Tolkien* appeared from Routledge in 2024. He has published frequently in many areas of literary studies, including world and postcolonial literature, and his coedited *Companion to the Australian Novel* appeared in 2023 from Cambridge University Press.

Sara **Brown**, PhD (she/her), is chair of the language and literature faculty at Signum University, U.S. where she has taught on courses with Corey Olsen, Verlyn Flieger, Dimitra Fimi, Robin Reid, Doug Anderson, Amy Sturgis, and Chris Vaccaro. Sara currently serves on the editorial board of *Mallorn*, the academic journal of the Tolkien Society, and is co-presenter on *The Tolkien Experience Podcast, The Rings of Power Wrap-Up, Rings and Rituals,* and *The Prancing Pony Podcast.*

Christopher **Cameron** (he/him/his) is a PhD candidate in English language and literature at the University of Waterloo studying twentieth-century British literature with a focus on narrative expressions of gender and national identity. His previous work has focused on Tolkien and the formation of identity through landscape and acts of walking.

Zachary Clifton **Engledow** (he/they) is a PhD candidate and Associate Instructor in the English department at Indiana University Bloomington. His primary research focuses on medieval romance and its intersections with queer and trans materialities, identities, and bodies. His work is featured in *Exemplaria*, and he has a forthcoming essay in *Studies in the Age of Chaucer* on trans psychoanalysis and "The Tale of Sir Thopas."

Gavin **Foster** (he/him) is a PhD candidate at Dalhousie University in Halifax, Nova Scotia. His research interests include J.R.R. Tolkien, Old and Middle English elegiac literature, and queer theory. You can find his research published in the *Journal of Tolkien Research* and *Florilegium*, and you can find his creative publications in *Open Heart Forgery*, *the tide rises*, and *The Dalhousie Review*, with more forthcoming.

Kristine **Larsen**, PhD, an astronomer at Central Connecticut State University, studies intersections between science and society, including the history of astronomy and depictions of science and scientists in popular media (especially in Tolkien). The author of *The Sun We Share* (2024); *Science, Technology, and Magic in* The Witcher (2023); *The Women Who Popularized Geology in the 19th Century* (2017); and *Particle Panic!* (2019), she received the 2020 Tolkien Society Best Paper Award.

Cordeliah G. **Logsdon** is an independent scholar who graduated in 2024 with a Master of Liberal Arts degree from McDaniel College in Westminster, Maryland. As an undergraduate student at McDaniel, they graduated summa cum laude in 2010, the recipient of the Makosky Award for Excellence in English for their thesis analyzing fantasy literature. They have a diverse academic background in English literature and language, philosophy, history, theater, and theology.

Danna **Petersen-Deeprose** is pursuing a PhD in English literature at Queen's University where their research focuses on queer and trans themes in speculative fiction. They have a master's degree from McGill University, where they studied the relationship between the sublime and the grotesque; a bachelor's degree from McGill University; and a certificate in publishing from Toronto Metropolitan University.

Robin Anne **Reid**, PhD (she or they), retired in 2020 and is engaged in several scholarly and creative writing projects which include the anthology *Race, Racisms, and Racists: Essays on J.R.R. Tolkien's Legendarium, Adaptations, and Readers* (working title, forthcoming, McFarland), and two monographs: *Webs by Women* (working title for a feminist reception analysis of Tolkien's legendarium) and *Atheists, Agnostics, and Animists: Secular Readings of J.R.R. Tolkien's Legendarium*.

Christopher **Vaccaro**, PhD, is senior lecturer at the University of Vermont, where he has taught courses on Tolkien and early medieval British literature since 1999. He is the editor of *The Body in Tolkien's Legendarium*, *Tolkien and Alterity* (co-edited with Yvette Kisor), and *Painful Pleasures*. His book, *Sadomasochistic Beowulf*, is set to be published this year.

Stephen **Yandell,** PhD, is a professor of English and associate dean at Xavier University in Cincinnati, Ohio. He teaches regularly on J.R.R. Tolkien and medieval literature, with research appearing in the *Proceedings of the J.R.R. Tolkien Centenary Conference, Tolkien and Alterity*, and *The Disney Middle Ages*. His work on C.S. Lewis appears in *Mythlore* and *C.S. Lewis: Life, Works, and Legacy*, and he has co-edited *Prophet Margins: The Medieval Vatic Impulse and Social Stability*.

Index

Abanes, Richard 3, 4, 5, 7
Abbott, Joe 89
abject 18, 77–91, 169, 172; *see also* Otherness
Abrahamson, Megan 7, 198, 199, 201, 214
Adam 62, 69, 174
adaptations 11, 14–15, 20, 166*n*3, 191, 198, 201, 205, 214–16, 230
aesthetes 127, 170
aesthetics 14, 16, 90, 127–28, 147
aglæcwif 85–86, 90; aglæca 86; *see also* Beowulf; Grendel's mother; translation
Ahmed, Sara 17, 51, 54, 176, 184
Aiavalë 208; *see also* Hands of the King
Ainur 18, 67, 109–10; *see also* bodies; genders
Alberto, Maria K. vi, 7, 20, 113, 120, 151*n*3, 189–200, 199*n*3, 200, 210, 229
Alcuin 51
Aldarion 33, 41, 116, 219, 226, 227; *see also* Ancalimë; Erendis; Tar-Ancalimë
Alexander, Michael 85, 89; *see also* *Beowulf* (poem); translation
allism 47; *see also* autism; neurodiversity
Alquallë 212; *see also* Hands of the King
alt-right 4, 12, 23; *see also* fascism
alterity 14, 22, 23, 37, 172, 173, 183, 186, 213, 216, 222, 223, 225, 230, 226; *see also* "Tolkien and Alterity" (Audas); *Tolkien and Alterity* (Vaccaro and Kisor)
amatonormativity 18, 107–22, 227; cishetero amatonormativity 119, 121, 227; compulsory amatonormativity 115, 116, 117; *see also* normativity
Amazon 2*n*2; *see also The Lord of the Rings: The Rings of Power*
ambiguity 35, 71–72, 81, 87, 96, 116, 119, 151*n*2, 192
Amendment 11 *see* The Labouchere Amendment
Amendt-Raduege, Amy 21*n*5, 89, 89*n*4, 128, 138, 221

anachronisms 45, 47, 52, 211
anal sex 147; *see also* sodomy
anathema 33, 130, 133, 173–74, 182–83; *see also* de Lille, Alain; Saruman
Ancalimë *see* Tar-Ancalimë; *see also* Aldarion; Erendis
Andróg 148
androgyny 47, 102, 109, 134; *see also* femininities; genders; masculinities
Angamaitë 135
angels 44, 48, 52, 176; *see also* Maiar; wizards
Anglachel (fan pseudonym) 20, 201–14; *see also* Hands of the King; "Writing a Green Sun"
Anglachel (sword) 149, 150; *see also* Túrin
Anglicanism 27, 40*n*8, 127; *see also* Buddhism; Catholicism; Christianity; Evangelicalism; Islam; Judaism; Paganism; Protestantism; religion
Anglo-Saxon 95, 97, 106; *see also* Old English; Rohirrim
Annatar *see* Sauron
anxiety 1, 3, 48, 53, 131–33, 145; castration anxiety 155, 163, 165
apocalypse 17, 18, 56–74; eschatology 13, 58; *see also* Christianity; genre; homophobia
Appendices 31, 32, 118, 125, 138, 183*n*7, 202
"Appendix A" 31, 34, 118, 120*n*9, 126, 129, 134, 136, 138
"Appendix B" 31, 32
"Appendix F" 183*n*7
Aragorn 19, 30, 31, 32, 33, 34, 36, 39, 83, 95, 131, 136, 138, 145, 202, 209–10, 217
archetype 90, 112, 219, 223; *see also* Jung, Carl Gustav
Archive of Our Own (AO3) 197, 199
Arda 37, 40, 56, 65, 72, 89, 111, 112, 114, 119, 120, 139, 189, 190, 193, 215, 222, 228; *see also* Beleriand; Middle-earth

233

234 Index

Aredhel 228; *see also The Fall of Gondolin*
Armitt, Lucie 77, 80–81, 89
Ar-Pharazôn 65, 113
Arthedain 135
Arthur, Sarah 6n4, 7
Arthur Pendragon 53, 223
Arthurian literature 44, 49, 53
Arul, Melissa Ruth 21
Arvedui 132–33, 135–36
Arwen 31, 36, 37, 38, 84, 90, 209, 218, 221, 222, 224
asexuality 33, 41, 42, 50, 61, 69, 73, 152, 153, 226, 227; *see also* bisexuality; gay; heterosexuality; homosexuality; lesbian; LGBQT+; same-sex relationships; straight
atheist 13, 22, 227, 230
athletes 170
Atlantis 59–60
Audas, Jordan vi, 7n7, 20, 215–28, 229
autism 13, 22, 45, 46, 54, 55, 227; *see also* allism; neurodiversity
auto-eroticism 150
Avari 38; *see also* Elves

Babel 60
Babylon 58, 70
bachelors 19, 31, 115, 117, 127, 153, 162, 226–27
Baggins, Bilbo 6n4, 9, 19, 20n1, 30, 37, 43, 45, 48, 49, 96, 109, 115, 116, 117, 127–29, 136–37, 153, 161, 211, 223, 227
Baggins, Frodo 6n4, 7, 14, 17, 19, 23, 27, 30, 37, 50, 60, 61, 77, 78, 80, 81, 82, 83, 88, 88n3, 95, 96, 114–15, 117–18, 120n8, 121, 126–31, 136, 137, 140, 144, 145, 152, 153–67, 173, 175, 178, 180–81, 182, 184n18, 186, 200, 211, 221, 222; *see also* Gamgee, Samwise; Frodo and Sam
Baggins, Ponto 128, 137
Baker, Dallas John 206, 214, 221
Baker, Deirdre F. 217
Baldassarro, M. Wolf 4, 7
Balrogs 50, 51–52, 95; *see also* Maiar
banned books 4, 7, 12, 13, 20, 22, 170; *see also* challenged books
Barfield, Owen 170, 223
Barraclough, Leo 21
Barthes, Roland 182, 184
Basil II 132
batman 31, 219; *see also* Gamgee, Samwise
Battis, Jes v, 3, 7, 14, 17, 18, 21, 43–55, 138, 183, 184, 217, 226, 229
Battle of Dagorlad 66
Battle of Five Armies 111
Battle of Maldon 95, 106

Battle of the Somme 27, 30, 138
beards 45, 47, 108, 112, 120n2; *see also* Dwarf women
Beleg 19, 20, 140–52, 189–200, 210; *see also* Túrin
Beleriand 35, 58, 59, 64, 140, 152, 192, 200, 214; *see also* Arda; *The Lays of Beleriand*; Middle-earth
Belshazzar 57, 63, 69–70, 72
bender 175, 176, 181; *see also* homophobia
Bennett, James 127, 138
Benshoff, Harry 57, 73
Beorhtnoth 94, 95, 96
Beorn 118
Beowulf (character) 60, 85, 86, 95, 98, 101, 105n4, 138; *see also* aglæcwif; *Beowulf* (poem); Grendel's Mother; translation
Beowulf (poem) 42, 69, 71, 85, 89, 90, 97, 98, 101, 106, 122, 138, 151n2, 152, 186, 224, 231; *see also* aglæcwif; Beowulf (character); Grendel's Mother; translation
Beowulf-poet 61
Beregond 29
Beren 34, 189, 207–8, 211, 213; *see also* Great Tales; Lúthien
Beren and Lúthien 189; *see also* Beren; Great Tales; Lúthien
Bernard, Carol A. 19, 153, 155–56, 158–59, 163, 166n4, 217
Best, Stephen 125–26, 138
bias 63, 174, 175, 198, 200, 226
Biden, Joseph 12
binaries 5, 12, 28, 40, 45, 51, 57, 64, 72, 78, 79, 82, 84, 87, 88, 99, 102, 103, 108, 109, 110, 111, 112, 117, 119, 119, 141, 153, 172, 175, 183, 203, 205, 206, 211, 213, 220; *see also* genders; non-binary
biology 36–37, 40n6, 89, 110; *see also* sciences
Birmingham 27, 35, 127, 165
Birns, Nicholas vi, 19, 33, 125–39, 229
Birzer, Bradley 60, 73
bisexuality 7, 104, 151, 211; *see also* asexuality; gay; heterosexuality; homosexuality; lesbian; LGBTQ+; same-sex relationships; sexuality; straight
blades *see* swords
Blessed Realm *see* Valinor
Bloomsbury Group 170
bodies 1, 16, 17, 22, 62, 66, 79, 80, 84, 88, 88n2, 90, 91, 93, 97, 99, 102, 103, 105, 106, 109, 126, 141, 143, 144–6, 147, 149, 151, 152, 158, 190–91, 201, 206, 225, 227, 230; Baggins, Frodo 77, 91, 144, 159; Beleg 19,

Index   235

148, 149, 195; Boromir 129; Celebrimbor 113; Eärnur 126, 129; Elves 109; Gollum 144, 163; *hrondor* 109; Istari 44; Orcs 22; Ringwraiths 144; Saeros 147, 148; Saruman 169, 181; Sauron 112, 113; Shelob 80–84, 87–88; Túrin and Beleg 19, 140, 147–51; *see also* embodiment
Bolg 111
Bolger, Fredegar 83
The Book of Lost Tales 145
The Book of Lost Tales Part I 58, 74
Book of Lost Tales Part II 56, 77, 192, 200
Booker, Susan 7
Boromir 33, 120*n*8, 126–31, 132, 133, 134, 136, 158, 202, 222
Boswell, John 68
Bowman, Mary R. 96, 106
Brake, Elizabeth 114, 120
Brandybuck, Meriadoc 31, 49, 83, 93–95, 98, 100, 102, 104, 109, 179, 182
Brandybucks 137, 179
Bratt, Edith *see* Tolkien, Edith Bratt
Brayton, Jennifer 7
Bree 68
The Bridge of Khazad-dûm 40*n*1, 52, 95; *see also* Moria
brotherhood 30, 143
Brown, Devin 6*n*2, 6*n*4, 8
Brown, Sara v, 18, 77–91, 105*n*1, 105–6*n*6, 166*n*6, 183*n*3, 226
Bruce, Alexander M. 95–96, 106
Brust, Annie viii
Buddhism 6*n*3, 8; *see also* Anglicanism; Catholicism; Christianity; Evangelicalism; Islam; Judaism; Paganism; Protestantism; religion
Bueno Alonso, Jorge Luis 97, 106
Bupu 47
Burgham, Olivia K. viii
Burgwinkle, William 144, 145, 152
Burke, Jessica 78, 89
Burns, Marjorie 78, 89
Busse, Kristina 191, 199
butch 102, 103, 106
Butler, Judith 18, 78, 79, 84, 89, 92, 93, 103, 105*n*6, 106, 137, 138
Byrthnoth 95, 96

calque 98
Cameron, Christopher vi, 19, 153–67, 229
camp 50, 52
Cannadine, David 128, 138
cannibalism *see* filial cannibalism
canons 8, 19–20, 41, 50, 90, 121, 129, 151, 152, 166, 189–200, 202, 210, 214, 229; canon kisses 20, 189, 192–96

Carpenter, Humphrey 40*n*12, 41, 74, 91, 122, 139, 167, 169, 176, 184, 186, 200, 222
Carter, Steven Brett 126, 138
castration 148, 164–65; anxiety 155, 163, 165; chemical 170; fear of 158–59, 163–65; female 165; symbolic 159, 163, 164; *see also* Freud, Sigmund; penis; phallus
Catholicism 1, 2, 6, 6*n*2, 8, 12, 13, 14, 27, 32, 34, 37, 38, 40*n*8, 40*n*9, 52, 58, 113, 162, 191, 203; *see also* Anglicanism; Buddhism; Christianity; English-Catholic; Evangelicalism; Islam; Judaism; Paganism; Protestantism; religion
Celeborn 31, 40*n*1
Celebrían 29, 31, 32, 33, 35, 40, 40*n*2
Celebrimbor 113, 199*n*2; *see also* Saint Sebastian
challenged books 7, 12, 13, 21; *see also* banned books
Chance, Jane 3, 7*n*8, 8, 14, 15–16, 21, 21*n*5, 22, 27–28, 33, 35, 37–38, 41, 43, 54, 69, 73, 77, 86, 89, 90, 106, 110, 126, 128, 139, 147, 151, 152, 166, 168, 173, 183*n*6, 184, 198, 217, 218, 219, 221, 222
Chanvisanuruk, Joel viii
Chaucer, Geoffrey 61, 152, 174, 230
The Chester Mystery Plays 60
Chick, Jack 2, 8
Chickering, Howell 85, 88; *see also Beowulf* (poem); translation
children 31, 32, 33, 36, 37, 38, 40, 67, 80, 82, 83, 116, 118, 127, 129, 130, 132, 134, 145, 212–13; *see also* fertility; reproduction
The Children of Húrin 145–50, 152, 189, 192–95, 198, 200, 228; *see also* Great Tales
Children of Ilúvatar 38, 110
chivalry 88*n*1, 95, 97, 143, 145, 147, 152, 173; *see also* courtly love; knights
Christianity 1–3, 6*n*1, 6*n*2, 6*n*4, 7*n*6, 52, 58, 68, 113, 178, 183, 190, 191, 203, 224; *see also* Anglicanism; Buddhism; Catholicism; Evangelicalism; Islam; Judaism; Neoplatonism; Paganism; Protestantism; religion
Círdan 120
Cirith Ungol 96, 159, 161
cisgender 20, 98, 104, 204, 205, 212; cis men 44, 99, 205; cis women 99, 108, 122, 205; cishetero 18, 115, 117, 119, 121, 227; *see also* genders; transgender
class 3, 5, 14, 21, 37, 136, 137, 217, 219, 220, 221
Cleanness 17–18, 56–74
closets 57, 71, 127, 168

Clover, Carol J. 86, 89
Coker, Cait vii, 8, 9, 200, 205, 214, 221, 225
colonialism 136
competition 146, 147, 173
concupiscence 174, 181, 185
condemnation 8, 82, 84, 86, 148, 180, 213
conservative 2, 173–75
conversion 2, 37–38, 40n9
Cooper, Gideon viii
corruption 175, 180
Cottage of Lost Play 58
Cotton, Rose 9, 117–18, 119, 128–29, 130, 162, 200, 205
Council of Elrond 29–30, 145, 160; see also Elrond
courtly love 142–43, 145–46, 198; see also chivalry; knights
Cowie, Elizabeth 182, 185
Craig, David M. 3, 8, 14, 22, 29, 41, 77, 78, 81, 82, 84, 89, 94, 106, 114, 120, 153, 166, 183n6, 185, 198, 199, 218, 226
Creed, Barbara 18, 77, 79, 81, 8a2, 84, 87, 89
Croft, Janet Brennan vii, 139, 185; see also Croft and Donovan
Croft and Donovan 8, 29, 41, 90, 120, 139, 199, 214, 216, 217, 218, 221, 222, 223, 224, 225; see also Croft, Janet Brennan; Donovan, Leslie A.
cross-temporal play 152n4; see also sadism
Crowe, Edith L. 84, 89, 111, 120, 128, 139, 216, 222
Cuiviénen 38
Cursor Mundi 60
Cúthalion, Beleg see Beleg

Dagor Dagorath 56
Daniel 62, 69–71
Dawson, Deidre 14, 21n5, 22, 184n16, 185, 222
De planctu naturæ 9, 139, 173, 186, 225
death 1, 31, 34, 47, 52, 60, 66, 73, 86, 94, 97, 128, 131, 136, 138, 145, 146, 156, 157, 160, 162, 172, 186, 195, 202, 207–8, 209, 212, 213, 219, 220, 225; Beleg 140, 149–50, 195; Edelman's death drive 64, 73, 139; Gil-galad 31, 32, 34, 39; Mabel Tolkien 34, 35, 169; Saruman 169, 177–80, 181, 192; Túrin 140, 149, 150
de Beauvoir, Simone 88
de Boron, Robert 53, 54
degendering 99, 104, 106; see also misgendering
degradation 145–50, 161, 175
degradation 145–51, 161, 175
de Lauretis, Teresa 172, 185

de Lille, Alain 9, 133, 139, 152, 173, 180, 186, 225
Denethor II (Anglachel) 201–14; see also fanfiction; Finduilas (Anglachel)
Denethor II (Tolkien) 129–30, 132–34
depravity 175, 180
depression 48
Dernhelm 18, 92–106, 109, 205, 226; see also Éowyn
despair 60, 159, 169, 175, 203, 206
destabilization 18, 50, 64, 105, 107–22, 192, 227
dialectic 173
Dinshaw, Carolyn 45, 52, 54
Dior 34
disorientation 140, 142, 149
diversity 3, 4, 5, 6n2, 13, 15, 16, 40, 40n6, 119, 135, 179, 190, 201, 207, 217, 222, 226, 230; see also *Tolkien and Diversity: Proceedings of the Tolkien Society Summer Seminar 2021*; Tolkien and Diversity Seminar
Dol Amroth 202, 212
domination 6n2, 8, 14, 15, 29, 59, 79, 118–19, 184; domination/submission 83, 117; see also sadism
Domínguez Ruiz, Beatriz 78, 91, 106, 218
Donovan, Leslie A. 77, 78, 79, 85, 90, 218, 222, 224; see also Croft and Donovan
Doriath 28, 34, 35, 189, 194, 197
Doty, Alexander 7n10, 8, 17, 20, 29, 41, 57–58, 73, 78, 90, 112, 121, 141, 152, 153, 166, 172, 182, 185, 191, 199, 211, 214
Douglas, Alfred 170, 185
Doyle, Mark 59–60, 73
Draft A 177–80, 184, see also Appendices
drag 48, 93, 104, 168, 218
Dragonlance series 47
dragons 2, 6, 8, 13, 45, 48, 85
Dragons of Autumn Twilight 47, 55
Driggers, Taylor 21n4, 22
duality 93, 102, 155, 163
Dúnedain 135
Dungeons and Dragons 2, 13, 45, 48; see also dragons
Durin's Doors 70–72; see also Moria
dwarves 18, 28, 40, 47, 70, 108, 110, 115, 116, 118, 119, 148, 197, 217, 225; women 108, 112; see also beards

The Eagle and Child 39
Eärendil 30, 34, 36, 40n9
Eärnil 131–33, 135
Eärnur 19, 77, 33, 125–39; see also Witch-King of Angmar
Easterlings 136

Edelman, Lee 63, 73, 130, 139
Edward the Confessor 132
Elbereth *see* Varda
Elboron 34
Eldacar 134
Eldar 31, 32, 38, 118; *see also* Elves
Elder Days 145
Elendil 30, 65, 134, 209
Elenwë 35
Elfhelm 100
Elfstone *see* Aragorn
Eliot, T.S. 60
Elladan 31, 35
Ellis, Havelock 170
Elrohir 31, 35
Elrond 17, 27–42, 59, 84, 145, 160; *see also* Council of Elrond; Rivendell
Elros 30, 32, 34, 36, 39
Elu Thingol *see* Thingol
Elves 7, 8, 18, 20n1, 21, 22, 27–42, 48, 59, 67, 88n1, 90, 108, 109, 110, 112, 114, 115, 118, 119, 120n2, 120n3, 138, 139, 140, 145–47, 182, 184, 184n16, 189, 190, 208, 209, 211, 213, 217, 219, 221, 223, 224; Avari 38; Eldar 31, 32, 38, 118; Elves of Eregion 35, 113; First Age Elves 28, 30, 35, 38, 67, 145; High Elves 32; Noldorin Elves 28, 31, 32, 36, 37, 120n3; Quenya 71, 118–19; Sindarin Elves 36, 37, 38, 119; Sindarin language 71, 223; Sylvan Elves 119; Teleri Elves 38, 120n3; Vanyar Elves 36; Wood-Elves of Mirkwood 108
Elves of Eregion 35, 113; *see also* Elves
Elwë 38
Elwing 34, 40n9, 227
Emanuel, Tom 6n2, 8, 13, 22, 60, 73
emasculation 148; *see also* castration
embodiment 104, 133, 219; female 83; *see also* bodies
emendations *see* revisions
Emmerson, Richard 58, 73
England's Criminal Law Amendment Act (1885) 169
Engledow, Zachary Clifton vi, 19, 140–52, 199n1, 230
English-Catholic 17, 27–42; *see also* Catholicism
Ents 111, 114
Entwives 111
Eönwë 113; *see also* Maiar
Éowyn 18, 78, 85, 90, 92–106, 109, 129, 205–6, 217, 218, 219, 221, 222, 223, 224, 225, 226, 228; *see also* Dernhelm
epic 44, 45, 47, 50, 52, 60, 73, 89, 194, 195, 222, 224
Eregion 35, 113–14; *see also* Elves; Sauron

Erendis 33, 116, 219, 226; *see also* Aldarion; Erendis
Erestor 199n2
Eriador 30
Eriol 58
eroticism 33, 45, 50, 107, 112, 113, 114, 117, 122, 131, 140–43, 144, 146, 149–52, 168–86, 196; erotic pleasure 33, 131, 162; erotic triangle 19, 153–67; erotics of suffering 99, 140–52, 151, 199n1; free love 175; "Uses of the Erotic" 114, 120; *see also* platonic love; pleasures; romances (medieval genre); romances (relationships); sex (intercourse)
Eru 56, 59, 64–65, 66–67; Ilúvatar 38, 110; *see also* gods
"Essay on the Istari" 44, 181, 183n10; *see also* Istari; Maiar; wizards
ethnicity 5, 13,14, 15, 134, 217, 218, 221
Evangelicalism 2, 12, 22; *see also* Anglicanism; Buddhism; Catholicism; Christianity; Islam; Judaism; Paganism; Protestantism; religion
excess 85, 94, 95, 96, 97, 115, 129, 142, 146, 150, 183n3
excommunication 174, 178, 180
Ezekiel 68

failure 15, 19, 31, 44, 48, 52, 53, 60, 69, 107, 125, 131, 133, 134, 138, 140, 142, 144, 148, 150, 151, 171, 185, 211
The Fall of Gondolin 34, 145, 189, 209; *see also* Aredhel; Gondolin; Great Tales
families 12, 13, 18, 27, 33, 34–35, 36, 50, 88n4, 100, 104, 105n5, 107–22, 128, 131, 137, 145, 155, 172, 183n4, 209; nuclear family 107, 117, 119
fandom 7, 7n11, 8, 120n10, 151n3, 190, 196, 199, 221
fanfiction 6, 7, 8, 11, 15, 17, 19–20, 105n3, 151n3, 182, 189–200, 201–14; fan fiction 7, 9, 199, 200, 215, 223, 229
Fangorn Forest 118, 175
fans 6, 7n11, 20, 50, 92, 175, 189–200, 205, 210, 219
fantasy 44, 45, 46, 47, 89, 191, 199, 218, 221, 223; Christianity and fantasy 1–7, 8, 9, 74, 203; fantasy films 7, 43, 162, 166n3, 218, 219, 220, 221, 223, 225; gender and fantasy 78, 91, 205, 214, 218, 220, 221, 222, 224; high fantasy 194, 214, 221; medievalist fantasy 48, 225; queer theory and fantasy 8, 21n4, 22, 126, 148, 182–83; race and fantasy 214, 220, 221, 224, 225; Tolkien and fantasy 21n5, 194, 201, 207; *see also* genre

238   Index

far-right extremists (FRE) 3, 11, 12; *see also* alt-right; fascism
Faramir 27, 29, 33, 129, 130, 132, 138, 156, 163, 202, 226
Farmer Giles of Ham 8, 23, 33, 42, 73n3, 74, 168, 183n1, 186, 226
fascism 12, 218; *see also* alt-right; far-right extremists (FRE)
fates 31, 35, 36, 37, 40n9, 45, 111, 136, 159–60, 165, 176, 177, 180, 183, 210
fathers 34, 35, 36, 44, 109, 111, 116, 129, 130, 131–33, 134, 155, 191, 194, 212; Elrond 3, 32, 33; Father Francis Morgan 4, 34, 35; Tolkien as father 27, 31, 32, 40, 179, 180; Tolkien's father 34, 36, 60
fëa 118; *see also fëar*
Fëanor 34, 35, 38, 120n3; Oath of Fëanor 56, 59; *see also* Maedhros; Maglor
fëar 109; *see also fëa*
fear 45, 47, 48, 66, 67, 82, 89, 90, 96, 100, 101, 135, 163, 165, 176, 177, 186, 212, 219, 225
Felagund, Dawn *see* Walls-Thumma, Dawn M.
The Fellowship of the Ring (book) 13, 20n1, 23, 28, 30, 31, 32, 37, 41, 49, 50, 52, 53, 56, 66, 68, 70, 71, 115, 117, 121, 141, 160, 162, 183n7, 186
female genitals 158, 165; *see also* Freud, Sigmund
female hero 92, 222, 226; *see also* heroisms; women
female masculinity 79, 82, 84, 88n2, 90, 129, 139; *see also* Halberstam, Jack; Shelob
femininities 18, 39, 77–91, 92–106, 108–9, 117, 129–30, 134, 146–47, 155, 157–58, 163–65, 166n4, 166n6, 175, 183n3, 212, 216, 217, 219, 224, 227; *see also* androgyny; genders; masculinities
feminisms 12, 15, 18, 22, 78, 82, 87, 88n1, 88n3, 89, 90, 91, 92, 94, 104, 106, 217, 220, 223, 224, 227, 228, 230; *see also* women
Fenwick, Mac 77, 78, 85, 90, 217
fertility 36–37, 227; *see also* children; reproduction; sterility
fetish 19, 144, 149–50, 153–67; *see also* Freud, Sigmund; penis; phallus
feudalism 194, 197–98
Fife, Ernelle 111, 121
Fighting Fantasy series 46
filial cannibalism 82–83, 89
Fimi, Dimitra 5, 8, 36–37, 38, 41, 134, 139, 218, 221, 222, 226, 229
Finduilas (Elf, Tolkien) 195

Finduilas (Human, Anglachel) 201–14; *see also* fanfiction
Finduilas (Human, Tolkien) 134; *see also* Denethor II
Fingon 108, 119, 199
Finwë 32, 39, 40n10, 120n3, 218; *see also* Gil-Galad; Míriel
Fionwë 29
fireworks 46, 49, 52
Fíriel 132
First Age Elves 28, 30, 35, 67, 145; *see also* Elrond
Flaming Classics: Queering the Film Canon 7n10, 8, 41, 90, 121, 152, 166, 214
Flieger, Verlyn 4, 5, 8, 13, 21, 22, 23, 39, 41, 169, 185, 222, 226, 227, 229
Fliss, William vii, 184n19
floods 58–61, 62, 64–68
folklore 41, 91, 154, 225
Fontenot, Megan 61, 73
Ford, Judy Ann viii
Forochel 135
Forster, E.M. 170
fosterage 27, 28, 33–35, 38, 40, 40n3, 40n4, 41; *see also* orphans
Foster, Gavin v, 18, 92–106, 205, 230
Fredrick, Candice 218, 226
Fredrickson, Nathan viii
free will 28, 25–38, 41
Freeman, Elizabeth 151, 152, 152n4
Freud, Sigmund 17, 19, 155, 157, 158, 162, 163, 165, 166, 172, 185; Freudian 88 n3, 163; *see also* castration; fetish; Oedipal triangle; penis; phallus
Frodo and Sam 14, 17, 19, 78, 81, 82, 83, 88, 114, 117–18, 130, 131, 137, 140, 153–67, 173, 175; *see also* Baggins, Frodo; Gamgee, Samwise
Fugelso, Karl 21, 22, 184, 226

Galadriel 31, 32, 40n2, 50, 56, 78, 82, 83, 85, 88, 89, 90, 120n9, 180, 218, 219, 221, 222, 223, 227
Gamgee, Gaffer 173
Gamgee, Samwise 14, 17, 19, 33, 78, 81, 82, 83, 88, 88n3, 96, 114, 117–18, 119, 128, 130, 131, 136, 137, 138, 140, 145, 153–67, 165, 173, 175, 182; *see also* Baggins, Frodo; Frodo and Sam
Gandalf 17, 43–55, 59, 66, 68, 70–71, 89, 93, 95, 97, 98, 106, 109, 112, 120n8, 127, 130, 132, 160, 162, 169, 174, 175, 176–80, 182, 183n1, 202, 207; *see also* Istari; Maiar; wizards
Gandhi, Mohandas K. 136
Garth, John 170, 185

Gawain 52, 61, 95; *see also Sir Gawain and the Green Knight*
gay 6, 7n10, 12, 22, 48, 73, 90, 104, 105, 106, 139, 146, 153, 161, 172, 192, 196, 199, 200, 211, 218, 219, 223, 227; *see also* asexuality; bisexuality; heterosexuality; homosexuality; lesbian; LGBTQ+; same-sex relationships; sexuality; straight
Gender Trouble 84, 89, 92, 93, 103, 106
genders 28, 29–35, 51, 77, 78, 79, 84, 93, 95, 98, 99, 101, 102, 103, 104, 105, 106, 108, 110, 111, 114, 117, 119, 134, 138, 163, 203, 205, 210, 213; gender binary 88, 108, 109, 111, 112, 119; gender fluidity 78, 84, 155, 157, 165; gender identity 84, 98, 100, 109; gender ideologies 107, 108, 110; gender-neutral 44, 99, 212; gender nonconformity 18, 79, 93, 102–3, 105n5, 112, 129–30, 137, 146; gender performance 18, 78, 83, 84, 92, 102, 103, 105; *Gender Trouble* 84, 89, 92, 93, 103, 106; non-binary 44, 51, 73, 99, 109–10, 119, 203, 205; *see also* cisgender; femininities; masculinities; transgender
Genesis 62–69
Genette, Gérard 17
genre 6, 14, 20, 21, 74, 194–96, 198, 199, 225; apocalyptic 18, 58–60, 62–4, 72; Christian 6n4; epic 44, 45, 47, 50, 52, 60, 73, 89, 194, 195, 222, 224; medieval apocalyptic 18, 56–74; *see also* fantasy; science fiction
Geoffrey of Monmouth 53
German 89, 100, 134, 192, 194, 199
Gil-Galad 30–33, 35, 39, 40n4, 40n10; *see also* Elrond; Finwë
Giles *see Farmer Giles of Ham*
Gilson, Christopher 121
Gilson, Robert 30–31, 170
Gimli 50, 118, 118, 119, 120n8, 120n9, 131, 145; *see also* Legolas; Legolas and Gimli
Girard, René 17, 19, 153–67
Glittering Caves 118
Glorfindel 199n2
Glosecki, Stephen 100–01
goddesses 89n5
gods 4, 5, 40, 51, 56–74, 97, 139, 162, 208, 209; *see also* Eru; Yahweh
Gollum 19, 22, 69, 82, 83, 144, 153–67, 169, 177, 178, 184n19, 217, 218
Gondolin 28, 31, 35, 58, 228; *see also* Aredhel; *The Fall of Gondolin*
Goodhew, Linda 6, 8
Goodrich, Peter 49, 54
Gorbag 110

Gordon, E.V. 61
Goselin, Peter Damien 78, 90
Gower, John 174
Grant, Patrick 78, 90
Great Tales 145, 189, 191; *see also*: *Beren and Lúthien*; *The Children of Húrin*; *The Fall of Gondolin*
Great War 29, 31, 170, 185, 222; *see also* World War I
Green, William H. 84, 90, 217
Grendel's mother 18, 73, 77, 79, 84–87, 89, 90; *see also* aglæcwif; *Beowulf* (poem); translation
Grima 69, 169, 174, 180, 182
Gummere, Frances B. 85, 89; *see also Beowulf* (poem); translation
gwegwin 109
Gwynne, Owain 7, 8

hair 47, 101–2, 108, 112, 120n3, 146–47, 197, 222, 226; *see also* genders
Haladin 115
Halberstam, Jack 17, 18, 79, 84, 88n1, 90, 92, 102–4, 105, 105n6, 106, 129, 139, 171, 185
Haleth 115, 120n8
Hall, Donald 171, 185
Hall, Radclyffe 170, 183n2
Halperin, David 57, 78, 90
Hands of the King 201–14; *see also* Anglachel (fan pseudonym); fanfiction
Haradrim 134–36, 225
Harris, Kamala 12
Hart, Lowell 6n5, 8
Headley, Maria Dahvana 86, 89; *see also Beowulf* (poem); translation
Heaney, Seamus 69, 73, 85, 86, 89; *see also Beowulf* (poem); translation
hearties 170
Hegel, Georg Wilhelm Friedrich 137
hegemony 171
Helcaraxë 35
Helms, Randel 185, 216
heredity 36, 29
heroisms 37, 38, 54, 61, 85, 90, 94, 102, 106, 137, 170, 189, 196, 202–7, 210, 211, 213, 214; female hero 92, 222, 226; northern heroic spirit 94–98, 102
heteronormativity *see* normativity
heterosexuality 31, 58, 104, 107, 1412–43, 152, 170, 175, 20; compulsory heterosexuality 112, 119, 126; *see also* asexuality; bisexuality; gay; homosexuality; lesbian; LGBTQ+; same-sex relationships; sexuality; straight

high culture 190; *see also* canons
High Elves 32; *see also* Elves
high mimetic mode 194
historical fiction 21*n*5; *see also* genre
Hithlum 146
The Hobbit (book) 6*n*2, 8, 12, 23, 28, 41, 43–45, 46, 48–49, 51, 53, 54, 73*n*3, 74, 90, 96, 97, 106, 109, 110, 111, 115, 121, 145, 194, 217, 218, 221, 225, 227
The Hobbit: The Desolation of Smaug (film) 225; *see also* Jackson, Peter
Hobbits 27, 29, 37, 44, 45, 50, 51, 53, 82, 86–87, 110, 127, 130, 155–56, 161–62, 165, 176, 180, 195; Hobbit women 109
Hocquenham, Guy 173, 183*n*8, 185
Hogwarts 48
Holmes, John 22
Homer 90, 138, 217
homoamory 29, 30, 42, 122, 141, 151*n*2, 152, 170, 175, 181, 186
homoeroticism 14, 23, 41, 113, 140–52, 153–67, 186, 220
homophobia 12, 18, 56–74, 114, 170, 174, 175, 176, 181; *see also* bender
homosexuality 5, 13, 14, 16, 17, 29, 62, 65, 72, 73, 107, 112, 113, 114, 117, 127, 133, 140, 141, 143, 151, 154, 161, 162, 165, 170, 176, 183*n*4, 183*n*6, 183*n*7, 185, 186, 206, 223; *see also* asexuality; bisexuality; gay; heterosexuality; lesbian; LGBTQ+; same-sex relationships; sexuality; straight
homosociality 31, 88*n*3, 142–43, 145, 146–48, 167, 225
honor 28, 38, 117, 126, 127, 175, 195
hooks, bell 64, 73, 172
hospitality 18, 49, 68, 69, 72
Howansky, Kristina 99, 106
Howie, Cary 144, 145, 152
hrondor 109; *see also* bodies; embodiment
Hrothgar 69, 98, 138; *see also Beowulf* (poem)
Hughes, Shaun F.D. 7, 9, 16, 21, 22, 23, 41, 121, 138, 152, 167, 200, 217, 219, 220, 221
Huor 36
Húrin 145; *see also The Children of Húrin*
hypermasculine 31, 110, 147, 148, 173; *see also* genders; masculinities

Idril 31, 39, 207, 209, 211, 213; *see also* Gondolin; Tuor
Ilúvatar *see* Eru
Imladris *see* Rivendell; *see also* Elrond
Imrahil 212
incest 82, 129
indecency 169, 170, 183*n*3
indeterminacy 63, 168, 169, 171, 176, 179; *see also* Saruman
inhospitality 68–69, 72; *see also* pride; sodomy
Inklings 1, 2, 8, 29, 39, 170; *see also* Lewis, C.S.; Williams, Charles
inspirations 40, 77, 96, 100, 194, 201
insults 146–47
International Congress on Medieval Studies vii, 6
intimacy 18, 105, 107–22, 172; male 19, 23, 121, 140–52, 153–67, 186, 196, 200, 220; same-sex 57, 63, 114–15
Isildur 30, 131, 132, 133, 135, 159
Islam 2, 221; *see also* Anglicanism; Buddhism; Catholicism; Christianity; Evangelicalism; Judaism; Paganism; Protestantism; religion
Istari 44, 50, 176, 183*n*9; *see also* "Essay on the Istari"; Maiar; wizards
Ivriniel 212

Jackson, Michael 47
Jackson, Peter 7, 8, 21, 50, 126, 147, 152, 183, 184, 198, 205, 216, 217, 218, 219, 221; *see also The Hobbit: The Desolation of Smaug* (film); *The Lord of the Rings* (film); *The Lord of the Rings: The Fellowship of the Ring* (film); *The Return of the King* (film)
Jaeger, C. Stephen 198, 199
Jagose, Annemarie 17, 19, 171
Jaques, Zoë 127, 139
Jehovah *see* Yahweh; *see also* gods
Jeremiah 60
Jericho 68
Jerusalem Bible 61
John of Patmos 58
Jonah 61
Jones, Jordy 102
Joshua 68
Judaism 6*n*2, 38, 176, 218, 225; *see also* Anglicanism; Buddhism; Catholicism; Christianity; Evangelicalism; Islam; Paganism; Protestantism; religion
Jung, Carl Gustav 78, 172; *see also* archetype

Kaye, Richard A. 113, 121
Keiser, Elizabeth 65, 73
Kennedy, Charles W. 85, 89; *see also Beowulf* (poem); translation
Khazad-dûm *see* Moria; *see also* The Bridge of Khazad-dûm
Kiernan, Kevin S. 86, 90
Kightley, Michael R. 223

Kilby, Clyde S. 6n1, 8
Kim, Sue 16, 22, 219
kin 90, 111, 135, 136, 146; *see also* kin-strife; kinship; kinslaying
kin-strife 134–35; *see also* kin
King, Virginia Elizabeth viii
kinship 53, 117, 137, 138, 175; *see also* kin
King Edward's School 29
kinslaying 56, 59; *see also* kin
Kisor, Yvette viii, 9, 14–15, 21n5, 22, 23, 40, 42, 89, 90, 100–1, 106, 120, 131, 134, 137, 138, 139, 142, 152, 166n2, 166n5, 172–73, 183n1, 183n7, 185, 186, 194, 196, 199, 200, 219, 221, 222, 223, 225, 226, 227, 231
kisses 19, 114, 149, 150, 151n3, 197; canon kisses 20, 189, 192–96
Klaeber, Frederick 85, 90
Klinger, Barbara 219
Klinger, Judith 77, 90, 223
Knight, Gareth 1, 8
knights 48, 51, 143, 145; *see also* chivalry; courtly love; *Sir Gawain and the Green Knight*
Komornicka, Jolanta N. 14, 22
Kristeva, Julia 17, 18, 19, 78, 80, 82–83, 87, 172, 185
Kuhn, Sherman 86, 90
Kullervo 194
kyriarchy 77, 83

Laanga 207
The Labouchere Amendment 169–70
Lacan, Jacques 157–58
Lady of the White Tower *see* fanfiction; Finduilas (Human, Anglachel)
Lancelot 53
Larsen, Kristine v, 17, 27–42, 81, 88n1, 90, 223, 227, 230
Larson, Bob 6n5, 8
The Last Alliance of Men and Elves 28, 29, 30, 40n1
Last Homely House *see* Rivendell; *see also* Elrond
The Last Unicorn 44
Łaszkiewicz, Weronika 205, 214
Latin Vulgate 174
Lau, Sam 73
Lauro, Reno 77, 90
Lawrence, D.H. 170
"The Lay of Leithian" 207, 208, 214, 221
"The Lay of the Children of Húrin" 145, 152, 192
The Lays of Beleriand 140, 146–47, 149–52, 192, 200, 214; see also Beleriand
Leaf by Niggle 39–40; *see also* Niggle

Legolas 50, 118–19, 120, 131, 145, 227; *see also* Gimli; Legolas and Gimli
Legolas and Gimli 50, 118–19, 227; *see also* Gimli; Legolas
L'Engle, Madeleine 44
lesbian 7, 74, 102, 104–5, 106, 126, 153, 183n3, 200, 211; *see also* asexuality; bisexuality; gay; heterosexuality; homosexuality; LGBTQ+; same-sex relationships; sexuality; straight
Letter #5 31
Letter #30 36
Letter #43 81, 174
Letter #96 58
Letter #131 114, 194
Letter #142 162
Letter #144 183n9
Letter #153 35, 36, 40n7
Letter #154 176
Letter #156 65
Letter #163 59
Letter #180 27
Letter #181 36, 176
Letter #195 58
Letter #213 27
Letter #214 128
Letter #250 38
Letter #257 59
Letter #294 36
Letter #345 37
Letter #347 134–35
Lewis, C.S. 2–3, 4–5, 8, 9, 13, 22, 36, 74, 121, 170, 216, 217, 218, 221, 223, 224, 226, 231; *see also* Inklings; Williams, Charles
LGBTQ+ 11, 12, 44, 50, 73, 200, 227; *see also* asexuality; bisexuality; gay; heterosexuality; homosexuality; lesbian; same-sex relationships; straight; transgender
Librán-Moreno, Miryam 121, 132, 139
Life of Merlin 53
liminality 17, 33, 34, 35, 37, 38–39, 40, 57, 91
Lindon 30
Lionarons, Joyce Tally 77, 83, 90
Liuzza, R.M. 106
Lochrie, Karma 141, 142–43, 152
Logsdon, Cordeliah G. vi, 6, 20, 105n3, 201–14, 230
Loki 44
loneliness 49, 169
Lopez, German 108, 121
Lord of the Nazgûl *see* Witch-king of Angmar
The Lord of the Rings (film) 16, 43, 126,

147–48, 162, 166, 166n3, 191; *see also* Jackson, Peter
The Lord of the Rings: The Fellowship of the Ring (film) 90, 166; *see also* Jackson, Peter
The Lord of the Rings: Rings of Power 20n2, 21,191, 229
Lorde, Audre 18, 114
Lorey, Christoph 190, 192
Lossoth 135–36
The Lost Road and Other Writings 29, 34, 35, 39, 41
Lot 57, 68–69
Lothíriel 9, 200, 205, 214, 221, 225
"Love, Not Wisdom" 197–98; *see also* fanfiction
Loy, David 6n3, 8
Lúthien 32, 34, 36, 38, 189, 207, 208, 209, 211, 213, 217, 220, 221, 226; *see also* Beren; Great Tales

Madame Mim 49–50
Maedhros 34, 118, 119, 199n2; *see also* Fëanor; Maglor
magic 1–5, 7n6, 7, 8, 44, 45–46, 48–50, 53, 54, 150, 158, 175–76, 208, 230; *see also* Istari; wizards
Maglor 34, 36, 118; *see also* Fëanor; Maedhros
Magnus, P. D. 2, 8
Mahtan 120n2
Maiar 36, 38, 43, 52, 113, 173; *see also* Balrogs; Gandalf; Istari; Saruman; Sauron; Valar; wizards
Mairon *see* Sauron
Majere, Raistlin 47, 54, 170, 181, 219–20, 227
Making Things Perfectly Queer 73, 172, 185, 191, 199
Man Alone 127, 129, 133, 135
Mandos 115
Manwë 29
Marcus, Sharon 125–26, 138
marginalization 7n7, 13, 20, 88n4, 172, 173, 192, 205, 215, 218
Marino, John 59, 74
marriage 28, 31–33, 36, 82, 107, 115–16, 118–19, 120n8, 128, 131–32, 135, 208–09, 212
masculinities 18, 32, 43, 47, 54, 77, 78–80, 83, 84, 87, 88, 92–106, 108–9, 110, 116, 125–39, 142, 146–48, 150, 163, 170, 173, 174, 181, 210; female masculinity 79, 82, 84, 88n2; masculine continuum 102–3, 106; *see also* androgyny; femininities; genders; hypermasculine

masochism *see* sadism
Matthew 62, 69
Maurice 170
McBride, Sam 218, 226
McCormack, Una 7n11, 8, 199, 205, 214, 224
McKellen, Ian 43, 50, 54
√mel 118–19
meletheldi 118, 121
Melian 36, 38
Melkor *see* Morgoth
melotorni 118
Mendro, Hannah viii
Menzer, Melinda 86, 90
Merlin (Arthurian) 18, 44, 49, 53, 54; *see also* wizards
Merlyn (White, T.H.) 46, 49–50, 53; *see also* wizards
Middle-earth 2–5, 6n2, 6n3, 8, 9, 13, 20, 20n1, 22, 23, 28–32, 35, 37–40, 40n3, 41–44, 50, 54, 56, 59, 63, 70, 74, 88, 90, 91, 94, 100, 106–8, 111, 114, 115, 118–22, 125, 126, 130, 135, 136, 139, 141, 144, 145, 152, 162, 165, 167, 181, 185, 186, 189, 190, 193, 194, 200–4, 206, 207, 210, 211, 213, 214, 218–21, 223–28; *see also* Arda; Beleriand
Milbank, Alison 158
Miller, Elizabeth 77, 227
Miller, John 93, 106, 108, 121, 220, 224
Miller, T.S. 77, 227
Milon, Anna 6n3, 8
Milton, John 77, 174
Mîm 148, 197
Minas Anor *see* Minas Tirith
Minas Ithil 133, 134
Minas Morgul 132, 133
Minas Tirith 68, 133–34
Mines of Moria 70; *see also* Moria
Míriel (Elf) 38, 120n3, 218
Míriel (Human) *see* Tar-Míriel
Mirkwood 46, 108
misgendering 98, 99, 106; *see also* degendering
misogyny 12, 81, 220
Mitchison, Naomi 176
Mithrandir *see* Gandalf
monsters 18, 46, 104, 106, 136, 163, 166, 168, 173, 180–81, 183n1, 183n3, 186, 225, 227; the monstrous-feminine 77–91
The Monsters and the Critics, and Other Essays 54
Monsters in the Closet: Homosexuality and the Horror Film 57, 73
Montefiore, Hugh 127, 129
moralities 1–2, 7n6, 17, 18, 96, 111, 114,

120*n*7, 120, 127, 170, 172–74, 180; Queer Moralities 27–74
Moran, Patrick 191, 199
Morgan, Father Francis 34, 35
Morgan le Fay 44
Morgoth 28, 34, 38, 39, 52, 56, 59, 65, 66, 69, 112–14, 145, 146, 148, 199*n*2
Morgoth's Ring: The Later Silmarillion Part One 31, 32, 36, 42, 67–68, 74, 109, 112–14, 120*n*3, 120*n*7, 122
Moria 70, 105–6*n*10, 111, 178
Mormegil the Black Sword *see* Túrin
Morse, Charlotte 63, 74
Mother Nature 79, 88*n*1, 90, 223
mothers 18, 28, 29, 33, 34, 35, 37, 38, 40, 53, 73, 77–91, 100, 106, 109, 116, 134, 135, 146, 155, 158, 166, 169, 183, 216, 223
Mulgan, John 127, 139
Mundburg 98
Muñoz, José 51, 54
mutability 70, 105, 171
mythologies 1, 5, 21*n*5, 21, 27, 28, 39, 52, 58–60, 67–68, 77, 85, 90, 91, 120, 145, 166–68, 174, 184, 194, 207, 209, 218, 221, 224; *see also* "Sketch of the Mythology"
"Myths Transformed" *see Morgoth's Ring: The Later Silmarillion Part One*

Nagel, Rainier 77, 90
Nagy, Gergely 157, 158, 167
Nargothrond 68
"Narn I Chîn Húrin" 145, 192, 193
Narnia 3, 5, 7*n*6, 7; *see also* Lewis, C.S.
narratives 19, 20, 41, 47, 49, 51, 56–74, 78, 82, 85, 96, 104, 105*n*3, 112, 125, 126, 131, 134, 138, 140, 144–46, 149–50, 171, 173, 178, 182, 189–90, 192–93, 196–97, 201–14, 223, 228, 229; narrative unreliability 110–11; narrators 68, 104, 110, 111, 115, 159
Narvi 70–71
Natis, Mercury 120*n*10
nativism 12
The Nature of Middle-earth 32, 42, 118, 120*n*10, 122
Nazgûl 59, 109, 144
Neave, Edwin 33
Neave, Emily Jane Suffield 33
Neoplatonism 55, 174, 178, 180, 183, 186; *see also* Christianity
Nessa 29
neurodiversity 17, 43, 44–45, 46, 53, 54, 226, 229; neurodivergent language 46; *see also* allism; autism
Nienna 115, 120*n*8
Niggle 9, 39, 42, 168, 183, 186, 226; *see also Leaf by Niggle*; Parish

Níniel 195
Noah 57–58, 62, 65–69
Noakes *see* Old Noakes
Noldorin Elves 28, 31, 32, 36, 37, 120*n*3; *see also* Elves
non-binary 44, 51, 73, 99, 109–10, 119, 203, 205; *see also* binaries; genders
Norman Conquest 132
normativity 14–15, 18, 27–42, 77–91, 107–22, 125–39, 144, 168–86, 196, 204, 206, 210; *see also* amatonormativity
northern heroic spirit *see* heroisms
Númenor 30, 39, 58–60, 65, 67–68, 116, 127, 131–32, 135–36

Oakenshield, Thorin 97
occultism 3–4
Odin 44
OED *see* Oxford English Dictionary
Oedipal triangle 154; *see also* Freud, Sigmund
Oedipus 194
ofermod *see* heroisms
Old English 44, 78, 90, 94, 96, 97, 100, 105, 106; *see also* Anglo-Saxon; Rohirrim
Old Noakes 27
Olórin *see* Gandalf
"On Fairy Stories" (Rohy) 9, 41, 139, 142, 152, 167, 185, 200, 220; *see also* Rohy, Valerie
On Fairy Stories (Tolkien) 61
Ondoher 131–32, 135
The One Ring 49, 50, 153–67, 217
oppression 30, 33, 39, 60, 83, 144, 181, 214
Opreanu, Lucia 14, 22
Orcs 8, 14, 21, 22, 29, 31, 32, 88, 110–11, 114, 120*n*6, 120*n*7, 121, 130, 134, 147–48, 152, 159, 173, 174, 183, 184, 190, 195, 216, 217, 220, 222, 224, 228; Man-Orc hybrids 130, 175; Moria Orcs 111; Orc-play 144–48; Orc women 110; *see also* races; racisms; species
Orgof *see* Saeros
orphans 28, 34, 35, 38, 41; *see also* fosterage
Orthanc 44, 175
Osgiliath 134
Otherness 7, 15, 20, 77, 78, 135, 136, 168, 172, 184*n*16, 215; *see also* abject
Oxford English Dictionary 40*n*11, 41, 175, 185
Ozment, Nicholas 175, 176, 185

Pacheco, Derek 43, 54, 106, 115, 120, 227
pacifism 180
Paganism 2, 9*n*3, 7*n*6, 8, 9, 89*n*5; *see also*

244 Index

Anglicanism; Buddhism; Catholicism; Christianity; Evangelicalism; Islam; Judaism; Protestantism; religion
pair bonding 114–15
Palantíri 44, 46
Parish 39–40; *see also Leaf by Niggle*
The Parlement of the Thre Ages 60
Parry, Owen 196, 199
Partridge, Brenda 77, 81, 88n3, 90, 164, 166n7, 167, 216
passion 3, 16, 29, 45, 51, 60, 62, 114, 141, 151n2, 156, 229
Patience 61–62
Patroclus 131
Pearl see *Pearl*-poet
Pearl-poet 56–74
Pelennor Fields 92, 93
penetration 19, 140–52, 199
penis 157–58, 165; *see also* castration; fetish; Freud, Sigmund; phallus; swords
Penre, Wes 5, 8
The Peoples of Middle-earth 32, 34, 39, 40n10, 42, 108, 122
Persaud, Christopher J. 191, 200
perversities 18, 80, 141, 144, 146, 147–49, 172, 175–76, 183n9; *see also* sadism
Petersen, Brooke viii
Petersen-Deeprose, Danna vi, 18, 105n5, 107–22, 227
Petty, Anne 78, 90
phallus 149, 158, 166n4; phallic sword 140–52, 164; *see also* castration; fetish; Freud, Sigmund penis; swords
philology 21, 27, 71, 138
philosophy 8, 13, 166, 230
Piatti-Farnell, Lorna 7, 8, 221
pipes 27, 53; *see also* smoking
pipeweed 46, 49, 52, 179–80; *see also* smoking
platonic love 107, 114, 119, 170, 174; *see also* eroticism; pleasures; romances (medieval genre); romances (relationships)
pleasures 19, 33, 45, 49, 50, 58, 73, 97, 115, 129, 131, 132, 140, 142–51, 162, 172, 182, 184, 185, 212, 231; *see also* eroticism; platonic love; romances (medieval genre); romances (relationships); sex (intercourse)
Plews, John L. 190, 192
Ponto II *see* Baggins, Ponto
popular culture 6, 21n5, 190, 229
Popular Culture and American Culture Conference vii, 1
postcolonialism 7, 15, 21, 138, 184, 217, 223, 229

power 5, 17, 18, 29, 31, 43, 45, 47, 50, 52, 53, 65, 78, 80–82, 84, 86–89, 95, 109, 112–14, 128, 133, 137, 144, 147, 154, 155, 158, 159, 163–65, 170, 172, 174, 176, 178, 183–84n10, 201, 203, 205, 209, 210, 214
presentism 211
The Pricke of Conscience 60
pride 36, 37, 58–60, 67, 69, 72, 95–96, 129, 133, 136, 138, 147, 168–86; *see also* inhospitality; sodomy
Progonoskes 44
progressivism 6, 12
pronouns 44, 71, 98–100, 102, 105, 105n2, 106, 110
prophets 60, 70, 73, 176
Prosser, Jay 17, 18, 92–93, 103, 105, 106
Protestantism 12; *see also* Anglicanism; Buddhism; Catholicism; Christianity; Evangelicalism; Islam; Judaism; Paganism; religion
PTSD *see* trauma
Pugh, Tison 8, 14, 16–17, 19, 21, 143, 151, 152, 184, 194–95, 199, 217
Purity see *Cleanness*
Purtill, Richard 2, 8

Quenya 71, 118–19, 120n10
Queripel, Rory 33, 41, 227

races 18, 20, 22, 23, 36–37, 41, 58, 73, 91, 83, 107–12, 120, 121, 125, 134–37, 175, 183n6, 184, 214, 215, 217–22, 224–28; *see also* Orcs; species
racisms 12, 23, 120n4, 121, 218, 220, 226, 228, 230; *see also* Orcs
Radagast 44; *see also* Istari; Maiar; wizards
Ragnarök 60
The Rainbow 179
Rateliff, John 194, 199, 224
Ray, Stella 90, 224
Rearick, Anderson 16, 22, 220
The Red Book of Westmarch 71
redemption 22, 96, 114, 119, 176–80, 221, 224
Reid, Robin Anne v, viii, 1–9, 11–23, 88n2, 88n3, 91, 94, 106, 120n4, 121, 198, 200, 206, 214, 220, 224, 227, 229, 230
religion 1–3, 6n2, 7n9, 9, 13, 56, 73, 74, 91, 162, 198, 203, 210, 223, 224; *see also* Anglicanism; Buddhism; Catholicism; Christianity; Evangelicalism; Islam; Judaism; Paganism; Protestantism
remediation 192–96
repression 131, 133, 147, 172, 174, 181–82
reproduction 33, 126, 129–32; mechanical

reproduction 23, 130, 139, 173, 185, 225; see also children; fertility; sterility
The Return of the King (book) 13, 23, 30, 31, 34, 42, 66, 92–94, 97, 98, 100–2, 109, 110, 112, 113, 117, 118, 120*n*9, 122, 129, 130, 134, 138, 139, 159, 179, 180, 183*n*7, 184*n*18, 186, 202
The Return of the King (film) 219; see also Jackson, Peter
The Return of the Shadow: The History of The Lord of the Rings Part One 115, 122
Revelation 58, 60
revisions 31, 32, 140, 145, 151*n*1, 180–82; see also Tolkien, Christopher John Reuel
Rhovanion 134
Riders of Rohan see Rohirrim
Riga, Frank 49
Ring of Barahir 135
Ring of Power see The One Ring
Ringbearers 118, 156, 159–60
The Rings of Power see *The Lord of the Rings: The Rings of Power*
Ringwraiths see Nazgûl
Risden, Edward 60
rivals 128, 134–35, 154–59
Rivendell 28, 30, 31, 33–36, 39, 40*n*2, 70, 128, 129, 131, 160, 202; see also Elrond
robes 45, 51
River Sirion 34
Rodas, Julia Miele 17, 43, 46, 54
Rohirrim 94, 96, 97, 100–1, 108, 134; see also Anglo-Saxon; Old English
Rohy, Valerie 3, 14, 16, 21*n*5, 33, 126, 130, 134, 142–44, 157–58, 173, 176, 198, 220, 225
role-playing games 45
romances (medieval genre) 142, 143, 147, 194, 219, 222, 223, 230; see also eroticism; platonic love, pleasures; sex (intercourse)
romances (relationships) 19, 33, 50, 52, 107, 118, 140; romantic love 142, 143, 172, 175; see also eroticism; platonic; pleasures; sex (intercourse)
Rose, H.A. 35, 41
Rosegrant, John 60, 74
Rosenthal, Ty 116, 120*n*8, 174, 183*n*6, 220
Rowling, J.K. 4–5, 7, 121, 224
Rubey, Daniel 216
Rubin, Gayle 183*n*5
Ruiz, Beatriz Domínguez see Domínguez Ruiz, Beatriz
Rushton, Cory 149, 152
Ryken, Philip 6*n*2, 9

Sackville-Baggins, Lobelia 81, 88*n*4, 89, 128, 138, 221
Sackville-Baggins, Lotho 128
Sackville-Baggins, Otho 128
sadism 77, 87–88, 144, 147, 151, 152, 173, 182, 231; sadomasochism (S/M) 138, 144–48, 151, 152*n*4, 182; see also domination; perversities
sadness 47–48, 97
Saeros 146–49
Saint Sebastian 113; see also Celebrimbor
saints 6*n*3, 9, 90, 113, 176
Salinger, J.D. 192
same-sex relationships 57, 63, 68, 107, 112–15, 121, 126, 130, 152, 170; see also asexuality; bisexuality; gay; heterosexuality; homosexuality; lesbian; LGBTQ+; sexuality; straight
Sangahyando 135
Saruman 19, 23, 44, 50–51, 69, 111, 128, 130, 133, 139, 152, 168–86, 225; see also Istari; Maiar; wizards
Satan 2, 4, 6*n*5, 8, 9, 58, 62, 69
Sauron 7, 21, 28–30, 59, 65–66, 110–14, 130, 133, 137–38, 159, 167, 173, 176, 178, 184, 199*n*2, 202, 217
Saxey, Esther 14, 22, 29, 31, 41, 183*n*6, 186, 220
Saxton, Benjamin 14, 23, 168–69, 183*n*1, 186, 225
Schmidt, A.V.C. 63, 74
scholomance 48
Schweicher, Eric 59, 74
science fiction 21*n*5, 185, 190, 223; see also genre
sciences 5, 36–37, 40*n*6, 79, 88, 90, 91, 223, 230; see also biology
Second Age 28, 35, 112–14; see also Sauron
secular 5, 12, 13, 230
Sedgwick, Eve Kosofsky 17, 19, 153–55, 161, 167, 171, 186
Sevelius, Jae M. 98–99, 106
Seven Mountain Mandate 13, 22
sex (intercourse) 51, 81, 82, 84, 114, 118, 120*n*8, 131, 141,142, 143, 147, 154, 166*n*4, 171–72, 174–75, 182, 183, 183*n*2; see also eroticism; platonic love; pleasures; romances (medieval genre); romances (relationships)
sex (sexual difference) 107, 108–9, 118; see also gender
Sexual Inversion 170
sexual liberation movement 174
Sexual Offenses Act of 1967 170
sexuality 5, 7*n*7, 7*n*10, 14–15, 19, 20, 23, 43, 84, 102, 104, 107, 110, 112, 115, 117, 119, 130, 134, 136, 137, 138, 140–42, 147–48, 151, 166*n*5, 169, 172–76, 182–83, 183*n*3,

196, 204, 210–11, 215, 229; female 77–91; male 19, 81, 168–86; *see also* asexuality; bisexuality; gay; heterosexuality; homosexuality; lesbian; LGBQT+; same-sex relationships; straight
Shadow of Mordor 191
Shagrat 110
shame 19, 140, 148–51, 160, 204
The Shaping of Middle-earth 28, 35, 42
Shaw, Adrienne 191, 200
Shelob 18, 77–91, 96, 105n6, 114, 159, 163–64, 166n6, 183n3, 218, 222, 227
Shippey, Tom 21n5, 61, 74, 97, 106, 200, 220
signification 144, 148
Sigurd the Volsung 194
The Silmarillion 6n1, 19, 29, 30, 34, 39, 48, 52, 56, 58–59, 64–65, 110, 115, 145, 189, 192–98, 199n2
Silmarils 34, 56, 59
Simons, M.A. 91
Simpson, Jacqueline 225
Simpson, Mark 63, 74
Sindarin (Elves) 28, 36, 38, 119; *see also* Elves
Sindarin (language) 71, 223
Sir Gawain and the Green Knight 52, 54, 63, 74, 143, 220; *see also* chivalry; courtly love; knights
Sir Gawain and the Green Knight, Pearl, and Sir Orfeo 54, 74
Sirion *see* River Sirion
sister-daughter 101
sister-son 101, 105n4
"Sketch of the Mythology" 28, 145
Slatton, Brittany C. 120n5
Sly, Debbie 78, 91
S/M *see* sadism
Sméagol *see* Gollum
Smith, Geoffrey Bache 30–31, 170
Smith, Mark Eddy 6, 9
smoking 47, 50, 52–54; *see also* pipes; pipeweed
Smol, Anna 16, 77, 83, 114, 130, 137, 140, 183n6, 198, 220
Sodom 18, 58, 62–63, 67–69, 72
sodomy 19, 133, 146–49, 173–74, 176, 180; *see also* de Lille, Alain; inhospitality; pride; Saruman
South Africa 27, 34, 35
Spates, Kamesha 120n5
species 28, 36–37, 40n5, 48, 83, 109–10, 175; *see also* races
spirituality 5, 6, 6n2, 6n3, 8, 9, 12, 59, 69, 137, 150, 175, 199n1
Stanley, Eric 86, 91

Steinwascher, Christiana viii
sterility 125–38, 149–50; *see also* fertility
Stern, Alexandra Minna 12, 23
"The Story Foreseen from Kormallen" 178
Strabo 51
Strachey, Lytton 170
straight 5, 14, 15, 48, 57–58, 64, 78, 112, 137, 153, 172, 176, 211; *see also* asexuality; bisexuality; gay; homosexuality; lesbian; LGBTQ+; same-sex relationships; sexuality
Straight, Michael 176
Strauss, Ed 6n4, 9
Stryker, Susan 17–18, 92, 104–5,
Sturgis, Amy H. 7n11, 9, 200, 205, 214, 229
subversion 18, 21, 57, 69, 77–78, 83–84, 87–89, 92–93, 105, 108, 203, 210, 213, 217
suffering 19, 28, 30, 38, 40, 66, 110, 140–52, 213
supernatural 1, 2, 7n6
surveillance 56, 62, 65–66
swords 19, 93, 140–52, 159, 164; *see also* Freud, Sigmund; penis; phallus
Sylvan Elves 119; *see also* Elves

taboo 153, 154, 161, 165, 198, 199n3
Tadie, Joseph 14, 23
The Tale of Tinúviel 145; *see also* Lúthien
"The Tale of Years" 30–31
Tally, Robert T., Jr. 120n6, 121, 228
Tar-Ancalimë 116; *see also* Aldarion, Erendis
Tar-Meneldur 116
Tar-Míriel 67
Tea Club, Barrovian Society 29–30, 170, 227
Teleri Elves 38, 120n3; *see also* Elves
Temple of Jerusalem 69
Tengwar 71
Testi, Claudio 6n3, 9
Thangorodrim 113
Théoden 97, 98, 100–1, 105n4; *see also* Éowyn; Rohirrim
theology 6n2, 8, 21n4, 22, 57, 63, 68, 186, 230
Thingol 146, 147, 148, 194
Third Age 32, 38, 40n3, 41, 125, 132, 137, 168, 179, 184n13, 184n14, 184n15, 186, 191, 202
Thompson, Andrea 83, 91
Thorin *see* Oakenshield, Thorin
Thorongil *see* Aragorn
Timmons, Daniel 14, 23, 38, 41, 91, 154, 167, 174–75, 183n6, 186, 220, 221
Tol Eressëa 59
Tolkien, Arthur Reuel 34, 36, 60

Tolkien, Christopher John Reuel 32, 41, 42, 54, 74, 89, 91, 122, 139, 145, 149, 152, 167, 178, 179–80, 184*n*11, 184*n*13, 186, 189, 200; *see also* revisions
Tolkien, Edith Bratt 37–38, 40*n*9, 222, 226
Tolkien, Hilary Arthur Reuel 28, 34–35, 169
Tolkien, Mabel Suffield 28, 33, 34–35, 37–38, 169
Tolkien, Michael Hilary Reuel 38, 81
"Tolkien and Alterity" (Audas) 7, 17, 20, 215; *see also* alterity
Tolkien and Alterity (Vaccaro and Kisor) 9, 14, 21–23, 42, 89, 90, 122, 139, 142, 152, 166, 185, 186, 199, 200, 225; *see also* alterity
Tolkien and Diversity: Proceedings of the Tolkien Society Summer Seminar 2021 121; *see also* diversity
Tolkien and Diversity Seminar 4, 8, 13, 22, 41; *see also* diversity
Tolkien at Kalamazoo vii, 16
Tolkien scholarship 1, 3, 6, 11–23, 62, 85, 140, 141, 143, 158, 172, 174–75, 190, 196, 223
Took, Peregrin 31, 53, 109
tragedy 29, 33–35, 60, 67, 97, 111, 127, 135, 136, 145, 175, 180, 194–96, 203, 204, 213
transformative works *see* fanfiction
transgender 18, 20, 43, 51, 54, 92–106, 109, 121, 201–15, 230; trans-coded 18, 92, 212; transmasculine 18, 98, 102–3; *see also* cisgender; genders
transgressions 18, 74, 83, 85, 88, 88*n*1, 105, 147
translation 7, 52, 54, 57, 61, 71, 72*n*1, 73, 74, 85–86, 89, 90, 184, 185, 201, 223; *see also* aglǽcwif; *Beowulf* (poem); Grendel's Mother
trauma 28, 31, 53, 60–61, 140, 149, 151
The Treason of Isengard: The History of The Lord of the Rings *Part Two* 178, 186
Tree and Leaf 95, 106
Trump, Donald 12
Tulkas 29
Tuor 36, 118, 207, 209, 211, 213; *see also* Gondolin; Idril
Turambar, Túrin *see* Túrin
"Turambar and the Foalókë" 145, 192–95
Turgon 31, 35, 39
Túrin 19–20, 38, 118, 119, 140–52, 189–200; *see also* Beleg
Turing, Alan 170
twins 28, 34, 38, 41, 42, 169
"Two Loves" *see* Douglas, Alfred
The Two Towers (book) 13, 23, 51, 52, 66, 80–81, 84, 86, 87, 101, 110, 111, 114, 122, 133, 139, 156, 161–64, 177, 183*n*7, 186
The Two Towers 13, 23, 51, 52, 66, 80, 81, 84, 86, 87, 101, 110, 111, 114, 122, 133, 139, 156, 161–64, 176, 183, 186
The Two Trees 59, 115

Ulmo 115
Umbar 134, 185, 202
Undying Lands *see* Valinor
Unfinished Tales of Numenor and Middle-earth 30, 42, 40*n*2, 44, 54, 113, 116, 122, 127, 139, 181, 183–84*n*10, 186, 192, 195, 200, 222
unnaturalness 65, 74, 79, 85
Urang, Gunnar 2, 8, 58, 74

Vaccaro, Christopher v, vi, viii, 1–9, 11–23, 29, 40, 42, 50, 54, 88, 90, 91, 106, 114, 120, 122, 132, 137–39, 143, 148, 151*n*2, 152, 166–86, 194, 199, 200, 221–23, 225, 226, 229, 230
vagina dentata 163–64; *see also* Freud, Sigmund; Shelob
Valar 28, 29, 34, 38, 65, 67, 110, 113, 115; *see also* Maiar
Valinor 28, 38, 39, 59, 65, 162
Valkyrie Reflex 78, 85, 90, 218, 222; *see also* Donovan, Leslie A.
Vanyar Elves 36; *see also* Elves
Varda 34
Venkatesan, Emily 228
Viars, Karen 9, 200, 205, 214, 221, 225
Victorian literature 113, 121, 126, 139, 225, 226
videogames 191
Vidumavi 134
Vikings 95
Vilya 30
"The Voyage of Earendel, the Evening Star" 56
Vulgate cycle 53
vulnerability 35, 46, 53, 133, 143, 147–48, 150, 176, 179

Waldman, Milton 194
Walker, Nick 45, 55
Walls-Thumma, Dawn M. 7–9, 198, 200, 226
Walz, Tim 12, 22
The War of the Ring: The History of The Lord of the Rings *Part Three* 177, 186
Warner, Michael 171–72, 182, 183*n*5, 186
Warnke, Mike 6*n*5, 9
warriors 8, 22, 28, 29, 54, 85, 94, 95, 97, 121, 127, 128, 130–33, 138, 190, 194, 195,

221; *see also* Battle of Maldon; *Beowulf*; heroisms
Wart 46, 49, 53
"The Waste Land" 60, 74
Watership Down 44
The Well of Loneliness 170, 183n2
Westron 71
Whipple, Amy viii
White, T.H. 46, 49, 53, 55
The White Council 30, 178, 180
Wiggins, Christopher 108, 122,
Wiggins, Kayla McKinney 175, 176, 186
Wiginton, Patti 89n5, 91
Wiglaf 101, 105n4
Wijman, Eva viii
Wilde, Oscar 136, 169
Williams, Charles 9, 74, 170, 217, 223, 226; *see also* Inklings; Lewis, C.S.
Williams, Donald 13, 22, 23, 227
A Wind in the Door 44
Wiseman, Christopher 30–31, 170
Witch-King of Angmar 19, 92, 95, 101, 109, 125, 127, 132–33, 135–36, 138
wizards 5, 13, 17, 19, 28, 43–55, 168–86, 207, 226, 229; *see also* Gandalf; Istari; Maiar; Saruman
women 37, 40n12, 79, 81, 83, 89–103, 108, 109, 110, 121, 127, 129, 131, 132, 142, 155, 183n2; characters 8, 9, 29, 37, 41, 66, 90, 91, 108, 109, 116, 120, 139, 140, 146, 198, 199, 200, 212, 214, 216–27, 230; cisgender 108; Dwarf 108; FTM 103–4, 106; Hobbit 109; Orc 110; transgender 99, 106, 12; women's liberation 94; *see also* female hero; female masculinity; feminisms
Wood, Ralph C. 6, 9, 23
Wood-Elves of Mirkwood 108; *see also* Elves
Woolf, Leonard 170
Woolf, Virginia 170
World War I 14, 29, 31, 88n3, 170, 191; *see also* Great War
World War II 170, 191
World Wars 5, 228
Wormtongue *see* Grima
"Writing a Green Sun" 211, 214; *see also* Anglachel (fan pseudonym); *Hands of the King*

xenophobia 12

Yahweh 60, 62–72; *see also* gods
Yandell, Stephen v, viii, 1–9, 11–23, 33, 39, 56–74, 168, 183n1, 183n6, 186, 226, 231
Yavanna 110, 115, 120n8
√yer 118–19
Yergeau, M. Remi 43, 45, 51
Young, Helen 226

Zagore 47
Zeikowitz, Richard 17, 19, 143–44, 147, 152
Zimbardo, Rose A. 89, 90
Žižek, Slavoj 168, 182, 183n1, 186